file copy

pub date: October 1993

COALITIONS
POLITICIANS
& GENERALS

BY SHELFORD BIDWELL
Gunners at War: A Tactical Study of the Royal Artillery
    in the Twentieth Century
Swords for Hire: European Mercenaries in Eighteenth-Century India
Modern Warfare: A Study of Men, Weapons and Theories
The Royal Horse Artillery
The Women's Royal Army Corps
The Chindit War: The Campaign in Burma, 1944
Artillery of the World (Ed.)
World War 3 (Ed.)

BY DOMINICK GRAHAM
Cassino
British Government and American Defence, 1748–56
No Subsitute for Peace (with Maurice Tugwell and David Charters)
The Price of Command: A Biography of General Guy Simonds

BY SHELFORD BIDWELL and DOMINICK GRAHAM
Fire-Power: British Army Weapons and Theories of War, 1904–45
Tug of War: The Battle for Italy, 1943–45

COALITIONS POLITICIANS & GENERALS

Some Aspects of Command in Two World Wars

DOMINICK GRAHAM
and SHELFORD BIDWELL

BRASSEY'S (UK)
London • New York

First English edition 1993

UK editorial offices: Brassey's, 165 Great Dover Street,
London SE1 4YA
orders: Marston Book Services, PO Box 87, Oxford OX2 0DT

USA orders: Macmillan Publishing Company,
Front and Brown Streets Riverside, NJ 08075

Distributed in North America to booksellers and wholesalers by
the Macmillan Publishing Company, NY 10022

Dominick Graham & Shelford Bidwell have asserted
their moral rights to be identified as authors of this work.

Library of Congress Cataloging in Publication Data
available

British Library Cataloguing in Publication Data
A catalogue record for this book is available
from the British Library

ISBN 1-85753-007-1

Typeset by M Rules
Printed in Great Britain by
The Bath Press, Avon

ACKNOWLEDGEMENTS

One of the pleasures of being engaged in military history is the readiness and good nature of our friends to share their knowledge and special expertise in a field that is almost always controversial. Graham spent the academic year 1987–8 at the Royal Military College, Kingston, Ontario where Barry Hunt, Keith Neilson, Ronald Haycock and Roy Prete offered him valuable advice on the First World War chapters. John English, then completing his thesis on the Canadians in Normandy, stimulated his thoughts on that subject. From Kingston, Graham was able to travel each week to the Military History Institute at Carlisle Barracks, Pennsylvania where the archives staff under Richard Sommers, and the Library staff showed him analyses of American Expeditionary Force operations written at the Army War College in the 'twenties and 'thirties. Robin Higham and D K R Crosswell at the University of Kansas introduced him to materials in the Eisenhower Library, Abilene. Terrence Gough, a member of the staff at the Center for Military History, Washington, in correspondence helped him to avoid some mistakes in the chapter concerning Pershing, although not all of them. Marc Milner, at the University of New Brunswick, guided him during continual conversations on shipping. Over the several years during which this book has been in draft, our mutual friend Carlo D'Este, straightened us out on US Army performance in the Second War.

Bidwell has to thank Brian Holden Reid, the Staff College, Camberley and Field Marshal Sir John Stanier for their valuable comments on his text.

Finally, as this is the authors' third and final joint work, Graham records how much he has enjoyed transatlantic cooperation with Bidwell since they met at a military history seminar at the Royal Military Academy Sandhurst in 1978.

From the first, our method of work involved intense mutual criticism and editing of our respective chapters. In the present book, Bidwell's input has been predominantly editorial. Only saintly patience on both sides enabled such a process to go forward over the five years during which our final text evolved.

Bryan Watkins maintained his faith in our book during the vicissitudes to which our publishers have been subjected, and his enthusiastic and constructive suggestions are a model for military editors.

Last, but by no means least, Mrs Jean Walter as a typist with an unerring sub-editorial eye has for the third time produced perfect copy for publication.

Having made these grateful acknowledgements we state formally that responsibility for any errors of fact or opinion is ours alone.

Dominick Graham
Shelford Bidwell

CONTENTS

INTRODUCTION

It may be said of the two World Wars that the first was not a world war and the second became one only after the Japanese and Americans intervened. To Europeans, they appear to have formed a continuum; a single European civil war with a truce from 1918 to 1939 in which a diplomatic revolution occurred. Not until 1941 did the civil war become the world struggle that ended the predominance of the European powers.

With the exception of Turkey, Germany's ally in 1914, which remained neutral in 1939, the same states fought the two wars. However, their relative power altered in the truce and the diplomatic revolution changed their alignment in the coalitions. Whereas in the First coalition of 1914 the British fought from first to last on the Continent alongside their French ally, in the Second they were ousted from it in the first year when France was defeated. Allies of the British in the First coalition, Italy and Japan changed sides in the diplomatic revolution. Her Italian enemy drew Britain into a Mediterranean campaign that lasted from 1940 until 1945. The Japanese made it impossible for Britain to defend her eastern possessions and also fight in Europe, a situation that British diplomacy had avoided in 1914 when Japan was an ally. After the French collapse in June 1940, Britain lacked an ally until the Soviets and the Americans entered the war in 1941. She then fought with the Americans, a more powerful ally by far than they had been in the First War when they entered late and played third fiddle to the French and the British.

The English-speaking allies of 1941-45 learned from their experience together a generation earlier, when the French were the main land power, although they retained inherited prejudices about each other. Unlike the Americans, the British had established an efficient war administration by the end of 1941 which gave them an initial advantage in dealing with their ally.

The wars were material struggles, won more by organising and applying a huge amount of war material than by employing it skilfully in specific battles. In the First coalition, Britain and France held the initiative in the politics which decided the production, distribution, and shipping of war material, and the employment of military manpower. In the Second coalition the Americans had the whip-hand in these matters. The balance of power in both coalitions was decided by the material means at the disposal of its members.

Most of the technologies of the Second war were developments from the First. Although the steps from propeller aircraft to jet and rocket propulsion were revolutionary, they came late and neither was decisive. On the other hand notable advances in electronics revolutionised political, economic, social and operational intelligence about the enemy's condition, his location and intention, and enabled the information to be rapidly distributed and, hence, acted upon. Speedy communications between political centres and the fighting fronts tended to increase the ability of commanders and staffs at the highest echelons to intervene at the level below them. Indeed, advances in communications, control and intelligence in the wider sense of the rapid processing, assimilation and use of information played a part in correcting the failure of the political leaders of the First coalition to control their generals in the field.

The title of the book and this brief introduction to it indicate that its focus is the relations between French, British and American politicians, their senior military managers, the supreme field commanders and their subordinate army group and army commanders in the two coalitions. Nevertheless, battle is the payoff. Armed forces are judged by how effectively they fight. So we have discussed field operations and tactics to illustrate the functioning of these senior echelons in the direction of the wars. That presented the problem of how to tell the story coherently at several levels. There had to be a frame of reference to link the directors at the summits with executors in the field.

Decisions were taken in both coalitions at four levels. At the political level, the Prime Ministers and the President of the United States worked through their chiefs of staff for military matters. At the next, the chiefs dealt with each other and with supreme field commanders, who, in their turn, directed army-group and army commanders. The concern at the top was with policy, civil and military, in the widest sense. Descending the ladder to the battlefields of armies, navies and air forces the concerns were increasingly operational and tactical. This gradation is well understood. What is less often considered is that stress was natural and unavoidable between each level of responsibility, not only because of personalities and national and service differences, but because the spheres of responsibility at each level were not discrete, and never could be. A political decision could not be separated from its application, requiring, as it did, action by many different civil and military authorities. Lower in the chain, operational and tactical considerations conflicted with strategy imposed from above in which political considerations played a major part. In theory, strategy should serve policy, operations further strategy and the tactics used in an operation offer it a chance to succeed. In practice, stress occurs at the junction of each category. A tactical battle may fail because equipment, training, the ground, the plan or the amount of troops available are inadequate for an operational task. A failed operation does not serve strategy and the policy suffers a set-back. The process of decision-making tends to unravel unless the implications of decisions at each level are pursued downwards and two-way communication maintained. The military admonition taught at staff schools, to think two down and sideways, obtains. It is not difficult at the lowest levels but is complex at higher levels.

Accounts of the stress between levels of command and staff responsible for policy and strategy, strategy and operations, and operations and tactics provide much of the material of the book. Stress would not occur if decisions were made entirely rationally, based on the facts, by men and women of saintly character. An intricate system of committees, which reached maturity in the latter stages of the Second coalition, was created to bring decision-making closer to dull perfection. It provided information which, at the international level, was intended to be normative, without national colour or personal bias, and concluded with a recommendation for action by a superior. National committees did much the same except that they served a national point of view, while individual service committees provided information and an identifiably service point of view. The origin of the committee system was the British Committee of Imperial Defence and its numerous sub-committees dealing with civil and military matters. Created at the beginning of the twentieth century. It developed between the wars and its success persuaded the Americans to adopt similar committees when they entered the war in 1941. By February 1942 the summit consisted of The Joint Chiefs of Staff Committee of the Americans and the British Chiefs of Staff which had originated in 1923. The two met together when required in the Combined Chiefs of Staff (CCS) which usually met in Washington and had a permanent secretariat. The development of this system and its numerous supporting committees and the national differences of approach to decision-making which it reveals, is a crucial part of our story.

We observed that battle is the pay-off. In the field there were sometimes conflicts between commanders over battle plans, particularly over the strategic setting and aims and their effect on the operational and tactical plans. As illustrations, we have chosen only two specific case-studies, one in each coalition. In the first, Sir Douglas Haig, the British Commander-in-

Chief on the Western Front from December 1915 until the end of the First coalition, clashed with David Lloyd George, prime minister from December 1916, over the correct military strategy to serve national policy. The specific issue was whether or not Haig should fight the battle of Passchendaele. He was in conflict with three of his army commanders Sir Herbert Plumer, Sir Henry Rawlinson and General Hubert Gough over an operational plan which he had imposed on them and which they considered tactically infeasible. From the Second coalition, we have chosen the actions of General Dwight D Eisenhower, Supreme Allied Commander in North-West Europe, following the defeat of the German armies in Normandy in August 1944. A disagreement occurred between Eisenhower and his subordinates as to how they should proceed. Eisenhower exhibited the opposite failing of Haig in that he neither directed nor coordinated their actions. These two examples at the core of the book illustrate stress at the junction points of policy, strategy, operations and tactics and the influence of personalities on the outcome.

Decision-making in the Second coalition owed much to experience in the First. In 1918, General Pershing, C-in-C of the American Armies in the field, challenged the authority of General Peyton C March, the Army Chief of Staff in Washington. George Marshall, Army Chief of Staff in 1941, learned from March's experience and imposed his will on subordinate field commanders and, like Sir Alan Brooke, his British opposite, established the authority of the Chiefs of Staffs over field commanders. Consequently, the powers of field commanders to make policy were markedly less in the Second than in the First coalition. President Roosevelt and Prime Minister Churchill did not have to struggle to establish their authority over them, as did President Wilson, David Lloyd George, and the various French prime ministers in the First coalition. Then, Haig, Pershing and their French military superiors tried to settle most issues between them to avoid political interference. Political influence over field commanders remained weak, even in the final stages of the First coalition.

The shift of power in the Second coalition to the chiefs of staff and the political leaders tended to politicise the control of Cs-in-C over their subordinates in international theatres. Political subjectivity sometimes eclipsed military objectivity. Even the Combined Chiefs of Staff, although concerned with policy, were inhibited from discussing candidly political reasons for military operations. For instance, in their arguments about Operation ANVIL-DRAGOON, the invasion of the South of France by American and French troops, the members advanced spurious military arguments in which they were more comfortable rather than lay their political cards on the table.

The management and politics of logistics were important in both coalitions. Pershing mismanaged his in the field and, at the higher level, American inability to provide guns, horses, ships and training facilities for the Expeditionary Force weakened his hand when he wanted to influence Allied military decisions. Eisenhower also mismanaged his logistics, and the similarity between the mistakes made by the Americans in the coalitions are striking. However, Marshall's staff experience in 1917 and 1918 convinced him that American economic power should be translated into proportional political and military influence in the coalition of 1941–45 in order to ensure that the British would not dominate the Second coalition. He ensured that Eisenhower's mistakes did not upset the balance between the Allies.

The part played by Marshall in the Second coalition was decisive. He was not the outstanding soldier of the war but he was a statesman, a model staff officer, and an astute but trusted politician. He pursued two goals for his country and the US Army. The first was to adhere to the allied plan to defeat Germany first and the second to ensure that, unlike 1918, the US Army should play the leading role in liberating Europe and receive the major share of laurels. In order to appease the Pacific lobby and the US Navy, led by Admiral Ernest King, he treated the Mediterranean as a sideshow and tried to ensure that the Allies closed with the Germans as soon as possible in the decisive theatre of war – North-West Europe. To ensure that the US Army played the decisive role there, he concentrated as many troops as possible in North-West Europe and as few as possible in the Mediterranean. He pressed for the ANVIL-DRAGOON landings and ignored the incorrigible fact of geography that the decisive part of the front in North-West Europe was in front of the Ruhr and was shared between the British Second Army and the US First Army. Rather than insist on concentrating forces opposite the Ruhr, he allowed Eisenhower to allot large forces to the American centre and right of the front although, as the representative of the Combined Chiefs of Staff responsible for overseeing the campaign, he knew that the CCS had set the Ruhr as Eisenhower's primary objective.

The multi-front war in which the Americans were involved strained even their material and manpower resources by the end of 1944. The mishandling of logistics by the European Theatre of Operations (US Army), the over-extension of the front by Eisenhower, which placed heavy demands on diminishing resources, a Congressional decision in 1943 to restrict the production of munitions, combined with unexpected demands from the Pacific, created a very serious crisis which might have been laid at Marshall's door in the autumn and winter of 1944–5, had it become public.

It was as well that the details of the muddle were concealed, for it would have put a different complexion on the dispute between Eisenhower and Montgomery over operations. Usually understood to have been about the single thrust versus the broad front advance after Normandy, it was fundamentally about logistics and concerned Marshall's political ambition for the US Army. By omitting those two elements from their argument, historians have been unable to resolve it, falling back on the familiar explanation that the conflict only concerned American and British personalities.

The British had no military institutional axe to grind like the Americans but, unlike the Americans, a persistent national policy regarding post-war Europe and the British Empire. The Mediterranean was essential to them as a highway leading to the East by way of the Suez Canal, and to the oil of the Middle East. The Balkans had long been an area of concern because Russia and Germany meddled there. The Americans, suspecting the British of plunging them into that caldron of intrigue from their base in Italy, would have none of it. Their geopolitical ambition lay in the Pacific not in Europe. Marshall's unconcern with the politics of Europe was understandable, but he shared the common view of American soldiers that military strategy should be divorced from politics. The education of the British senior ranks made it clear that that was impracticable but their difference with the Americans on the subject made agreement over strategy difficult.

In their concern for the Mediterranean, the Middle East and Turkey, the British appeared to the Americans to be following the 'Easterners' strategy of the First coalition and to be incorrigibly opposed to a Western strategy of invading northern France. The similarity of British strategy in the two coalitions is clear but the interpretation of the Eastern strategy of 1914–18 as an alternative to the slaughter of the Western approach in either war was wrong. In the First coalition they had hoped to delay a major intervention on the Continent until 1916, when the Germans and French would be weakened. They were forced to commit themselves to the Western strategy when supporting the Russians proved fruitless, the French insisted on a major British commitment to the Continent and British finances and war material did not stretch to supporting both allies. In the Second, they had no option but to use a peripheral strategy until the Russians had weakened the Germans and sufficient American divisions were available to make invasion practicable.

This book concerns the relations of the French, the British and the Americans in two coalitions. The stresses in the coalitions lay at the junction points between policy, strategy, operations and tactics. The system of committees in the Second coalition was designed to iron out the stresses that had occurred in the First, which to a remarkable degree they did. However, the personalities on the pages of this book ensured that the events of the Second coalition were as dramatic as those of the First.

In the opening section of the book we discuss the origins and functions of army staffs and survey military development before and during the wars. The section ends with an introduction to the problems of the coalitions with which the rest of the book is concerned. In the second and third sections, respectively, we record civil-military relations in the First and Second coalitions. In the First coalition, policy, military strategy and operations were not coordinated. By the end of the Second it could be said that politics, not the cold logic of the staff appreciation prevailed. In the conclusion we consider whether or not this development had gone too far.

CHAPTER 1

THE MILITARY MIND

Let us have some system to start with, and if it is not perfect we can improve it.

HAIG, AT THE GENERAL STAFF CONFERENCE
AT THE STAFF COLLEGE, 1907

The direction of the British and American war effort in the two World Wars revolved around a fundamental question: how could governments, inevitably concerned with great strategic decisions when the prosecution of war demanded a total effort in terms of economic resources and man-power, make the best use of expert military advice? This in turn led to another question almost as difficult: once the commander-in-chief in the field had been given his mission, how much latitude should he be allowed? We see, for instance, Sir John French being dissuaded from disengaging the BEF from operations in 1914. In sharp contrast, in 1917–18 the Prime Minister, Lloyd George, strove to frustrate Douglas Haig's single-minded intention to break German resistance by unremitting offensive action and failed. There was a further complication. The military link between the head of state and the commander or commanders in the field, the chief of staff, had the delicate task of, on the one hand, explaining the ineluctable principles of war to his masters while protecting the field commanders from political interference, and on the other of guiding and restraining his subordinates; no easy task, bearing in mind that generals are selected pri-marily for their strength of character, not to say the bloody-mindedness of which Montgomery is the extreme example.

Things were different if the roles of head of state and supreme strategist were combined in one person, and when military operations were simple enough to be directed by a general on horseback: 'The man on the white horse'. (It is not without significance that the names of the chargers of Alexander the Great, Napoleon and Wellington are still in popular memory – Bucephalus, Marengo, Copenhagen.) But for Ludendorff, Foch, Haig, Pershing or Eisenhower the business of modern war was too complex and involved too many momentous and interacting factors for one man to manage. What was required was a collective brain, an educated military mind, with the function of advising statesmen in peace-time on the danger areas where threats might arise and the preparations or precautions that military wisdom recommended, and in time of war to recommend to statesmen and field commanders alike the possible options and best course of action.

There was nothing new in the idea of a group of experienced and capable officers assembled *ad hoc* to assist commanders in the field, as can be gathered from their old titles. The personal assistant of the commander of a regiment was his 'adjutant', dealing with discipline and the transmission of his orders and instructions, the quartermaster was responsible for billeting camps and supplies. (From the French *maréchal de logis* the modern term *logistics* is derived.) The 'adjutant-general', the 'quartermaster-general' supervised these matters from general headquarters. The system of selection was based on the personal preference of the commander and, in the case of his aides-de-camp, that as well as being intelligent they could afford the high quality horses necessary to carry out their errands rapidly, often under fire. The French General Bourcet conceived the idea of a 'general staff', permanently established and suitably trained, but it did not survive the Revolution, and would not have appealed to Napoleon Bonaparte, the supreme example of 'the man on a white horse'.

A true 'general staff' has been defined as:

A central military organ assisting the supreme military authority of the state . . . particularly in determining and implementing intellectually the higher directions which are to govern military activity.

Such an organ has to be much more than a bureaucracy toiling at its desks and organised in separate departments concerned with every phase of military activity, such as existed in the United States before the reform of its staff system at the end of the nineteenth century. Its members must have responsibility for action and be held responsible for the results. 'Command' and 'staff work' have to be regarded as closely connected, not separate activities.

The simplest way to set this question of a 'general' staff, as existed in the armies of the principal belligerents in 1914–45, in perspective is by a short historical digression, explaining how one of the most important innovations in the history of modern warfare came to be universally adopted.

10

In the early years of the nineteenth century it had become apparent that the Prussian Army, the most renowned war-machine in Europe was, without a Frederick the Great to grip its control levers, badly in need of reform and re-animation. Its command system had become ossified and authoritarian, it was bound by regulations and slow to react to the emergencies of operations; weaknesses exposed by the humiliating defeat it suffered at the hands of Napoleon at the double battles of Jena-Auerstadt in 1806. King Frederick William III of Prussia, a far-seeing man, had already accepted the offer of an outsider, a distinguished mercenary officer, Major Gerhard Scharnhorst, the son of a small-holder born in Lower Saxony, to undertake the reforms which led to the creation of an élite of outstanding young officers trained in the art of command and able to serve in any branch of staff duties; operations, logistics and intelligence. Scharnhorst's collaborators were the equally famous Gneisenau and the philosopher of war Clausewitz. To educate the new 'general' staff the Prussian *Kriegsakademie* was established; a 'war college', it will be noted, not a mere staff school.

The success of the venture was due to the value placed on education in nineteenth century Prussia and the fact that the principal source of officers was the sons of the landed gentry of East Prussia, the 'youngsters', or '*junkers*' as they came to be known. The Junker families, traditionally martial, and loyal to the Prussian throne, were firmly wedded to it by being favoured for officer commissions, with the added advantage of a free education in the officer cadet schools. Protestant in religion, Puritan in outlook, poor and therefore frugal and with a strongly moral code, the *esprit de corps* of the General Staff was reinforced by its sense of identity as Prussians, and a moral outlook which governed the behaviour of an officer and a gentleman. Looking back on his career Heinz Guderian, one of the pioneers of mechanised warfare, listed the prerequisites for appointment to the General Staff in order as

1 'integrity of character and unimpeachable behaviour and way of life both on and off duty',
2 'military competence; a man had to have proved himself at the front, have an understanding for tactical and technical matters, and a talent for organisation',
3 'powers of endurance both physical and mental',
4 'to be industrious',
5 'of a sober [i.e., calm] temperament',
6 'determined'.

He goes on to strike a chord familiar to all armies when he says that strength of character and 'warmth of personality' were as important as sheer intellect.

Finally, and this is at the heart of any successful staff system, 'its members were trained to judge events and make appreciations both operational and tactical, according to a definite and uniform system. From this basic uniformity it was hoped to create a wide uniformity of decision'. There was no rigidity in this mental process. It is notable that the German General Staff was not guided by any fixed set of principles, like those set out in the British *Field Service Regulations* in the interwar years. They were regarded as implicit in sound military thinking. The General Staff was not separated from the rest of the officer corps. Its members regularly alternated between staff and regimental appointments, to keep the 'feel' of commanding troops; theory was always refreshed by practice. Similarly, although the General Staff was divided into two main branches, its members were liable to serve in either.

The Great General Staff (*Grossesgeneralstab*) was, in effect, the military element in the war ministry. The Chief of the General Staff was, in peace, the professional head of the army and through the war minister the military adviser to the head of state, the Kaiser. In war, he took command of the armies in the field. The 'great' staff was concerned with gathering and analysing information concerning foreign armies and the topography of possible theatres, the organisation and training of the army in peace, contingency plans for war and preparing in immense detail elaborate schemes for mobilisation; calling up the reserves and moving millions of men, horses and guns to the frontier.

The General Staff attached to the various headquarters in the field from GHQ down to divisions (the *Truppengeneralstab*) performed the same function as the older staffs it superseded, planning and monitoring the three main spheres of activity, operations, logistics and intelligence, but with one unique difference. Originating in the days when high command appointments were awarded to aristocratic or princely candidates, and continuing when vacancies were filled by General Staff officers, the *Truppengeneralstab* was held collectively responsible for the advice given to commanders *and that they accepted and acted on it*. The Junker caste was traditionally blunt spoken, and saw no difficulty in reconciling respect for rank and discipline with their duty to offer candid and sometimes unpalatable advice to their generals. If his advice was not accepted, the officer concerned had the right to record the fact in writing; a necessary precaution, since in the event of failure the custom was to dismiss the chief of staff together with his erring master.

The formal machinery for this was institutionalised in the *Generalstabdienstweg*, the separate staff line of command and control extending downwards in parallel to the normal hierarchical chain of command.

The surviving records of the Second World War, when conversations between headquarters were taped, reveal the continual and searching nature of staff consultations on the situation and enemy intentions, with the aim of arriving at an agreed staff opinion. It was customary in all armies for commanders to despatch a chief of staff or a senior staff officer to assess a situation in person or to convey his wishes to a subordinate commander, but a German General Staff officer on such an errand was not merely a messenger or a rapporteur: he could issue orders for immediate action without reference back to his own commander.

Such practices were totally foreign to the General Staffs and commanders of the supposedly more 'democratic' British and US armies. When, to take two British examples, General Alan Cunningham's chief of staff in the Western Desert, perceiving that his commander was on the verge of breakdown, summoned General Auchinleck to come forward and see the situation for himself, and Montgomery's chief of staff in 21st Army Group in North-West Europe, de Guingand, warned him that his tactlessly expressed objections to General Eisenhower's plans might lead to his dismissal, both were regarded as bold but unheard of actions from a mere staff officer.

The question that arises here is this. If the Prussian-German General Staff was so perfect, how did it come about that Germany was so signally and disastrously the loser in both World Wars? It is partly answered in our third chapter dealing with the causes of the deadlock on the Western Front, but the basic causes lie outside our self-imposed terms of reference. In both wars, German capabilities fell far short of German war-aims, and in the second, the awful dilemma of reconciling patriotism and loyalty to the state was too difficult for the simple Junker ethic to resolve. What seems beyond doubt is that the German General Staff remained in a class by itself in the direction of the operations. As we will clearly demonstrate, wars are not won by armies alone, no matter how well they are equipped or how bravely they fight. In the end, their part is dictated by and subordinate to national strategy and political direction.

The first army to profit by the Prussian example was the British, the spur to reform being, as it was later in the US army, public realisation of the failure in logistics and administration in the Crimea, causing great and unnecessary suffering to the troops. Formal training of British staff officers began on 1 April 1858. Realisation of its operational ineptitude had to wait for the lessons of the South African War. The British Army, it should be understood, may have been backward compared with the armies of the European powers, but it was perfectly satisfactory for the purpose for which it existed, which was to provide as cheaply as possible an imperial gendarmerie capable of fighting colonial wars, together with a small expeditionary force for coalition war in Europe; a traditional eighteenth century role, hopefully embarked upon in 1914 and yet again in 1939. The organisational backbone of the army was the 'regimental system', by which the individual regiments of cavalry and infantry were virtually autonomous, recruiting their officers on the basis of class and affluence acceptable to the peculiar outlook of each. Until the reforms of the early 1970s it was difficult for an infantry or cavalry officer to live on his military salary.*

No attempt was made to attract the best of the output from the public schools, which provided the bulk of the officers, the army being content to accept what was left over after the learned professions had taken the cream of the material as far as brain-power was concerned. The quality of the intake was skimmed further by the competition for vacancies at the Royal Military Academy, attended by the engineer and artillery candidates, and the Indian Army, both fields offering interesting and adventurous careers and better pay. In fact until 1939 there was little need for the majority of cadets choosing the infantry and cavalry to exert themselves unduly. Provided they did not fail the Sandhurst course, they could be sure of a place in the regiment of their choice. There was nothing inconsistent or incompatible in this with the policy that the Army should be the least possible burden on the Exchequer, and trained and equipped only for minor colonial operations. It produced a corps of infantry composed of the little, closed societies known as 'regiments' renowned for their morale, *esprit de corps* and durability under the stress of war. As in the Prussian Army, the qualities of loyalty, integrity, courage, leadership and determination were essential but, unlike the Prussians, intellect was not; indeed, it was regarded with the suspicion that the British have for anything resembling cleverness. The trouble was that something more than brave officers was required to make the best use of the heroic battalions that had fought at the Alma and Inkerman, who starved outside Sebastopol or died in the pestilent hospitals of Scutari.

* Exact figures are difficult to arrive at, but by way of example, in 1932 the parents of successful candidates in the entrance examination for the RMC Sandhurst and RMA Woolwich were informed that the absolute minimum allowance for an ensign in the Foot Guards was £400. In polo playing cavalry regiments it may have been four figures. In unfashionable infantry regiments, perhaps £100–200.

No British Scharnhorst appeared with powers to reform the British Army root and branch. That was not the British way. Progress was step by step, with compromise and modification to adjust an alarming foreign idea so as to allay the suspicion and resentment of the deeply conservative officers of the infantry and cavalry. Nevertheless, the Staff College, created in 1858 as one of the post-Crimean reforms, was to become the most influential and respected of British military institutions. No concession was made to the feelings of mature officers who, as many saw it, were forced to become schoolboys again; sitting at desks in class-rooms, writing essays and learning campaign histories by heart; necessarily, since the higher military education of army officers at that period was a perfect blank. This was in due course corrected by lengthening the Sandhurst course to two years and improving the curriculum at Sandhurst and Woolwich. Seventy years later, the curriculum at Sandhurst and Woolwich had become so advanced that it would have surprised those pioneers of the Victorian age, including as it did military history, the principles of strategy, tactics, military administration, some basic economics and constitutional theory and aspects of Imperial defence.

The British Staff College was from the first in effect a War College. It reached the peak of its influence, perhaps, in the inter-war years when Fuller, Dill, Brooke and Montgomery* were among the senior instructors and the student body provided the successful senior commanders and senior staff officers of the Second World War. The brilliant innovation of the British Staff College was self-instruction by peer groups, a mental discipline necessary for men who would in their professional life have to work in teams under physical and emotional stress. The unit of instruction was the 'syndicate', a group of seven to ten students, who learnt by mutual discussion and criticism. Important exercises were carried out as a team, the syndicate members playing the parts of the staff officers who would be found in planning. The role of the directing staff was to act as guides and authorities on matters of fact and to devise exercises in the form of realistic military problems, for which they offered suggestions but never exclusively correct solutions. Basic position papers on, say, infantry tactics in jungle warfare, or the system for the evacuation and treatment of wounded, known as 'précis', were discussed in syndicate with a designated student acting as chairman, while a member of the directing staff sat listening, ready to advise on any particular point. Individual syndicate solutions were mercilessly dissected in open forum by the spokesmen of the

---

* Major General JFC Fuller, Field Marshal Sir John Dill, Field Marshal Viscount Alanbrooke and Field Marshal Viscount Montgomery.

other syndicates, who in turn had to defend their own team's solution. What the attendant directing staff were looking for was rational analysis, lucid exposition, a practical solution taking military realities into account and, all important, the capacity to accept trenchant criticism with unruffled composure.

To assist officers unskilled in logic and the logical analysis of problems the Staff College devised a set procedure of the 'appreciation of the situation' under the headings: OBJECT, CONSIDERATIONS AFFECTING ITS ATTAINMENT, COURSES OPEN TO THE ENEMY AND OURSELVES, THE COURSE RECOMMENDED as it emerged from the argument and the proposed PLAN OF ACTION, which had to be set out in sufficient detail to enable the staff to issue the precise orders for a set-piece operation, such as a deliberate attack or protracted defence or, for an open-ended operation such as a temporary defence, a reconnaissance in force, pursuit or exploitation, the briefer 'operation instruction', leaving the method to be employed to the commander concerned.

The British Army (like the French and the United States armies) did not follow German practice in one significant respect, the corporate responsibility of the General Staff and the *generalstabdienstweg*. British commanders were extremely jealous of their power and authority, and when staff spoke to the staff or the commander of a subordinate headquarters they were careful to emphasise that they were conveying their chief's wishes. The British Army, in characteristically British fashion, avoided a total radical change and grafted the new on to the old. The idea of a 'General' staff was conceived by RB Haldane when he was Secretary of State for War, in 1907, as part of the wider reorganisation of the British Army involving the creation of an Expeditionary Force and a Territorial Army. His principal assistant was Douglas Haig.*

It assumed responsibility for operations, planning, training and intelligence and 'staff duties', the allocation of man-power and warlike equipment in accordance with general staff directives. It was also the regulating branch of the whole. The ancient offices of the Adjutant-General, the Quartermaster-General and the Master General of the Ordnance, responsible for personnel management, supply and transport and equipment respectively continued to exist, and their representatives, though trained at the Staff College, were regarded as separate and, by implication, inferior in status to the General Staff, distinguished by the titles of their appointments, e.g., 'Deputy', Adjutant General or 'Assistant' Quartermaster General. Compared with the simple division of staff duties

---

* See John Terraine, Haig: The Educated Soldier, (Leo Cooper 1990), pp 42–43.

distinguished by letter or number as finally adopted in the German, French and United States armies, British staff nomenclature was baffling to all but the staff itself. The chief of staff might be so-called, or a 'Major-General General Staff'. The operations officer in a brigade was 'the Brigade Major', his administrative colleague was 'the Deputy Assistant Adjutant and Quarter Master General'. The role of 'Chief of the Imperial General Staff' was never strictly defined. He was by custom, the principal military adviser to the government, the professional head of the Army, but only *primus inter pares* in the Army Council, together with the Adjutant-General, the Quartermaster-General and the Master-General of the Ordnance, the chairman being the Secretary of State for War. When Lord Kitchener, who believed that he required no military advice was appointed Secretary of State in 1914 the situation became confused. It became more so when Lloyd George sought alternative advisers when the advice offered by the CIGS was unpalatable.

During and after the First World War it became fashionable to deride 'the gilded staff', and accuse it of remoteness from the men in the firing line and incompetence. The real handicap under which it suffered in 1914 was that a cadre strong enough to cope with the enormous and unexpected expansion of the army was never built up. Professor Bond has pointed out that the total number of officers qualified as PSC (Passed Staff College, the official qualification) in 1914 was 447, of whom eighty-four had been killed in action by the end of 1915, and 219 altogether by the Armistice, or 46 per cent. In fact, considering the size of twentieth century armies, and the unprecedented complexities of modern war, the service rendered by a staff of hastily trained war-time officers and the small cadre of staff-trained officers from Camberley and Quetta (the Indian Army Staff College) deserves our admiration.

The reaction of the French High Command to the shattering defeat of their army by the Prussians in the war 1870 was to blame it on two military shortcomings, a mistaken defensive strategy, and the absence of a General Staff on the Prussian model. The first was to have a disastrous consequence in the First World War, when a war doctrine that the overriding strategic and operating principles of offensive action and attack *à outrance* was advocated with religious fervour by Foch and Grandmaison, regardless of the defensive potential of modern fire-power. A true general staff was created, responsible for personnel, intelligence, operations and logistics, and the *Ecole Supérieure de Guerre* was established in 1875.

As regards potential candidates, the French had a great advantage over the British. The Army was a career open to talent. The Ecole Militaire for cavalry and infantry cadets, and the Ecole Polytechnique, which conferred degrees in science and engineering, ranked with the *grandes écoles* of a nation prizing education and intellect. The horse artilleryman Foch and the military engineer Joffre were Polytechnicians. Pétain was an infantryman who, before 1914, perceived the defensive potential of modern small arms fire and the folly of infantry attacking in mass. What the French did not accept was the idea of the staff as an exclusive *corps d'élite* with the positive duty of imposing its collective view on commanders, or of a *Generalstabdienstweg*. The Napoleonic image of the commander as the ruling genius persisted too strongly for that. Foch, dynamic and volatile, treated his chief of staff, Weygand, as no more than a superior adjutant. The performance of the French high command in 1914–18 presents some strange contradictions. It pursued an offensive strategy at hideous expense in human life in Lorraine in 1914, at Verdun in 1916 and again in the Nivelle offensive in 1917, the last precipitating a widespread mutiny. But that was due not only to the feeling in the infantry that it could stand no more, but serious failures in welfare, man-management and administration; later rectified by Pétain (who in that role can be seen as the saviour of France).

The Staff itself was extremely bureaucratic, smothering the front-line troops in paper. (The British, when they took over French trenches, were amazed by the litter of abandoned documents.) Such rigidity was corrected by the tradition of individual initiative and self-reliance inherited from the post-Revolutionary armies, and what was called *le Système D*. A whole class of French officers had learnt their soldiering in the overseas empire, commanding outposts and small forces in operations very unlike those analysed at the *Ecole Supérieure de Guerre*, without any definite orders, and as likely to be engaged in road-building, keeping order or introducing French culture to the natives as fighting. They learnt how to cope, to manage – se débrouiller –and so arrived in a practical fashion at what the Germans called *Auftragstaktik*. ('Mission directed tactics'; in plain language on being given a mission or faced with a novel problem, dealing with it promptly and in the light of common sense and the circumstances.) The Germans arrived at the idea of fighting in loose, self-sufficient groups by logical thought. The French fell into it naturally.

The history of the United States Army is one of gradual evolution from the patriotic militia, part of the US military myth, which unaided had defeated the British in 1812 and 1814, to a small permanent force of regular volunteers, then to the huge expeditionary force of 1917 which, once it had found its feet, was equal in skill and prowess to all the armies engaged on the Western Front, and finally to the giant war machine of the Second World War. In the debate on defence, the advocate of a properly trained

and officered force prevailed and the government was persuaded to establish the United States Military Academy at West Point. Modelled on the
Ecole Militaire and *Ecole Polytechnique*, it aimed to educate officers for
service in all arms – a military university, not a mere cadet school.
Admission to a four year course culminating in graduation and a regular
commission was by written examination and sponsorship by the President
of the United States, or a senator from the applicant's state. Tuition was
free. Rich and poor alike could secure for their sons what every American
aspired to, a college education. When, therefore, the Americans decided to
create a general staff on the German model, they had a well-educated
corps of officers on which to draw.

Any hopes that the United States would be free from the curse of war
were soon disappointed. In 1846, the army was engaged in a minor war in
Mexico. The Civil War of 1861–1865 proved to be one of the bloodiest
conflicts fought by large armies. No sooner was it over than the Army
began its long involvement in what in modern terms was an anti-guerrilla
or counter-insurgency campaign against the American Indians, which kept
it fully occupied for a quarter of a century until 1891, when the Indians
wars were officially declared over. In 1898 there was war with Spain that
exposed serious deficiencies in operational command, in administration
and arrangements for the welfare and training of the mass of volunteers
who rushed to the colours. In 1916–1917, an expeditionary force commanded by Brigadier-General John J Pershing, whose aide-de-camp was
Captain George S Patton was sent to Mexico to suppress the Villasta 'ban-
dits'.

The impact of the Civil War was tremendous, but it was emotional and
political. The US army did not distil from it a military philosophy or tactical doctrine to prepare it for the twentieth century. (More attention was
paid to it in Britain than America; there Henderson, the professor of military history at the Camberley Staff College in the 1880s, was one of the
leading authorities on the subject and used it as a text.) The formative
experience for the post-bellum US Army was the long haul in the vast
spaces of the Middle West, where it was scattered in isolated posts, condemned to long periods of tedium interrupted by occasional skirmishes
with the warlike but elusive Indians, cut off from the main stream of society, and without the sense of mission that animated the French and British
colonial forces. The Indians were simply a nuisance, to be suppressed or
extirpated.

Where the United States Army was fortunate was in having a core of
energetic officers who did not allow it to stagnate mentally. Three are
notable. The foremost was Emory Upton, an artilleryman who was only

twenty-six at the end of the Civil War, having commanded both a cavalry and an infantry division. He reverted to the rank of lieutenant-colonel and filled the empty hours of peace-time soldiering by writing a book on all-arms tactics based on the lessons of the war, and persuaded the Army to adopt it as an official manual. He was appointed Commandant of Cadets at West Point in 1870 and in 1876, when his tour of duty was over, was sent on an official mission to Europe and India to study the British-Indian, French and German armies. What impressed him most was the German General Staff system and the *Kriegsakademie*, which in due course the US Army was to copy. Emory Upton firmly believed that, one day, the US Army would be engaged in a foreign war against a first class enemy, and that the correct policy was to build up a cadre of properly trained and educated officers suitable for the highest command and staff appointments.

The first training establishment for serving officers to be set up was the artillery school at Fort Monroe. In 1875, a progressive commandant, Colonel George W Getty, who considered that young artillery lieutenants required something more than purely technical training, added courses in 'military art and science', embracing geography, military history and military law. Two years later, Emory Upton joined the school as chief instructor in these subjects.

Acting on a suggestion made to him by Emory Upton in 1881, General Sherman, then the Commanding General of the US Army, established a cavalry and infantry school at Fort Leavenworth, which in 1887 followed the example of Fort Monroe and expanded its course to two years to include general military studies. One of the additional instructors appointed was Arthur L Wagner, who as a lieutenant had won the Gold Medal of the American Military Institute and for three years had occupied the chair of Military Science at Louisiana State University. He remained at Leavenworth for eleven years, becoming chief instructor in 1893. He wrote a study of the campaign of Königgratz in the light of the experience of the Civil War, and introduced a practical system of instruction which included 'staff rides', i.e., 'tactical exercises without troops' (or TEWTs), map exercises and 'appreciations of the situation'; in US terminology, 'estimates' of the situation. While Upton was the practical soldier, whose authority was derived from experience of battle, Wagner was the complete academic, but he was the spiritual founder of what was to become the US Army Command and Staff School at Leavenworth to this day.

The third of a distinguished trio who played an important part in professionalising the officer corps of the US Army was Tasker Bliss, like Upton an artillery officer. After attending the course at Fort Monroe, he was posted to West Point as an instructor in military science and French.

Ordered to prepare a series of lectures on the Russo–Turkish War, he took the trouble to learn German and Russian the better to study the sources. German was to prove useful when he, in his turn, was sent to study the European military systems at first hand. Like Upton, he was deeply impressed by the *Kriegsakademie*. In 1884, Commodore Stephen B Luce, USN, a veteran of the Civil War with first-hand experience in joint naval military operations, proposed a Naval War College in which officers could study grand strategy, and, having convinced the authorities, was appointed its first president. Luce believed that a study of naval strategy should incorporate lessons both from naval and military history, and the Army met his request for a suitable instructor by attaching Bliss. (His naval colleague was no less than Alfred Thayer Mahan.*) When, therefore, a reforming Secretary for War, Elihu Root, decided to set up an Army War College, an ideal candidate for the post of president was waiting in the wings.

Elihu Root was a distinguished corporation lawyer whose appointment was a consequence of the war with Spain in 1898. Like the Crimean and South African Wars, it had aroused a frenzy of patriotism, followed by disillusion when the degree of military incompetence displayed was revealed, and in particular a breakdown in the administrative arrangements that had caused great and unnecessary suffering. Considering that for a quarter of a century American generals had had no experience in handling large bodies of troops, and only theoretical understanding of anything other than constabulary and anti-guerrilla operations, they had done well to bring the campaign to a successful conclusion, although their conduct of operations may not have been a model of the military art. The scandal arose from the treatment of volunteers inside the United States. The Secretary for War, Russell E Alger, had unwisely given way to the popular enthusiasm which led to a rush of volunteers. Some 600,000 were accepted, too many for the army to accommodate and train and more than it could use, of whom 80 per cent spent their service in squalid camps without hearing a shot fired and 917 died of disease. Under pressure from press and public President McKinley first ordered an enquiry which only produced eight volumes of uninformative verbiage that satisfied no-one, and then reluctantly accepted the resignation of the luckless Alger. Root was a brilliant choice, and moreover enjoyed two advantages without which no reformer of an entrenched institution can prosper. He had an open mind

* Alfred Thayer Mahan (1840–1914) was author of many books about the
influence and practice of seapower. After examining British maritime strategy in
the 18th century and noting the lack of American naval power in the war of 1812
with Britain he devoted himself to advocating a strong navy. Great battles enabled
the victor's trade to flow freely and closed the seas to his enemy.

and was uninhibited by institutional loyalties, being an outsider. The institution in question had been discredited and badly shaken. The US Army higher command structure might have been deliberately designed with the objects of protecting vested political and bureaucratic interests, blocking innovation and promoting inefficiency.

Root's professional experience had given him an insight into the working of the great and growing commercial enterprises of the United States. What he found in Washington was totally at variance with all sound managerial principles. There was a 'Commanding General of the Army' – not a 'Commander-in-Chief', constitutionally that was the title of the President – but though he was responsible for the discipline, training and readiness for war he had no executive power. All administrative matters came directly under the Secretary for War, who was assisted by a number of staff departments, or 'bureaux', responsible for artillery, ordnance services, medical services, personnel, supplies, pay, military law, and building and works, such as the construction and maintenance of coastal defences. The specialist bureaux also exercised direct supervision over the specialist arms and services, the engineers, signals and quartermaster units. Financial control was exercised by Congress, which budgeted separately for each bureau (in the same fashion that the British Parliament divides military appropriations into 'votes'), and through its committees kept close control over the smallest details of expenditure, so any alteration or initiative could be indefinitely delayed. Each bureau therefore had to keep in touch with the committee concerned and tended to by-pass the Secretary. There was no coordinating staff branch. For instance, the modernisation of the coast artillery, involving the use of electric power and electrical fire-control systems bogged down in five different bureaux unable or unwilling to coordinate their separate roles. There were no bureaux for intelligence, mobilisation or operational plans. Elihu Root's achievements reveal his outstanding ability as an organiser, and also his considerable skill as a politician and advocate, bearing in mind that the American constitution was designed to give Congress complete control over the armed forces as a safeguard to liberty. What in other armies could be decided internally and promulgated by order or regulation in America required Congressional agreement and legislation.

Root's reforms attacked the bureaucrats head on. Dual civil-military control was patently absurd. The military commanders all down the line had constantly complained that they had responsibility without power. The post of Commanding General was abolished, and in its place the post of Chief of Staff of the Army established, who was the professional head of the US army and the adviser on all military matters to the Secretary of

State. A General Staff was finally established consisting of four numbered sections or branches: G1, personnel, discipline, manpower; G2, intelligence; G3, operations, plans, training, military doctrine; G4, supply. The bureaux dealing with technical arms and services were retained and retitled 'Special' branches of the staff.* Henceforth there was to be only one chain of command from top to bottom; commander to commander.

Root's other important innovation was the creation of a War College for the higher education of officers, but with a different function from the German *Kriegsakademie,* which was purely educational and attended by young officers, like Leavenworth in the United States and Camberley in England. The students at the United States War College were mature officers, already trained in staff duties. They learnt by doing. The War College combined the functions of a department for long-term contingency planning and a research institute. The students were invited to consider the scenarios of possible threats and draw up, in considerable detail, suitable contingency plans of campaign. This was also the practice at Camberley where, in the inter-war years, the students were asked to consider the defence of Singapore, and forecast the plan used by the Japanese with remarkable accuracy. Fortunately, exercise RED-ORANGE held at the US War College in 1919 was not prophetic, its scenario being a joint invasion of the United States by the British and Japanese mounted from Canada.

Such were the four military brains whose fate it was to wrestle with the most intractable problems ever faced by soldiers in the history of war. The first was the division of responsibility between soldiers and statesmen when to wage war successfully demanded the mobilisation of the entire resources of the state. The second was the administration and maintenance of morale of armies in the field counted in millions, of which perhaps only 10 per cent were fighters or located in the artillery zone of fire. The third, whose factors had been dimly perceived by a few prophets, was the technological revolution in the art of war which led to the deadlock on the Western Front. It is to perceptions by the General Staffs of war doctrine, or the operational art, and a technical analysis of the tactical factors prevailing on the Western Front that we now turn before examining the problems of command facing Haig and Pershing in the First World War, and Eisenhower in the Second.

* See Chapter 8 for the details of staff organisation under Pershing.

CHAPTER 2

THE OPERATIONAL ART

The ultimate overthrow of the enemy demands offensive action. A successful defensive unless followed by offensive action can only result in averting defeat. The offensive tends to confer the initiative, and with it, liberty of action, to force a defensive conduct on the enemy, to raise the morale of the forces and to depress that of the enemy.

FIELD SERVICE REGULATIONS VOLUME II (OPERATIONS) 1924

In 1903 the future Marshal Ferdinand Foch, then a lieutenant-colonel and an instructor at the *Ecole Supérieure de Guerre*, published his collected lectures on the operational art under the title *Des Principes de la Guerre*. They were a strange mixture of the metaphysical and the practical, with evidence on every page of the ardent personality of the author. Foch, like all the generals who commanded armies in the First World War, was a fervent believer in offensive action, and that the 'engagement' – the battle – was the decisive act in war. The operational art, the interpretation of topography, the use of signal communications, an understanding of the capability of the three arms, skill in manoeuvre, all had only one purpose; to bring about an engagement on the most favourable terms. Foch went beyond that. There was no place in his philosophy for defence, let alone withdrawal. Superior will-power gave a commander the upper hand, but final success in battle could only be gained by the determination of the infantry. In his final chapter, on the modern battle, he only recognised the effect of the great increase in fire-power insofar as it helped the infantry to close with the enemy: 'The laurels of victory are on the point of the enemy bayonets. They must be plucked *there* . . . they must be won in hand to hand fighting, if one really means to conquer.' It was the doctrine that led to appalling casualties in the opening battles of 1914. The French were not alone in this delusion. It was shared by the Germans, Prussians and Russians. (The British had had their lesson in South Africa.) In 1914, the German infantry advancing shoulder to shoulder in line were massacred by British rifle fire and shrapnel shell.

24

On the practical side, Foch devoted three out of his twelve chapters and eight maps to an analysis of the advance-guard action at Nachod (in 1866), an instructive example of the encounter battle which, as was then generally agreed, would be the opening manoeuvre in any great war. The operational art, in fact, was then indistinguishable from the art of manoeuvre. Foch made clear his belief that the best guide to the study of warfare is military history, and that from it could be deduced 'principles of war', guide-lines or precepts based on experience; in his words 'indisputable truths' – 'verités indiscutables' – 'principes de la conduite des troupes à la guerre'. Apart from the offensive principle, which was implicit throughout his lectures, Foch identified economy of force, security and strategic surprise, but while he was at pains to argue that though principles applicable to every phase of war in every age existed, they were only for guidance, not slavish application. In his preface to the English edition of his book, he compares them to 'the fires lit by shepherds on a storm-bound coast to assist the uncertain navigator'. He quotes with approval the exclamation of General Verdy du Vernois when faced with the confused situation at Nachod: 'To the devil with history and principles! What is the problem?'

In fact there were a number of principles, real or so-called, jostling for the attention of the student of warfare. The post-war British manual, the Field Service Regulations, listed seven: Economy of Force, Security, Surprise, Cooperation, Mobility, Concentration and Offensive Action. General 'Stonewall' Jackson recognised only two: Surprise and The Pursuit; never allow a shaken or defeated opponent to recover. The British came to regard as the first and essential principle the choice of the correct Object, or Aim. Montgomery later coined 'Balance', apparently meaning dispositions proof against an unexpected attack and equally suitable to seize an opportunity to strike a blow, what Foch called 'freedom of action', the Initiative – making the enemy dance to your tune – and to have a 'Master Plan' and stick to it. Clausewitz, by contrast, observed that 'no plan survives contact with the enemy', which perhaps prompted Liddell Hart's advice that a plan should have many branches; Flexibility. Liddell Hart also invented a nebulous theoretical concept, the Indirect Approach; more than a principle, a universal formula or law governing all tactics and strategy. To these could be added Unity of Command, obvious enough, especially in a coalition war, the adage 'march divided, fight united', Speed and Audacity; the last two central to Napoleon's method of making war.

The German General Staff did not believe in a codification of principles at all, holding that the properly educated soldier should be able to appreciate any situation objectively on its merits and reach the correct conclusion. Clausewitz says: 'Theory cannot furnish the mind with formulas for solving problems, nor can it mark the narrow path on which the solution is supposed to lie by planting a hedge of principles on either side', but elsewhere says there are always those of inferior intellect 'who have to be helped along by routine methods tantamount to rules. These will steady their judgment and also guard against eccentric and mistaken schemes, which are a great menace in a field where experience is so dearly bought'. As Clausewitz says, a good general is not necessarily a 'man of learning'; true to some extent of the British Army, which is why the British Staff College taught its students to follow the formalised, logical procedure of the 'appreciation' – a perfect example of 'a routine method tantamount to a rule'.

It was not necessary for generals to be 'men of learning' because the basic concepts of the operational art are simple. Manoeuvre warfare can be compared to a rough, body-contact game like American football; indeed American officers freely used terms such as 'end run' and 'carrying the ball' as metaphors. When the only maps available were small in scale, unreliable and ungridded, and communications limited to the electric telegraph and telephone, a great deal depended on the intuition of the general, and how he read the battle after the first collision of armies approaching each other like blindfolded wrestlers feeling for a grip. The general practice was to advance on a broad front, which masked the objective and also speeded up concentration, since there was not one long column to coil up but several short ones. The counter to that was to take advantage of 'the interior line', anticipate the enemy concentration and to strike with full strength at his isolated corps so as to defeat them in detail. Hence the principle of mobility, meaning that armies should be free to manoeuvre, not shackled to their supply lines, and never await attack in a fixed defensive system or fortifications. Mobility alone made it possible to implement the principle of pursuit which the Germans pressed to its logical extreme. The *objective* in war was the enemy army, and the *object* (or *aim*), its 'annihilation', not literally, but its reduction to a state of impotence beyond recovery. The ideal attacking manoeuvre was, therefore, encirclement, as seen at Sedan in 1870 which later in the days of the *Panzers* took the form of the double penetration that joined hands deep inside the enemy position, trapping everything inside the ring. (The '*Kesselring*', a term borrowed from the German system of driving game for sport, with the guns in the middle and the drivers surrounding them in an ever contracting circle.)

When Foch was lecturing, such manoeuvres still seemed perfectly feasible. Napoleon, the model and exemplar for every French student of warfare, brilliantly exploited the interior line when at bay in the valleys of the Seine and Marne in 1814, where he defeated the Allied armies invading

France in detail and in succession at Champeaubert, Montmirail, Vauchamps and Montereau, only failing when a force exhausted by marching and reduced to some 23,000 effectives met 70,000 fresh troops at Arcis-sur-Aube. In 1864, General Robert E Lee, withdrawing across the North Anna river, did not block the crossing places, but held his main force between them, concentrating in turn against the widely separated Union columns.

But the golden age of generalship was soon to end. A turning point is clearly visible in 1914, at the battles of Tannenberg and the Masurian Lakes, when two Russian armies converged on the province of East Prussia. The German Eighth Army, commanded by Hindenburg with Ludendorff as his chief of staff, was handled in masterly fashion, routing one and then defeating and pursuing the other back into Russian territory. The price of victory was 100,000 men or about 40 per cent of the German strength.

Manoeuvre had become costly through a combination of mass armies, henceforth to be numbered in millions, and the intensification of firepower. There was ample room for manoeuvre on the Eastern Front, but even there the cost of the fighting in August and September in Galicia in 1914, when the Russians succeeded in driving back the invading Austro-Hungarian armies was: Russians, killed and wounded 250,000 plus the loss of 40,000 prisoners of war; Austro-Hungarians, 300,000 plus 100,000 taken prisoner, perhaps 50 per cent of the armies in the field. When, in June 1916, the Germans came to the aid of their ally, their highly successful offensive operations cost them 90,000 casualties.

At this point we should emphasise that we are not concerned with the validity of different concepts of the operational art or the mistakes of generals, but how the art was perceived in a changing military environment. On the Western Front there was a deadlock broken only in the spring of 1918, marking the change from the old to a totally new form of warfare. The inter-war years were a period of re-assessment, taken up with a debate on whether the deadlock on the Western Front was a freak effect, a fulfilment of the prognostications of the author Bloch* and a permanent state of affairs, or an interim period in which fresh operational methods could be devised. The correct path to the solution was followed by the Germans and Russians. In essence it was made possible by what Liddell Hart called 'The ratio of troops to space'; there had to be 'room for manoeuvre'. Henceforth it would be necessary to fight for space, not by the method of prolonged attrition, but by a violent breakthrough followed by its exploitation in depth behind the main line of resistance.

* Jan Bloch, or Ivan S Bliokh, a Polish railway magnate, writing in Russian, published an immense work of five volumes, in 1899, on the effects of fire power.

The issues in the post-war debate on the future of war, whose reverberations are heard today, were greatly oversimplified. Manoeuvre, that is to say the principle of mobility, had to be restored to its place, and the magical weapon for this purpose was to be the tank, and with it 'mechanisation', the substitution of the internal combustion engine for the horse and the legs of the infantryman. Both were indeed profoundly important innovations, but were attended by difficulties which could easily have been foreseen. Weapons have always generated their own antidotes. The mine and the high-velocity anti-tank gun were to become to the tank what the machine gun and barbed wire had been to the infantry. The theorists Fuller and Liddell Hart and even the highly practical PCS Hobart relegated infantry and field artillery to subsidiary roles, to be confounded by events, but the new 'queen of the battlefield' turned out to be the fighter-bomber; the Stormoviks, Hurricanes, Messerschmitts, Focke-Wolfs, Thunderbolts and Mustangs. The search for manoeuvre, for formulas, for a magic weapon proof against any counter-weapon, led the pioneers of armoured mobility to forget that the ability to conduct operations, whether fluid or protracted static battles, a pursuit, a river crossing, a landing on a defended coast or an air-land battle rested on five pillars; the morale of the troops, logistics, command and control, intelligence, and adequate resources. These were the *preconditions* for success.

Volumes have been written about morale, but we are no nearer to a complete explanation of its nature since Julius Caesar made a practice of exhorting his legions before battle. We know its ingredients: discipline, sympathetic leadership, attention to the welfare of the troops and thorough training, which inspires confidence when facing the hazards of battle. To these can be added the good fortune of success in the first experience of battle. We know how to measure it. Good units and therefore good armies are durable in numerical terms of the number of combat days they can remain at fighting pitch before the stress on individuals and the attrition of trusted junior leaders finally take their toll, and by the desertion rate. Neither propaganda about the villainy of the enemy nor the justice of the cause have any predictable effect, since the interaction of psychological and social factors is too subtle and complex to make any confident assertions as to why, for instance, the German army in 1944–45 fought so long and with such determination long after any hope of victory had vanished, or why the brave, patriotic French collapsed in weeks in 1940. The Americans and British soldiers, well supplied and equipped, well trained and with a just cause, were by any criterion inferior in durability and fighting power to their German opponents.

A well run supply organisation has always been an essential component of generalship, but in the two World Wars 'logistics' took on an entirely new dimension. Statistically the figures are varied by a number of factors such as the distance between the Base Area and the rear boundaries of the combat formations which operate their own supply services forward of rail head and whether operations are fluid or static battering. On the Western Front not only were immense and unexpected tonnages of artillery ammunition in demand by mid-war but the back-up of medical services, ordnance and supply depots, reinforcement holding units, battle-schools, police and prisoner of war camps, began to absorb more manpower than there was in the firing line and these units required headquarters and staffs to administer them. A ratio of nineteen men in the rear areas to one in the line is sometimes mentioned. In the later war, in the same theatre, the proportions were doubled. Theatre-based air forces required aviation fuel and ordnance while armoured and mechanised forces required a vast combined tonnage of motor fuel and ammunition. (An armoured division in intense operations needed 900 tons a day.) If, as experienced by the Eighth Army in the Western Desert and the US forces in France in 1944, a long section of the line of communication has been operated by trucking, the fuel bill becomes astronomical and the number of forward units capable of active operations severely limited. (We discuss these problems in Chapter 8 and, in particular, in Chapter 15.)

There are two ways of organising the administration and supply organisation of an army in the field. It can be either managed by the General Staff which ensures that it has early warning of requirements through its antennae with front line units or it can be command-managed by placing the whole logistic apparatus from the rear boundaries of armies to the ports of entry under a single commander so as to free the commander-in-chief to concentrate on operations. That is only workable if the logistics commander is made entirely subordinate to the operational commander and wholly 'in his mind', since it is yet another principle of war that operational and logistic factors are inseparable. As we shall show in Chapter 15, it was the Americans' failure to observe this principle that led to the administrative chaos within their Communications Zone (COMMZ) in France in 1944–5.

In modern defence jargon command and control is abbreviated to 'C3I' (Command and Control, Communications and Information) in recognition of the fact that it is a manifold of 'command', in its literal sense of issuing orders and instructions, 'control' which is the monitoring of the operation that ensues, while both depend on the signal communication network which makes possible the two-way flow of information and intelligence along the command chain. ('Information' and 'Intelligence' are not quite the same thing: 'C3I^2' would be more exact. It is a question of usage rather than definition. 'Information' refers to the location and activities of friendly troops, while 'Intelligence' is the order of battle, dispositions and possible intentions of the enemy. 'Information' can also mean information concerning the enemy collected by various agencies and processed into 'intelligence' by the intelligence branch of the General Staff; G(inf), G2, 1C, according to the army.) Fast moving, fluid operations extending over large areas are unmanageable unless the staff can provide commanders at every level with up-to-date information of the location, movements and combat effectiveness of their own units. In the First World War and, indeed, sometimes in the Second there was a complete information black-out from the moment when the attackers crossed the start-line and disappeared into the smoke-screen and when reports that the attack had either stalled or reached its objective, eventually reached headquarters.

No communication network is wholly proof against breakdown or enemy action, and the remedy is what the Germans termed *Auftragstaktik,* or 'mission-directed tactics'. The term is misleading, suggesting as it does a tactical formula, whereas it is really an idea central to the whole art of command of modern armies, whose operations are continuous, and whose sub-units are engaged in fluid battles widely extended in frontage and depth. It is not a new idea. Long before anything resembling modern warfare began to evolve, it was recognised, albeit reluctantly, that the close grip of events maintained by the commander in the field could not be extended beyond his field of vision. A classic example, taught to cadets at Woolwich in 1932, is the order given by Napoleon to Grouchy, his cavalry commander, when the Prussians under Blücher withdrew, battered but not beaten, from the field of Ligny, in 1815. Napoleon assumed that Blücher would fall back on his lines of communication and told Grouchy to follow him up, which he did, following the letter of his orders. Blücher, however, marched off to join Wellington at Waterloo. Had Grouchy been told to follow the Prussian army wherever it went and harry it, things might have turned out rather the worse for Wellington. In its simplest interpretation *Auftragstaktik* means giving a subordinate his mission and leaving him to use his judgment. In its more profound sense it demands that initiative should be exercised at every level of command. This, in turn, requires that the officer corps is intelligent, militarily well educated, imbued with a common doctrine of war and informed about the commander's intention.

Between 1915 and 1918, as we explain in the next chapter, the impact of technology began a radical transformation of intelligence gathering methods which accelerated between 1939 and 1945. This, in turn, unlike any previous war, led to a contingent of the best civilian brains being drawn into the intelligence-acquiring and the intelligence-processing agencies. The working rules that were adopted in both wars (but not always strictly observed) involved a separation of function. Acquisition agencies should be sternly discouraged from having ideas about strategy. The first processing should be by dispassionate specialists within those agencies but only for reliability or classification. The military implications are the business of the intelligence branch of the general staff. These in their turn have to be insulated from pressure from the operations branch or, worse, a strong-minded commander, to serve up interpretations of the evidence that agreed with their hopes or convictions. A classic example of this last was the relationship between Haig and his Brigadier-General Staff (Intelligence), John Charteris, who felt that it was his duty to tell Haig nothing that might shake his confidence in his current plans. Usually this took the form of rating German morale as low which, apart from being incorrect, was bad intelligence practice, as it is too often based on the interrogation of prisoners of war, who are dejected, or deserters, who have a natural grudge against the units from which they have fled. In the Second World War, the information that two SS panzer divisions were refitting within easy reach of the objectives of the British airborne division about to be engaged in MARKET GARDEN ('Arnhem') in 1944 proved all too true, but the intelligence staff officer who pressed this unwelcome evidence too vehemently was relieved of his appointment.

Finally there is the question of resources. The fact that has to be recognised is that they are expendable in terms of human life and of equipment and weapons. The underlying idea of beginning a war with a single, overwhelming stroke, whether it was in the form of the Schlieffen plan or the later blitzkrieg was to avoid the need for vast reserves of men and material to make good the losses of a prolonged war of attrition. In modern warfare the resources required consist of a pool of man-power available for military use, the basic combat strength counted in divisions and material, which has to be measured in both quantity and quality. The critical factor in both wars was the availability of infantry replacements. In numerical terms, infantry is the easiest arm to form but by far the hardest to train to the exacting standards of modern warfare. The British Army in the earlier war and both the British and the US Armies in the latter suffered from a serious wastage of high-grade assault infantry units. The rule of thumb for assessing casualties used to be that in any one action the units in the forward zone suffer 25 per cent casualties of all kinds, of which another 25 per cent might be fatal, or some 6–8 per cent of the total casualty figure, almost all in the rifle companies of infantry battalions. It is always difficult for British students of warfare, whose perspectives are distorted by the British David and Goliath myth and the British tradition of minimum par-

31

ticipation in land campaigns to grasp the powerful advantage conferred by numerical superiority. One of the legacies of the Western Front was the universal horror at the final count of British dead, some 750,000, roughly the number lost by the French from a smaller population between the outbreak of war and the spring of 1915. That, and the committal of some fifty-seven United Kingdom divisions plus a tank corps and an air force was seen as a terrible aberration, the consequence of departing from traditional British strategy. Seen in isolation, the total British casualties distorted the historiography of the war and the verdict on British generalship.

No such minimalist illusions have inhibited German strategy. In 1914, the German armies deployed in the west were over a million strong. In 1941, Hitler assembled 145 divisions for the invasion of Russia; not enough as it turned out. The Americans, measuring their needs by their experience in 1918, deployed some sixty divisions in North-West Europe, although the United States was also involved in full scale war in the Pacific.

When the French, the Germans and the British came to assess the lessons of the Western Front each, predictably, revised its military doctrines in light of their own bitter experience. France had provided the battle ground and suffered most bitterly. The offensive *principle* was abandoned in favour of defence based on a fortress barrier, backed by a powerful army, equipped with powerful and well designed tanks, but the French generals failed to organise distinct, mobile, armoured formations capable of counter-offensive operations, the necessary tactical corollary to a strategic defence. For so logical, so 'Cartesian' a nation, in military matters French military men remained remarkably conservative, even romantic. The most heroic but ridiculous episode of the fall of France in 1940 was a last ditch defence attempted by the staff and students of the cavalry school at Saumur, the survivors rounding up the horses and leading them off to safety, in the hope that the cavalry of France would be reformed, once more to ride sword in hand against the enemy.

The German General Staff, secretly re-created in defiance of Treaty obligations, formed an independent air force and elite all-arms mobile formations based on the tank to spear-head their old-fashioned infantry armies with horse-drawn artillery. The '*blitzkrieg*', as the British came to call the new German tactics (owing a great deal to the brief but startling success of deep penetration tactics they used in their final throw in March–April 1918), was not a radical or revolutionary change in the operational art but a perfect example of the workings of the German military mind, applying sound thinking from first principles to make best use of mechanised infantry and artillery, tanks and, most important, close air support, orchestrated into a single war-machine.

The United States Army was fortunate in that it emerged from its brief engagement on the Western Front without severe loss and had good reason to congratulate itself on its performance. Like the British, it suffered in the Second World War from the disadvantage of having to create a huge army and air force from too small a regular base. However, with a sound operational doctrine, sound organisation and the backing of the largest and most efficient industrial base in the world it produced the fully mechanised, superbly equipped army and air force which ultimately ensured victory in the West.

The evolution of British military thought in the inter-war years was contradictory, even paradoxical. When the post-war euphoria of victory waned, the prevailing mood was determination never again to become fully involved in a war in Europe or, indeed, in any war at all. Britain reverted to her role as a naval power and the Army, deprived of its own air arm, reverted almost immediately to its role of an imperial gendarmerie.

At the same time there was a remarkable flowering of radical military thought inside the British Army, an institution noted, as we have seen, for conservatism and anti-intellectualism, judged even by the standards of armies as a category. It was the work of a small number of gifted officers who had been attracted to the Royal Tank Corps (as it became) by the belief that the future of land warfare lay in the restoration of mobility, and that the key to this was the armoured fighting vehicle. Lindsay (infantry), Pile and Broad (artillery), Martel and Hobart (engineers) were practical soldiers, primarily concerned with tank design and tank tactics. By far the most influential was Major-General JFC Fuller, originally an infantryman, who had served as the principal operations staff officer to the commander of the Tank Corps in France. He was the first to conceive the idea of an autonomous armoured force based on the tank, as opposed to its role as an automotive armoured cannon designed for the close support of infantry. Genius is perhaps too strong a word, but he was at least one of the most powerful and imaginative minds to appear in the British Army, besides being a brilliant interpreter of the lessons of military history and the highly articulate advocate of the armoured idea.

Fuller's friend and colleague, Captain Basil Liddell Hart, was more of a synthesiser and a publicist, with a passionate interest in every form of military activity from infantry drill to armoured warfare and a concept (or nostrum) lying at the heart of all strategy and tactics, 'the Indirect Approach'. There is much to criticise in the work of both Liddell Hart and Fuller, and it is certainly true that the experience of the Second World War, though it affirmed the importance of armoured, mechanised mobility like the first, confirmed in the long run the decisive nature of numerical

33

superiority, and the utility of infantry and massed artillery. That, however, does not derogate from the value of that work. If it did nothing else (and it did much more), it stimulated debate, and the more provocative the propositions advanced, the greater the stimulation.

British opinion on all this was divided. The army chiefs accepted that the post-war economic situation made the dismantling of the huge, victorious war-machine of 1918 inevitable, nor were they prepared to dispute a policy that gave priority to the security of the Empire, even though it meant reducing the regular army to its pre-war status without even the nucleus of the up-to-date expeditionary force that had existed in 1914. They and the core of surviving regular officers were perfectly content, indeed happy, to revert to a small, all-regular force organised on the cosy regimental system. All the same, the lessons of the war were not forgotten. The *Field Service Regulations* were revised, and in 1924 the War Office issued *Volume II (Operations)*. Its author was Brigadier Aspinall-Oglander (the author of the official history of the Gallipoli campaign), assisted by Fuller, who contributed the section on the principles of war – Security, Economy of Force, Cooperation, Offensive Action, Mobility, Surprise, Concentration (note the order) which, with the addition of the principle of the Object, remained the guidelines for British commanders until long after the Second World War.* Their appearance stimulated a historical study of British strategy by Major-General Sir Frederick Maurice, a soldier and scholar of distinction who had been Director of Military Operations in the War Office until 1918 and who in 1927, after retirement, was appointed to the chair of Military Science at Kings College in the University of London.† He gave a number of lectures on strategy, the nature of war, whether the lessons of military history could be expressed as 'principles', and if so, what they were, fleshing out the staccato paragraphs of the FSR with many illuminating examples from past campaigns, together with insights on the impact of tanks and air-power on modern war.

Maurice's *British Strategy: A Study of the Application of the Principles of War* was published in 1929. It represents the orthodoxy of the day, but it can still be read with profit. *British Strategy* is neither as profound or as stimulating as the works of Fuller, which were wide ranging and widely

---

* Colonel, later Major-General, JFC Fuller was a senior instructor at the Camberley Staff College at the time, and published his own *Lectures on FSR II* in 1931.

† Maurice was dismissed in 1918 after he had publicly contradicted Lloyd George's statement to the House of Commons on the strength of the British Expeditionary Force in France before the German offensive of March, 1918.

read. Fuller's *Foundations of the Science of War*, (1926) and his Staff College lectures, published as *Lectures on FSR II* [Field Service Regulations] (1931) and *Lectures on FSR III (Operations between Mechanized Forces)* (1932) help to form the opinions of students destined to hold high appointments in the Second World War.

In Europe, the serious work was done in Russia and Germany, understandably, since the former officers of both the Tsar and the Kaiser had felt the sting of a defeat which they believed had been brought about by a collapse on the home front and not by the Army's failure in battle. Both groups were accustomed to planning and executing operations on the largest scale. Neither had any illusions about their cost, or failed to perceive that however ingenious or thorough the tactics, the attacker had to pay for their success in blood. Both saw clearly that the problem lay in maintaining the continuity of the offensive. As we explain in our next chapter, after grievous trial and error, G Bruchmuller, a German artillery officer, the British General Sir Julian Byng, assisted by his artillery commanders, General J Monash, the Australian and the Russian General Brusilov, had all demonstrated that it was possible to break into the strongest defensive line. The problem that remained unsolved was how to break out into the open and maintain the momentum of the offensive before the gap could be sealed off by the counter-offensive formations held in reserve. Tactical innovations are so simple that they often occur simultaneously to different armies. The difficulty lies in persuading the conservative military to accept them, and the detailed mechanics required for execution. All the same it was, notably, two officers of the Red Army who pioneered what came to be known as the 'deep battle'. Generals Tuchachevskii and Triandafillov. (Both shot in Stalin's purge of the Red Army Officer Corps in the late 1930s.) Essentially, the method they suggested was to exploit the break-in using a 'shock army' of massed armour, as already anticipated by Fuller in his 'Plan 1919', supported by aircraft and, the real innovation, the use of parachute troops dropped in areas behind the main defensive system to block the movement of reserves to the threatened point. Not only were these two brilliant officers shot but their teaching and writings were declared taboo by Stalin. It was not until after the Russian victory at Stalingrad and their subsequent crushing defeat of the Germans at Kursk in 1943, that Stalin realised the need for new tactics to carry the Red Army forward into Europe. He therefore lifted the ban and it was on the basis of 'deep battle' that Operation BAGRATION swept the Russian armies westwards to Berlin, an advance also made possible by the provision of hundreds of 4-ton lorries and jeeps from the great storehouse of the United States. This was the first time that the Red Army had such mobility for its logistical support and was in stark contrast with the plight of the Germans, who had lost most of their motor transport and were relying increasingly on horse-drawn wagons .

Whether the idea of 'blitzkrieg' (for want of a better compact name for armoured-air-airborne offensive operations) was arrived at independently by the re-created German General Staff, how far it was a development of the infiltration tactics so successfully used in the final German offensive in March-April 1918 on the Western Front, whether it was inspired by the writings of Fuller or, more likely, reinforced an idea already born, or whether the doctrine was lifted bodily from the Red Army, with whose staff the Germans had enjoyed a close liaison is obviously of great historical interest to students of warfare, but not relevant to the theme of this part of our chapter, which is concerned with the differing perceptions of the operational art of the belligerents of 1939–45. The French, as we have seen, had decided upon a purely defensive strategy based upon fortress-like defences. The British were at first reluctant even to contemplate a second intervention on the continent on the scale of the last. Even when the British Government decided that war with Germany was inevitable, the most it was prepared to offer, in a re-run of 1914, was to send a small expeditionary force to re-inforce the powerful and, as it was believed, invincible French Army. In the East, Stalin had believed that his pact with Hitler in 1940 had obviated the risk of German aggression altogether. As for the Germans: their *Blitzkrieg* doctrine was entirely suited to their intention to wage offensive war with the political aim of gaining territory (*Lebensraum*) from an unprepared or demoralised opponent. This is not to say that armoured formations with close air support had no role in the defence. Clearly they had great potential in the tactical counter-offensive, but that role differed essentially from the 'blitzkrieg' designed for the rapid overthrow of an unprepared opponent making full use of strategic surprise.

The United States Army looked at the operational art from a totally different angle. It believed that in 1918 it had made a brief but successful debut in modern warfare from which it had emerged after some hard fighting, with its self-confidence greatly enhanced. Its military doctrine was basically the same as the German, since its senior officers when modernising its staff structure and education had studied German ideas and German methods closely. When the Second World War broke out the Americans did not repeat the mistake they had made in the First. They made the best use of their late entry into the war to build up and modernise their land and air forces, keeping three considerations in mind: that armoured-air forces now dominated land warfare; that the strategic aim would be to regain and liberate North-West Europe, which demanded offensive action; and that in turn demanded well equipped and well organised forces capable of inter-arm cooperation. The Americans recognised that the advent of the tank did not reduce the importance of infantry and artillery. They also made no bones about the importance of numerical superiority, and the inevitability of heavy casualties even in successful operations.

In the context of the third of these considerations, the British policy in the Second World War of withholding a significant portion of military manpower from active operations to the point that in the very crisis of the battle for North-West Europe infantry divisions were being disbanded for lack of infantry re-inforcements is explicable. As George C Marshall, who was more sympathetic to the British scruples than most American generals, said, British policy stemmed from the experience of 1916–1917 on the Western Front, which the United States had been spared. That also accounted for the British tactics, scorned by the Americans, of deliberate planning and cautious execution, of which Montgomery was the supreme exemplar. In fact, the operational problem dictated whether audacity or deliberate, systematic methods were appropriate. For instance, when Patton entered Lorraine in 1944 and encountered the German field fortifications around Metz, he had to revert to the deliberate methods employed in the earlier war. To emphasise this, we run ahead of the argument in this chapter to glance at the situation the Red Army faced in 1942.

The operational problem faced by Joseph Stalin was the same as that of the French and British in the earlier war, except on a vastly larger scale. The survival of the USSR demanded that the German invader should first be halted and then thrown out of Russia. Stalin's adoption of 'annihilation strategy' carried no Clausewitzian gloss: he meant it literally. The German armies were to be destroyed, Germany occupied and reduced to such a condition that she could never again threaten the Soviet Union. Stalin had no military education or experience. He was not even, like Hitler, an enthusiastic amateur. What he had was a clear mind, and an understanding of organisations. When it came to the pinch he could choose good generals, he could tell a good plan from a bad one, and if ever a war-lord deserved the epithet bestowed by Liddell Hart on Clausewitz: 'the Mahdi of mass', it was he. Any fool (Stalin might have said) could see that victory could only be won by superior numbers and resources. By the mid-summer of 1944, when the Red Army was ready to begin its general offensive, its order of battle was 166 divisions of all types, 9 independent rifle brigades, and included over 30,000 pieces of artillery and 5,200 armoured fighting vehicles. The air force, whose sole task, like the Luftwaffe's, was support for the army, had 6,000 light bombers and fighter-bombers. On the ground the

Red Army had a superiority of about three to one in every respect. If it took the lives of 3 or 10 Russian soldiers to kill one German it was a matter of only statistical interest. No-one knows exactly what the Russian battle casualties were to this day.

Having made himself chairman of the State Defence Committee, the People's Commissar for Defence, Supreme Commander-in-Chief of the Armed Forces, and arranged for the political control and supervision by the NKVD ('The People's Committee for Internal Affairs') over the field commanders, Stalin's power was absolute, and unchallengeable even by his professional military advisers. He attended to every detail of all major plans, exercising control through a small committee called the *Stavka*, whose military members were the chiefs of staff of the armed forces, often sent out to take operational command of a 'front' when it was engaged in a crucial operation. (A 'Front' was a group of armies associated with a particular sector of the front in general.)

Stalin's strategy was simple and consistent. Not a yard of ground was to be surrendered for however good a reason without a fight, and if lost it was to be immediately regained by counter-attack. The reinforcements for counter-strokes he doled out with a grudging hand, while he built up reserves bit by bit; first for armies, then by fronts and finally his strategic reserves. The appalling losses of 1941 were made good by superhuman efforts in the war factories and mass recruiting from every ethnic group in the USSR. New units were formed by slinging together the newly produced weapons and raw recruits with the least possible delay. A man hastily taught to use a rifle or a machine gun became an infantryman, the more intelligent were as hastily taught to man the simple but robust and effective heavy weapons; the tanks, artillery and mortars. In the artillery the battery commander was often the only literate man able to read an order or draw up a gun-programme. By American and British standards the Red Army was primitive, but combat is a good schoolmaster, and the simplest of methods combined with Draconian discipline and the hardihood and frugality of the Soviet soldier made the Red Army a formidable fighting machine.

Stalin began his defensive-offensive operations earlier than his marshals would have liked, but he had an instinctive understanding that it was the way to wear the German armies down and gradually gain the initiative. He understood that a defensive victory had to be exploited immediately by a counter-offensive, as at Stalingrad and Kursk where, before the German armies could disengage, a deep thrust from north and south threatened to encircle them. When he was ready he began the final advance (Operation BAGRATION)which, after much hard fighting against the best professional soldiers the world has ever seen, ended in Berlin. Nice distinctions between a strategy of annihilation and of wearing out or attrition are unreal, since both work together in all operations. The German armies in the east finally ceased to exist. The significance of those vast and terrible battles on the Eastern Front, so remote from American and British experience and understanding, is that they are the ultimate example of the real, brutal nature of the operational art.

The great advantage enjoyed by the rival commanders in the Second World War was that the problems of modern warfare had been solved in the crucible of the Western Front. The deadlock had been broken. The question was how best to make use of what had been discovered. Even Stalin grasped that. To understand what such problems were, and what solutions emerged it is necessary to appreciate afresh the exact causes of that deadlock and the interaction between tactics and technology. This is the subject of our next chapter.

CHAPTER 3

THE LONG THIN BATTLEFIELD

In the Salient the whole world seems brown and mired. Up here you realised just how thin this mud-world was. The green countryside browned gradually. There was a kind of bruised and trampled verge before the vermiculated lines of the old trench systems appeared – bay and traverse, bay and traverse – and beyond them the erratic spoor of duck-board and fascine tracks across the mud, the pools in the craters flat and opaque like pennies. From this range I could not see any men, but I knew they were down there in their hundreds of thousands, hiding. It seemed such a miserable, attenuated strip to be fighting over.

A VIEW FROM AN OBSERVATION BALLOON, WILLIAM BOYD,
THE NEW CONFESSIONS pp. 151–2

The causes of the deadlock on the Western Front have been extensively discussed, but not always recognised. In this chapter, at the risk of some oversimplification, we treat the question as fundamentally one of the interdependence of technology and tactics. Why did the General Staffs of the four main continental powers ignore the lessons of recent military history? The American Civil War had clearly demonstrated the consequences of the combination of large armies supported by railways, increased fire-power and rapidly constructed lines of trenches and field fortifications: heavy casualties and prolonged operations. The South African War had demonstrated that a small army of marksmen using magazine rifles backed by a few but well handled modern artillery units could hold in check an army organised and trained on the European model, until its leaders changed their ideas. The answer to that question is that the General Staffs attached no importance to what they deemed to be the operations of second-rate colonial armies in remote theatres, and less to the opinions of a Polish civilian Bloch (see page 27), an intruder in the field of military expertise.

The prevailing tactical theory was that if attacking formations were suf-

40

ficiently dense, enough men would survive the fire-storm to overwhelm the defence when bayonets were crossed. Tactical formations were line and column at close interval. The French advanced in the style of 1870 without any systematic artillery preparation. The British infantry and artillery observers were astonished to see German battalions advancing in unbroken line with linked arms 'who went down like targets on the range when the rope is cut.' In attack the British themselves were little better. The future Field Marshal Montgomery has described his first attack, at Le Cateau – 'no reconnaissance, no plan, no covering fire' and a loss of seven officers and forty men. It took three years to invent all-arms tactics.

The German plan for invading France, known by the name of the Chief of the Great General Staff who conceived it, Field Marshal Graf Alfred von Schlieffen, was to pass a mass of manoeuvre of four armies with a total strength of some 940,000 horse, foot and guns through Belgium, which would then pivot on the area of Verdun and wheel left, or south, on Paris; the outermost army directed to the west of the capital. The aim was to cut it off from the rest of France, so paralysing the centre of government, at the same time cutting the French railway network at its nodal point. After that, the way would be open to finish off the French armies attacking across the frontier into Lorraine and Alsace with a flank attack, or envelop the French frontier fortress system, or both, as opportunity offered.

The Schlieffen plan failed, for a number of reasons worth recounting, because they serve to remind us that the art of war is neither itself a science, nor a game, and that generals and staff officers responsible for plans require above all the gift of prescience. There had been no war in Europe for forty-three years and the failure was due as much to lack of imagination as of experience. The planners ignored the possibility that violating the neutrality of Belgium would add not only the Belgian but the British Army to the total of their opponents. The effect on the troops of a march of 300 miles in August heat which left the infantry exhausted and footsore and the horses broken down when they reached the area of decision was totally unforeseen. The arrangements for command and control were hopelessly inadequate, there being no intermediate headquarters like an 'army group' for the control of the huge right wing, which fell into disorder. The outer army passed east instead of west of Paris, so exposing its right flank to the most famous counter-attack in history. Von Schlieffen's successor, Helmuth von Moltke 'the younger,' acutely conscious of the dangers of a two-front war, took counsel of his fears. The situation on the Eastern Front proved alarming, and making the decision which probably led ultimately to Germany's defeat, Moltke sent his reserves to the Eastern Front and ordered the armies in France to consolidate on the line of the River Aisne.

There followed the exciting 'race to the sea' and, before the year had ended, the two sides were facing each other along a line of contact whose active front was between Compiègne and Noyon, with a loop including Verdun, thence north past Ypres to the North Sea coast between Nieuport and Ostend. From St Mihiel to the Swiss border the front remained inactive by mutual consent. This was to dictate the whole strategy of the war in the West, since the fortification of the line of contact was to dictate its operational-tactical pattern. France had been saved, but only at the cost of leaving the North-East with its rich industrial assets in the hands of the invader.

Von Moltke was replaced by the Minister of War, who was also a soldier, Field Marshal Erich von Falkenhayn, a fervent advocate of the offensive. The German positions were organised for protracted defence based on a policy of not yielding a yard of French territory. The Allies, the French, British and Belgians, followed suit, but their defences were designed more as assembly areas and jump-off lines for a succession of offensives; rather as in siege warfare, which in some respects the ensuing operations resembled, when the besiegers' defensive works are intended as an insurance against a sortie by the besieged. The parallel should not, however, be pressed too closely. A protracted defence involves methods also used in siege warfare, but a siege is essentially a different operation. The besieged are 'invested', or cut off from re-supply or reinforcement, while mobile forces are deployed outside the enclosing perimeter ready to counter-attack a relieving army, as at Stalingrad. German policy was not consistently defensive, although it made strategic sense to hold on in the west until the situation on the Eastern Front turned sufficiently in Germany's favour to allow a large enough force to be switched to the Western to enable an offensive policy to be mounted. The operational cliché was that a policy of protracted defence should only be adopted as preparation for a future offensive. That, however, ran counter to Falkenhayn's deepest instincts. In a terrible chapter, perhaps the most terrible chapter of the history of the war, he initiated the offensive at Verdun with the deliberate aim of bleeding the French armies to death by beating off their counter-attacks. The outcome of the war was in fact decided by the relative rates of attrition, but the intention of both sides was to achieve a break-through; in the symbolic colours of the newly born British Tank Corps, 'through mud and blood to the green fields beyond.' In practice there is no choice between a policy of annihilation and wearing down, or attrition, or between manoeuvre and headlong, frontal attack. All these are at work at once, and may, or may not, bring about the collapse of morale of one side or the other.

Some writers who should have known better seem under the impression that the trench barrier came into existence fortuitously as a consequence of the great increase in fire-power. An extreme example is Professor Norman Stone who, in an aside to his valuable study of the Eastern Front refers to the Western expressing precisely that notion: ' . . . the sudden discovery that soil proved to be the best defence against artillery . . .' and that ' . . . to the generals' bewilderment a line of trenches began to snake across France and Flanders, and both sides found their attacks slackening and failing against a seemingly 'unsoldierly' defence . . .' This is an interesting example of prevalent attitudes and opinions on the subject of generalship in the First World War; of the deeply entrenched belief in the stupidity, lack of imagination and obstinacy of 'the generals', which we propose to examine. It also reveals the pitfalls of writing military history without some basic knowledge of the military art. Anyone who has opened a general work on the history of warfare would know better than to write in so supercilious and sarcastic a fashion. The use of earthworks as protection against projectiles is as old as the invention of cannon. (Of what else besides that universally available and easily worked substance, soil, did the besiegers of masonry fortresses build their batteries and defences to protect their investing troops?) The use in mobile warfare of long, continuous chains of batteries and redoubts connected by trenches or breastworks has a long history. One has only to recall the Lines of Brabant and Ne Plus Ultra in Marlborough's wars, Wellington's Lines of Torres Vedras, and the increasing importance of such entrenched lines in the American Civil War; at Spotsylvania, for instance, and the 'Dimmock' Lines at Petersburg, which cost the Union troops so dearly to storm. As firepower increased, the more the infantry resorted to the spade; Fuller, in writing of the Civil War, coined the apt term 'mobile entrenchments'. The use of mines, as at Messines, has a history going back to the invention of gunpowder. The German High Command, having determined to hold on to the valuable tract of France it had captured, deliberately set its engineers and tacticians to building what in an earlier age might have been called 'the Lines of France and Flanders'

The term 'trenches' is misleading in itself, although it was possible to walk at the bottom of a trench all the way from the North Sea to the tiny strip of Alsace held by the French abutting on the Swiss border. On the German side, it was an elaborate system of fortifications, in the form of a combination of successive trench lines interspersed with villages and farm buildings converted into strong points and concrete pillboxes, backed by artillery deeply dug in, many guns in pits with overhead cover, and concealed from ground observation by careful siting. The main defensive 'line' was in fact a zone protected by echeloned belts of barbed wire covered by artillery defensive barrages and enfilading machine gun fire. Even the communication trenches were fire trenches sited to contain the flanks of a break-in ('switch lines') and, where the ground permitted, deep underground shelters were provided for the infantry garrisons proof against heavy artillery fire. This defensive system did not come into being at once, but gradually evolved to meet the ever-increasing weight of Allied artillery fire and changes of tactics in the successive Allied offensives. Falkenhayn, their Commander-in-Chief, began with the concept of one strong line backed by reserves. The battle of Neuve Chapelle in 1915, a tactical milestone, showed that a single line could always be breached, but that exploitation could be checked by even a rudimentary system of strong points and machine gun nests out of range of the attacker's artillery. The next step was a second complete line and later in the *Siegfriedstellung* ('Hindenburg Line') a third, with strong points in between them, as encountered at Cambrai by the British tanks. (At Cambrai the third line had not been completed.) The whole system, as finally developed, was in great depth, some five to six miles, and the defensive tactics were not based only on men firing from behind cover, but on mobile action by infantry groups skirmishing, using the strong points as fire bases and pivots. As an attack progressed, it was faced with graduated counter-attacks from the reserve companies of battalions up to whole divisions retained in true reserve, i.e., uncommitted and clear of the defence system, ready to seal off and crush any major penetration.

It was in the availability of strong reserves that the 'Lines of France and Flanders' differed from all previous patterns. In the eighteenth and nineteenth centuries it was not possible to maintain armies in the field large enough to man a fortified line continuously from end to end. The defence had to rely on holding the strong points and observing the unmanned stretches by patrols and vedettes. It was always open to a skilled commander to make a surprise attack, or to attack by night, or to lure the reserves away by strategem and penetrate an unmanned sector. On the Western Front, the ratio of troops to space was such that wherever the initial assault was to be made, it was inevitably given away by the preliminary massing of the artillery, the preparatory bombardment, and where the gaps were being cut or blown in the wire. Even in 1918, when Ludendorff's last desperate offensive succeeded in a complete rupture of both the British and the French fronts, the defence held, if only just. The deep salients which resulted were eventually contained and vulnerable to counter-attack, since where the attackers halted to consolidate they no longer enjoyed the protection of the elaborate defences from which they had emerged.

The result of this negation of the offensive principle was the bizarre phenomenon of the self-adjusting battlefield, returning like stretched elastic to its natural boundaries. All the major battles of the Western Front except the last, in the summer of 1918, were fought within the limits of a strip of ground as sharply defined as the area of a mediaeval tourney or a football gridiron, temporarily bulging out in one direction or another, but normally no more than 30 – 50,000 yards wide; enough to accommodate the quick-response counter-attack units and the opposed heavy artillery batteries. The 'players', as was found time after time, were confined to the 'pitch'. The numerical balance between the two sides was such that attrition rates conferred by fire-power could kill off the attackers faster than they could be reinforced, so preventing a decision until one side or the other collapsed. Both sides, however, persisted in striving for a break-out into the open, but they were without the means of exploitation. New weapons, better applications of old weapons, were of no avail because of the truism that there is no innovation in war that cannot be countered and superseded by another. Progress is dialectical, from thesis to antithesis, and never finished, except by superior numbers, or a collapse in morale. That is in fact what happened. As the German High Command had long foreseen, even before the possibility of a large British army had entered into their calculations, a war on two fronts was to prove fatal. When we consider the Western Front it is essential to avoid an Anglocentric view, and to keep in mind the fact that when the German army was caught in the meatgrinder of its own making at Verdun, there fighting battles as terrible for its own infantry as they were for the British on the Somme and in Flanders, it was engaged in equally costly battles in the East. That was to be true of the war in Europe in 1944–1945.

Today we have the advantage of viewing the First World War with the knowledge of the Second in which, after all the object lessons of the Western Front, a fresh generation of generals took two years longer and far greater casualties to bring to a successful conclusion. When we consider the generalship of the First, therefore, we have to make allowance for the fact that in 1914 all the commanders were the heirs of a military philosophy that had taken a century to formulate, only to be faced with a revolutionary situation for which they were mentally unprepared. It is an insufficient explanation to say that they were stupid, or were inhibited by 'authoritarianism' as variously defined, or were deeply conservative. The outbreak of war coincided with a surge forward in applied science, engineering and technology, of which the increase in simple fire-power was only a part. That had long been the subject of discussion.

Such speculations were based on arguments à priori, as was Foch's belief that the same effect would be an advantage to the offensive. There were in fact no statistics based on experiments which took into account such factors as the degradation of accuracy under the stress of battle, or when weapons are fired at increasingly longer ranges, or the effect of deliberate dispersion of the target pattern. It was simply assumed that longer ranges and higher rates of fire would increase lethality, without any examination of the mechanics of the process, or any strict definition of the term 'lethality'.

The attitude of military and civilian students of warfare towards 'science' was ambivalent. In the nineteenth century, a little-known and less understood class of person, 'the scientists', began to be regarded as the possessors of a new form of wisdom. All human activities could be profitably examined scientifically, so it naturally followed that there could be a science of war; meaning the discovery of formulas which if correctly followed would lead to success. It is significant that Foch, an artillery man, in his first lecture used a mathematical notation to express the interaction of military factors, ('f(a), (b), (c), (d)..') What was not understood was the philosophy of science, the scientific method; the process of observation, the construction of a hypothesis to account for a pattern of cause and effect, its validation by experiment and further reference to a wider field of observation ending in the formulation of a theory. That is an approach not easily applied to the study of war, whose 'experiments', i.e., battles, are not easily replicated. (It is not, of course, *impossible*. Some practical questions can be analysed using mathematical models such as the effect of fire-power on a notional target array or the balance of advantage between mobility, weight of armour and armament in tank design and so forth, but the parameters require to be strictly defined and care taken not to arrive at wider, more general conclusions than the assumptions warrant.)

The generation of officers who arrived at high command in time to face the deadlock on the Western Front were not scientifically minded in the sense given above. Even the highly educated German General Staff officers could not look beyond the operational frame-work of historical examples. The more open-minded, like Haig, were aware of the importance of innovation, but only in the sense of new 'gadgets', as Sir Lawrence Bragg called them. Others could not see beyond the traditional arms, and the *arme blanche*. Foch, speaking of the use of aircraft for reconnaissance before the war dismissed them as 'pretty toys'. Ironically, the popular interest in science led to science fiction, with the result that its application to war became identified with fiction and fantasy; mere entertainment, like H G Wells short story describing huge tanks ('pedrails', on tracks) and his *The War in the Air*. A didactic writer in this vein was the future Major-General Sir Ernest Swinton, an officer in the Royal Engineers and one of the co-inventors of the tank as used in France. In 1911 Swinton published in book form, under the title of *The Green Curve* and the pseudonym 'Ole Luk-Oie', a number of short stories concerned with the future of warfare that had already appeared in *Blackwood's Magazine,* an unserious periodical concerned with Imperial adventures or comical incidents in a pastiche of Kipling's style, the favourite reading of army officers. In his foreword, Swinton modestly describes them as 'sketches originally written for the entertainment of soldiers', but among them were previews of the devastating effect of field artillery fire directed by air observation, the explosion of a huge mine (then regarded as an obsolete aspect of siege-craft) and an attack by aeroplanes on engineers re-building a vital bridge over a river.

The reality outdid Swinton's imagination. It is worth recalling the time-span of military evolution in the First World War and its extent. A spectator at one of the great battles of the nineteenth century, in 1870 for instance, or the Alma in 1854, where the fashionable Russian ladies drove out in their carriages to watch the expected defeat of the French and British, might not have noted any startling difference between those engagements and the frontier battles of 1914 in which the French infantry in blue and red charged – in mass formation, bands playing, colours flying, field and general officers mounted – until they were struck by the German heavy artillery fire. By 1918, the only spectator who enjoyed a wide view of a battle was the pilot of an aircraft: it was difficult for a front-line soldier to see what was happening a quarter of a mile away. The change was total and it was the 'gadgets' that had done the trick. Curiously, it was the scientifically advanced Germans who led in purely tactical innovation, while the British, who exploited science and technology to overcome their difficulties, had perforce to start from a position far behind the Germans who, at first, excelled in artillery technique, the key to the whole problem.

Of course, the conventional view of operations in 1915–1917 is that the deadlock was caused by the impregnability of entrenchments protected by barbed wire and covered by fire from defiladed machine-guns, and only overcome by the invention of the tank, a weapon mishandled (of course) by Haig, who committed it prematurely to action during the battle of the Somme. It is important to understand that the true tank, the principal weapon of future mechanised armoured mobile forces, was not technically feasible until the better suspensions (such as the famous Christie design), more powerful and more compact engines and better armour, were developed in the 1920s and '30s to provide the mobility and protection essential to its task. The original tank was a slow ($2^1/_2$ miles per hour), barely bullet proof, tracked, automotive gun platform capable of crossing trenches, crushing barbed wire, and bringing cannon and machine-gun fire to bear at close range, 500 yards or so. The French, with their usual precision in the use of military terms called it a '*char d'assaut*'. This is not to say that it was not a seminal invention, and one that men of vision like Fuller perceived would dominate future wars. The tank was simply one way of employing artillery fire efficiently. The Russians saw this long before anyone else, fitting their T34 tanks with a long 76mm (3in) gun in 1941.

Field artillery techniques were improved by retaining the advantage of long range from defiladed positions, and off-setting the inherent disadvantages due to the inherent loss of accuracy as the range increases by using the techniques of greater accuracy in target location and the process known as 'predicted fire', i.e., by calculation.

A new dimension, literally, was exploited by air-power which apart from direct attack and the battle to control the air-space provided a flow of information to enhance the effectiveness of artillery in one way, and to help convert intelligence operations from the crudity of intuition and agents or 'spies' to a science. Artillery intelligence converged on the same goal. The whole was linked together by the new 'wireless'. Wireless telegraphy between formations had been in use since 1914. By 1918 sets for communication , from air to ground and on the tactical level from the front line to the rear were gradually coming into use, promising to break the silence which followed when the assault troops had disappeared into the smoke of battle. All these developments were interlinked and cross-fertilised with each other. Sir Lawrence Bragg, who was deeply involved in technical artillery intelligence recalled after the war that 'There was an almost impassable barrier between the military and scientific minds. The military thought us scientists far too visionary and gadgety to be of any help in the field; the scientists could not understand why their brain-waves, which seemed to them such war-winners, made no appeal to the military mind.' Yet the results finally achieved are a matter of historical fact. As Bragg himself recalls, eventually he was given *carte blanche* to recruit anyone he wanted, being allowed to visit training depots, ask for everyone to be paraded for him, give the order; 'Bachelors of Science, one pace, step forward!' and remove any who filled his requirements.

Haig, who was no scientist, and to whom the philosophy of science meant nothing, was acute enough to perceive that the 'gadgets' were important, as can be seen from his diary. He actually grasped that the technical revolution embraced not only weapons systems, but also made possible radical changes in the acquisition and evaluation of intelligence. Colonel Hemming, a colleague of Bragg, a scientifically minded artillery officer, has recorded how when he was a mere captain in the artillery intelligence section of a corps headquarters, Haig, who was visiting, went out of his way to consult him personally early in March 1918 as to whether he

Table 3.1 Inventions and Innovations 1915–18

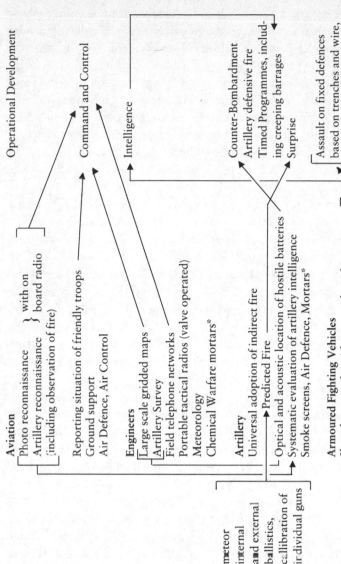

State of Operational Art 1914

Horsed Cavalry
Rifle and Bayonet
Infantry
Heavy Machine-guns
Horse-drawn field and medium artillery – heavy artillery used for short range direct fire
Mechanised heavy guns
Command & control by liaison, telegraph, civil telephone network, Marconi type 'wireless' telegraphy between formation HQs.
Optical air reconnaissance, reporting on landing or by message dropping.
Tactics based upon mass attacks, later extended lines.

Note

* Mortars
ie. short range high-angle artillery pieces, firing a heavy 'bomb' were introduced to throw gas filled projectiles, or to cut wire with HE.
Then as a trench weapon, easily transported and of 2" and 3" calibre.

(Middle column — Inventions and Innovations)

Aviation
Photo reconnaissance
Artillery reconnaissance (including observation of fire) } with on board radio
Reporting situation of friendly troops
Ground support
Air Defence, Air Control

Engineers
Large scale gridded maps
Artillery Survey
Field telephone networks
Portable tactical radios (valve operated)
Meteorology
Chemical Warfare mortars*

Artillery
Universal adoption of indirect fire
Predicted Fire
Optical and acoustic location of hostile batteries
Systematic evaluation of artillery intelligence
Smoke screens, Air Defence, Mortars*

meteor
internal and external ballistics, calibration of individual guns

Armoured Fighting Vehicles
Slow, heavy tanks with guns and machine-guns
Speedier light tanks
Wheeled Armoured Cars
Prototype SP artillery
Armoured bridgelayers and supply tanks

Infantry
Decline of Rifle and Bayonet
Increase in automatic fire
First steps towards light mortars* as infantry weapons
Organic signalling equipment

Operational Development

Command and Control

Intelligence

Counter-Bombardment
Artillery defensive fire
Timed Programmes, including creeping barrages
Surprise

Assault on fixed defences based on trenches and wire, counter machine-gun fire

Exploitation, reconnaissance and pursuit

Tactics based on small groups of fire teams in open order

Inter-arm co-operation: air/tanks/artillery/infantry

would be able to detect the artillery build-up which would reveal the thrust line and possible date of the expected German offensive, ordering him to report his conclusions to him in a telegram marked for his (Haig's) personal attention.

The historian AJP Taylor in his *The First World War*, fell into the same error as Norman Stone. Of the Western Front he says: 'The opposing lines congealed, grew solid. The generals on both sides stared at these impotently and without understanding. They went on staring for four years'. It may be an emotional necessity for some to believe that all generals, and the generals of the First World War in particular, were dolts, but such a statement is unhistorical, to say the least. It is always a good rule in history to resist the temptation to look at the attitudes and the events of the past with the eyes of today. No staff or civil service organisations, such as boards or committees, existed to consider the application of technology to military requirements. No profitable avenue for examination had been identified; no lists of scientists or others with qualifications drawn up. Progress was by chance and individual initiative. It was not until the Second World War that the discipline of 'operational analysis', or 'operational research', came into being, and some time before it was accepted by professional soldiers. Bragg was not alone in the frustration felt by British scientists after the outbreak of war in 1914. Yet the fact remains that those much abused generals presided over a successful revolution in the art of warfare.

What we are concerned with here is not so much the actual changes but the sociology of innovation in a conservative and authoritarian world. It is an error to gibe at men like Falkenhayn, Haig, Joffre, Foch, Nivelle and Ludendorff, in the belief that, when confronted by the defences they themselves had created, they reacted as it were like a horde of Mongols riding in search of some rich territory to lay waste when suddenly confronted by the Great Wall of China. They knew very well what they had to do, and proceeded to do it. The formula for forcing the passage of a fortified line was well understood: sapping forward, the counter-battery battle, the breach, the assault. Ideally, the attack would be made over a wide front so as to extend the garrison and create gaps for exploitation; either by isolating the separated sectors and dealing with them piecemeal, or ripping an open breach to provide a path wide enough for a large, mobile force to pass through. All that was basic to the operational art of two previous centuries and continued to be used on every front in the Second World War.

The difficulty in 1915 was that though the formula was well known, the techniques for realising it were, for the moment, lacking. Barbed wire, extremely resistant to artillery fire, had superseded the ditch and the abattis, the defences were widely dispersed earthworks with a low profile, presenting poor targets for the artillery, which, on both sides, had retreated into positions invisible to ground observers.

The technical innovations of the First World War included those so obvious and convenient that they neither demanded expensive new resources nor trod on the corns of the traditional arms. The infant air forces, for example, themselves an innovation, were only too pleased to extend their role of reconnaissance to the support of the ground troops, first by acting as observers for the artillery and later by direct attack using bombs and machine-guns. By 1918, the old Royal Flying Corps and the new-born RAF had brought army/air cooperation in the British army to a peak of efficiency not to be seen again until late in 1942.

Some developments, however, were so esoteric, such as those in the artillery world involving cartography, the interpretation of air photographs, meteorology, interior and external ballistics, acoustics, electricity and chemistry, to say nothing of aviation and the systematic, logical evaluation of intelligence data, that few senior officers knew of the existence of the problems involved, let alone whether they were soluble. The pioneers were therefore able to carry on their work unhindered by bureaucracy, military protocol, or the interference of the ignorant or uninitiated.

A great deal depended on individual enterprise. A sergeant, Coles of the British Royal Engineers, designed a theodolite for the field use of 'flash spotters' (observers engaged in fixing hostile batteries by cross-observation of the flash of discharge), in which the angular reading was visible in the field of view (so that it could be read without losing the target) and was sent off to a firm making optical instruments in England to help produce it. Lucien Bull, the French scientist who originated the idea of fixing hostile batteries by acoustics, ('sound-ranging') began his experiments with a borrowed electrocardiograph. Lieutenant-Colonel HH Hemming, Royal Artillery, a pioneer of flash-spotting who invented a device to ensure that the cross-observers were observing the same flash, bought the necessary electrical relays from a second-hand junk shop in Holborn when he was on leave in England. The 'sound-ranging' apparatus was highly sophisticated, involving as it did faint electrical impulses from widely separated receivers, which recorded the shape and time of arrival of soundwaves on a film, from which both the location and the calibre and type of gun could be accurately deduced. A device required to record the faintest electrical impulses was made by a corporal in the Royal Engineers, Professor Tucker, as he became.

In contrast, the 'Stokes' mortar, the prototype of all the infantry mortars in service today, succeeded by virtue of its extreme simplicity; a smooth barrel and a finned bomb propelled by a small arms cartridge fired by percussion. Equally simple was the 'flapjack', a signalling device to be used in trench warfare, no more than a rectangular screen with flaps elevated on a pole, and operated by pulling a cord that exposed the white interior surface of the screen and so transmit the morse alphabet.

Radio communication in the form of 'W/T' – 'wireless telegraphy' for morse transmissions at first used spark transmitters and primitive receivers. The invention of the thermionic valve which could rectify and amplify a signal and produced a 'continuous wave' led to greater efficiency and eventually 'R/T', or radio telephony, although the full extent of the command, control, communication and intelligence revolution was not realised until the Second World War.

Innovation of equipment was, in general, not premeditated or the result of a 'staff requirement', but the coincidence of a need with the 'brainwave' of sometimes a humble, sometimes a senior officer. Finally, for major innovations, a powerful advocate or sponsor became necessary before resources were allotted for production, and an 'establishment' table drawn up for equipment and manning. It was then that obstacles multiplied, either from sceptics who objected to innovation on principle, or felt that it offended the traditions of their arm of the service. The Royal Horse and Royal Field Artillery were especially guilty in this latest respect, as regards 'scientific' gunnery, but its officers were eventually forced to toe the line.

The epoch-making Battle of Cambrai provides a good example of a benevolent supporter in high command. During the planning stage, the artillery commander of one of the infantry divisions, Brigadier-General HH ('Owen') Tudor put up a proposal to rely on the force of tanks assigned to lead the attack to gap the wire obstacles, dispensing with the usual preliminary bombardment and to rely entirely on the new gunnery to produce a completely predicted programme opening at Zero Hour. This met with strong objections from officers of his own arm, who argued that it was too risky to entrust the whole of the vital artillery programme to the unchecked work of the surveyors, the locating units and the battery officers, and demanded permission at least to carry out preliminary registrations by fire, which, of course, would forfeit surprise. Fortunately Tudor's proposals had the unwavering support of the army commander, General Sir Julian Byng, and the reliability of the new gunnery was completely vindicated. The barrage and the counter-battery programme came down exactly as predicted, surprise was complete, the break-in battle succeeded with negligible casualties and a subsequent inspection confirmed that 90 per cent of the hostile batteries had been accurately engaged.

Although the Battle of Cambrai disappointed British hopes of a complete break-through, it marks an epoch in the development of modern warfare.

Its significance in the context of this chapter is that it was a clash between innovation and tradition: the new technical and the old tactical. Byng disposed of 378 battle and 98 auxiliary tanks, an assault force of eight divisions, each with an attached tank battalion, organised in two corps: 1,003 guns and howitzers, of which 277 were in the heavy category from 5 inch to 15 inch; 289 reconnaissance, artillery observation and light bomber aircraft of the Royal Flying Corps. Four cavalry divisions awaited the opportunity to ride out beyond the Hindenburg Line, and eleven more infantry divisions could be drawn on for a reserve. The reasons for failure were numerous, but fundamentally it was due to the fact that in the British Army technical innovation had not been accompanied by tactical reform. Inter-arm cooperation was rudimentary, and the use of cavalry for exploitation proved a fiasco.

The Cambrai sector was also the scene of a trial run of the new German infantry tactics, used in the counter-attack to drive back the British, and later with devastating effect, against the weakened defences of the British Fifth Army in March 1918. It was based on the revival of the old custom of grouping the best soldiers in special assault units (formerly 'grenadiers', in 1918 'storm troops', and in the Second World War 'grenadiers' or 'panzer grenadiers' once more). The German flair for training and combining discipline with initiative produced small groups of men carrying their own heavy weapons to infiltrate deep into the enemy position, by-passing strong points, overrunning the artillery positions and threatening formation headquarters, until the whole defensive system began to disintegrate.

Tactical and technical innovation are, naturally, interlinked, since new weapon-systems require new methods of application, but there is an important difference in the actual process of innovation. One is an intellectual exercise, carried on by an elite assisted by sponsors intelligent enough to understand the value of its ideas. Tactical innovation may well originate from a single bright idea, or from a staff reassessment of the lessons of previous operations, but it cannot be brought about simply by the issue of orders and instructions, or pamphlets, or new manuals. The fighting units have to be re-educated from generals down to corporals and privates. A sad example of the consequence of ignoring this basic rule was the arbitrary reorganisation of the British infantry divisions early in 1918, and the adoption of a poor copy of the new German system of flexible defence in depth; by decree, without consultation, or time for retraining and re-indoctrination. The Fifth Army, over-extended in frontage *and in depth*, was completely overrun and only the determination of Haig and the valour of the troops prevented a total collapse of the British position.

TE Lawrence, writing about guerrilla warfare made a perceptive observation deserving wider application: that the commanders of regular troops arranged the bodies of their soldiers in ranks, but the leader of guerrillas had to set the ideas in the minds of his followers in order. Before the new attack tactics could be introduced, there had to be a profound alteration of attitude in the minds of officers brought up to believe that the secret of command and control was absolute obedience to the letter of written orders, inculcated by drill. It is a very reasonable, or at least understandable attitude. Drill is often spoken of disparagingly, but in the broadest sense it was the most significant invention in the history of warfare. It imposed order on chaos, enabled a few to command many, made the art of manoeuvre possible, and without it inventions such as gun-powder or fire-arms, momentous as they were, would have been of little use. Even after the continental armies abandoned the closely packed formations of 1914, battalions went into action in lines or 'waves' in extended order, a formation imposed by trench warfare and the use of the linear barrage. It required a minor tactical revolution to change to fighting in small groups or 'fire-teams'.

The tactics of infiltration by loosely organised groups may have come about by an evolutionary process rather than a single flash of insight. What may have happened is that in the confused alternation of 'mopping-up' and the local counter-attack, battalions and companies fall into disorder, or at least into looser groupings, which gave scope for individual initiative. Small parties of grenadiers against cleared trenches, bombing their way from traverse to traverse; a Lewis gunner and a few of his mates went off to stalk a troublesome machine gun 'nest', or a junior leader gathered together what men he could find to make a local counter-attack. This trend could have been general throughout the armies. It was especially congenial to the Dominion troops, Australians, Canadians and New Zealanders from self-reliant pioneer societies, or the French with their Gallic independence of mind whose military tradition derived more from the revolutionary armies than the strict system of General Martinet. The great change in tactics, therefore, probably started from below, in the form of a popular movement, the produce of the psychology of men in dangerous or difficult situations, who gather round any leader who seems sure of what he has to do. Be that as it may, the idea of a systematic application of such local initiatives originated in a French mind.

As early as 1915 a Captain Laffargue put up a paper entitled *L'Etude sur l'Attaque*, laying the basis of a completely new approach. Its essence was the use of élite assault groups backed by squads of machine gunners to infiltrate the enemy position, using the line of least resistance to advance to the greatest depth, and leaving obstinate centres of resistance to the more formally organised units following behind. This was printed and circulated to units by the French general staff, but without, apparently, any other intention than to provide an interesting topic for discussion. It made no impact on disciples of Foch, Grandmaison and Ardant du Picq, whose ideas were very different. To them, Laffargue's proposals seemed a delegation of responsibility, even a surrender. Were the commanders of regiments and battalions to abdicate and leave the outcome of battle to *sous-officiers* and corporals leading a handful of skirmishing scallywags? In 1916, a copy of Laffargue's paper, found in a French position, fell into the hands of the German General Staff, who found it stimulating and in accordance with their own, possibly already half-formed ideas. An innovation requires a favourable climate to take root, and the Germans were looking for tactics, both defensive and offensive, less rigid and costly than they had used in the Somme battles and at Verdun. With its usual thoroughness, combined with imagination and operational flair, the General Staff adopted it. When Ludendorff launched the great *Kaiserschlacht* offensives of March/April 1918, the German Army had organised and trained eight spearhead infantry divisions of élite 'storm troops', fully trained in the new style. Had they been accompanied by a mechanised exploiting arm, or even if they had not used up their horsed cavalry in the infantry role, things might have turned out much worse for the British and French armies. In the event, by 1918 the German Army as a whole was only a pale shadow of what it had been at the beginning of 1916, and the victorious advance of the élite storm divisions petered out from the sheer fatigue of marching; as had happened in August 1914. That halt was also due to a serious breakdown in discipline. The euphoria of success had so gone to the heads of the advancing infantry that they paused to loot houses and cellars on their line of advance and soon many were drunk and incapable – a situation which would have been inconceivable with the regular soldiers of the old German Army. The evidence of this comes from the pens of their own officers, deploring the orgy in their post-war memoirs.

The unexpected collapse of the German armies was due to the fact that they were worn out, that the salients the *Kaiserschlacht* offensive had created were vulnerable to counter-attack, as dictated by the logic of 'the long thin battlefield' and by the arrival of a fresh, eager reinforcement in the shape of the Americans. But that was not all. An all important feature was the combination of new artillery tactics, improved infantry tactics, tanks and close air support, the prototype of the warfare of the future.

We have dwelt at length on the Western Front because it was the laboratory in which modern warfare was designed and tested and, equally important, it had a profound effect on the attitudes of the two great democracies who once more were to be allied in the Second World War. It was during the First that statesmen and soldiers of the United Kingdom and the United States were forced to recognise the intimate linkage-between strategy and politics, and that coalition war demanded both a generalissimo and proper machinery at the level of government to decide on strategy and run the war; the former was created only in 1918, under the spur of a great emergency, but the latter had to await the Second coalition of 1941–45 to come to fruition.

All the future belligerents interpreted the lessons of the Eastern and Western Fronts to suit their own ideology, their own circumstances, or their own ambitions. The future Western Allies' hopes and plans were based on avoiding war and on defence against aggression. France collapsed and fell out of the war in 1940 not so much as the result of faulty military doctrine or inadequate armaments, being at least in material terms a great military power, but because of lack of will. Twenty-two years had not been long enough to recover from the human losses of the earlier war. After fighting alone for 18 months, the British were joined by the Americans to form the Second coalition. In the First, the three principal allies had had roughly equal strengths on the Western Front by the autumn of 1918, American dependence on French weapons and British shipping being balanced by their own enthusiasm and self-confidence. In contrast, in the Second World War the United States emerged as a super-power and the arsenal of the free world, while the British Empire, in decline, was its client. War-wise and well commanded as the British Army was when the untried US army entered the war, the American generals were not at all disposed to accept the tutelage of the British, whose pretensions they felt exceeded their prowess.

In the later chapters of this study, we advance some harsh criticisms of the senior American officers responsible for the conduct of the campaign in Northwest Europe; we hope with due regard for objectivity and for the historical background. British officers, notably Brooke and Montgomery, considered their American colleagues operationally illiterate, and made their views known with insular lack of tact. In theory, American military doctrine, based on the study of military history and reinforced by the success of the American Expeditionary Force in the hard fighting of 1918, was sound, based on the same principles as the British and, perhaps more significant, the German. The grand American plan for making the best use of military manpower in terms of job selection and training was arrived at by logical analysis of the problem and the application of businesslike methods. The organisation of their combat formations was superior to the British, allowing the component units to be grouped in a way appropriate to the mission in hand, very like the German 'battle-groups'; the infantry 'regimental combat teams' of all arms, the armoured 'combat commands', subdivided into 'task forces', an expressive term now in general use.

American weapons, American motor transport and American military equipment in general was designed to meet accurately defined military requirements, sophisticated but at the same time suitable for mass production. The United States Army was better equipped than any other belligerent, and the British were only too pleased, if not noticeably grateful, to get their hands on as many Sherman tanks, jeeps and self-propelled artillery as possible by virtue of the generous policy of 'lease-lend'.

Later we recount the bitter quarrels over joint strategy and operational methods which afflicted the Anglo-American high command in Northwest Europe from September 1944 onwards. Those differences of opinion, so vehemently pursued by both sides, were not the cause of the rancorous antagonism that marred the final victory but its consequence. There is a saying that no plan, good or bad, survives the first clash of arms. It seems equally true that no arrangement for the conduct of a coalition is proof against the friction of jealousy, the natural rivalry of armies and the real goals of its members. Politics, not the cold logic of the Staff appreciation, prevail.

CHAPTER 4

A COALITION BEDEVILLED

It is not a choice between a maritime or a continental strategy but a delicate judgment of how to apportion scarce resources between the two.

FIELD MARSHAL LORD CARVER, ROSKILL MEMORIAL LECTURE,
CHURCHILL COLLEGE, CAMBRIDGE, 16 FEBRUARY, 1989.

General Philippe Pétain once said to Brigadier General Fox Conner that he had always rated Napoleon as 'a devil of a general' until his own experience taught him how fortunate Napoleon had been in being able to fight without allies.* Experience of coalition in the First World War impressed on the Americans and British the need to agree a common strategy, and to set up an elaborate political and military apparatus to realise it. Even so, they encountered great difficulties in the Second, only overcome by the boon of a common language, and by virtue of the brutal fact that when the alliance was faced with an apparently irreconcilable difference of opinion, the vastly superior power of the United States enabled it to impose its own solution. In 1914 no such machinery existed for regular consultation or even for satisfying the first rule of warfare, unity of command. The British government did not think it necessary, and gave it little thought. The French were not by temperament inclined to favour cooperation and compromise, unless the outcome was strictly in accordance with French interests, and as for unity of command, to be sure Gallic logic demanded it, but Gallic pride demanded that it be exercised by a French commander-in-chief.

For two centuries British strategy had been to fight in Europe only as a member of an alliance. As for defining roles and responsibilities successive British governments had found that the national commanders had been perfectly capable of managing their affairs between themselves, as Marlborough and Eugene had managed, Wellington and Blucher, and

---

* Fox Conner was chief of staff to General Pershing q.v.

Raglan and Canrobert in the Crimea. In 1914 the British and French, fight-ing on the same side for only the second time in their history, soon found that such simplifications were obsolete. The natural rivalry between allies and the temptation to press for a strategy that favoured the selfish war aim of one side or the other, sharpened by the prodigious investment in wealth and man-power necessary to wage modern war, demanded a far greater return than the gain of a slice of territory here or the establishment of a buffer state there. Governments, assisted by the speed of modern commu-nications, kept a close watch on operations as well as strategy, and the generals in the field soon found that every important decision had a polit-ical dimension, involving their own government's goals, and therefore their relations with each other. This aspect of the struggle on the Western Front can be seen as a pattern of unforeseen emergencies, gradually compelling the partners to take a more rational, ecumenical view of how the war should be managed. The relationship between the Entente commanders was not quite as straightforward as it was on the other side, where Falkenhayn could thump the table with his fist, bellowing the while at his Austrian colleague Conrad von Hotzendorf: 'Are you aware that you are speaking to a *Prussian Field Marshal*?' Difficulties of coordination and cooperation on the Western Front were intensified when the United States entered the war with the firm intention of keeping its newly raised armies independent of any particle of foreign control. Genuine unity of command was only brought about late in the war by fear of impending disaster, in April, 1918.

This burden pressed heavily on the politically unsophisticated generals who found themselves in command on the outbreak of war, and later led to the fraught relationship between the commander-in-chief of the British Expeditionary Force Douglas Haig and Prime Minister Lloyd George in 1917. Before examining how the winning team – Foch, Haig and Pershing* – managed their affairs it is first necessary to explain the strate-gic viewpoint of the governments of the three Allies, beginning with the French, since it was the fortunes and misfortunes of the French that proved the determining factor in the evolution of the alliance. First, for emotional, political and economic reasons there could be only one French goal, the ejection of the invader from the soil of France. Second, this had to be achieved as soon as humanly possible because, with a smaller population than Germany, France could not for long endure a haemorrhage of French blood. The ultimate aim of the French was to recover the status of France

* Ferdinand Foch – see Chapter 2; Major-General (later General of the Army) JJ Pershing, US Army and C-in-C American Expeditionary Force.

as a power, indeed the leading power, in Europe, badly damaged by the defeat of 1870 and the miserable face of French internal politics after it. The growth of the British armies in France to parity with the French in size and prowess in 1917 and in 1918 the fresh American army a million strong, threatened to reduce France to a third, insignificant place at the post-war conference table, a position too humiliating to contemplate. It was therefore essential to the French to control the war politically so that, as far as possible, the armies of her allies acted only as ancillaries to her own and under French direction, thereby conserving French soldiers to strike the decisive blows, leaving France as the leader of the victors.

Britain entered the war after much hesitation, and then only on the pretext of honouring her treaty obligation to defend the neutrality of Belgium. No formal agreement with France had been entered into, but growing British uneasiness caused by the ambition and military power of Kaiserene Germany had led to the creation of official and unofficial channels of communication between the two countries. In this, one famous actor on the political-military stage, General Henry Wilson, a convinced Francophile, played a leading part. The pre-war reforms of the British Army had included arrangements to mobilise a small but highly efficient force to be sent to France, and its deployment area had been already more or less settled. The British Government intended to follow Britain's historic policy, The Royal Navy would be responsible for the defence of the Empire and Britain's vital trade-routes. The real role of the British Expeditionary Force was to stake Britain's claim in the post-war political settlement. She would use her political and financial muscle as the principal means of supporting her allies, especially Russia; numerically a great power, requiring only a supply of munitions to exert satisfactory pressure on the Central Powers – Germany and Austria.

British war-aims were imperialist, brought about by the rivalry with the German Empire. It was expected that the whole military man-power of the Empire would be placed without question at Britain's disposal, but an Imperial strategy had two separate aspects. There were the white, English-speaking Dominions, valuable auxiliaries, later to be acknowledged as the Empire's best troops, their homelands too remote from the theatre of war to be under any military threat. Then there was India, for emotional reasons the 'jewel in the crown' of the Empire, its rule delegated to a British viceroy (or Governor-General) and an all-British civil service; self-sufficient and providing a valuable army from its own financial resources. The security of India, and therefore the sea-route through the Mediterranean, the Suez Canal and Aden was a vital consideration for British strategists. When the Ottoman Empire entered the war on the side of the Central Powers in

November 1914, the British were inevitably drawn into an overseas or 'eastern' strategy, since the Turkish frontier included the east bank of the Suez Canal and its seaboard included the eastern shore of the Red Sea and part of the north-western coast of the Indian Ocean.

The potential threat in that sensitive region of a primitive but tough army supported by advisers from the German General Staff could not be ignored, and the opening of theatres of war in Mesopotamia and Sinai were inevitable. The Dardanelles adventure of 1915 was a reaction to this threat but also sprang partly from Winston Churchill's ambition, as First Lord of the Admiralty, for the Royal Navy to play a leading part in guiding Imperial strategy, and partly from the need to open a safe, warm-water supply route to Russia. When it became clear during the course of 1915 that Kitchener's foresight in forming a huge army was correct, but that it had to be used to avoid the collapse of France, and the sooner the better, the British government had perforce to abandon its traditional strategy, for the simple reason that it could not afford to finance the war effort of its allies let alone provide them with arms and at the same time arm and equip a huge modern army of its own to fight on the Continent.

It is an enduring belief that there were two rival British strategies, an 'Eastern' and a 'Western', and that the eastern strategy was conceived when the German defences on the Western Front proved impregnable. The opposite is really the case. The British began the war intending only a limited liability intervention in Europe together with a far-flung defence of her eastern empire, which from first to last absorbed a numerical strength of the order of a million Imperial troops (Egypt, Sinai, Palestine, Aden, Gallipoli, Salonika and Mesopotamia) but, because of the French imperative, Britain had to commit her new armies and later her conscript armies to a major effort on the Western Front. Lloyd George's later manoeuvres in diverting British troops badly needed on the Western Front elsewhere were made simply to shackle Haig. As far as there was any debate between a group of 'Easterners' and another of 'Westerners', it was between orthodox strategists like Haig and the Chief of the Imperial General Staff, General Sir William Robertson, and against the tendency to dissipate resources which might bring about a quicker result on the Western Front. It was perhaps necessary to send men and equally important, guns, to prop up Italy, but a waste of time opening a subsidiary theatre in that strategic cul-de-sac Salonika. Lloyd George understood, as far as he could understand any military question, that Germany had to be defeated on the Western Front. What he really wanted was to shift the burden of that task to the shoulders of others; French, or American[1]. (How the idea of an 'Eastern' strategy grew up as a panacea is not easy to explain or understand. After the war it was suggested that the casualties of the Western Front could have been avoided – by the British. The seeds of that idea were sown in the self-justificatory writings of Winston Churchill and Lloyd George, and their desire to discredit Haig. The simplistic idea of a sort of strategic outflanking move to avoid assaulting the German defences in France chimed with the post-war ideas of Liddell Hart and his 'indirect approach' theory. Shortly before 1939 he readvocated the strategy of 1914, complete with the despatch of a tiny, token force to France.)

British and French strategy was, therefore, determined by the realities of war and force of circumstances. The American case was different. The United States entered the war from self-interest only in April 1917, defying public opinion, which preferred to avoid entanglement in Europe, because, in the long run, it was not in the interests of the United States, her mediation having been rejected, to allow Western Europe to descend into chaos, or to come under German hegemony, however isolated or insulated Americans felt themselves to be from Europe. In addition, the French and Americans had emotional ties dating back to 1776. There was another additional and equally powerful motive. The President, Woodrow Wilson, was a man of missionary zeal. He did not seek territorial aggrandisement or other material advantages for his country. His aim was a moral one: to promote a lasting peace and to rearrange the map of Europe according to the principles of natural justice. He defined the aims of the peace in his Fourteen Points – as a wag unkindly observed, four more than those brought down by Moses from Sinai. It would be a happy circumstance if when the war ended the principal victor was the United States, the possessor of a fresh, powerful army equal in size to the worn-out British and French armies put together, its commander also the commander-in-chief of the Allied armies. With such superiority and the lustre of bringing the war to a successful end, the United States could act as the arbiter of Europe. In 1914, Kitchener had the same ambition for his armies.

The American experience of 1917–1918 profoundly affected the military outlook of the United States and shaped its policy a quarter of a century later, so an account of it is contained in the final chapter of this section. Here it is enough to say that though the reforms to its general staff and command system made under the Secretary for War, Elihu Root and Tasker Bliss had been of great benefit, the US Army itself, as a modern fighting force, simply did not exist. There was no divisional or corps organisation, no peace-time organisational structure into which newly raised units could be fitted, and no officer of rank above major-general. Its officers' knowledge of modern warfare was zero. It had no tactical doctrine, except the somewhat outdated one of the supremacy of the rifleman and rifle fire, using its one up to date American weapon, the 0.3 inch Springfield magazine rifle. Tanks and even light field artillery would have to be supplied by France, since American industry was not geared to provide the munitions for a great modern conflict in quantity or quality. The two great American assets were an ample supply of physically fit and enthusiastic recruits and its commander-in-chief elect, Major-General John J Pershing. His colossal task was to go to Europe, prepare a base there for a million strong army, train it, assemble it into divisions and corps, and then command it in the field. Pershing's directive was clearer than those given to Sir John French (C-in-C BEF) and later to Haig, and a good deal more uncompromising. The American Expeditionary Force was not in any circumstances to be introduced into the battle piecemeal, whatever the emergency, whether by battalions or divisions, although temporary attachments to formations in the line purely for instruction and experience were permissible. The AEF was to fight under its own United States commander as an army, later two armies, and in its own sector. Carried out to the letter such a policy meant the AEF could not possibly be ready to fight efficiently until the spring of 1919. It was to be upset by that ever inconvenient factor in planning, the actions of the enemy. Pershing had to throw his partially trained divisions into battle before the war ended in 1918; gloriously, with the fresh laurels of Belleau Wood, St. Mihiel and Meuse-Argonne on the colours of the US Army and Marine Corps, for which the usual price was exacted.

The path of General Pershing was to be far from smooth, and his difficulties great. At least his government was behind him and his relations with the French and his mission had been clearly and unambiguously defined. Sir John French had enjoyed no such advantages. The administrative arrangements for mobilisation and moving the BEF to its concentration area were as flawless as such arrangements can ever be, but on the political side much had been left in the air. There had been no preliminary discussion of the delicate question of cooperation at the command level. The French Ambassador in London believing that the government was fully committed, had expressed his dismay that Britain had not immediately declared war on Germany when France had rejected the German ultimatum demanding French neutrality. The French high command had assumed, although it had no formal assurances on the subject, that the BEF would for operational purposes come under the orders of the French commander-in-chief. Sir John French had been warned for duty by the CIGS, General Sir Charles Douglas* on July 30, but on August 2 he found

---

* French, as CIGS, was expected to take command of a British Expeditionary Force, but had resigned in protest over the government's handling of the dispute

it necessary to ring up a friend, the newspaper proprietor Sir George Riddell, to ask if he knew whether Britain was about to declare war, and if so, was the BEF definitely being sent to France, and under whose command? He himself was engaged in discussions with the French military attaché, but that was no substitute for establishing in good time a rapport between himself and the French commander-in-chief, and between their respective staffs. This way of carrying on was due inevitably to the prudence of the British Government in refusing to take any step which might bind it prematurely to an obligation to go to war on France's behalf, but it was none the less inefficient. Sir John was also to be afflicted by the mutual dislike and misunderstandings that arose between himself and the newly appointed Secretary of State for War, Kitchener; Herbert Horatio, Field Marshal Viscount Kitchener of Khartoum, 'K of K'. The two men, well known to each other from South African days, met again in their new capacities for the first time at a Council of War called by the Prime Minister, I II I Asquith, on August 5.

Kitchener, as a serving officer, was an unusual choice, although it was common practice in France and Germany to employ distinguished soldiers as Ministers of War. In England there was no constitutional objection since Kitchener, though on the active list (on which field-marshals remain for life), being a peer was a Member of Parliament. It seemed a sensible way of making use of the outstanding military capacity of a man too senior and of too great a reputation for any post such as CIGS or the Commander-in-Chief of the Expeditionary Force, and the only one suitable for him, Commander-in-Chief of the British Army, had been abolished. Asquith, whose initiative it was, called his choice a gamble, and the gamble lay in Kitchener's personality. He was the arch-hero of British Imperialism, who had made his reputation in the Sudan as the victor of Omdurman and the avenger of Gordon and, as Chief of Staff to the old hero Lord Roberts, had restored the sagging reputation of British arms in South Africa and ruthlessly crushed the guerrilla resistance of the Boers in the last phase of the war. That he was a brute did not injure him in the eyes of the British public. 'Get out of my sight, you drunken swabs',* was their hero's genial greeting to members of the press corps eager to interview him

---

* 'Swabs', like 'beggars', was a Victorian euphemism, used in print or polite society for two coarse expressions as much used then as today, by gentlemen.

---

over the proposed use of force in Ireland. Charles Douglas was a nonentity hastily appointed.

on his victorious return from South Africa. He was a formidable figure, whose charisma was such that his saturnine expression, his moustachios and piercing eyes on a poster was by itself almost sufficient to pull in the volunteers for his new armies. He had plenty of brains, having been trained, like Joffre, as a military engineer, and his military judgment was sound, as shown by his foresight in recognising the need for a mass army in what was he perceived to be a long war, and the energy with which he set about raising it. Fitted with a *pickelhaube* he could well have been England's answer to Erich von Falkenhayn. Like him, Kitchener proved to have an inner weakness behind the facade that led him to vacillate when faced with the need to take important decisions. But Kitchener's style was not Prussian. Visitors to his room in Whitehall found him gracious, thoughtful and unhurried. Like many successful commanders, he was an actor who chose his roles carefully . By nature, Kitchener was secretive and domineering, belonging to the generation which saw the new-fangled General Staff conceived by Haldane and Haig as an undesirable novelty. He neither sought nor accepted advice and, indeed, was much admired for his Olympian habit of making his own decisions, keeping his own counsel, and carrying even the details of his plans in his own head. He disliked and distrusted what we would now call 'structured organisations': he was the great *dis*-organiser. It was entirely characteristic of his methods that in building the 'Kitchener' armies he made no use of the Territorial Force so painstakingly set up by Haldane. Asquith's gamble was whether such a man would, or even could act in a constitutional manner, directing the nation's war effort on land as agreed by the Cabinet, and guide the decision of his colleagues with professional advice as tendered to him by the Chief of the Imperial General Staff. They soon found that he was not disposed to do either. Kitchener's attitude was: they wanted the best professional advice? They should have it – *his*. The CIGS and his staff's business was to concern themselves with the nuts and bolts of staff duties. The channel for the government's views to the commanders in the field, and their guide for operational matters would be – *himself*. In short, he arrogated to himself the role of 'War Lord'.

The great shortcoming of Kitchener, which so impaired his outstanding military ability was that he lacked political *nous*, and was totally deficient in that sensitivity for the feelings of others that is part of the make-up of the best leaders. Sir John French was a man who needed careful handling. As a commander in the field, faced with awful responsibilities, he required encouragement. Kitchener tended to scold or lecture him as if he were an adjutant dealing with an unsatisfactory subaltern, on one occasion ticking him off for daring to write directly on some subject to the Prime Minister.

Their relations worsened, and this in turn reacted on Sir John's relations with the French. In consequence, that period of the war when Sir John with Kitchener breathing down his neck was trying to cooperate with Joffre, the French Commander-in-Chief, who was guided in a more tactful way by the French War Minister, Charles Millerand remains the paradigm of a mismanaged coalition.

The first misunderstanding arose from the directive Kitchener gave to the Commander-in-Chief of the British Expeditionary Force of the British Armies in France.[2] It was so hedged about by warnings and qualifications as to be unworkable if interpreted either in the letter or the spirit; had it been intended to fill the mind of a commander about to be thrust into the vortex of a great war with doubt, it could not have been more skilfully worded. The object was 'to support and cooperate with the French army'; in a later paragraph exquisitely redefined as 'every effort will be made to coincide with the wishes and plans of our ally'. All the same, Sir John French should keep 'steadily in view' that the man-power available to the BEF for replacements and reinforcements was 'strictly limited', and that 'the greatest care must be exercised towards a minimum of losses and wastage' (sic). The 'gravest consideration' should be given to any 'forward movement' made independently of the French 'where your Force may be *unduly* exposed to attack'. (Author's italics.) Any such proposals were to be referred to 'me' (the Secretary of State for War) in good time for the government's decision to be conveyed to the Commander-in-Chief. Had Sir John French been a Chinese general versed in the military philosophy of the mythical Sun-Tzu he might have understood how to cooperate without actually fighting, or fight without incurring casualties and avoid provoking his opponent by 'forward movements' lest he struck back, but neither the French nor, more importantly, the Germans were bound by such restraints.

The only clear and positive statement in the directive was: 'I wish you distinctly to understand that your command is entirely an independent one, and that in no case will you come under the orders of any Allied general'. Neither the text of this document nor some more suitable paraphrase for diplomatic channels was conveyed to the French government, nor was there any verbal communication on the subject and, worse, Sir John French was not aware of that. He was, therefore, also unaware that Joffre was firmly under the impression that, for operational matters at least, the BEF was under his command.* Difficult as it is to believe, the French only learnt of the true state of affairs by chance, through a conversation between Lord

---

* Joseph Jacques Césaire Joffre (Marshal of France 1916) graduate of the Ecole Politique, engineer service, Chief of Staff 1914, C-in-C 1915, relieved December 1916 by Nivelle – q.v.

Esher and Millerand in Paris. Small wonder that the touchy Sir John reacted so strongly to what he construed as Joffre's presumption. According to Esher, he only learnt the true state of affairs from him on April 15, 1915 although, it has to be said, the differences continued between him and Joffre. If there is any scientific law that once muddles and misunderstandings, together with the resentment they generate, have taken root, they proliferate and intensify, then the history of Anglo-French cooperation from the retreat from Mons till the Battle of Loos in September 1915 can provide a doleful case-history to support it.

Sir John fell out with the French on two levels: with General Lanrezac, who commanded the neighbouring French Fifth Army, during the retreat from Mons, and then with Joffre over his intention to disengage the BEF to rest and re-equip. Only Joffre's passionate appeal persuaded him to take part in the Marne and stand on the Aisne. Sir John later put forward a sensible but tactless proposal to prepare a 'fortified camp' around Boulogne, rousing French suspicions that the British, if pressed too hard, might run for their boats. Joffre was possibly influenced by this thought, but more probably by the fact that as the French Commander-in-Chief he, and not the civil government, was responsible for the war zone including the German-occupied territories when, after the BEF had marched north from the Aisne to the area Armentières-Ypres, he took steps to prevent the British sector becoming a British-dominated enclave. He inserted a French corps between the right flank of the Belgian Army on the coast and the left flank of the BEF, and kept it there. In the first phase of extending the front to the north he sent up a single French division, the 42nd, later reinforced to an army corps. This he designated 'the Army Group of the North', with Ferdinand Foch as its commander. What Joffre wanted from the British was for their commander to accept his orders and plans, and also for them to increase their small force; and more, to become emotionally involved in the battle for France. When the French Government pressed for an increase in the size of the BEF, Kitchener gave assurances of a million men in 1915, for which he had no authority. The story goes that Joffre's grim aside when he was told this was that he only wanted *one* man, but he would make sure that one man was killed. That is as may be. What it shows is that Le Ver ('the slug'), dogged and unimaginative in operational matters though he was, was not so stupid as his critics believed when it came to the politics of war.

After so inauspicious a beginning, it might be wondered how the British and French managed to carry out any effective, coordinated operations at all. One powerful reason was the next move of the enemy, that ever inconsiderate upsetter of pre-conceived arrangements and plans. The battles on the Marne and the Aisne in September 1914 gave the Allies only a brief moment of respite. Falkenhayn, who had stepped into Moltke's shoes, was not a man who gave up easily or was shaken in his adherence to the offensive principle by even so severe a setback as the failure of the Schlieffen plan. For the moment there was a great gap on the Franco-British left and the right flank of the Belgian troops who, having escaped from Antwerp, were aligned roughly along the River Yser on the coast. Falkenhayn decided to try a new thrust in the north directed at the Channel ports to cut off the BEF from its direct communications with South-East England and so upset its logistics and depress its morale. Falkenhayn, therefore, had as good if not better reasons for fighting the First Battle of Ypres, and later the Second, as Haig had for choosing the same area for his offensive in 1917, the Third Battle of Ypres called Passchendaele. What followed is sometimes rather dramatically called 'the race for the sea.' In fact, it took the form of a hard fought encounter-battle in the gap. In the North, the Belgians, fighting well and flooding the low ground, successfully blocked the coastal route. The French moved in on their right, and the BEF marching north from the Aisne fought a succession of desperate engagements at La Bassée, Armentières and finally for the low ridges overlooking Ypres from the East. It was still a war of manoeuvre, with one emergency following another for which the 'Old Contemptibles' were perfectly suited.* Sir John, who could always rise to the occasion, had at that moment neither the time nor the inclination to consider the requests and orders of the French in light of the ambiguities of his directive.

A second, and unlikely blessing was the coincidence at that juncture of two such high-spirited men as John French and Ferdinand Foch. Sir John's feelings towards the French were at best, ambivalent. He admired French valour, but so far had not been impressed by French officers, considering them not quite gentlemen, unreliable, even a 'low lot'; a regrettably English attitude. Of Sir John, Foch made a complete conquest. Whatever his idiosyncrasies may have been, deficient as he may have been in the qualities required for the highest command in war, Sir John could always respond generously to a call for action and a sympathetic answer to a request for help. What clinched their relationship was the crisis at Ypres when Haig's 1st Corps line was broken and his last reserves committed. Foch forbade withdrawal, but he sent in eight French infantry battalions and six field batteries to Sir John's unconcealed relief and gratitude. It was at First Ypres that Foch revealed his flair for driving a three-horse team without

---

* The origin of this honourable soubriquet was a mistranslation of the Kaiser's comment that the BEF was an 'insignificant' little army, as indeed it was, numerically.

cracking his whip; employing all his personal magnetism, his panache and his habit of giving the shortest and clearest orders. (During the preparations for the Marne, his new chief of staff, Maxime Weygand, unused to Foch's style, translated one of his brief verbal orders into the voluminous instructions customary in French staff duties, only to receive a severe ticking off, and be told to tear them up and convey what Foch had actually said to his corps commanders, and no more.) Foch had soon modified his ideas about wild offensives delivered *à la bayonette* at the *pas de charge*. His method was to hold on to ground firmly, not yielding an inch, because that would only encourage the attacker, keep a reserve as the only way a commander could influence a battle apart from mere exhortation, and try to bring about a situation in which he himself could resume the offensive.

Weygand, describing his chief's style of leadership, said:

> He avoids any word or allusion which might wound their (his allies) *amour-propre*. He never utters a complaint or reproach to those with whom he is associated in the struggle. They are doing the best they can. He does his best to help them. He never tries to command them in the strict and military sense of the word. This situation is out of place between allies. He persuades. His first words are never of blame or criticism, however widely his views differ from those he is talking to. He even starts by approving anything he finds acceptable. Then he tries to bring the other over to his own point of view. Usually he is successful. If he encounters resistance or objections he puts his ideas down on paper, which he leaves . . . [them] to consider. Much good grace and warmth temper his strength . . .

Although Sir John continued to have his tiffs with the French, his inherent good military sense told him that only one commander could grip the situation and take important decisions. During the discussions about the combined offensive of which the British share was to be the Battle of Loos, in September 1915, he recorded in his diary that the final decision had to be left to Joffre, to whom he refers as the 'generalissimo'.

In 1915 the diverging aims of the British and French did not arise from conflicting operational opinions between Sir John French on one side and Joffre on the other, but between their respective governments, and in this the British cannot be said to have dealt openly or candidly with their ally. Kitchener, in turn, was hampered by having to impress the views of the British Cabinet and War Councils on Sir John French, yet leaving him to mediate the British aim of avoiding too deep an involvement in the battle of the Western Front with the offensive strategy of the French, implemented by Joffre. Kitchener's trouble, common to war lords as a category, was that while he was a great doer and achiever, he had no marked gift for self-analysis. He seemed not to understand his role as a politician nor, judging by his actions, did he communicate his war aims to his colleagues. Naturally secretive and new to politics, he lacked what counted in the long run, a 'constituency' in the cabinet and parliament. His public support was immense; but the public was fickle. Politically he was isolated. This was partly the fault of the Prime Minister, Herbert Asquith, who did not pull the Cabinet together, as did Winston Churchill in the Second War coalition government. Asquith did not lack intellect but took neither his responsibilities nor the war seriously. He was lazy and drank too much. When bored in meetings he wrote letters to his inamorata, and he worked to a peace-time programme of leisurely evenings and weekends devoted to relaxation. He might have been running the Zulu or Crimean War. Kitchener may be described simply as a dyed-in-the-wool Imperialist, but initially the strategy he preferred was shared by most of his colleagues. They favoured providing money and arms to enable the Russians to fight the Germans and assisting any potential British allies in the Eastern Mediterranean who might help them. As 1915 wore on, diplomatic attempts to build up Allied fronts in the Eastern Mediterranean to this end failed and the Russian government's financial incompetence absorbed sterling credits that Britain needed for her own armament. Kitchener had raised his large army as a strategic reserve and it began to appear that, in future, military aid might be more effective in helping the Russians. The question was when and where the army should be employed. In the Near East he preferred that Indian and ANZAC troops look after the Suez Canal. Kitchener agreed with most of his colleagues that Britain should commit only limited forces to the Continent and he did not want the Kitchener Armies to be frittered away there or in the Mediterranean. He hoped that the French would hold their own on the Continent until, at the end of 1916 or in early 1917, they and the Germans would be exhausted and British formations could enter the battle decisively. In the meanwhile he would give Joffre as much encouragement as possible without committing the major part of the British Army to fight beside the French.

Kitchener's balancing act, if it were ever practicable as more than a general idea, collapsed before the end of 1915, when Sir John French was replaced by Sir Douglas Haig. The first blow was the fiasco of the Dardanelles, which extended from March 1915 until the end of the year. Kitchener's vacillation over the Dardanelles destroyed his standing in the Cabinet. The second was the ferocious fighting on the Western Front in 1915 in which the French suffered 1,430,000 casualties to be added to the

995,000 of 1914. The British and Dominion troops, fighting off the German gas attacks at the 2nd Battle of Ypres, and attacking at Neuve-Chapelle, Aubers Ridge, Festubert and Loos suffered about 200,000. Although Kitchener advised caution on the new commander of the BEF in 1916, French demands made it impossible to withhold the Kitchener armies from the fighting so that the strategic die was cast in favour of the Western Front. The collapse of the Anglo-British attempt to defeat the Turks in the Dardanelles had removed, for the time being, any hope of an alternative in the Mediterranean.

At this stage Kitchener's influence on British strategy had waned, partly because events on the Continent were beyond his control and partly because Asquith's lack of leadership in the Cabinet allowed the persuasive Winston Churchill and Lloyd George to take charge.[3] In pertinacity and power of advocacy Kitchener was no match for Winston Churchill who conceived the Dardanelles plan. Kitchener should have opposed such a venture, particularly as early as March 1915, before the new armies were ready and in the midst of a crisis over munitions. Rightly, he calculated that the security of India and therefore Egypt was all-important to the Empire, but that it could be safely left to the government of India and the Indian army. As an experienced soldier with some knowledge of the Near East, Kitchener could have argued against Churchill on the grounds that:

1 it ignored the temper of the new regime in Turkey,
2 it underestimated the fighting power of the Turkish army, equipped as it was with German artillery and advised by German officers,
3 overestimated the ability of warships to operate in enclosed waters covered by the fire of shore batteries and sown with mines, and
4 such operations demanded the simultaneous and coordinated action of naval and land forces.

As a 'naval person', as he later called himself, Churchill should have been aware that this has always proved to be the case, and modern technology had increased the advantage of coastal defences. Churchill won his argument by default, though, and the ill-fated Dardanelles venture was duly launched on 18 March.

The total failure of the Dardanelles venture had consequences more far-reaching even than the waste of 40,000 excellent United Kingdom and ANZAC troops and 10,000 equally valuable French (figures further inflated by a long sick list caused by malaria and dysentery) who would have been 'better employed' in France or Flanders. It removed the persuasive voice of Winston Churchill from the British War Council and Cabinet, and

71

implanted in him and the British Army a morbid fear of amphibious assaults on a coast defended by a resolute enemy. It did not, however, cure Churchill of his obsession for strategic envelopment in the form of far-flung adventures in the Eastern Mediterranean and the Aegean. Kitchener had neither firmly opposed the naval operation nor supported it with adequate land forces. Indeed, he supported the idea that a naval force could do the job alone – because he lacked trained divisions, as yet. When it became a failed land operation and he had to decide to evacuate Gallipoli at the end of the year, his reputation never recovered. In the meanwhile Joffre had continued his bloody offensives on the Continent, compelling Kitchener to commit his new armies as the Germans opened their Verdun offensive in February 1916, and Sir Douglas Haig was committed to a major offensive on the Somme in July.

There was another powerful reason for the Allies to maintain pressure on the Western Front in 1915 beside the French determination to free their country. The Dardanelles was designed to defeat the Turks and open the sea route to Russia. The Russians were everywhere in retreat and Allied offensives on the Western Front were intended to attract German troops away from the Russian front. This succeeded only too well in that the Germans were never in trouble from the Allied offensives, almost broke through at 2nd Ypres and at Verdun in early 1916. Nevertheless, the need to coordinate offensives on the two fronts and to assist the Russians indirectly continued to be a strategic factor until the Russian collapse in 1917.

After Kitchener was drowned in June 1916, on his way in the cruiser *Hampshire** to an assignation in Russia where the Cabinet thought he would be harmlessly employed and temporarily out of the way reporting on Russia's war effort, he was succeeded by the rising star, Lloyd George. Lloyd George's capacity for mischief was curtailed by being bound by the conditions, insisted on by William Robertson,[†] who became CIGS in December 1915, that he (Robertson) had the right of direct access to the Cabinet and to communicate with field commanders. Thus Lloyd George

---

* Kitchener sailed for St Petersburg in the cruiser HMS Hampshire, mysteriously sunk off the north of Scotland, possibly by a submarine or a mine floating loose from its moorings. No U-Boat has been identified operating in that area, or claimed a sinking in it at that time. Its loss remains a mystery.

† William Robert Robertson, b 1860 at Welbourne, Lincolnshire, son of the village tailor and postmaster. Entered domestic service as a footman. Enlisted in the 16th Lancers and rose to rank of Troop Sergeant Major. Commissioned 1888 into the 3rd Dragoon Guards. Chief of the Imperial General Staff, December 1915–February 1918.

could not act as a filter between Robertson and the Cabinet or interfere directly with field commanders as had Kitchener earlier.

Robertson was to play a part of immense importance in the conduct of the War throughout his two years as CIGS. Not only was he a brilliant administrator and a professional soldier to his fingertips but, whilst he was at the War Office, Haig had a stout-hearted champion to guard his back when the political going got rough. Although Robertson and Haig did not always see eye-to-eye on tactics – and Robertson was by no means alone in this – they were as one over the importance of the need for British strategy to be firmly anchored to the Western Front. In consequence, it is worth looking more closely at the figure of 'Wully' Robertson – as he was affectionately known throughout the British Army. In the 1880s, it was most unusual for a serving Warrant Officer to be granted a combattant commission and even more unusual for such a man to become a graduate of the Staff College and later its Commandant – Robertson was the first to do either. Going to France with French as Quartermaster General (later Chief of Staff) of the BEF in 1914, he soon made his mark once again, as his later selection to become CIGS showed. He was a remarkable and, indeed, a unique character. Blunt almost to the point of rudeness and so laconic in his speech as to seem almost inarticulate, he was at his best on paper. He never abandoned his native Lincolnshire brogue to the day he died, nor would he ever do other than to drop every aitch. This last characteristic became immortalised in the story of the occasion upon which he was ordered to inform General Sir Horace Smith-Dorrien, the commander of the 2nd Corps in the BEF, that he had been sacked. Smith-Dorrien and French had long been at loggerheads and the dismissal was essentially a question of personalities, making it difficult for French to undertake the unwelcome task himself. Quite undaunted, Robertson walked up to Smith-Dorrien with the cheerful cry of 'Well, 'Orace, you're for 'ome'. Despite his homeric struggles in Haig's defence in Cabinet, Robertson often felt that Haig was not as appreciative of his loyalty as he felt he had a right to expect. After the war, he was heard to exclaim, as he got into a taxi having listened to Haig speaking at a reunion of senior officers and making no mention of him: 'Well. That's the last time I'll go fartin' with Alg.'

Haig had his own constituency among influential politicians, and the confidence of King George V, a strong character, well versed in politics who exercised more influence in military matters than a monarch was expected to do in the later war or today. His strongest ally was, however, the Prime Minister, Asquith, who had confidence in Haig. Haig's opinion of 'Squiff', (Victorian slang for tipsiness, 'squiffy') was that even when in his cups he was cleverer and more clear-headed than many other men when sober.

Haig therefore entered on his immense task with the advantage of what soldiers term a firm base in London. In France his position seemed unassailable too. He had the prestige of a commander of a force that was no longer the 'BEF', but a great and growing group of armies approaching, if not equal to the French Army in numbers, but steadily improving in tactics and combat skills. He could deal with the French as a peer, not as a refractory junior member of the team as had Sir John French. His reputation in the British Army was formidable, and there was no one who cared to challenge it. Wisely, he maintained good relations with Joffre so that politicians would hesitate to take the responsibility for operations from his shoulders by intervening, as had Kitchener earlier. His relations with Joffre rested on goodwill, flexibility, self-interest and, above all, on the latter's strong political position. Nevertheless Haig often disagreed with Joffre, and resented his hard-headed businessman's approach to Anglo-French relations. 'Another curious letter from Joffre' he wrote in his diary on 28 March 1916. '(He) wants 2,000 men and 1,000 workmen in exchange for the 68 heavy guns he left behind when the British took over their line. This cost the British 150,000 men to take over . . . the truth is that there are not many officers in the French Staff with gentlemanly ideas. They are out to get as much from the British as they possibly can.' By and large Haig preferred to deal with Foch, his equivalent army group commander when the latter was commanding the French northern armies, as had Sir John French. But so long as Haig had to play a subordinate role in operations and politics did not intrude unduly, he grumbled, occasionally exchanged angry words, but was comfortable with Joffre whom he respected for his toughness. Haig, it is sometimes forgotten, was a man of the world, well-informed, who had travelled abroad, spoke French well enough for social purposes (naturally relying on interpreters for a precise translation of important statements or documents), had excellent manners and a good humoured acceptance of human foibles. He was careful always to give Joffre a lunch that was good by exacting French standards when the old man visited his GHQ; it made for smoother discussions. No great talker, unless he had something to say, he accepted Joffre's system of commanding by conference, of which no fewer than fifty are recorded, at which such wide ranging issues, as the international scene, the Eastern Front and the Balkans were discussed. Between these conferences and Haig's personal contacts with Joffre, whom he accepted as 'generalissimo', the coalition was managed tolerably well until Joffre fell and was replaced by Nivelle in December 1916.[4]

The dynamic factor in the coalition when Joffre commanded was his determination to use the British to mount diversionary attacks or to relieve

French troops for the offensive. When the Germans attempted to bleed the French white at Verdun, the French needed the British to mount a major offensive on the Somme and to maintain it from July to December. It absorbed the Kitchener armies although Haig was only too aware that they and their commanders and staffs were for the moment little more than a 'militia' and wished to delay the attack until later in the summer when they would be better-trained. By the New Year of 1917, Haig believed that the French were in decline and looked forward to launching a British offensive in Flanders. For the time being, though, General Nivelle continued the offensive strategy of Joffre and wanted the British to take over more line to enable him to form a reserve for an offensive in Champagne while they mounted a subsidiary attack at Arras. Haig remonstrated but agreed to play his part. The result was a disastrous French spring offensive that caused many French divisions to mutiny and led to the inescapable conclusion that the initiative in the coalition had passed to the British. The fate of the coalition depended, it seemed, on concealing the French army's impotence from the Germans by keeping the British front active.

Relations between the two armies thus entered a new phase in May 1917. Until then, Joffre and Nivelle had treated the British as unprofessional, if stout-hearted, allies to be used as they determined. After that date, the British was the more reliable and effective army and Haig was determined to prove it in Flanders.

David Lloyd George entered this drama in January 1917, soon after he became Prime Minister when Nivelle was attempting to convince Haig to play his part. As he did not share Haig's belief in the maturity of the BEF, he opposed his plan for a campaign in Flanders and supported Nivelle. Further, he planned to create a unified allied command controlled by the politicians and, as a step in that direction, to subordinate Haig's armies to Nivelle in the coming offensive.[5] When Haig agreed to cooperate with Nivelle, as he had with Joffre, the wind was taken out of his sails. After the French offensive failed and his confidence in Nivelle proved to be unfounded, he had no recourse but to depend on Haig and the BEF.

The actions of Lloyd George and Haig in the new circumstances unfold in the next chapters, when Haig proceeded with his Flanders campaign and Lloyd George with his attempts, by indirect means, to check his independence.

Lloyd George had distinguished himself as a liberal statesman and social reformer before the war when he held the offices of President of the Board of Trade and Chancellor of the Exchequer. His political future was temporarily blocked by his avowed pacifism, but he saw the justice and wisdom of assisting Belgium in August 1914. In 1915 he became Minister of

Munitions, in 1916 Secretary of State for War, and then, in December, Prime Minister of a Liberal-Conservative coalition formed with the express object of sinking party differences and winning the war.

Winston Churchill's drawback as the war leader of Britain in the Second World War was that warfare was his passion, he had vast experience and he knew too much. Lloyd George, on the other hand, did not understand its principles or basic truths, and had no rapport with its practitioners. Militarism can be identified as an inability to distinguish between the reason for armies and the romantic elevation of warfare and the military virtues as things morally sublime. There are politicians, and Lloyd George was one of them, who are astute, even brilliant, but suffer from a parallel delusion that the subtle activities of building a constituency, of manipulating opinion, forming cliques and pressure groups, of creating political devices and structures and arriving at purely political goals by an exquisitely indirect approach, are ends in themselves. Lloyd George did not understand the necessity for an orderly system, to examine policy options and arrive at sound decisions. In rightly seeking a supreme Allied war council and a supreme military commander he did not grasp that neither would have the authority or means to execute plans, without proper staffs. They could not be created by politicians sitting in conferences. Indeed, it was the impracticality of his ideas that created friction with military leaders. Lacking Winston Churchill's ability to converse with his military men on the same wave-length, he could not learn from them the character of the British, French and American armies, or the true relationship between their leaders. He did not understand that unity of command would come about when the generals themselves found it necessary in a crisis. The system of command would then be cooperative rather than hierarchical because the Allies had not developed methods in common, let alone a joint staff to direct their armies. Indeed, Lloyd George did not understand the functions of such a staff.

None of the Allied armies had the unique authority and ability of the German staff which could coordinate divisions of diverse ability and of different nationalities, teach common methods, maintain standards, and replace and renew the quality of defeated divisions. Even in the Second coalition such a common staff only came into existence on the Allied side at the level of the Chiefs of General Staff and in the supreme headquarters of General Dwight D Eisenhower. The authority and practices of the German staff originated in the 19th century, as we have seen: no Allied staff acquired such authority over operations in either of the Western coalitions. Indeed, even the national staffs had to learn, or unlearn in the case of the French, during the wars. Nevertheless, a start had to be made to create something better than the *ad hoc* cooperative arrangements between

Haig and Joffre in 1916, Nivelle in early 1917 and then with Pétain until March 1918. Political control had to be established over the generals. In November 1917, the four allies, France, Britain, America and Italy set up a 'Supreme War Council' based in Versailles. A chiefs of staff committee was to coordinate or control strategy, it was never really clear which, with the powerful lever of a specially created central reserve at its disposal. All agreed when Foch was made its chairman. The British representative was General (later Field-Marshal) Sir Henry Wilson, articulate, mercurial and politically astute, an officer with whom Lloyd George felt he could work. In early February, this arrangement was in the melting-pot because Foch lacked power and authority to do more than advise the Cs-in-C. Lloyd George saw a solution by readjusting the relative powers of the CIGS and the British representative. He wanted to curtail the power of the CIGS by revoking the Order in Council of 27 January 1916 which authorised Sir William Robertson to communicate orders to Haig in the field. These orders would, instead, be issued by the British Representative at Versailles at Foch's bequest. On principle, Robertson objected both to the proposed power of the British representative and to the reduction of those of the CIGS, who would remain an adviser to the War Council but with reduced executive power. The particular issue was the control of British central reserves which he insisted should continue to be controlled by the CIGS and the C-in-C. As a majority of the War Council agreed with him, Lloyd George changed his tactics. He decided to leave the powers of the CIGS unchanged but to make Wilson CIGS and Robertson British Representative. The post of British Representative would, therefore, remain comparatively unimportant. Lloyd George felt that he could control Wilson but not Robertson. Robertson declined the Versailles post. On 16th February, the Official Press Bureau announced that Robertson had resigned as CIGS and was appointed to the Eastern Command. It was untrue but, having refused to accept the new arrangement, he had to go. On the 18th, Wilson was appointed CIGS in his place.

Sir Henry Rawlinson, commander Fourth Army, was sent to Versailles instead. Haig was deprived of Robertson's valuable support in London where Lord Milner became Secretary of State for War with Wilson his CIGS. Pétain, busy restoring the French Army to health, was Haig's superior as French C-in-C. Convinced that his Third and Fifth armies on the BEF right wing were vulnerable to the coming German offensive in March, and being uncertain of the support that he could expect from Pétain, Haig opened a correspondence with London demanding that lawful commands from the French be precisely defined. As things stood, Haig's original directive from Kitchener had not been modified or abrogated. Thus the onus was passed to the War Council to hand over, if they would, the BEF to French command. Haig knew well enough that they would not allow Lloyd George to have his way in this respect.

On 21 March, 1918, the German offensive for which Haig had warned Captain Hemming to be on the alert, burst on the British right. No theatre reserves had been formed by the War Council's military committee. When the Germans had driven a great U-shaped salient into the British front, Haig called on Pétain to send French reserves to cover Amiens in the British rear. Pétain, thoroughly alarmed, moved slowly and appeared to be covering the routes to Paris. It looked to Haig as though the Germans might drive a wedge between the BEF and the French and advance towards the mouth of the Somme. He called for Wilson and Milner to cross from London and, with Clemenceau, the French prime minister, to appoint Foch as supreme commander.

Thus it was an emergency that forced on the Allies a measure that could not be brought about earlier. Foch's powers of command were limited, nevertheless. In the first place he had a small staff which could not plan and execute joint operations. He guided rather than ordered his subordinates. His real power lay in persuading them to form reserves and make them available in the months of April to June when the Germans struck on the British front on the Lys in Flanders in April, and on the Aisne and the Marne on the French front in May and June. On the Lys, the French fought with the British, on the Aisne the British fought with the French, and on the Marne three armies were involved and the Americans first made a name for themselves.

The precedent set by Foch, that of direct intervention in operations with a small tactical headquarters, was one of the options open to General Dwight Eisenhower as Supreme Commander Allied Expeditionary Force in 1944. Foch, as a Frenchman, was determined that the fighting should terminate with French armies in a position to influence the peace. In particular he wanted the Rhineland to be occupied permanently by the French, and to share the eviction of the Germans from the Low Countries with the British, although they had entered the war for Belgium and fought and shed so much blood there. The political ambition of the French High Command was not ended, by any means, by the creation of the Supreme War Council. For them, the disgrace of the War of 1870 and the Dreyfus Affair, and the bloodletting since 1914 demanded that the honour of the French Army be recognised by the terms of the peace settlement.

CHAPTER 5

LLOYD GEORGE: MAN IN A FROCK-COAT

The nation that will insist on drawing a broad line of demarcation between the fighting man and the thinking man is liable to find its fighting done by fools and its thinking done by cowards.

GENERAL SIR WILLIAM BUTLER, *AUTOBIOGRAPHY*

Before assessing Haig's responsibility for the disastrous 3rd Battle of Ypres it is necessary to examine the part played by Lloyd George and his political colleagues who eventually authorised him to mount it.

As Prime Minister, Asquith assembled a War Cabinet and a War Council, but both were too large and clumsy for the effective direction of a war of unparalleled complexity and size.[1] When Lloyd George[2] succeeded Asquith as prime minister of the war-time coalition between the Liberal and Conservative and Unionist Parties, he formed two small and what should have been workmanlike bodies; a War Cabinet, which consisted of two great pro-consular figures of outstanding administrative ability, both peers, Alfred Milner[3] and George Nathaniel Curzon[4], and two members of the House of Commons, Bonar Law and Arthur Henderson[5], and a new War Policy Committee (WPC) which, besides the members of the War Cabinet, included General Jan Christian Smuts.[6] Smuts, soldier, holist philosopher and supporter of the Imperial idea, had fought in the army of the Boer republics in 1899–1902 and was regarded by both Lloyd George and Churchill as a man of profound sagacity. There was therefore no lack of talent. The Prime Minister sat as chairman of both with Bonar Law as his deputy.

Such bodies could not operate by light of nature. They required elaborate machinery to collect information on every subject from the departments of state and the service chiefs, prepare position papers and briefs, draw up agenda and record and circulate decisions. The Committee of Imperial Defence, an advisory body with the Prime Minister as chairman, had gone into suspended animation on the outbreak of war. Instead, there had come into being the War Cabinet Secretariat organised by Maurice Hankey.[7] Under his energetic and guiding hand it developed 'ideas' and 'machinery' (or procedure) divisions, and sections to attend to civil, political and military matters. Hankey's scope was limited by the fact that he was not a Permanent Under Secretary of State in the Civil Service hierarchy, nor equal to one in status, nor did his Secretariat correspond to a department of state; he was without executive power. As well as Hankey's Cabinet Secretariat, Lloyd George had set up his own at 10 Downing Street, facetiously termed the 'Garden Suburb'. There existed, therefore, at least in embryo, the sort of organisation for the management of the war effort elaborated and perfected by Churchill in the Second World War. The problem was how to make it work and adjust it in the light of experience. Running so great an enterprise requires the balancing of political, military and economic factors and the vision to hammer out consistent policy as well as the ability to deal with urgent, day to day events, or crisis management, as it is now called. To this has to be added the efficient, systematic discharge of business. All this makes a tall order.

The deficiencies of the machine as operated by the Prime Minister were only too apparent when the WPC undertook its first major review in June 1917. Its task was to find a solution to the German submarine offensive. A course proposed was Haig's land offensive at Ypres to capture the German bases at Ostend and Zeebrugge from which short-range U-boats had access to the northeastern approaches to the Straits of Dover, the British East Coast ports and the Western Approaches. This was neither the only nor the best option. One third of the ships lost from the Channel and Western ports were victims of Flanders-based U-boats slipping through the Straits of Dover, which had yet to be effectively blocked by improving the minefield between Dover and Calais. Other practical measures were attacks by fast patrol craft, raids to block the harbour entrance (as eventually undertaken at Zeebrugge in April 1918) and aerial bombardment. Above all, there was the fiercely debated proposal to assemble merchant ships in convoys escorted by the Royal Navy as the principal answer to the German unrestricted submarine warfare declared in February 1917. In fact, the first experimental convoy had reached the United Kingdom safely on 10 May. The Atlantic Convoy Committee had been established within the Admiralty on 17 May and, on 6 June, it recommended that the convoy system should be adopted.

It seemed that a combination of measures by the Royal Navy to meet the submarine crisis was either in place or could have been ordered by Admiral

Sir John Jellicoe,[8] the First Sea Lord. Jellicoe had been appointed in November 1916, after twenty-seven gruelling months in command of the Grand Fleet, and was believed to be tired and ill. Lloyd George considered that he was deeply pessimistic and inconsistent in his opinions and proposals. In 1916, Haig and Admiral Bacon, who commanded the light naval forces entitled 'the Dover Patrol', had discussed an amphibious operation against the enemy held Flanders coast, using General Rawlinson's Fourth Army and, with remarkable prescience, a force of tanks landed on the beaches from flat-bottomed barges, only for Jellicoe to turn it down. Nevertheless, the landing remained part of the plan for the battle of 3rd Ypres now designed by Haig and under discussion by the WPC in June 1917. When Jellicoe spoke strongly to the WPC in favour of Haig's Flanders plan as a solution to the U-boat crisis he seemed to have reversed his position and to be showing lack of confidence in convoys. The Prime Minister and the WPC believed that he was trying to shift the burden of responsibility for adopting the correct anti-submarine strategy from his own shoulders to theirs.[9]

Earlier, Lloyd George had determined to bring about the removal of Jellicoe although the Admiral was a naval hero and had powerful political backing. He had to maintain a delicate balance for he headed an uneasy coalition of bitterly opposed factions, and had himself appointed Edward Carson,[10] a staunch Conservative and Unionist, as First Lord of the Admiralty. The First Lord was a politician, the civil head of the Navy who corresponded to the Secretary of State for War, and Lloyd George feared that if he too obviously interfered to bring about Jellicoe's dismissal over his head, Carson would resign. At this point the political and strategic options piling up proved too great an obstacle for either the Prime Minister or the WPC to make a timely and rational decision on the Flanders ports, submarines and Haig's plan.

While all this was pre-occupying Lloyd George, his nice domestic calculations were interrupted by a crisis in the strategic situation of the Allies engaged on the Western Front mentioned in Chapter 6. Information from Russia made it clear that the Russian armies were incapable of and unwilling to attempt further offensive action, and that it was doubtful whether they even had a defensive capacity. Both the British and French armies had suffered heavy casualties in 1916, on the Somme and at Verdun. Great hopes had been pinned on the offensive so confidently planned by General Nivelle, launched on 16 April, but by the first week in May it became all too clear that it had been a ghastly failure. How complete was the demoralisation in the two groups of armies employed was not yet clear, perhaps not even to the French high command (it was some time before it degenerated into actual mutiny and wholesale refusal to enter the front line), but they were vulnerable to a counter-thrust. Were the Germans to take advantage of the situation in Russia and reinforce the Western Front with divisions from the Eastern, the situation would be dangerous indeed. The one bright hope was assistance from the United States which had declared war on the Central Powers in April, but units of the US Army were unlikely to be fit to take their place at the front until the early summer of 1918, at the earliest.

It was quickly decided that nothing less than an immediate summit meeting between heads of state could resolve how to meet this emergency. Accordingly, on 4 May 1917, M. Paul Painlevé, the Minister of War, with his military advisers, who included General Pétain (shortly to be nominated Commander-in-Chief in place of Nivelle), met Lloyd George, who was supported by Haig and Robertson, in Paris. Their conclusions were unequivocal. Their armies would remain on the defensive until the American Expeditionary Force was equipped and trained. All three would then make a concerted effort. This was the promise that Pétain, in his task of restoring discipline and healing the wounds in French morale, had had to give his troops. In the meantime, the British would undertake strictly limited local offensives to draw German attention from the French. Their operation at Arras, launched in support of the Nivelle offensive, was serving that purpose. Much to Lloyd George's relief, Haig agreed that the British Army would cooperate in this strategy. Haig's interpretation of what was a 'limited' operation and what a 'break-through' offensive was more elastic than Lloyd George or the French understood. An operation mounted in the Ypres salient to occupy the U-boat bases on the Belgian coast was not within the parameters of the Paris agreement, although Haig was to argue with the unexpected help of Jellicoe, that it was, or ought to be. Whether 3rd Ypres was limited or strategic, plagued, confused and soured the relations between Lloyd George and Haig for ever.

The shortcomings of the WPC were evident in the way it handled the connection between the U-Boat crisis and the Third Battle of Ypres. Apart from the domestic political factors which influenced its judgment, there was a structural weakness in the process for reaching decisions. There was no suitable inter-service staff to coordinate the views of the Admiralty and the War Office and to present analyses of strategic problems to Hankey's secretariat. Hankey received from the Services only their preferred course of action, not the appreciations with the advantages and disadvantages of alternatives as well as the chosen course which the staffs were trained to write. Hankey, himself a former naval officer, had been at pains to lay before the new WPC a brief summary of the options and, at first, its members agreed with his view that in terms of cost benefit an offensive launched from the Ypres salient was too drastic a method for achieving a limited result.[12] In any case, the short-range U-Boat threat would not be eliminated by the course recommended by Haig and Jellicoe; it would merely lengthen the journey of the U-Boats to their target areas by forcing them back to German ports. This view, sound enough, was Hankey's own but had not been discussed, let alone agreed, by the Services.

When we look back at the bumbling and ineffectual attempts (as they seem to us) of Lloyd George's administration to direct the war in 1917–1918, we should keep in mind that nothing like the carefully structured and complex apparatus of joint and combined inter-service staffs and their specialist ancillaries could have sprung into being, even if the politicians had willed them. Nevertheless, the experience of these last years of war gave rise to the efficient system that the British enjoyed soon after the start of the Second World War. The essence of that system was that ideas generated at the top could be referred downwards for service scrutiny and comment as to their practicability, and the planning branches of service staffs produced proposals for inter-service scrutiny at the professional level and upwards for examination for their political and grand strategic implications. To create such a system required a revolution in thought about the role of government in peace as well as war. For the first three years of war, the prevailing assumption was one that had remained unchanged for the two preceding centuries: that there was a clear-cut division of responsibility between the civil and military authorities. The services were responsible for operations in the field and at sea and the head of state, as represented by Cabinet, for all civil and political affairs. When total war demanded the integrated management of grand strategy *and* operations, and also of the whole fabric of the national economy, including shipping and agriculture and civilian morale, the politicians were not mentally prepared to undertake it. This was demonstrated by their inability to respond to the daily demand to spend hours mastering the contents of papers pouring out from the Services and every civil department of state. Consequently, Service staffs considered submitting arguments with full documentation a waste of the hours spent in compiling them. How to intervene when something was going wrong, to master the facts and take appropriate action was something the politicians, with few exceptions, did not undertake systematically but should have. Furthermore, manpower, shipping, the submarine threat and the strategy in the new circumstances of the entry of the United States into the war and the imminent collapse of Russia should have been foremost in their minds, not domestic political manoeuvring.

Perhaps this is a counsel of perfection to which the war-time coalition could not hope to subscribe, bearing in mind that inter-party politics before 1914 and since had been as bitter as at any time in Parliamentary history. Unlike Winston Churchill in the later war, Lloyd George could not often depend on a bipartisan approach. The 'Welsh Wizard' might radiate authority, his oratory could dazzle an audience or charm the birds out of a tree, his deftness in political manoeuvre might be unrivalled, but the fact was that he had become an outsider, in both senses of the word; he was to the followers of the ousted Asquith in his own party a usurper, and supported only grudgingly by the Conservatives and Unionists, who did not trust him. With the war going badly, he had to dissemble his lack of confidence in the First Sea Lord, the CIGS and the Commander-in-Chief in the field, and trim whatever ideas he had about a better direction of operations to political realities.

According to one story, in dealing with a flagging and pusillanimous Jellicoe, Lloyd George is supposed to have stridden into the Admiralty on 30 April 1917, planted himself in the First Sea Lord's chair and ordered Jellicoe to adopt the convoy system forthwith. This is part of the Lloyd George myth. Arthur Marder described the interface of the two men as 'cautious knowledge' versus 'the valour of ignorance'. It appears that Hankey, who accompanied Lloyd George, described the meeting as amicable, even cordial. In any case, the Admiralty had already undertaken a trial for Convoy, and the wily Lloyd George was manoeuvring to be acclaimed as its father when the admiralty officially adopted it in May. However, Lloyd George's own comment to Hankey about convoys a week earlier (on 22 April) had been: 'Oh well, I have never regarded that matter as seriously as you have.' The remark reveals Lloyd George's opacity to the most vital strategic questions which he regarded as no more than the professional foibles of the military mind.[13]

It should have been obvious that it would take some time before the convoy system was able to operate at full efficiency. The naval units themselves required to be trained in new tactics and, a far more difficult task, the masters of merchant vessels, a famously independent class of men and antipathetic to the 'brass-bound' Royal Navy, had to be drilled to sail together and manoeuvre in company. The longer the Prime Minister hesitated to dismiss Carson and Jellicoe, the longer it would take for the convoy system to be established and the more the losses in shipping would pile up. All these problems, convoy, shipping, the distribution of scarce labour between the armed forces and industry were interlocking, and demanded urgent positive solutions. The same spirit of political expediency and the consequent delay in arriving at positive decisions was the dominating factor in the causal chain which led to 'Passchendaele'. It seems doubtful if Lloyd George was capable of understanding the logic of logistics. His obsession with political adroitness blinded him to the connection of military cause and effect. He sought to prevent a major offensive in the Ypres sector. He could have ordered a systematic evaluation – an 'appreciation of the situation' – to examine what other measures could achieve the various agreed short term objectives of the Paris conference at less cost. Instead he conceived the idea of hampering Haig by removing resources from the Western Front to the Mediterranean, to strategically irrelevant theatres like northern Italy, where he sent British units untrained and ill-equipped for mountain warfare, Salonika, where they died of disease, and the Near East. All three increased the logistic burden and demanded a share of the already shrinking fleet of merchant shipping.

There is no doubt that Lloyd George opposed Haig's plans for a strategic offensive at Ypres. It is on the record that he was outvoted in the WPC after its final discussion on the subject, when it gave Haig permission to go ahead, on 25 July.[14] Unfortunately, the whole involved topic has been obfuscated by Lloyd George's sustained effort after the war to denigrate Haig and prove that he had himself acted correctly at every turn of events and that he alone had been the great architect of victory. It is more correct to say that he was right to oppose the Third Ypres plan, but that he did so for the wrong reasons. It is not an apology for his deviousness and delays to explain them as the ineluctable consequence of his insecure position as a Prime Minister without his own constituency. He had dished his chances with the Conservative/Unionist establishment, with which the Service establishment was closely allied, over the business of placing the BEF completely under the command of the egregious Nivelle, as opposed to ordering its Commander-in-Chief to cooperate with his French colleague and regard him as the senior partner. Haig, after all, had worked loyally and harmoniously with Joffre, and with Nivelle, whose débâcle had redounded to the discredit of Lloyd George's military judgment.

It would have been a happy outcome had Lloyd George and Sir William Robertson[15], two self-made men, achieved a rapport. Had the CIGS and a Chief of Naval Staff, or whatever title the Royal Navy preferred, been linked in a chief of staff's committee and recognised constitutionally as the professional heads of their services and principal advisers to the government the decisions linking 3rd Ypres with the U-boat crisis might have been avoided. Unfortunately, Lloyd George did not recognise that the proper channel to the commanders in the field was through the CIGS. Instead, he saw Robertson's simple adherence to military realities and his loyalty to Haig as obstacles to be removed. Robertson, a straight-forward, plain dealing man had been disgusted by Lloyd George's handling of the Nivelle period and did not trust the Prime Minister. Yet, had Lloyd George asked Robertson for an objective military assessment of the prospects of 3rd Ypres, knowing, as the CIGS certainly did, of the appreciations that his own Director of Military Operations, General Maurice, had drawn up on the subject, and that his Director of Military Intelligence, General Macdonogh had written on the morale of the German Army, he would have received a negative recommendation. Furthermore, Robertson knew of Rawlinson's and Plumer's misgivings about the operational plan; if not of their details. Lloyd George himself had no access to informal Service channels or gossip or private letters. Nor did he bother to read the contents of circulating official papers. Instead of clarifying the connection between the submarine war and the Ypres solution to it, he pursued his tactical aim of removing Jellicoe and Carson. The method was to separate Haig from Jellicoe.

It is a good rule in politics, as in war, to pick off opponents one by one. On the subject of Third Ypres, Milner supported the view of Lloyd George, while Curzon and Smuts were in favour of it or, rather, they preferred Haig to Lloyd George, as being the more reliable on matters of strategy. The decisive vote was in the hands of Bonar Law[16], whose view it was, as leader of the Conservatives, that his followers would not stand for any more interference with Robertson and Haig. Lloyd George had decided that his first move should be to purge the Admiralty, in which he had the support of Milner. It was notoriously inefficient, it had only accepted the creation of a naval staff on the lines of the army's general staff shortly before the war on the insistence of the First Lord, then Winston Churchill. (At whose request Haig had written a paper showing how it might be done.) The Royal Navy's performance at Gallipoli had been inept and at Jutland an opportunity to destroy the German High Seas Fleet had, it seemed, been bungled. Lloyd George was not prepared to give Jellicoe the excuse that he had been hampered in his task by Lloyd George's refusal to allow Haig to assist him by clearing the Flanders coast, and he was too shrewd to take on the Admiralty, the War Office and the Commander-in-Chief in France simultaneously.[17]

When Haig was in London to attend the meeting of the WPC, he concerned himself with the efficiency of the Admiralty staff. He had been largely responsible for setting up the General Staff before the war under the great Secretary of State, R.B. Haldane, and had been used by Churchill in his battles with Admiral Fisher to introduce a similar staff for the Royal Navy. One of Haig's friends, Sir Eric Geddes, an industrialist with a gift for organization, had improved the efficiency of the French railways serving the BEF. Geddes, now Controller of the Royal Navy, had been appointed to inject efficient management into its affairs. He asked Haig to call on him for a discussion of the problems in the Admiralty. Acting on a suggestion of Lord Beaverbrook, a man adept in political manipulation and an ally of Lloyd George, Haig agreed to meet Lloyd George and Geddes to discuss what could be done about the Carson-Jellicoe regime at a working breakfast. To rule the service chiefs by dividing them was certainly an intriguing idea worthy of Beaverbrook and likely to appeal to Lloyd George. Nothing more can be deduced from the meeting than the interesting possibility that the Prime Minister may not have opposed the 3rd Ypres plan as strongly as he might so as to retain the support of Haig against Jellicoe and Carson.[18]

Thus far we have presented the bare bones of the complicated problem facing Lloyd George and the WPC over 3rd Ypres and touched on the embryonic apparatus at their disposal to solve it. Now we have to answer two questions about the relations of Lloyd George and Haig over the latter's plan to fight a great battle in Flanders which was overtly designed to contribute to the U-boat war. The first was how well was Lloyd George, by experience and personality, fitted for his great role? Second, how successfully did he assess the merits and defects of Douglas Haig, who dominated the military field, even more than the admirals and his own superior, the CIGS?

Lloyd George's assets were that he was an extremely clever man, he had vast political experience, he was a great orator, he enjoyed popular support, he radiated authority and he had what every successful leader must have, the urge to dominate. His trouble was that in modern war inspirational leadership is not enough. Lloyd George had no system and was intellectually lazy. The WPC under his chairmanship was a talking shop, seldom sticking to its agenda and almost never reaching positive conclusions which could be passed by the secretariat to the appropriate departments for action. The only occasions on which some system prevailed was when his deputy, Bonar Law, took the chair. Its members sometimes complained that they only learned by chance of decisions that the Prime Minister had arrived at in private conversations or at dinner parties. Lloyd George, like Churchill in the later war, was a talkative man who enjoyed conversation, and one who was naturally attracted to men as articulate as himself, and also put off by men who, in his view, lacked imagination and pointed out that his strategic ideas were castles in the air without solid foundations. Unlike Churchill, however, who devoured every piece of paper given to him in long hours of close reading, and constantly demanded to be supplied with facts and progress reports, Lloyd George was seldom at any pains to master a brief.

Compared with Churchill, who had made a life long study of warfare, Lloyd George was at a disadvantage, but it was a disadvantage he took no pains to remedy. As no less an authority than Wavell later pointed out, strategy is governed by a few, easily understood maxims or principles. Yet it was said of Lloyd George that never from first to last did he grasp the significance of possessing the 'interior line'; nor, as his actions showed, did he understand the great principle of concentration. He did not understand what generals *did,* but what was worse, he made no attempt to find out. It was unfortunate that the two men on whom he could and should have relied to enlighten him in friendly conversation on the subjects of strategy and the operational art (Robertson and Haig) were, though capable of writing lucidly and convincingly, notoriously inarticulate, especially in the parry and riposte of wide-ranging conversation about ideas. (This seems to have been a Victorian and military characteristic. In Victorian literature the garrulous man is often portrayed as lacking in bottom, insubstantial, a weakling; the ideal was the 'strong, silent man', saying little and never revealing his feelings. Soldiers were almost all authoritarians, insisting on unquestioning obedience to orders and abstention from questioning established ideas. As for conversation, the first thing impressed upon a newly joined subaltern was that he should not speak until he was spoken to. At the same time he was required to learn a list of topics barred from polite conversation, which included everything connected with his profession beside the arts, politics and religion).

In the Second World War, Churchill found his Commander-in-Chief in the Middle East, Sir Archibald Wavell, almost monosyllabic in conversation. It was that trait, as much as any other, that led to a breakdown in confidence between the two and, ultimately, to Wavell's removal, despite Sir Alan Brooke's efforts to explain that taciturnity was not the same as incompetence. As CIGS, Brooke had to act as interpreter between Churchill and Wavell's successor, General Sir Claude Auchinleck and, later, General Sir Bernard Montgomery in North-West Europe. In the First World War, however, the Commanders-in-Chief in the field were regarded as superiors of the CIGS. It was, after all, only a decade since the Commander-in-Chief at the Horse Guards had been abolished and the CIGS had not yet assumed his unchallenged position as professional head of the British Army. Indeed, the constitutional relationship of the CIGS to the Secretary of State, the Prime Minister and the Cabinet had not been established by precedent let alone by tradition. When, therefore, Lloyd George was faced with a military situation with which he was dissatisfied, and the circumstances of which he did not understand, he felt he had no other option than to replace the men he held responsible. With Haig, such a step was politically impracticable. In February 1918, he was to pluck up enough courage to replace Robertson by a manipulation in which he was crass enough to replace him by the charlatan Sir Henry Wilson, trusted by no-one. Haig remained unassailable because he was trusted by the Army, his power of command was formidable and, like Lloyd George himself, there was no-one willing to replace him.

The character and capabilities of Douglas Haig have been exhaustively dissected, but one side of them seems to have passed unobserved. Haig, in his own way, was every bit as shrewd a politician as the Prime Minister. In his strategic, as opposed to his tactical ideas, he was as rigid in his military beliefs, as it may be presumed, he was in the tenets of his Calvinist religion, but in his political dealings he had a strong sense of the possible. He could distinguish between the important and the unimportant. He understood the need to have a constituency. He cultivated his friends, not least King George V, whose complete confidence he enjoyed, and who gave him sound advice on how to guard his corner. In the words of the Thai proverb, he had observed 'that the bamboo bends in the gale, but it does not break'. Haig not only obeyed orders, he thought it improper not to do so. He cooperated with Joffre, because it was the sensible thing to do. He accepted his position under Nivelle, and avoided expressing any sign of satisfaction when Lloyd George's initiative, so wounding to himself and 'his' army, proved so wholly mistaken. When someone's head was demanded for the collapse of the Fifth Army, he accepted the dismissal of its commander, General Sir Hubert Gough (who was not to blame and whose reputation was restored after the war). One of Haig's amiable but unsoldierly weaknesses was excessive loyalty to his personal staff. He liked to have as advisers men with whom he felt comfortable. He suffered the humiliation of having his chief of staff and his chief of intelligence relieved on orders from above. He patiently acquiesced. It was when he was not given a positive order, or at least a clear cut directive, that Haig's obsessions prevailed over his military judgment. Ever since the First Battle of Ypres, when until the last moment all seemed lost, he had been convinced that the balance of victory always inclined to the general whose will to continue the offensive never faltered. It was that that led him into prolonging the Somme battle and then the Third Battle of Ypres long beyond the moment at which costs began to exceed benefits. In fairness, it should be added that it was his obsessive insistence on offensive action and never giving up that yielded the fruits of victory in August 1918, but we are here concerned only with what was the correct action to be taken in June, 1917.

Bearing in mind that the machinery for answering such questions was only evolved after great difficulty and trial and error twenty-six years later, it has to be recorded that of the three bodies concerned, the General Staff at Haig's GHQ, the General Staff in the War Office, and the WPC, none made any attempt to examine the various courses by which policies agreed at hastily convened meetings could be implemented, other than by mounting a costly offensive in an unsuitable sector; and one furthermore already condemned after exhaustive appreciations by the present Director of Military Operations in the War Office when serving on Sir John French's staff in GHQ BEF. The most imaginative course might have been to revive the plan for an amphibious assault on the U-boat havens, combined with air attack, which could have achieved the double object of a contribution to the anti-submarine offensive and of attracting the German reserves to the north and away from the French.

Two distinct but connected tactical/technical innovations had made it possible to strike telling blows against the weaker sectors of the elaborate Siegfried defensive system. One was the 'break-in' elaborated by the civil engineer turned soldier, the Australian General Sir John Monash, who developed it in meticulous detail and demonstrated it in its final, perfect stage in a local operation at Hamel in July 1918 and later in August and September. The other was the seminal battle of Cambrai in November 1917 already described. These techniques were ready to use in the mid-summer of 1917, but the point is not whether their adoption might have altered the course of Third Ypres, but that no staff study was put in hand to examine their feasibility, or whether they afforded a means of striking short, telling jabs to keep the attention of the German High Command fixed on the northern sector. Cambrai was an after-thought, embarked on after Third Ypres had been closed down. The conjunction of Byng, General Hugh Elles, commanding the Tank Corps and Brigadier-General Tudor was fortunate, but fortuitous. (See Chapter 3 Page 5)

'Passchendaele' remains the paradigm of the defects of the British high command in the First World War: the head of state striving to direct grand strategy without the faintest understanding of its guiding principles, while his commander-in-chief in the field had one simple aim, to continue battering at the German war-machine until it cracked, cost what it may. The instrument that should have served both lay to hand in the shape of the General Staff, modelled on the German Great General Staff, but never used. The supreme irony was that the Commander-in-Chief, who by the verdict of history was responsible for 'Passchendaele', was himself one of the most accomplished staff officers of his day. Unfortunately, when in command he chose to become an inspirational if obstinate leader, instead of using the instrument he had helped to create. The lesson was not forgotten. In the Second World War the division between the 'Frocks' and the 'Brass Hats' disappeared. Churchill was his own Minister for War, and 'Warlord', who kept his CIGS constantly at his side, formulating grand strategy from a basis of knowledge, and able, in his maddening, prodding way, to talk on equal terms with the commanders in the field.

In the next two chapters we look at Third Ypres in some detail and seek to evaluate Haig's personal performance as the initiator and commander of one of the bloodiest battles in the history of war. A Calendar of Events, to which the reader will find it helpful to refer, is to be found on pages 121–5.

CHAPTER 6

HAIG: MAN ON THE WHITE HORSE: PASSCHENDAELE I

The art of war is like medicine, murderous and conjectural.

VOLTAIRE

The Third Battle of Ypres – 'Passchendaele' – was a terrible ordeal for both the British and German armies, even by the standards of the First World War. For British historians and in public memory it remains the supreme example of the horrors of war and of the crassness of the generals of that era, but three quarters of a century later it deserves a cooler appraisal. Its planning and its outcome rested squarely on Haig's shoulders. He would have been the first to acknowledge it.

Historians are generally agreed that the account of Passchendaele in the British official history is flawed. Sir James Edmonds, the series editor, quarrelled with the 'author', GC Wynne,[1] who was expected to produce a purely factual, depersonalised account, or 'campaign narrative' but Wynne, a considerable scholar and authority on the Western Front and the German Army, had other ideas. They disagreed over the question of whether Haig or the commander of the Fifth Army, General Sir Hubert Gough bore the greater share of the blame for the failure of an ill-considered, ill-planned, imperfectly executed and unnecessarily prolonged battle. Unable to convert Wynne to his view that the major share was Gough's, Edmonds edited Wynne's narrative and added a retrospective chapter of his own. He believed that his final account was well-balanced but Wynne strongly disagreed and refused to allow his name to appear on the title page when the volume was published.[2]

In fact, neither historian got to the bottom of the story.[3] Three survivors, Gough himself, General Malcolm his chief of staff, and Sir John Davidson, Haig's chief of operations, offered the official historians their recollections in 1944 and 1945, but differed over matters of fact. Gough contradicted Haig's diary upon which Wynne had relied too heavily, and Davidson some of the official papers. As neither Edmonds nor Wynne revisited the battlefield they could not relate Gough's plan, or those of Rawlinson and Plumer to the topography. In short, the official historians did not reconcile the testimony in Haig's Diary with the evidence of the surviving witnesses and the sequence of events, including the making of the plans, recorded in the official papers. Edmonds' attempt to do so and to save Haig's reputation distorted the story.

When Edmonds wrote that, finally, he had 'got to the bottom of the business' he really meant that he had let sleeping dogs lie; further controversy would harm the reputation of the British Army and be unsuitable for official history. Here we are not under the same constraints as official historians. What Edmonds found too controversial is the salt in the subject; the problems of personality and clash of aims that hamper the exercise of high command in coalition war. It has to be accepted that commanders, like politicians are, even should be, ambitious, self-willed men who pit themselves against other men of similar mettle. None needs to be a saint; they often find it politic to hide the truth from others, and sometimes from themselves as well. Sir Douglas Haig survived the attempts of Lloyd George to remove him and to curtail his authority because he was politically astute and had political allies. Until the middle of 1917, he was shielded from responsibility for strategy by successive commanders-in-chief, first Joffre and then Nivelle, who were regarded as responsible for the coordination of Allied operations. The Asquith and Lloyd George governments found that their commander-in-chief's qualified subordination to a French generalissimo conveniently curbed his activities; it suited Haig as well, for instance in relieving him of the main responsibility for failure on the Somme, a battle initiated by Joffre. But in the interval between the mutinies in the French Army in April and May 1917, when Nivelle was replaced by Pétain, and the crisis caused by the German offensive in March 1918, which brought Foch to supreme command, Haig took upon himself sole responsibility for a great British campaign. Haig's failure to make a success of Passchendaele made him vulnerable to Lloyd George's criticism for the first time.

The planning and execution of the offensive was bedevilled by lack of clarity about its object and confusion about the operational method to be employed: its tactics were dictated by the topography of the Ypres salient. As a result, it was a costly effort which not only failed to achieve its strategic object, but even to break through the German defences. The innovatory Battle of Cambrai which followed, the successful last ditch defence against the German onslaught in March 1918 and the leading part played by the BEF in the final victorious battles of August–November, count as nothing in the balance-scales against Passchendaele when weighing the competence of Haig as a military commander. It is to this question of Haig's competence that we offer an answer.

As we explained in Chapter 4, Kitchener had expected the French and German armies to be exhausted by the end of 1916 and had hoped to preserve the New Armies until then. Before his death in June 1916, knowing that Haig had his mind set on breaking through the front on the Somme or in Flanders, Kitchener advised against it.[4] It would require a destructive battle of attrition which the Cabinet was as much against as he was. The German onslaught on Verdun demanded that the British Army fight a major battle to ease the terrible pressure on the French, nevertheless. So Haig was committed to Joffre's battle on the Somme. The question that concerns us, as it did Kitchener, is the kind of operation Haig intended to mount.

The debate over Haig's competence revolves about his own, obsessive, interpretation of the offensive principle; a principle soundly based and, it must be emphasised, regarded as valid by all the high commanders of the day. Like Foch, Haig believed that the successful general had to be a man of unyielding will-power, though he never expressed it with the same metaphysical fervour. He thought that to have a clearly defined, valuable goal encouraged the troops and commanders at every level. What is certain is that it was part of Haig's operational and strategic doctrine that a major offensive should have as its aim a strategic goal deep in enemy territory beyond the fortified defensive zone, and that the first step to break through it should be a single, continuous thrust, to maintain the momentum of the attack, keep the initiative and prevent the enemy from using his reserves to build up a new line of resistance in the rear. In principle, there was nothing unsound or impracticable in this idea (like most operational concepts, simple to the point of being obvious), but as the necessary conditions and weapons did not exist in July 1916, the Somme became a battle of attrition. In Haig's opinion, while weapons and conditions might not have existed in 1916, they did in 1917. He was confident that the new armies which constituted the bulk of the BEF had been seasoned and hardened by their ordeal on the Somme, and that they were fully mature and superior to the French, whose armies had shot their bolt and were incapable of further serious effort; a view formed after Verdun and reinforced by the outcome of the Nivelle offensive in the spring of 1917. It followed that the initiative had passed to the BEF, and its subordination to French direction had ended.

In this respect, Haig enjoyed the support of his principal staff officers and his army commanders. When it came to the kind of initiative that the BEF should take, he did not. Haig was convinced that the German Army was approaching exhaustion, an illusion fed by his chief intelligence staff officer in GHQ, Brigadier-General John Charteris who showed him over-optimistic and baseless reports of a decline in German morale in the later stages of the Somme and at Arras in April 1917. Here Haig's commanders ventured to differ. Nothing in the previous year's fighting or the Battle of Arras supported such a view, but their most profound area of disagreement was over the tactics of position warfare. General Sir Henry Rawlinson, who had played the leading part as commander of the Fourth Army in the Battle of the Somme, a man with an analytical mind and a considerable tactician, had concluded, before that battle began and in defiance of Haig, that the only way to force a way through a defensive system in depth was by a series of methodical attacks with limited objectives, pausing after each to prepare the next. A year later, he was of the same opinion. On 4 May 1917, in a conversation with Brigadier General John Davidson, then Haig's chief of operations, he said that he did not think that a strategic operation was timely when Davidson showed him the casualty figures for Arras, he agreed that the BEF was wasting away. If they continued to live at the present rate they would have to reduce either the number of divisions or the number of battalions in divisions by the end of June. 'Personally,' Rawlinson wrote in his diary,

'I am of the opinion that we ought to limit ourselves to small offensives all along the line assuming a general defensive attitude. Otherwise, should anything happen on the Russian front which enables the Boche to bring over 30 or 40 divisions, we shall be in a bad way until the Americans arrive.'[5]

Essentially, all those concerned with planning Passchendaele, General Herbert Plumer, later even the impetuous Gough, their chiefs of staff and especially Davidson at GHQ, shared Rawlinson's view. It was this fundamental difference of opinion on the *strategic* level between the commander-in-chief and his subordinates which bedevilled the planning and execution of the battle from start to finish. Nevertheless, Haig's critics closed ranks in the face of David Lloyd George's behaviour towards the BEF after he became Prime Minister. His attempt, at Calais in February 1917, to subordinate the BEF to Nivelle by removing Haig's right to appeal to the British Secretary of State for War over Nivelle's head, not only angered Robertson, the CIGS, who saw that the BEF might be endangered by being used piece-meal in ill-considered French operations and the British Government lose its ability to influence strategy on the Western Front, but also all senior officers in the BEF who had had dealings with the French. They knew that although Joffre had hankered after subordinating the BEF to his own headquarters, Haig and he worked together as equals without any more formal arrangement than had operated in General French's time. They were astonished, even insulted, when Lloyd George attempted to place them under Nivelle's orders. Haig had recognised that Joffre, until he fell out of favour, had the solid backing of his own government. He was much less happy with Nivelle who lacked Joffre's political ballast, having become a sudden favourite promoted over the heads of Foch and Pétain on the strength of his tactical success at Verdun. Haig saw himself subordinated to a man who depended on winning a great victory to remain in political favour, under an arrangement that altered his working relationship with the French high command by opening the door to political interference. After the Calais conference, it required no encouragement from Haig for his senior staff to regard Lloyd George as an enemy, even a traitor who trusted the French more than the BEF and employed devious means to bring them under political restraint.

When the Americans entered the war in April 1917, Lloyd George's opinion that the Allies should wait for the American Expeditionary Force to arrive in strength before undertaking another strategic offensive was widely supported in the BEF, not least by Rawlinson. Haig objected for two reasons. First, he thought it undesirable to allow the Americans, any more than the French, to determine the final outcome of the war: second, in his opinion and also that of the French General Staff, only a handful of American divisions could be fit for action by the summer of 1918 and the Allies could not be passive until then. Such a fundamental difference in opinion about strategy was bound to cause a clash of wills. Haig was determined that the BEF should seize the initiative in Flanders before the Germans transferred about fifty divisions from the Eastern Front with which to finish the war before the Americans could be effectively engaged. Lloyd George was equally determined to thwart Haig's intention.

Haig was perfectly clear what his correct course of action should be. What he sought was a strategic argument sufficiently strong to persuade the War Cabinet to allow him to mount a full scale offensive with the Ypres salient as its base, the aim being to clear the enemy from the area enclosed by the northern sector of the front, the enemy-occupied stretch of the Belgian coast and the Dutch frontier. He found it lying to his hand in a combination of the German submarine offensive that threatened the whole British war effort, and the desperate state of the French Army in

May, 1917. As to the first, the British had always regarded the presence of a hostile power in the Low Countries as intolerable. One outcome of 'the race to the sea' in 1914 and the subsequent bitter fighting was that Ostend and Zeebrugge fell into German hands: ideal bases for their short-range (as opposed to their ocean-going) U-Boats. From then onwards regaining control of the Belgian coast was a British aim.

The original proposal for a thrust from Ypres towards the coast had been made by Sir John French. When Haig succeeded him as Commander-in-Chief, he obtained Joffre's agreement to shift the British effort northwards into Flanders when the Somme objectives had been reached. Falkenhayn's unexpected offensive at Verdun, which made the battle on the Somme primarily a British battle and extended its duration almost until the end of 1916, postponed the Flanders plan. In the autumn of 1916, the Germans resumed their submarine offensive which soon turned into a life or death struggle. On 20 November 1916, the War Committee of the British War Cabinet examined the problem. Next day, Mr Asquith, then Prime Minister, drafted a note to the CIGS as a guide to the views of the War Committee for the benefit of Robertson, Haig and the First Sea Lord, Sir John Jellicoe, who were to discuss the matter on 23 November. The note included this instruction:

> There is no operation of war to which the War Committee would attach greater importance than the successful occupation, or at least the deprivation to the enemy of Ostend, and especially Zeebrugge. I desire, therefore, that the General Staff and the Higher Command in France, in consultation with the Admiralty as necessary, shall give the matter their closest attention . . .[6]

It was this statement that led to Haig's second arrangement with Joffre for a British offensive in Flanders after a proposed renewal of the Somme offensive in the early spring of 1917.

In January 1917, Haig renegotiated the arrangement with Joffre's successor, Nivelle, when preparations began for the spring offensive of 1917. Nivelle planned a major French break-through in Champagne supported by a powerful preliminary attack by the British at Arras. When that had been carried out, the British, as before, would side-step to the north to the Ypres sector. Haig wrangled with Nivelle over the arrangements. He cannily resisted a demand that he should take over part of the French front to allow Nivelle to form a general reserve, since he felt that it would be difficult to persuade the French to re-occupy it in time for the Flanders offensive, when the British in their turn would require to form a reserve. He was overborne by Lloyd George's partisan support of Nivelle. A related question which exercised Haig's staff was whether Nivelle would break off his battle when it became obvious that it had failed in its purpose, a break through. They envisaged a slogging match developing which would absorb British reserves intended for Flanders as well as the remaining campaigning weather. Haig was not prepared to harass Nivelle on this question provided that the battle in Champagne began early enough for his Flanders venture to be completed before the autumn rains. His staff warned that more time was required for the army to recover from the Somme, and for the ground at Arras to dry for the use of tanks, and it recommended a later start than Haig desired. Without saying so outright, the thrust of their argument was that unless Nivelle broke through the German defences quickly, there would not be time for an operation in Flanders that year. Haig ignored them, choosing to accept half a loaf from Nivelle rather than resort to unreliable support from his own politicians.

Meanwhile, on the German side, Hindenburg and Ludendorff (his chief of staff and the real commander), who had replaced Falkenhayn in August 1916, decided to revert to a defensive strategy in the West. They improved the German defensive system (as explained in Chapter 2) and shortened the line to create the necessary reserves by withdrawing from the arc to the chord of the line between Arras and Craonne – the Siegfried or Hindenburg Line – laying waste the ground relinquished. Nivelle attacked without the close reconnaissance and detailed preparations necessary to break into so strong a position. The French divisions, already worn out and dispirited by being rotated through the furnace of Verdun, suffered heavy casualties, and refused to fight any more or even be sent into the line. That, for the moment, ought to have removed a great break-through offensive in Flanders from the realm of practical possibilities.

Indeed, the Allies were now in a situation in which a false move might lose the war. Not one, but two of the armies of the Entente were incapable of undertaking offensive action, or even in a condition to meet one with any hope of success. It was not until October that the Bolsheviks seized power in Russia and March, 1918, that the Treaty of Brest Litovsk was signed and hostilities between Russia and Germany ceased, but from March 1917 onwards war-weariness and the infection of revolutionary ideas paralysed the Tsarist Army. It was only a matter of time before the Germans would be able to transfer the bulk of their forces from the Eastern to the Western Front as Rawlinson feared. This was the situation when Lloyd George visited GHQ on 6 May to ask Haig what he could do to help the French. Haig had already ordered General Plumer, commanding the Second Army in the Ypres salient, to be ready to launch what was to be known as the Battle of

Messines from late April onwards, either as a separate operation if Nivelle failed, or as part of the general Flanders offensive if he succeeded. The aim was to secure the tactically important 'Messines ridge' on the southern, or right face of the Ypres salient and included exploding nineteen huge mines under the German positions. When Haig suggested messiness as a suitable first step Lloyd George was delighted, and turning on his famous but deceptive charm was cordiality itself not omitting to congratulate the Army on its success at Arras. It seemed to Haig, whose experience so far of Lloyd George's methods inspired only dislike and distrust, that the Prime Minister had had a change of heart and, now agreed that the BEF had come of age and was the Entente's best and, at that moment, only military asset. After the war, seeking to detach himself from any part in the ruinous Passchendaele affair, Lloyd George averred in his *War Memoirs* that he had been kept in the dark about the full extent of the collapse of the French Army, and that although GHQ had received a communication from the French a few days after the Paris conference, giving the full details, they were not passed on to the War Cabinet. He argued that he would never have allowed Haig to fight the campaign had he known that the French could not provide their quota of limited, diversionary attacks. (A consistent theme of Lloyd George in his *War Memoirs* is that the CIGS and the Chief of Naval Staff habitually concealed the essential facts from the War Cabinet and the War Council for their own ends.) Exactly what the French revealed at the Paris Council about the state of the French Army is not known, but no doubt Pétain himself made it clear to Lloyd George that the French Army was incapable of any major offensive action, even if he did not provide him with the statistical details of what was fast deteriorating into a full scale mutiny. Lloyd George was, after all, a highly intelligent man with a politician's sensitivity to atmosphere and the nuances of a dialogue: he was sitting at a table with two Frenchmen who faced disaster, and it is impossible that he left the conference unaware of how dangerous the situation had become.[7] Haig used this lacuna to argue, also after the fact, that the precarious state of the French Army compelled him to continue Passchendaele into the autumn. In fact the French Army had by then recovered and needed no such assistance.

Haig's amiable meeting with Lloyd George at GHQ on 6 May was the point at which things went wrong for him. He tended, when discussing a course of action on which his mind was already made up, either to resent criticism or to assume that when the critic was tactful enough to cloak his misgivings in partial agreement or approval qualified with guarded reservations, he was in fact expressing his total endorsement of Haig's plans. That is evident from time to time in Haig's diary. It is possible that the

'Welsh Wizard', whose charm was notoriously deceptive, misled Haig into the belief that he would agree to turn Messines into the preliminary stage of Haig's cherished strategic offensive in Flanders, as had been Haig's intention before the mutinies. It is more likely that Haig had calculated that success at Messines would persuade the War Committee to allow him to continue, whether or not Lloyd George agreed. In the light of his action on the next day, 7 May, that must be the conclusion.

When Lloyd George left for London, Haig held an Army Commander's conference at which he announced not only that Messines would start on 7 June under Plumer, but that the rest of the Flanders operation would follow several weeks later after Hubert Gough, commander of the Fifth Army, had completed his plans for reorganisation and his army had transferred from the Arras front. It may be pointed out that although Lloyd George had not agreed to this sequel, it was essential to move Gough's army from Picardy to Flanders so that it would be ready if the War Cabinet authorised the offensive that Haig desired. However, only limited attacks, like Messines had been agreed at Paris and a strategic operation such as would have required Gough's Fifth Army, had been rejected. Haig, it is safe to assume, hoped that the U-Boat crisis, a national matter not discussed at the Paris conference, whose solution was crucial to the safe transport of the American Expeditionary Force to Europe, would incline the War Policy Committee to allow Gough's Fifth Army to be employed if that would help. The shipping losses were daunting: 875,000 tons of shipping had been lost in April 1917 alone, and a projection showed that if the haemorrhage continued unabated, the losses could not be borne beyond November. Naval opinion was that if the Belgian based U-Boats and surface raiding craft could be eliminated, the resources of the Dover Patrol could be redeployed for the anti-submarine campaign on the North Sea and Atlantic routes.[8]

It so happened that long before Haig, Rawlinson, Plumer and Gough together with their distinguished chiefs of staff and Haig's own Director of Operations, John Davidson, began to wrestle with the operational and tactical problems of the Third Battle of Ypres, Davidson's predecessor, one of the best military minds in the British Army, had been working on the tactics appropriate to war on the Western Front in general and in the Ypres salient in particular. Brigadier-General Frederick Maurice, who became the Director of Military Operations in the War Office when Haig replaced Sir John French, was both a scholar and an experienced soldier. Maurice's appreciations for Sir John French were always, as such papers should be, elegant, logical and dispassionate. In writing them he resisted pressure to serve up opinions which chimed with those of his commander-in-chief.

Maurice first considered the essential characteristics of the Western Front and the apparent inability of either side to stage a decisive break-through. As he repeated in *British Strategy,* he concluded that imperative as the interaction of modern fire-power and tactics were the primary cause of the stalemate was the high ratio of troops available to space.[9] The defender was able to feed strong reinforcements into the battle faster than the attacker could bring up his artillery and fresh units to exploit the initial break-in. He therefore concluded that a break-through at one point in the front would not be successful unless the enemy had been weakened by a protracted battle of attrition elsewhere; in Maurice's term, a *bataille d' usure.* A break-through had to have a strategic objective, even if its location might be tactically unfavourable. Between a break-through battle and a *usure* there was a profound difference. The former predicated a continuous advance whose momentum was not allowed to slacken until open ground suitable for a manoeuvre battle had been reached. (And also, a break-in on a front wide enough to ensure that the forward move of the artillery and fresh units to be used for exploitation were uninterrupted by enemy fire over the flanks, and deep enough to deny the enemy observed fire over the ground gained.) A *usure,* Maurice argued, had to take the form of a succession of carefully staged attacks, each objective being chosen as ground vital to the defence to entice the defender to counter-attack; so reversing the advantages of attack and defence. Artillery observation had to be excellent and road and rail communications sufficient to maintain a prodigious supply of ammunition for bombardments from which the defender suffered disproportionately, particularly as he was driven back into less well-prepared positions. The attacking divisions had to be reinforced, re-supplied and trained, and brought to the front more quickly, by a comfortable margin, than the enemy's. Unfortunately, the prolonged bombardment, then deemed necessary, created an obstacle to forward movement, while the defenders withdrew on to roads and field railways in working order. As it took the Germans three weeks to bring drafts of men from Germany, incorporate them into an exhausted division, train the division and get it back into the line, battles had to be fought at least every ten days or the Germans could withstand *usure* almost indefinitely.

It is repulsive to students of warfare that the object of the *usures* of the First World War was simply to gain an advantageous balance of casualties inflicted, rather than to capture ground, points of strategic significance or a favourable position for manoeuvre. In fact, as is often the case in warfare, practice seldom followed theory, however persuasively or rigorously

101

argued. 'Pure' *usure*, such as the notable attack by the Canadians on Hill 70 in August 1917, was rarely attempted. Even the German high command at Verdun, where a *usure* was deliberately conceived with the object of bleeding the French army to death, strove for a break-through at the same time. Moreover, technology and tactics were not static on the Western Front but evolving. By the end of 1917, as already explained (in Chapter 3), new artillery techniques, new infantry tactics, and the combination of tanks, artillery and air power at Riga and Cambrai were shown to be a way out of the deadlock by other means than pure attrition.[10] In 1915, Maurice concluded that the French would have to play the leading role in *usures*, probably until the late summer of 1917 when the British would have acquired the resources to maintain them. In the meanwhile, mere diversionary attacks, such as Loos in the autumn of 1915, were wasteful, ineffective and irrelevant, an unfortunate consequence of the BEF's subordinate role in offensives planned to suit French strategy.

When Maurice turned his mind to the Ypres salient in the light of this general theory he found that it offered no tactical advantage to compensate for the disadvantage of attacking out of a salient. He conceded that Ostend, Zeebrugge, Bruges, Ghent and a front line ending on the Dutch border constituted together an attractive strategic goal, and one that was attainable if an offensive in Flanders coincided with a major French offensive elsewhere that forced the German High Command to thin out their garrisons in the north to increase their reserves in the central sector. Otherwise he concluded, the tactical objections to an offensive in the north were overwhelming. First, the start-line for an attack in the Ypres salient was overlooked throughout its length from the east. Second, if the attack succeeded in reaching the Dutch frontier, the new front would require more divisions to hold it than the existing direct line from the Ypres salient to the coast. (An important consideration, except in the unlikely event that the German High Command decided on a general withdrawal.) It would loop eastward and northeast to the Dutch border, forming an appendix served by only two single-track railways from Dunkirk-Furnes-Lichtenfelde and Hazebrouck-Ypres-Roulers, while the Germans would have behind them six double-track railways connected to the main German system through the Antwerp-Brussels-Charleroi network. The Belgians, whose existing front was protected by inundations along the Yser, would find it impossible to advance across them against German opposition. They could play no part in the offensive, therefore, and in the new line on the Dutch border would be deprived of the protection from inundations that they had enjoyed in the old.[11]

After Maurice left for the War Office, his staff at GHQ continued to write studies of positional warfare through 1916 and the first half of 1917. In 1917, they pointed out, regretfully, that the BEF had never fought a battle designed specifically as a *usure*, though two of its major operations had inadvertently become battles of attrition and, moreover, in sectors unsuitable for the purpose. (Loos and the Somme.) At the Somme, Haig had intended a strategic break-through battle, while the commander of the Fourth Army who was to plan and carry it out, General Rawlinson, a far better tactician than Haig, appreciated that the methods of a *usure* were more likely to succeed; the clash of opinion was to be carried forward to the following year, when Rawlinson shared responsibility for the initial planning of the Flanders offensive with Plumer. The Battle of Arras, in which three British armies were engaged had, on the insistence of General Nivelle, been limited to a purely diversionary operation, the break-through role being reserved for the French. General Allenby, commanding the British Third Army, a cavalryman who was ill-suited by temperament to what he felt to be the shackles of trench warfare and was known at this time as 'The Bull', had to be restrained by GHQ from attempting a break-through at the outset, using the new artillery methods with tanks. In fairness to Allenby, it must be said that when moved to command in the Middle East, where he had substantial cavalry forces under command and ample room for manoeuvre, he would prove to be a master of mobile warfare – but the Western Front was not his scene.

Maurice's final verdict was that the Ypres sector of Northern Flanders was unsuitable for either type of offensive. Next he considered the operational utility of the Salient itself. A shallow curve in the line, not a deep indentation, it contained an historic city of only symbolic value, but one whose surrender might damage Belgian morale. The sensible course, favoured by Maurice, the staff at GHQ and Plumer's staff, was to shorten the line by straightening it out, placing the city in the front line. The alternative, to establish a viable defence in depth by driving the enemy from the system of low but commanding ridges south of the city and extending north east into the German position, ending at the significant village of Passchendaele, would be a difficult operation with no commensurate reward.

Here arose a nice point concerning the first principle of war, one all too often overlooked in the convoluted process of obtaining agreement on strategy in a coalition, and between the services, the various commanders-in-chief and their governments. Military pedants insist that the first step in making a plan is to define the aim, in the singular. To have two aims is likely to lead to dissipation of effort: four invites first confusion and then disaster.

1 The secret aim of Haig was to win a great victory with the BEF alone, untrammelled by French desires or objections.

2 Haig's overt, or manifest aim complying with the wish of both governments, was to distract German attention from the French sector of the Western Front.

3 He also proposed an operation calculated to assist the Royal Navy in the submarine war.

4 There was also the insistent but unformulated aim of strengthening the British grip on an area regarded by the French and the Germans as vital, which guarded the BEF's supply lines from the Channel ports and had been the immediate cause of Britain's entry into the war.

It will be seen that none of the first three necessarily predicated an offensive out of the Salient: *aims* and *benefits* were being confused.

CHAPTER 7

PASSCHENDAELE II

Haig initiated his Flanders offensive on 5 March 1916, by giving Rawlinson, who was about to take command of Fourth Army, and Plumer, who was commanding Second Army in the Salient, the task of fighting the battle together after the conclusion of the Somme. The operation was to have two phases . In the first, the high ground upon which the Germans stood was to be taken, Rawlinson's Fourth Army making 'the main attack' north-eastward with his right moving through Frezenburg–St Julien–Langemarck–Passchendaele while his left pivoted on the Houthoulst Forest. Plumer's Second Army, after taking the Messines Ridge, was to 'endeavour to advance its left north-east along the ridge running roughly from Wytschaete to Broodseinde'. In the second phase, Rawlinson would break out towards the coast from the line Passchendaele–Staden. Although it was a two-army attack, Plumer had only his left engaged after his centre had taken the Messines Ridge and his right moved up the Lys valley. Plumer, though, who had to take the higher ground and act as a shield for Rawlinson, had the more difficult task, despite GHQ naming Rawlinson's 'the main attack'. The inter-army boundary, which was a problem in subsequent plans, was the Ypres–Roulers railway. (See Sketch 1). That was Plan One.[1]

In December 1916, in response to the agreement between Joffre and Haig for 1917, Davidson issued Plan Two for Ypres. This brought in Gough's Fifth Army to replace the Fourth Army which remained on the Somme to take over part of the French line. Fifth Army was to take the Messines Ridge and then advance with its left on the Ypres–Comines Canal

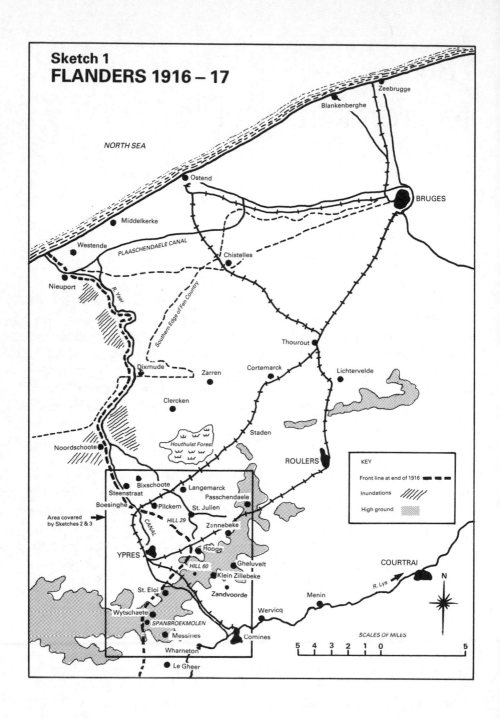

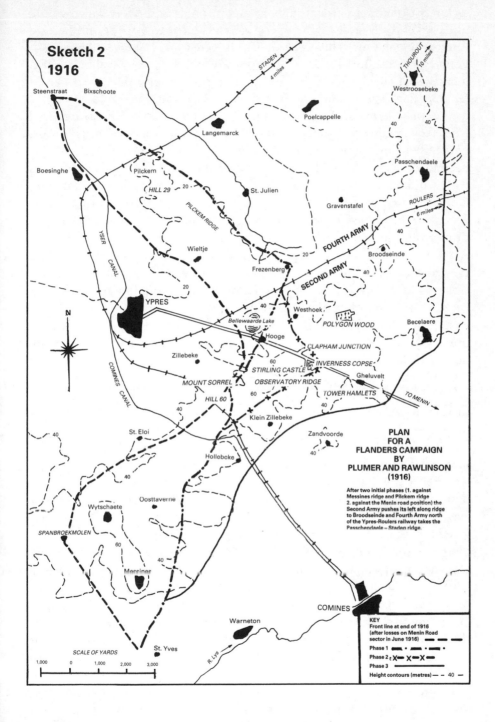

Sketch 2 1916

Steenstraat · Bixschoote

STADEN
4 miles

THOUROUT
10 miles

Westroosebeke

Poelcappelle

Boesinghe · Pilckem

Langemarck

Passchendaele

HILL 29 — 20

St. Julien

PILCKEM RIDGE

ROULERS
6 miles

Gravenstafel

FOURTH ARMY

Wieltje

Broodseinde

YSER CANAL

20

Frezenberg

SECOND ARMY

YPRES

Bellewaarde Lake

Westhoek

POLYGON WOOD

Becelaere

N

Hooge

CLAPHAM JUNCTION

Zillebeke

INVERNESS COPSE

COMINES CANAL

STIRLING CASTLE

MOUNT SORREL

OBSERVATORY RIGE

Gheluvelt

HILL 60

TOWER HAMLETS

TO MENIN

Klein Zillebeke

St. Eloi

Zandvoorde

Hollebeke

PLAN FOR A FLANDERS CAMPAIGN BY PLUMER AND RAWLINSON (1916)

Wytschaete

Oosttaverne

SPANBROEKMOLEN

Messines

After two initial phases (1. against Messines ridge and Pilckem ridge 2. against the Menin road position) the Second Army pushes its left along ridge to Broodseinde and Fourth Army north of the Ypres-Roulers railway takes the Passchendaele – Staden ridge.

COMINES

Warneton

St. Yves

R. Lys

KEY
Front line at end of 1916 (after losses on Menin Road sector in June 1916)
Phase 1
Phase 2
Phase 3
Height contours (metres) — 40 —

SCALE OF YARDS
1,000   0   1,000   2,000   3,000

as far as Comines to provide a flank guard for Second Army which would undertake all the rest of the operations assigned to Fourth and Second Armies in Plan One. Thirty-five divisions were to be employed (Sketch 2).[2] Plan Two was short-lived, being replaced by the Haig–Nivelle arrangement which envisaged a rapid advance at Ypres after a break-through in Champagne. The assumption that the advance would be rapid, in consequence of a German defeat in Champagne, had not been explicitly removed from the planning criteria when Gough took over in May 1917 after Nivelle had failed,[3] although neither Plumer nor Rawlinson had accepted it. Second Army's role in Plan Three was reduced to taking the Messines Ridge and advancing its left south of the Menin road to Zandvoorde and Gheluvelt to provide a flank guard for Fourth Army. Second Army's right was contracted, there being no advance towards Comines and, after objections from Plumer, even Zandvoorde ceased to be an objective. Fourth Army's role was to take the rest of the high ground. Attacking from the line Hooge–Steenstraat, its right was directed on Broodseinde, the centre on Gravenstafel Ridge and St Julien and the left on Langemarck and Bixschoote. The objective named by GHQ in the first phase was 'the Passchendaele-Staden ridge'. The second phase of the operation was the break-out to the coast as in Plan One. The Menin road was the army boundary given by GHQ. In forwarding his outline for the execution of Plan Three, Plumer observed that 'the centre of gravity of prospective operations' had, 'in accordance with the C-in-C's instructions been transferred further north' requiring him to shorten his right flank and relinquish the main advance to the northern army.[4]

Plumer and his chief of staff, Major-General Charles Harington, the men on the spot, coordinated Plan Three until the other army commander, whether it was Rawlinson or Gough, arrived from the south. Rawlinson had previously commanded a division and a corps at Ypres and he had seen eye to eye with Plumer over how to carry out their task since it had been given them in 1916. Both men immediately perceived the inherent contradiction in their strategic mission. Its axis of advance was *north-east*, but the topography of the Ypres Salient dictated that the natural line of exit was *south-east*. In the First and Second Battles of Ypres, the Germans, conversely, had perforce to attack *north-west*, their lines of communication extending back to Comines, Menin and Courtrai on the River Lys. After the Second Battle, they had organised a deep belt of defences on the arc of high ground commanding the city on the south, east, north-east and north. The base-line of Haig's proposed offensive had to be approximately the line Ypres–Steenstraat, which meant that the right flank of the designated army (Rawlinson's Fourth) would skirt the line of the railway from Ypres to Roulers, exposing it to counter-attack and artillery fire from the numerous enemy batteries defiladed behind (south-east of) the high ground.

In greater detail, (see sketches 1 and 2), the enemy defences ran from the Wytschaete–Messines Ridge (in the event, the objective of the battle by Plumer's Second Army) thence to Mount Sorel and what was known as the 'Observatory Ridge', to Hooge on the Messines road, north-west along the Pilckem ridge to the Ypres Canal. The Menin road, lying across this defensive arc like an arrow on a bow, marked the natural 'centre' line of operations designed to clear the heights, and also a convenient inter-army boundary. (This may seem pedantic to the general reader, but axes of advance and boundaries are an essential part of command and control.) If there had to be *two* operations, a main advance on the left and a local, limited offensive to clear the German defences on the right, it inevitably meant that the deeper the Fourth Army pressed into the enemy positions on the left the further the alignment of the inner flanks of the Second and Fourth Armies would diverge, leaving a gap held by the unsubdued and aggressive defenders. The outline plan put forward by GHQ suggested that the Second Army's attack should curl round, following the stave of the 'bow'. 'Rolling up the enemy's flank' in a manner reminiscent of Frederick the Great's 'oblique order' was a pretty notion, but it required an opponent more passive than the German Army. It raised obvious tactical difficulties, such as the choice of successive start-lines at ever varying angles, the movement of the supporting artillery and, of course, the capture of the high ground on the Menin Road. Herein lay the core of a long dispute over tactics between GHQ and the responsible army commanders that continued throughout the planning of the Third Battle Ypres in 1916 and 1917.

Rawlinson and Plumer appreciated that three preliminary operations before the main advance were essential. Plumer had to clear the Messines–Wytschaete ridge and Observatory Ridge. As Rawlinson needed a secure start-line and concealed gun positions for his main advance he decided that the long, low ridge extending across his front named after Pilckem, the village at its northern end, must be taken. Until these two preliminary operations had been completed the third, to take the key to the German position, the high ground from Observatory Ridge to Polygon Wood on either side of the Menin Road, could not begin. Both were essential to enable the necessary guns to be re-deployed against the Menin Road. With the Menin Road position in his hands Rawlinson could extend his grip on the high ground as far east as Becelaere and northwards to Broodseinde, while Plumer pressed down the Menin Road to Gheluvelt. Each would thus support the other. From the high ground astride the Menin Road and the spur protruding into the Lys valley east of the

Messines Ridge, the German positions facing Plumer's centre could be overlooked and outflanked. With Gheluvelt safely in Plumer's hands, Rawlinson could half turn his back, as it were, on the enemy to his south-east and begin his drive north-east towards the line Passchendaele–Staden, indicated by Haig as a phaseline (rather than an objective) on the way to the coast.

Plumer and Rawlinson never persuaded Haig to accept the necessity of these systematic preliminary operations. Obsessed by the idea of a rapid advance, Haig asserted that a series of initial operations would lose surprise and lead to a battle of attrition. He dismissed Plumer's argument that the attack on the Menin Road sector could not begin until the Messines Ridge, which overlooked it, had been taken and a few days allowed for regrouping the artillery. Nor would he accept that the preliminary capture of the Pilckem Ridge was essential to seize gun positions for the assault on the Menin Road, insisting that tanks could drive the enemy from that vital sector although the Tank Corps advised against it. He refused to budge in the months before Arras started only conceding that if Nivelle's offensive failed he would order a preliminary operation to clear the Messines Ridge.[5]

Rawlinson agreed to compromise by forgoing his preliminary Pilckem Ridge operation provided that Plumer took the Messines Ridge first and then joined him in a concerted attack on the Menin Road sector, and that no more than three or four days elapsed between Messines and the next phases of the operation. Otherwise Rawlinson foresaw himself in the uncomfortable situation of attacking the toughest part of the enemy position with his right while Second Army supported him with only a defensive flank instead of a vigorous attack towards Gheluvelt. He recorded in his diary that the trouble he had with the French XX Corps in the Maricourt salient, on the Somme in August 1916, was 'following him to Ypres.' (At Maricourt, the French attacked at right-angles to his own thrust in order to provide themselves with a defensive flank for their own crossing of the Somme and left Rawlinson's right flank exposed for most of August.)[6]

On 7 May, Haig announced at the Doullens army commander's conference that Gough was to command the main (left) attack at Ypres instead of Rawlinson. Gough had a reputation as a thruster and it was generally agreed that he was better suited to break-through operations. Rawlinson heard indirectly that he had been dropped in late April but Haig did not inform him directly, let alone explain the reason. Rawlinson recorded that it was because neither he nor Plumer believed a break-through to be possible, particularly after Nivelle's failure and the prospective interval of many weeks, during which the Germans would strengthen their positions and reinforce the Ypres front, before Gough could begin.

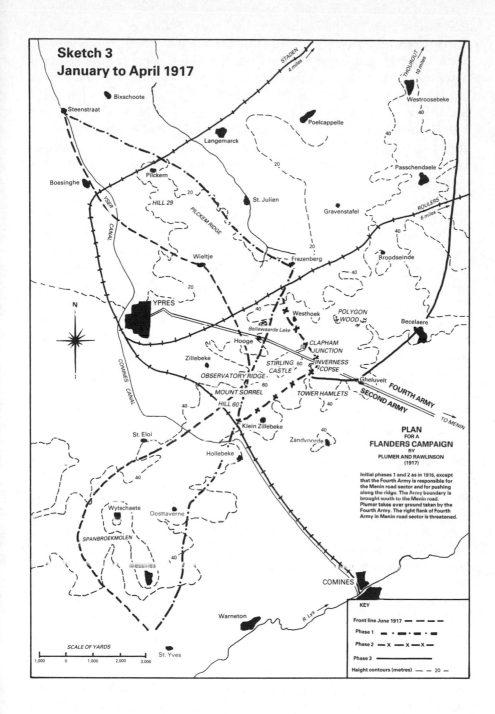

Sketch 3
January to April 1917

STADEN
4 miles

THOUROUT
10 miles

Bixschoote

Steenstraat

Westroosebeke
40

Poelcappelle

Langemarck

40

Passchendaele

Pilckem

HILL 29

St. Julien

Boesinghe

20

Gravenstafel

ROULERS
6 miles

YSER CANAL

PILCKEM RIDGE

40

Wieltje

Frezenberg

Broodseinde

20

40

YPRES

20

POLYGON WOOD

Westhoek

Becelaere

Bellewaarde Lake

40

Hooge

CLAPHAM JUNCTION

Zillebeke

STIRLING CASTLE 60

INVERNESS COPSE

COMINES CANAL

OBSERVATORY RIDGE

60

Gheluvelt

FOURTH ARMY

MOUNT SORREL

TOWER HAMLETS

SECOND ARMY

HILL 60

40

40

TO MENIN

St. Eloi

Klein Zillebeke

40

Zandvoorde

PLAN
FOR A
FLANDERS CAMPAIGN
BY
PLUMER AND RAWLINSON
(1917)

Hollebeke

40

Initial phases 1 and 2 as in 1916, except
that the Fourth Army is responsible for
the Menin road sector and for pushing
along the ridge. The Army boundary is
brought south to the Menin road.
Plumer takes over ground taken by the
Fourth Army. The right flank of Fourth
Army in Menin road sector is threatened.

Wytschaete

Oosttaverne

SPANBROEKMOLEN

40

Messines

COMINES

Warneton

R. Lys

KEY

Front line June 1917

Phase 1

Phase 2   X   X   X

Phase 3

Height contours (metres)   20

SCALE OF YARDS

1,000   0   1,000   2,000   3,000

St. Yves

N

111

Gough received a file of GHQ directives and previous plans on 14 May from one of Haig's staff. He began to plan the operation on the 23rd but no one briefed him about the details of the long-standing disagreements between GHQ on one side and Plumer and Rawlinson on the other. Plumer never advised Gough about the unsuitability of the central sector for tanks or the necessity to concentrate all his artillery against it. At Doullens, on 7 May, Haig commented that Plumer's occupation of the Messines ridge on 7 June would solve the problem of the Menin road and allow Gough to attack simultaneously across the front without first taking the Pilckem ridge or staging any other preliminary operation, as Rawlinson and Plumer recommended.

On the 13th May, Major-General Launcelot Kiggell, Haig's Chief of Staff, gave Gough Haig's directive to take 'the Passchendaele–Staden ridge' and Roulers as his first objectives. Gough was to push down the Menin road, still the army boundary, with his right to Gheluvelt, at the same time pushing north-eastward to Becelaere and Broodseinde and Moorslede; his centre was to move by St Julien and Langemarck to Passchendaele. Plumer's role had been reduced to taking over the high ground captured by Gough. A glance at the map will indicate it was not an operation of war. Gough had to seize the firm base, formerly Plumer's task, *and* advance north-eastward *away* from it; to advance south-eastward and north-eastward at the same time out of a small bridgehead. Further, whereas Rawlinson and Plumer had stipulated an interval of only a few days between their phases, so as to keep the Germans off-balance, Kiggell gave Gough to understand that the lapse of six weeks between the Messines ridge operation on 7 June and Gough's battle on about 25 July (which in the event allowed the Germans to recover and changed the conception of the battle entirely) had not altered Haig's intention of a rapid break-through to Staden, Passchendaele and Roulers, as in January, when Plan Three was inaugurated. He left Gough to discover that although the inter-army boundary ran at almost right-angles to his north-easterly thrust, Second Army had not been directed by GHQ to participate in the drive to Gheluvelt. In consequence, the Germans could enfilade his units from commanding ground on the right (south) of the Menin road, for which neither army was responsible.

The matter of his flank consumed Gough throughout June until it led him to quarrel with Plumer. That would not have happened had Kiggell managed their relationship more adroitly and had he clarified Haig's directive in the light of the problems already raised by Plumer and Rawlinson, but ignored by GHQ, which were bound to arise again with Gough. The root of this dispute was that GHQ had allowed an operation once seen as a two-army attack to become a one-army attack with minor support from another; Plumer having virtually opted out, and the reinforcing divisions originally earmarked having been used up at Arras. Kiggell simply lacked the guts to confront his master on such great issues as a Chief of Staff should. Gough lacked neither courage nor the intelligence to see that the current arrangements were impractical, but he was not prepared to outface Haig either. In any case, unlike Rawlinson and Plumer, he believed that a break-through, as opposed to a *usure,* was feasible. Fresh from his limited success at Arras, Gough believed that there was an opportunity to break through in the first forty-eight hours. Accordingly, in his outline plan, presented at a conference attended by Haig and both army commanders on 14th June, he disclosed his intention to advance on a broad front as far as Broodseinde on the first day.[7] Haig naturally accepted it.

When Gough presented his outline plan the success at Messines was fresh in everyone's minds. Haig felt strongly that Plumer had lost an opportunity to exploit it, although the plan had not envisaged a deeper advance and exploitation was only mentioned by Haig as a possibility late in May. During the conference on the 14th Gough spoke of his concern about the security of his right flank as it advanced towards Gheluvelt in the Menin road sector. Haig considered that problem solved. Messines was secure, and he had transferred the IInd corps on Plumer's left to Gough's command on the 8th; moving the Second Army boundary southwards to Observatory Ridge to give all the Menin road sector to the Fifth Army. (Except in Sketch 16 the Official History (OH) does not mark army boundaries in its sketches, an omission that helps to conceal the eccentricity of Haig's setting of the battle and the problems that it caused the army commanders. Sketch 14 (OH) indicates that the boundary of Fifth Army's IInd Corps and Second Army's Xth Corps passes through Klein Zillebeke and Zandvoorde so that all the 'Gheluvelt plateau' is in Fifth Army's zone.) Haig had earlier told Plumer to use the IInd Corps to jump the Germans holding the Menin road sector, but Plumer had refused, arguing, as he had when Haig rejected the Rawlinson-Plumer plan for a preliminary operation between Bellewarde and Observatory Ridge, that it was necessary to redeploy the artillery and mount a carefully prepared attack. He had tried to convince Haig for over a year that that was essential and was not to be stampeded into action. Given instructions to use the IInd Corps himself, Gough tested the front but decided not to risk wasting it, since it was assigned the most difficult task in his future operation in July. By the 14th, Gough knew that simply shifting the IInd Corps to his command could not help him unless Plumer attacked vigorously on the general line Klein Zillebeke–Gheluvelt and the army boundary were re-orientated to run north-eastward; otherwise his right flank was merely exposed further south. He asked for this, but Haig only told Plumer to 'act offensively', not to intervene directly.[8]

There was a clash of personalities between Gough and Plumer at the conference. Plumer was older than Haig and had been an instructor at the Staff College when Haig was a student. To some degree he still retained the upper hand. After he had failed to persuade Haig of the hard facts of the topography by patient explanation, he determined to save his troops from the consequences of Haig's obduracy by doing as little as possible for Gough. Gough was inclined to overlook difficulties but once he had found how they could be overcome, he was headstrong and impatient with those who obstructed him. Nevertheless, although he needed Plumer to attack alongside him, he was not prepared to insist that Haig should force him to do so. Thus, unless Haig helped Gough, the scene was set for a serious row between a frustrated Gough and an obdurate Plumer. Haig should undoubtedly have held a frank round table discussion with the two Army Commanders, but that was not at all his style. Lofty and remote, he made it appear that Gough was making a fuss about nothing.

In such circumstances it is the duty of a General Staff to work behind the scenes to reconcile differences of opinion between the various Commanders it serves, but the idea of a *Generalstabdienstweg* had never really caught on in the British Army, clashing as it did with a deeply engrained tradition of personal loyalty. Kiggell lacked both the necessary authority and the respect of strong-minded men like Harington, Chief of Staff of the Second Army, and Malcolm of the Fifth, and was too timid to put the dissenting views of their respective commanders squarely before the Commander-in-Chief. Kiggell's door was not, as it should have been, always open to the Chiefs of Staff of the Armies for informal, unscheduled discussion, as a result GHQ was cut off from external advice and opinion. Davidson, Haig's chief of operations, chatted regularly with Harington, with Rawlinson and Montgomery, his Chief of Staff, but Davidson was also in awe of Haig and could not persuade Kiggell to act where he himself feared to tread. The deadlock was complete because Haig was a formidable man, feared by everyone except Plumer, who had his measure, but even he had no intention of taking the ultimate step of defying him openly. In short, once his mind was made up, Haig was impervious to reasoned argument.

Such was the state of affairs at Ypres when Haig left for London to appear before the new War Policy Committee, only formed on 9 June. When Haig attended on the 19th, 21st and 22nd June, the agenda included the U-Boat crisis and a discussion to consider whether an offensive at Ypres should be part of the solution. Haig knew perfectly well that to obtain permission to launch it he had to convince the Committee that he planned to carry out only the limited attacks that had been agreed at the Paris conference, which could be broken off at any time. He did that and, to improve his case, conveyed the impression that limited attacks could lead to ousting the Germans from the coastal ports, if that were part of the desired solution to the U-Boat crisis. He also suggested that if the German railways to the coast were cut, this would force a major retirement from Belgium and a consequent withdrawal opposite the French. He asserted that the enemy had been markedly weakened in the previous year and would not be able to withstand his continual systematic attacks. He argued that although the French were weak and required him to relieve the pressure on them by attacking at Ypres, yet they would be capable of helping him by short, sharp attacks of their own, as they had agreed in Paris.[9] This ability to prevaricate came naturally to Haig, who could keep mutually exclusive ideas in his head at the same time disregarding their logical incompatibility if it did not suit him. A gift was dropped into his lap by the sudden and unexpected intervention of the First Sea Lord, Admiral Sir John Jellicoe, who declared that the whole anti-submarine campaign would be jeopardised if the U-boat havens at Ostend and Zeebrugge were not eliminated. Even so, Haig's eloquent exposition of his plan did not win outright permission, only to continue the preparations. The offensive's planned opening date was 25 July, and the three week long counter-battery battle which was to precede the final bombardment and infantry advance was due to begin shortly. It can be imagined, therefore, that Haig was much on edge when he returned to France. The WPC only gave its agreement to him a month later, when the gigantic logistic preparations for the battle were virtually complete and events, as so often occur in war, had generated their own momentum.

While Haig was in London, Gough was trying to persuade Plumer to help him in the operations on the Menin road sector by attacking vigorously towards Gheluvelt and Zandvoorde on his flank. Plumer, already as close to being mutinous over GHQ's directions for the battle as that shrewd old soldier was likely to be, had no intention of playing that game. After the meeting on the 14th, Plumer had been told 'to secure the right flank of Fifth Army against attacks from the southeast from the outset and during the advance'. This woolly directive had no effect, so Davidson went to Harington to try to make him persuade his master to consider taking Zandvoorde, or at least Klein Zillebeke and the Hollebeke spur. On the 18th Plumer declined to take Zandvoorde and agreed to take the other places only when Fifth Army had taken Inverness Copse, on the Menin road, and handed over guns and gun areas. On the 25th, Gough demanded a conference with Plumer which Kiggell chaired. In February 1944, Gough recalled for Edmonds what occurred:[10]

> I asked that the Second Army should actively protect my right and broaden the front of attack to take in the whole of the Gheluvelt plateau. Haig, who was to have been there had been called to London so he was represented by Kiggell. I pressed my point rather hard and Plumer did not like it and finally lost his temper and said: 'If you are going to ask me to take my part in attacking, I shall make such demands for artillery support that I know you cannot meet' he added: 'I have been in the Salient for two years and I am not going to get into another one.' I did not think this was the right tone in which to discuss such a problem but Kiggell was not a strong enough character to dominate the conference. Nothing was settled at it, and Haig must have agreed with me for within a week or two orders were issued to bring my suggested plan into force.

Gough's memory of so dramatic a meeting was probably accurate but in 1945 he accepted the official account of the sequel in recording that, on his return from London, Haig sorted out the dispute. On that point the historians accepted the version of events in Haig's diary. It is wrong.[11] Gough's decision to seek a meeting with Plumer and Kiggell was sparked by the appeal to him of Lieutenant-General Sir Claud Jacob, whose IInd Corps advance was going to be enfiladed by the enemy from Tower Hamlets in Second Army's sector. Haig records that he was told about the problem by Jacob himself on the 27th and, at a meeting called for the 28th to hear Gough's final plan, he reported the matter to Gough and told him that he had transferred two more divisions to him from Plumer to cover the flank. His version of the meeting on the 28th was:

> I urged the importance of the right flank. It is, in my opinion vitally important to occupy and hold the ridge west of Gheluvelt in order to cover our right flank and push along it to Broodseinde. The main battle will be fought on and for this ridge, so we must make our plans accordingly. The main difficulty seems to be at the beginning of the attack, in advancing from a comparatively small salient to the attack of a wider area. I impressed on Gough the vital importance of the ridge in question and that the advance North should be limited until our right flank has really been secured on the ridge.

This entry exemplifies Haig's habit of self-deception, to the point of claiming other people's ideas as his own. In this case, inspired by hindsight, he made *post facto* entries in his diary which made it difficult for official historians to discover the truth. For reasons that will be apparent shortly, Davidson supported Haig's account. In fact, Haig only returned from London on the 27th, spoke to Jacob on the 29th after the meeting and gave the order for the transfer of one division, the 24th, on the 30th June. On that day he ordered Plumer to 'act offensively' in response to Gough's appeal at the meeting on the 28th. The evidence that it was Rawlinson, Plumer and then Gough who were concerned about the 'Gheluvelt Plateau' and that it was Haig who had consistently refused to treat it as a special problem, is quite clear from the plans submitted by Rawlinson and Plumer and Gough's concern expressed at the meeting on the 14th.[12]

Haig gave Plumer no specific orders on the 28th that would make the battle a two-army attack. He simply transferred the Second Army division responsible for Tower Hamlets from Plumer to Gough. He accepted Gough's plan to attack simultaneously from Observatory Ridge on the right to Steenstraat behind the Pilckem ridge on the left, and to attempt to penetrate up to two miles. The first objective, the 'Passchendaele–Staden ridge' and the final one, 'the coast', remained. Gough's intention was to take the objectives quickly not, as Haig told the War Policy Committee, by careful stages. In the Official History Edmonds thought it necessary to explain away Haig's acceptance of Gough's plan although Haig had already accepted its outline on the 14th. Plumer, he argued, spoke in favour of it and Haig was in the habit of allowing his army commanders to carry out his plan in their own way.[13] Edmonds argued that when so careful a commander as Plumer favoured a plan, Haig would naturally have agreed to it. Gough, on being offered this explanation, told Edmonds that he would not recognise the Haig he knew in this version. They were all scared of him and did what they were told. He regretted that he had not insisted on more open discussion. Haig got the plan that he wanted: it did not need Plumer to speak for it. On reflection, Gough commented:

Plumer was a wily old fox and would quite likely have urged such a course knowing that he would in no way be responsible for the job.

[Wynne omitted Plumer's intervention from his draft. Edmonds inserted it but omitted Gough's comment. The report of Plumer's intervention was Davidson's; Gough did not recall it.]

Objection to Gough's plan was widespread, nevertheless. On the 26th, Davidson had written a theoretical counter-plan to that of Haig and

Gough which was on Haig's desk when he returned on the 27th. It was developed from his memorandum of 13th June and was written to supplement Haig's introductory statement before Gough presented his outline next day.

In it Davidson envisaged that the operation might relapse into a *usure* and suggested that closer objectives should be chosen for their defensibility against counter-attack.[14] Haig paid no heed to it: he wanted to have his cake and eat it. His own remarks included this explanation of his intentions:

> Underlying the general intention of wearing out the enemy is the strategical objective of securing the Belgian coast and connecting with the Dutch frontier. The nature and size of the several steps which will be required before that objective is reached must depend on our *effectives* and number of guns available ... the next step will be a battle to secure the Passchendaele–Staden–Clercken ridge as a basis for a further advance into Belgium. We hope to launch the first part of this second battle stage on July 25th.

Haig's oracular statement meant that Messines, the first step, had been completed and Passchendaele–Staden was the second. His 'further steps' referred to the operation after the Passchendaele ridge had been taken, not to Gough's immediate battle. On the 14th and later, Davidson doubted whether Passchendaele could be reached in one step. Later he convinced the historians that Haig held the same opinion.

That Haig and Davidson were not in accord is evident from an incident on the 30th, when Malcolm issued a Fifth Army memorandum along Davidson lines which Haig criticised savagely. Malcolm was explaining Gough's flexible, phased advance in which Fifth Army would go as far as possible on the first day and then fight as the ground demanded to inflict the maximum casualties on the enemy, rather than choose objectives on a map which corresponded to enemy defence lines or Haig's strategic objective:

> 'The fundamental idea which will underline all our actions is that our one object is the defeat of the German army. That is the task that has been set us and, by comparison, the capture of this or that piece of ground or even so many guns is a matter of minor importance.' There would have to be a series of battles on a grand scale, on broad frontages and at short intervals, he went on. They would have to be thought out ahead of time so that the ground actually occupied would be suitable for the next battle.[15]

Malcolm was describing a *usure* along Maurice lines, much as Davidson's memorandum on the 26th described it: a phase that might follow Gough's rush to gain territory immediately after the initial bombardment had stupefied and disorganised the enemy. That did not suit Haig. He wrote critical comments in the margin which, incorrectly, appeared in the Official History as an instruction to Gough.[16] He ringed the use of the first person pronoun and was angered by Malcolm's philosophising. On objectives and the purpose of the operation he scribbled:

> See report of Doullens conference, 7 May. Section 1, 4th paragraph, and section 3b, and OAD 479, section 1: 'Capture the Passchendaele–Staden ridge.' Briefly, 'wear out the enemy but at the same time have an objective.' I have given two, 1st the P–S Ridge; second the coast.

In 1945, explaining to Edmonds what had been in his mind when he wrote his memorandum and his inability to get Wynne to understand, Malcolm said:

> Wynne makes me tired. We have repeatedly emphasised that the British commanders had to make up their minds between a stage by stage ambush and a break-through . . . Haig decided that he wanted a break-through and Charteris was telling him that the Germans were on the point of cracking – the break-through was the policy. It then became obvious that this aim could not be achieved on the same lines as at Messines. What Wynne is quite incapable of grasping is that the two forms of operation have little in common. A commander cannot achieve a break-through by merely beating off counter-attacks which may never come. When Plumer took over [at the end of August] the idea of the break-through had been abandoned.[17]

It had annoyed Haig to have the disparity between his aims and the plans for the battle played back to him by Malcolm. He had told the Committee in London that limited attacks would achieve strategic objects. Malcolm's memorandum in 1917 agreed with Maurice's in 1915 that they would not, particularly at Ypres. Even if the methods shortly to be used at Cambrai to achieve a break-through (a fully predicted bombardment from guns held silent until zero hour and the massed use of tanks) had been considered for use at Ypres, which they had not, the conditions were unsuitable. In London, Lloyd George had derided Haig's apparent intention to defeat the German Army 'single-handed'.[18] Here was Malcolm telling Fifth Army that was precisely what Haig intended! His references to a *usure* and carefully chosen tactical objectives, rather than Haig's strategic ones, were equally unwelcome for they suggested that Ypres was to be a Verdun for the Germans. Indeed, Haig eventually tried to make it just that: he was to claim that Passchendaele had bled the German Army white. The historians followed Haig in jumping on Malcolm because, like the small boy watching the procession, Malcolm pointed out that the emperor was naked. Permission to proceed with his offensive was given to Haig only days before the opening of Gough's attack, 31 July. Asked by the War Policy Committee on 20 July what was his first objective, Haig gave them the baffling reply: 'The Ridge extending from Stirling Castle by Passchendaele, Staden and Clercken to near Dixmude' and that he would attain it by a series of limited advances.[19]

The Third Battle of Ypres started on the 31 July and its course has been described and analysed at great length and in great detail. There is no need for it to be refought in these pages. Briefly, Gough obediently began his assault, taking the Pilckem ridge in his stride and was immediately checked along the line of the Steenbeck, and a mile down the Menin road after taking Hooge. Plan One had called for thirty-five divisions. He had only nine for his main assault, and three to secure the important central sector. (In the Battle of Messines on 7 June Plumer had used nine divisions to advance two and a half miles and secure the Wytschaete–Menin ridge.) The fact was that limited operations were not cheap. Vimy Ridge (9–12 April) had cost the Canadians 9,937 casualties; Arras (9 April–27 May) the combined First, Third and Fifth armies 158,660. Haig's armies were already running short of trained infantry. Then it began to rain, and Gough pressed his attacks through an unexpectedly wet August. The continual bombardment churned the sodden ground into porridge, impeding movement, and providing those scenes of bogged tanks and artillery that illustrate every work on the battle. Worse, low cloud and rain prevented the Royal Flying Corps from launching ground attack sorties in support of the infantry, and even more important, artillery reconnaissance and fire-direction in the counter-battery battle. More than once Gough requested Haig to call off the operation, but Haig insisted on carrying on, to draw the Germans away from the French front. In fact, by the end of August, the French armies had recovered, and Pétain had felt able to stage some successful local attacks of his own to restore the self-confidence of his troops.

Then Haig, in an impulsive change of plan and tactics, handed the main thrust of the operation over to Plumer, instructing him to revert to the old Plan One by advancing north-east along the 'stave' of the 'bow'. Plumer, in his methodical way, took Polygon Wood and Broodseinde in two successful sub-battles, but the autumn rains began in October and the subsequent struggle was, once more, as much with the mud as the enemy. There was a certain irony in Haig's belief that the troops fought better with a tangible objective in view. The battle petered out in November when the Canadians captured what was left of the insignificant village of Passchendaele, a mere reference point in Haig's intermediate phase line, whose name has usurped the title of his battle, and become a by-word for British military incompetence. That was not all. Haig insisted that the ground gained, an over-extended and more protuberant salient, should be held as a winter line, for which it was quite unsuitable. Such roads as there were ran parallel to the front, and with Zandvoorde, Gheluvelt and Becelaere on high ground still in German hands, the German artillery, safe in covered positions could take it from the flank. After a voluntary withdrawal in March, the front line was flung back to the outskirts of Ypres by the German spring offensive in April 1918.

There is no doubt that it was a battle equally terrible for both sides, but historical opinion is agreed that though Haig may have claimed that it was part of the great 'wearing out' process that prepared the way for the final victory, the balance of attrition was against the British. As accurately predicted, the supply of infantry ran out, and the United Kingdom divisions had to be reorganised with only nine instead of twelve battalions, with all the temporary confusion in terms of reorganisation, command and control and tactics that it entailed.

'Passchendaele' might have lost the war. In March 1918, the German Seventeenth, Second and Eighteenth armies, reinforced by divisions from the Russian front, hurled themselves against the depleted Third and Fifth. Only by their fingernails and 'with their backs to the wall' were Byng's and Gough's troops able to hold their ground after a confused and disorderly retreat. On 27 May, the German Seventh Army served the French in the same fashion, and were held on the Marne between Chateau-Thierry and Epernay.

Then the German armies in their turn were overstretched and physically and morally exhausted. The combined French, British and American onslaught in the summer of 1918 was a fresh chapter in the war, and a merciful deliverance.

CALENDAR OF EVENTS

March–April 1916 – PLAN ONE

First edition of the campaign written by Plumer and Rawlinson. Plumer's southern army to push its left along the ridge. Rawlinson's northern army has its right flank on the army boundary and pushes northeast towards Roulers, Passchendaele and Staden. Rawlinson's named the main attack but Plumer has more difficult task. Both insist on preliminary operations against Messines, Pilckem and the Menin road sector. Army boundary is the Ypres–Roulers railway.

17 November 1916
Joffre and Haig agree to a campaign in Flanders in 1917.

20 November 1916
Asquith requests plan to take Belgian coast.

December 1916
Davidson issues Plan Two. Fifth Army takes over Messines front and advances with left on the Commines Canal to cover Second Army's right flank. [Second Army to take over former role of Rawlinson's northern and Plumer's southern army.]

11 December 1916
Nivelle replaces Joffre.

6 January 1917
Kiggell orders Plumer to prepare new plan. A rapid advance in expectation of Nivelle's success in Champagne in April. The main drive is shifted northwards at Haig's instruction. Rawlinson given the task of driving north-east along the ridge. Plumer to form defensive flank and to push to Gheluvelt to provide base for Rawlinson. Rawlinson's named main attack. Both men again propose preliminary operations. Refused by Haig on grounds rapid not systematic operations required, using tanks on the Menin Road. Army boundary is Menin road.

January 1917
Haig and Nivelle in London to negotiate over British take over of French front, dates of offensives etc.

26 February
Calais conference. Lloyd George arranges with Nivelle clandestinely to place British Army under his command removing, in effect, Haig's right to appeal in case of operations that endanger it.

February–April

Correspondence between Plumer and Haig and GHQ concerning the problem of attacking the Menin road sector using tanks. Haig continues to resist Plumer and Rawlinson plan for preliminary operations.

April

Plumer, who is in charge of the plan, is corrected by Haig when he suggests that Messines will be a separate preliminary battle.

7 May

Haig announces Flanders operation at Army commanders' conference at Doullens. Messines scheduled for 7 June and the rest of the Flanders operation several weeks later. The date Gough planned later was 25 July. Delays brought the start to 31 July.

14 May

Gough given Flanders file by Colonel McMullen, the staff officer responsible for liaison with the army commanders. He was also the planning officer of the landing of tanks and infantry from the sea on flat-bottomed barges. Admiral Bacon, commander of the Dover Patrol, did not receive Jellicoe's support for it. Rawlinson was to have command and the scheduled date for the landing was 8 August.

7 June

Messines begins. Battle ends on 14 June, although the advance was complete in twenty-four hours.

8 June

II Corps transferred to Fifth Army when Plumer refuses to use it on the Menin road sector to exploit Messines. Gough later declines to use it until his offensive starts when it has the most difficult task.

14 June

Gough presents his outline plan at a conference of the army commanders. He will set objectives as much as two miles deep but does not expect to reach them necessarily. He raises problem of his right flank where Plumer is only to occupy ground taken by Gough or to provide a defensive flank. Haig thinks he has solved the problem by handing over II Corps and taking Messines before Gough attacks. Orders Plumer to support Gough by advancing towards Gheluvelt.

123

19-27 June

Haig is in London for the War Policy Committee meetings.

23 June

Davidson has failed to persuade Plumer to attack Zandvoorde and Gheluvelt. Gough has show-down with Plumer at meeting chaired by Kiggell. Plumer refuses to do what Gough wants.

26 June

Davidson writes his memorandum, printed in the OH, proposing a series of limited operations instead of the Gough-Haig plan to take Passchendaele-Staden rapidly. He wrote much the same in his memorandum on the 13th. Haig ignores it.

27 June

Haig returns from London and hears of the row between Gough and Plumer. Jacob, II Corps commander, complains to Gough about the danger of enfilade fire from his right flank unless Plumer attacks vigorously on his right.

28 June

Conference at which Gough presents his final plan. It is accepted by Haig. Haig concedes the flank problem by taking another division from Plumer. Plumer speaks for Gough's plan. OH claims that was why Haig accepted it.

30 June

Haig attacks Malcolm for his memorandum which suggests that after the first rush forward a series of limited tactical objectives, in the *usure* style, may be necessary.

31 July

Battle opens. Pilckem ridge taken and ground taken on Menin road. On the whole it is a disappointment. Attacks continue through a wet August with small gains.

7 August

Translated German document shows that their defensive system is based on prepared counter-attacks by whole divisions held out of field gun range during British bombardments and barrages. This seems to strengthen Davidson's belief in limited, tactical advances. Logically, it led to handing over the operation to Plumer at the end of the month and the limited attacks that he mounted in the Menin road sector on 20th and 26th September, and 4 October. These attacks were in the style proposed in Plan One, to the extent that they first thrust eastward (20th September) then north-eastward on 26th September, and 4th October. Gheluvelt was never taken, however, and no more ground was gained in that direction after 20th September. In a sense, the battle of the Menin road on 20th was the preliminary operation that Plumer and Rawlinson had proposed and Haig declined.

CHAPTER 8

AND A THOUSAND STERN WARRIORS

While the literary man is laying down the law at his desk . . . the wretched man who has to do the work finds the matter settled for him by pestilence, want of shoes, empty stomachs, heavy rains, hot sun and a thousand stern warriors who never show on paper.

CHARLES KINGSLEY, WESTWARD HO!

When America declared war, on 6 April 1917, she was unprepared to fight. The War Department had no plan, no field commander, only the nucleus of a general staff and her total land force, including National Guard units in federal service was 200,000 officers and men. There was not a single complete field division. A selective service act had been recommended to the Congress on 2 April but it was not until 18 May that it became law. Her war industry had been producing small arms ammunition and weapons for the Allies, but she had no production runs of field or heavier calibre guns. There was no mobilisation scheme for men, horses or motor transport, nor the shipping to transport a substantial force to Europe when it was raised.

Initially, the President intended to provide the Allies with immediate credits and supplies and eventually, after a period to raise an army and train it, to send an expeditionary force to Europe. The pace of his modest and leisurely plan had started to accelerate just before Major-General John J Pershing arrived in Washington from the Mexican border on 10 May to find that he had been appointed to command a single division, as yet non-existent, that was to be sent to France immediately as a morale booster. Before Pershing left for Britain on the 28th in the SS *Baltic,* his 1st Division was already being envisaged as the forerunner of a substantial American contingent of indefinite size. So the immediate questions Pershing was told to answer upon his arrival in Europe were: how large a force should be sent? How soon must it arrive? And he was instructed to prepare its bases, its training areas and its future zone of operation. The Administration would then address the tasks of raising, equipping, supplying and transporting it to Europe. These matters and committing the American Expeditionary Forces to battle were to consume most of Pershing's time from May 1917 until the end of the war.

The main instigators of the enlargement of American vision during May, cautious as it was, were a British mission under Lord Balfour that reached Washington on 22 April and Marshal Joffre's Franco-Italian one which followed it on the 25th. Both were after credits, which they duly received, but their military object was to obtain an immediate infusion of men into France. Major-General Tom Bridges, a distinguished cavalry veteran of the Mons retreat, asked for 500,000 men to be drafted to serve in the British Army. The French asked for 90,000 skilled and semi-skilled men to replace potential French combat soldiers on the Lines of Communication, that voluntary enlistment in the French Army should be permitted and that small American units up to battalion size should be incorporated in it. But Joffre, who had heard about Nivelle's failure in Champagne on his way over, asked particularly for one complete division of Americans to encourage his countrymen.

Not surprisingly, the Americans agreed only to this last request, and reluctantly. The War College Division of the General Staff had recommended in February and March that, in the event of war, regulars should be retained in the United States to train the new divisions and not despatched overseas in regular divisions. In August 1914, Douglas Haig and other British officers had been of the same mind about the BEF. In the American case, unlike the British in 1914, it would be many months before a significant composite force could be readied and the shipping collected to transport it. In line with their proposal, the War College Division had recommended that when divisions had been raised they should be trained in the United States and not receive their initial training under British or French instructors in Europe. As to the idea of allowing volunteers to serve in foreign armies – once merged with an Allied Army, they would never emerge. When questioned about the War Department's intentions, the deputy Chief of Army Staff, Major-General Tasker H Bliss, was cagey, saying that the French were perfectly aware that the Americans were unprepared to send a 'serious' expedition for 'serious' business, and that the general staff had made no plan for the 'prompt' dispatch of considerable forces. The United States having sent a 'small' force for moral effect, the French might imagine that it would be followed quite soon by a large force for 'physical' effect. Thus far, the United States had no plans to do so.

That was strictly true. Plans did not exist. But plans and intentions were not the same thing. Bliss did not intend to get ahead of both the President, who had prevented the War Department preparing for war, and the Congress which, he hoped, would pass the legislation and vote the money expeditiously, but which had not been enthusiastic for war. Nevertheless, Pershing had been instructed that he was to be C-in-C of American *forces*, not simply a divisional commander, and that he was to establish all the necessary bases for successive contingents of troops. The size and organisation of the force was to be at his recommendation, which seems a remarkable delegation of responsibility, until one remembers that an initiative was not expected from political quarters and that he was the appointed AEF Commander-in-Chief. Nevertheless, in June, a commission under Colonel Chauncey Baker followed Pershing to France to advise Mr Newton D Baker, the Secretary of War, on the establishment of the American Expeditionary Forces in France. The Commission and Pershing's staff cooperated over their report, which was submitted on 11 July. On 1 July, in the meanwhile, Pershing had called for a million men to be ready to participate in operations by the summer of 1918, to be expanded to nearly twice that number subsequently, and for the infrastructure of such a force to be created in the United States. In round numbers, that meant about thirty divisions; 1,328,488 men, counting a divisional slice as 44,283. The supply services would require 24 per cent of the whole and 3,000 replacements per corps of six divisions per month were demanded. Later, plans were considered for the AEF in France to have eighty divisions, one hundred divisions and sixty-six divisions respectively. By the Armistice about forty-two divisions were in France.[1]

Pershing, whose nickname 'Black Jack' was earned in the 10th Cavalry in which he commanded black Americans in Cuba, had recently been promoted to Major-General, the most senior rank in the American Army, for his work on the Mexican border in pursuit of Pancho Villa in 1916–17. Of only six officers of that rank, all but Pershing could be ruled out, on grounds of age or health, for command of the AEF. In France, he had to adjust his mind from small police actions to a huge war. More over, the war was not the open affair that the American Army was still envisaging but a positional war of material which Pershing had not had recent opportunity to study, although he had been an observer in the Russo-Japanese War. The fate of the 19th and 21st British New Army divisions at Loos, in 1915, might have illustrated for him what could befall new American divisions if they were committed to battle prematurely on the Western Front. Trained for open conditions and eager to succeed, the two British divisions had been rushed into the struggle for Hill 70 under a misconception that a break-through had been achieved. Both were slaughtered and routed. Their men had been in the army for about a year; it was their divisions' first action. In the battle of the Meuse-Argonne of September 1918, when most Americans had had less than a year in uniform, and were in their first stern test, AEF casualties were 122,063 and divisional performances were patchy. At Loos, in much the same period of time, the British and French suffered about 100,000 against a more effective enemy in stronger positions. It is not our aim here to contrast performances but to stress Pershing's daunting task in preparing the AEF for such a war quickly and starting with few advantages but enthusiasm and determination. The measure of ignorance which Pershing brought to his task might have been not entirely to his disadvantage could he but have recognised it.

Indeed, our purpose is to describe the command and staff problems of the AEF not its battles, which were comparatively insignificant until the Meuse-Argonne offensive, which continued from the end of September 1918 until the Armistice. Pershing's achievement was in getting his army into the field in a condition to fight. First, there had to be created, virtually, a general staff in the field to write the tables of organisation and establishments for his divisions, and to whip them into shape when they arrived. The General Staff had to conduct a protracted struggle over logistics with AEF service chiefs, its own Line of Communication staff and with the War Department. Pershing, himself, had to withstand a continuous and sometimes acrimonious cold war with his two allies over the shipment, strength, deployment and disposal of the AEF. Throughout, taking advantage of a general staff in Washington as immature as his own in France, Pershing denied its legitimate authority over the AEF and bickered with it incessantly. None of these matters was discreet. Each impinged on the others continuously, creating tension and demanding changes in staffs and in methods, themselves unsettling. We attempt here to communicate that impression and not a false one of order and clarity where in fact confusion reigned. Under pressure, certainly partly of his own making, Pershing proved to be unable to master training and operations as well as administration and coalition politics. Coordination suffered. Urged by Washington and London to devolve powers and responsibilities for the latter, he resisted because they were symbols of his political position as C-in-C. A degree of delegation was nevertheless forced upon him from above. If his management of some of these matters can be faulted, for example when he resisted offers of French and British trench warfare training in favour of open warfare to the detriment of his troops,[2] his stamina and determination to maintain his independence and that of the AEF command admiration. Pershing was totally committed to the AEF and it can be said of him, as of Haig, that he did not distinguish between his own ambition and the good

129

of the AEF which he commanded. In all, the American experience of these matters that concerned AEF relations with its allies probably left a more lasting impression on the Army and on American conceptions of the war than did AEF operations in the field, and were to be an important influence on their relations with the British in the Second World War, as we shall see in the second half of this book.

Pershing's portrait shows him to be determined, strong and fit; not intellectual, like Bliss, but a field-hardened leader. Yet he held a law degree, earned while a professor of military science at the University of Nebraska. Life had dealt him a hard blow when his wife and all his children save one lost their lives in a fire in 1915 while he was absent on duty. Ambassador Lloyd C Griscom, who became his liaison officer in London, comparing Pershing and Haig said:

> They were, to a striking degree, of the same type. Self-contained, direct, honest and incapable of intrigue. They had great respect for each other but when they met for a conference the very similarity of their reserved characteristics prevented them from indulging in an open, free and frank discussion, which might have had a very important influence on the conduct of the war.[3]

Pershing's vision of what was required of his army was clear. It had to be able to shoot straight, to march fast and far, and to learn to manoeuvre under fire in small units. His was a conception of war close to Haig's in 1914, and one that many British commanders were trying to restore in the British army at this time. They had found it difficult to inculcate in battalion commanders unused to accepting authority, junior leaders who did not survive long enough to discard the experience of months of trench fighting, and men who seldom used their personal weapons. Pershing believed that although his Americans were inexperienced at all levels and were untrained in open or trench fighting, they had less to unlearn. Perhaps that was making a virtue of necessity. Pershing was the only officer in the American Army who had commanded so much as a brigade. He was to be desperately short of junior officers who even had field experience in the tough Moro country of the Philippines, in Cuba and recently on the Mexican border – the nearest American equivalents to experience in South Africa for the British. The total number of War College or Staff College graduates in the whole regular army was 379 out of a total of 3,885 regular officers with more than a single year's service.[4] Add to this the burden of adopting strange weapons, for while the US army's rifle was the satisfactory Springfield,[5] it would have to learn to use French machine-guns and

French artillery equipment.[6] The task facing Pershing's officers resembled that of Kitchener's officers when training the New Armies. With that in mind he adopted Kitchener's approach, which was to avoid committing them to battle for as long as possible.

Pershing's organisational ability, particularly his conception of the role of the staff, had not been formed, as had Haig's, by the experience of creating a general staff, let alone an Imperial General Staff, in peace. Unlike Haig, he did not see the general staff as an army institution which would guide the army's development and its operations. Rather, it was an extension of his own staff, its individuals were his executives, not part of a larger élite group with a professional ethic which had members in the War Department too. He regarded himself as the Commander-in-Chief, not just of the AEF but of all American armies serving under the President. He was inclined to treat the Army Chief of Staff in Washington as an assistant of his AEF chief of staff.

The battle within the Washington War Department to establish the supremacy of the Chief of the Army Staff was only won decisively when Peyton C March returned from France in 1918 to become Chief of Staff and to make it clear in his General Order No. 80 that there could be only one door to the sanctum of the Secretary of War and that was guarded by the Chief of Staff and the War Department General Staff.[7] A decade earlier, a similar battle had been fought in London. In the later nineteenth century, the mainly civilian British supply organisation had been progressively militarised, but it operated within a civilian dominated War Office, quite separate from the operational staffs working for the Commander in Chief. The first reform leading to the creation of a British version of a general staff was the abolition of the appointment of Commander-in-Chief and the removal of his staff to the War Office. Most senior British officers then regarded the general staff as the instrument that would 'throw the civilian clerks out of the War Office.' It was more than that; it was also the means of controlling and harnessing the service chiefs of administration – the Quartermaster-General and Adjutant-General, for instance – either by making them part of the general staff or by making them submit to staff control. These were the heads of service corps, bureau chiefs in American parlance, which, in Washington, still insisted on their independence in 1917, only allowing the general staff officers to coordinate their actions. In truth, the American bureau chiefs' attitude was that of civil servants operating in an entirely peace-time environment, their activities closely linked with the country's civilian ones; which, of course, was the case in practice. However, in the twentieth century, war departments had to be a bridge from the civilian zone of the interior to the Army, not simply an extension of the former. A War Department had to prepare contingency plans for mobilisation and for controlling armies in war. For that purpose, it had to contain both a bridgehead element forward, whose criteria were war conditions, to integrate the war department with the field army, and a near-bank element which handled the acquisition of war materials. On the near shore were the service of supply elements. One authority, the staff, had to control both shores and the bridge between them.[8]

It was the bridging organisation that had yet to be properly established in Washington when Pershing arrived in France, regarding himself in no way subordinate to the General Staff at the War Department. Clearly, neither he nor his Chief of Staff, his fellow cavalryman Lieutenant Colonel James G Harbord, had absorbed the development of other staff systems at that stage. Nor can they have understood the relevance to their own case of what had gone on in their own War Department, for they created in GHQ in France a small War Department with the same unresolved contradictions between staff and bureaux. GHQ was divided into a general staff and an administrative and technical staff. The latter was termed the 'personal staff', a misnomer, surely. The former was initially divided into three sections, for Administration Combat and Intelligence. The head of each section was an 'assistant chief of staff'. The personal staff, which included all the bureaux, had direct control of logistics in the widest sense. Harbord acted as the mouthpiece of Pershing and was nominally controller and coordinator of both staffs but a lack of coordination between the staffs was soon evident. The heads of bureaux took their problems direct to Pershing, as their War Department superiors went, by law, direct to Secretary Baker in Washington, cutting out the Chief of Staff; also, they communicated direct with Washington, as did Washington with them. Harbord's response was to try to make it unnecessary for bureaux to approach Pershing, by handling their problems himself or through one or other of his staff sections. Consequently, he increased his general staff sections to five; Administrative Policy, Intelligence, Operations, Coordination and Training Policy. All military staffs face similar problems and Pershing's reacted to the logistics one by creating the important coordination section which was a combination of what the British might have called 'General Staff Duties' and 'Q(Ops)'. It might have been termed the logistics section but for the fact that it was the Administrative section that dealt with railways and some other logistical matters and the Coord Section with orders of battle. Its parentage seems to owe much to Wellington's division of his staff into the Adjutant-General's (Administrative) and Quarter-Master General's staffs. Since training was soon to be the main occupation of American divisions in France, the new, fifth section was formed to handle it.

The difficulty of making Pershing's, so-called personal, administrative and technical staffs function smoothly in the service of supply, continued until the Armistice. The Coordination Section was, in fact, largely designed to control their work. Later, the staff sections adapted the French nomenclature to their needs so that Administration became G1, Intelligence G2, Operations G3 and Logistics G4, with G5 as the extra Training section, although the division of responsibility between G1 and G4 continued to differ from French or British practice.

The personal staff was huge and curiously designed. Its size reflected the idea that the functions of supply were extensive and its relationship to the General Staff that its members were experts who well understood their work and required the general staff to play only a coordinating role in a generally smooth and routine process. This conception seemed to follow from there being a French civilian zone of the interior in France which provided an administrative infrastructure. US Field Service Regulations (1914) determined that an overseas theatre of operations should be divided into a Line of Communication Zone and a Zone of Advance. The former would be under a commanding general who would be directly responsible to the Commander-in-Chief and would handle supplies received from the Zone of the Interior in the United States, classify, store them in a Communications Zone in France and transport them to combat troops in the American Zone of Advance. It was not until 18 September, that Pershing cabled to Washington a 'Service of the Rear project', a new term corresponding with French terminology which suggested the function of service rather than the command of territory, the L of C. To American minds at the time, the term 'service' suggested a staff rather than a command task. In 1917, the appointed commanding general (CG) of the L of C was one of many bureau chiefs in Pershing's Personal Staff, which included the chief quartermaster, the director general of transportation the Adjutant General, the general purchasing agent and several others. Until an L of C was actually created, the CG L of C had nothing to command and when, as a staff officer, he attempted to coordinate the numerous functions nominally his responsibility, he was caught up in the struggle for the staff's legitimate authority over bureaux and in a conflict with the General Staff.

This situation continued until almost the end of the year. It is a legitimate criticism of Pershing that having been given a primary responsibility to build a logistical bridgehead to handle the flood of divisions that would eventually arrive, he did not do so while the size of the AEF was still small; it numbered under 90,000 on 31 October and by the end of the year still only 175,000. Like the Red Queen in *Alice Through the Looking Glass*, he would have to run to stay in the same place. Colonel Hagood one of the men who, to an extent sorted out the situation, described some of the things that he found at the time the L of C was established in December a month after his own arrival in France.

> The Advance Section (one of the echelons of supply) did not exist at this stage. There was chaos on the railways, conflict between bureau chiefs at AEF GHQ and the L of C, and need to choose between the British and French systems or to modify the American one; there was ignorance among Americans as to how any system worked; that a ship lay at one base waiting to be unloaded 42 days; that one brigade commander told him that his men had gone as long as 12 days without potatoes, 8 days without any vegetable component and that it was a common experience to do without bread.

In December, he observed, a Board of which he was chairman, had laid down, *inter alia,* how a French innovation, the 'Regulating Station', and automatic supply worked, standard scales of supplies by classes laid down and how to maintain the formations without 'the bondage and slavery of red tape under which the Army had struggled all the dreary years of peace. For instance, food for a whole division could now be obtained merely by telephoning a supply depot and giving its total strength.'

The reader should reflect that one of the unlauded achievements of Haig and others of the British War Office and Expeditionary Force staffs in the Haldane years before 1914, was to overhaul the supply system so that once the front settled down it worked smoothly, until the French railways broke down under the strain in 1917. Then Eric Geddes was appointed to refurbish the system, working directly for Haig. As early as November 1914, according to Colonel George Owen Squier, the American Military Attaché in London and the only foreigner allowed to visit the BEF at this time, it was a remarkable system. Kitchener had sent for Squier and asked him to visit the BEF with the specific purpose of briefing the Americans on the demands of modern war. He told Squier that the American Army should learn all it could before its inevitable entry into the fight. Unfortunately, Squier's meticulous and detailed account of how the BEF administration worked was shelved by the War Department in Washington. (Squier had an outstanding intellect; a scientist, inventor, artilleryman, signals officer who, after becoming head of the aviation section, was appointed Chief Signal Officer, a post he held until 1923. 'Ironically, he was not a good administrator, but became immersed in the scientific and technical aspects of the war.')*

---

* Note supplied by Terrence Gough, Staff Support Branch, C.M.H. Washington, November, 1989.

By the final month of the war, although the American service of supply creaked, it worked. On the other hand, forward supply in armies, corps and divisions was still chaotic. In large part that was owing to a grave shortage of horses, abysmal horse management and shocking motor vehicle maintenance. But the Meuse-Argonne was also the AEF's first difficult supply operation in a battle area with virtually no roads. With huge divisions and inexperienced divisional staffs, the outcome was predictable. Our concern here is to describe, in outline only, the reform of the L of C which Hagood's board had initiated in December, 1917. It removed the CG L of C from GHQ at Chaumont to Tours, on the Loire, and made him directly responsible to Pershing. He was intended to have the staff sections for administration and coordination to serve him, together with most of the bureau chiefs. Liaison elements of staff and bureaux were to stay at GHQ. Hagood suggests that Pershing simply did not understand the principles involved because he allowed the bureaux' chiefs to stay at GHQ and the staff sections to send their deputies to the L of C instead of their chiefs. In the meantime Colonel Moseley, who had become assistant chief of staff (Coord or G4), virtually ran the Advance Section, L of C, and the crucial Regulating Station which controlled the flow of men and supplies into railhead from the rear and out of it forward to armies. Moseley's argument was that Operations had to determine what was sent forward. A feud continued over Regulation between the staff of the CG L of C and G4 at GHQ until the end of the war.* In the meantime, the confusion between the director of railways, whose system crossed other command boundaries and ran from ports to the front, the chief quartermaster, whose supplies were carried on the railways, and various commanders in whose base areas functions such as berthing, unloading and enrailment, storage and consignment of supplies were conducted in other hands, also continued. Supplies of the right kind and in the right quantities still did not reach the front.

It was not until July 1918, that the War Department, which knew of the chaos in the AEF from its bureau chiefs and was being besieged by Congressional demands to 'civilianize' the L of C, proposed sending out the great engineer and builder of the Panama Canal, George Goethals, to sort out the muddle. Goethals was Acting Quarter-Master General from December 1917 to April 1918, when he became Director of Purchase, Storage and Traffic and a general staff officer. But March, who was proving a ruthlessly efficient Chief of Staff, had made Goethals 'Mr Supply', and had removed the power of the bureaux to thwart him. March's instruc-

---

* The feud continued in France in 1944, as Chapter 15 describes.

tions to Goethals might have been the model for George Marshall's to General Brehon Somervell, head of the Army Service Forces in Washington in the Second War:

> You are given complete charge of all matters of supply. You can make any changes in personnel, methods, and general set-up necessary to get results and don't bother me with details. I hold you responsible for results, and I will take all the responsibility for anything you have to do to get them. When you need more authority or specific authority in any particular case, come to me, and you will get it.[9]

The War Department's plan to send Goethals, had been instigated by the President's close confidant, Edward M House, who had proposed that Edward Stettinius, a member of the JP Morgan banking firm, be sent to take charge of logistics. This was at a time when the question of the rate at which American divisions could be shipped to Europe and equipped was being continuously and acrimoniously discussed in London, Paris and Washington at prime ministerial and ambassadorial level. The state of American logistics, in particular the incapacity of the L of C to absorb an accelerated flow of men and materials, became a political issue. A civilian, though, would not be acceptable in France for he would neither have the knowledge nor the legitimate authority to correct the situation. Goethals' nomination allowed Baker, the Secretary of War, to propose a different solution. As a distinguished senior soldier he could be made 'coordinate with Pershing, rather than serve under him,' Baker explained when he presented the idea to Pershing. March was being infuriated by Pershing's changes of plan, demands for supplies at short notice, and arrogant assumption that all his demands should be instantly satisfied regardless of shipping limits or production. Goethals would dampen down Pershing's volatility, March believed. He approved of Baker's placing Bliss on the Supreme War Council where he handled military-diplomatic matters in France in 1918. If Goethals were installed Pershing would be confined to military training and operations.

Pershing's reaction was predictable. The War Department was not only interfering but also infringing the principles that there be a single commander in a theatre of war and that the commander control his own logistics. The L of C must not be a War Department bridgehead in the Zone of the Armies. But Pershing was nobody's fool for he knew that his power to control the disposal of his armies and their build up depended on the negotiations that he had largely, and quite successfully, conducted with the Allied governments and their Cs-in-C in France, and in those negotia-

negotiations his supply system had become a handicap to him. So he called on Harbord, who had recently been appointed to command the 2nd Division, to assume command of the L of C. Pershing toured the supply system with Harbord and was convinced that the latter could put matters to rights. Changes were made and the dispute between railways, base commanders and the QM Corps was ended, although the railways were not being satisfactorily run even in September. Virtually, Harbord became a second chief of staff, one responsible for the service of supply, with two staff branches, G1 and G4, to serve him. However the tug of war between G4 at GHQ and Harbord's own staff continued. Who had been right was still undecided in 1941, after Moseley, Hagood and Harbord had written books on supply in the AEF, successive War College courses had studied the matter, and the United States had entered another war.

Pershing was convinced that March was behind the plan that he had averted and that March was trying to extend his authority into the AEF. On 18 August, he wrote to Secretary Baker suggesting that the problem lay in the War Department General Staff, which had not yet reached that point of perfection which would enable matters to be handled systematically. He fully realised, Pershing continued, that it was difficult to get the perfection that Baker should have because some of his staff were unsatisfactory. 'The system should be one thoroughly tested out, such as in operation here, and upon which every successful army organisation must depend.' His letter reflected the view of Harbord that Pershing was responsible directly to the President through Baker and that March was a trouble-maker. Pershing's letter was breath-taking in its pomposity and blind to the defects of AEF staff-work; wisely, Baker did not show it to March who wrote later:

> As the AEF increased in size, General Pershing's inability to function in teamwork with his legal and authorised superiors increased, until it reached a point where he refused to obey Foch's orders abroad; and on August 18, 1918, wrote a letter to Secretary Baker, behind my back, in which he said, in substance, that while we seemed to have sufficient energy it was badly directed, and better results would be obtained if an officer from his staff were put in charge of the War Department General Staff. He wanted a rubber stamp for Chief of Staff at home, so he could be entirely independent of any supervision or control . . . I did not know about this particular letter until after the war. There certainly would have been a showdown if I had.[10]

March was unimpressed with boards, of which he had tried to rid the

War Department, awash with them when he took over, and commented scathingly on Pershing's addiction to them in the AEF. It showed Pershing's lack of understanding of how his own general staff should operate.

As is so often the case, both parties to the dispute within the AEF over control of logistics were right; Harbord and Hagood, his chief of staff, in arguing that the CG L of C was really a chief of staff responsible directly to Pershing, and Moseley who insisted that the general staff at GHQ had to control forward supply and direct the policy of the CG. Each had almost suggested a solution, one that was later to be adopted successfully by General Bernard Montgomery: to split GHQ into a main and rear element. In the former presided the Chief of Staff; in the latter, the Chief Administrative Staff Officer who was his equal. The latter was in effect both the commander of administrative areas and the coordinator and controller of the numerous functional services as far forward as railhead or the rear army boundaries. However, while he had access to the C-in-C, he also received directions from the chief of staff, when necessary, and the latter was 'the first among equals'. Unfortunately the officers who were to design the American supply system in the European Theatre in 1944 seem not to have read the records of 1917 and 1918, although the men sent to sort things out from Washington by General Brehon Somervell, Mr Supply of 1944, were perfectly aware that the mistakes of 1917–18 were being repeated. The nub of the issue was that American commanders insisted on addressing only the command mission in supply, and not the general staff function. In turn that error stemmed from drawing a line between command and staff functions that precluded staffs from what they called 'operating'. In practice staffs have to operate, to provide commanders with extra arms and legs.

Before turning to the question that had brought the Goethals proposal to a head, the flow of American divisions to Europe and their disposal and control, we must discuss how Pershing decided the basic question of their outline organisation. If he had studied the French and British experience by the middle of 1917, instead of accepting his allies' self-serving advice, a few relevant facts might have influenced him to reach a different conclusion from the one he did in July 1917. Of course, infantry suffered by far the heaviest casualties and were always scarce. Fire-power, both in the infantry and in the artillery, had been steadily increased. Necessarily, that increase had been at the expense of the cutting edge of the division, the man with a rifle and bayonet. In August 1917, there were eight artillerymen in action at Ypres for every ten infantrymen. Divisions had not altered much in size, because at the same time as riflemen decreased, their effectiveness was their own 'trench' mortars, light machine guns, and rifle grenades. The combat and service divisional slices had grown because of a larger corps and army artillery, the creation of the tank corps and the air arm, *inter alia,* and the complexity of the maintenance of an increasingly technical army. Tactics had responded to technical change, albeit a step or two behind. Before the end of 1917, the practice of attempting to overcome several lines of a trench system by sheer weight of infantry and an obliterating preliminary bombardment of several days was obsolescent. As we have seen, it came to an end, signally, at Cambrai in November. This was marked by changed organisations.

Why, then, did Pershing propose very large infantry divisions, relatively weak in artillery although strong in medium machine guns? Major General Fox Conner, who succeeded Harbord as Pershing's chief of staff, said that an Act of Congress in 1916 had established divisions with three brigades of three regiments of three battalions for a total strength of 28,256. By the time that this was approved on 30 May 1917, it had been agreed that two brigades of six regiments were sufficient but that the strength of companies should be raised from 150 to 250 men. Each of the twelve battalions in a division was to have a company of 12 machine guns beside four rifle companies.[11] It is interesting that having three levels of command was like the German organisation of 1914, soon abandoned in favour of two, like the British and French. Pershing asked for this organisation, Conner assures us. At the Armistice, American divisional establishments were 28,105, and the Superior Board of the AEF in 1919 recommended that the future war establishment be increased to 29,199. Fox Conner and Pershing himself, on the other hand, regarded this figure as 'way too large', and recommended 16,875. Disagreement on such a scale at that stage is strange, particularly as, Hewes tells us, at the outbreak of war the War Department had actually been planning on divisions of about the French and British size, not large ones as Fox Conner said. 'The change to large divisions occasioned much work and no little confusion, new tables of organisation and equipment had to be prepared,' and the plans for accommodation had all been based on the smaller establishment.[12] Pershing's comments on the 1919 Board recommendation was that the future organisation should be suitable for American continental conditions and not specifically designed for the European continent.

It is generally believed that Pershing's proposal in July 1917 had been inspired by the British and French missions' suggestion earlier in Washington that the Americans field large divisions although, at that time, their own bayonet strength had been reduced for tactical reasons. However, it was not until the beginning of 1918 that the British were forced to adopt the nine battalion standard for want of manpower, although the French took that step earlier. For their part, the Germans adopted smaller divisions earlier still, because they found them easier to move and supply, but they formed more of them. It seems probable that the missions reasoned that large American divisional establishment would suit their own desire to acquire American infantry and machine gunners in quantity for themselves. Their argument that the AEF could not provide staffs for more smaller divisions, was appealing, but was sophistry for the divisions had an extra level of command, the brigade, and they must have known that managing divisions of such size would be difficult except in static positions. That was probably their real point, for the French envisaged the Americans holding the line to release their own divisions to attack, and large divisions strong in infantry were suited to static tasks. In practice, in the type of semi-open warfare that had become normal in the dog-fight conditions of mid-1917 and was to be commonplace in 1918, the American divisions being twice the normal size, were unmanageable and exceedingly difficult to supply. The abundance of riflemen invited the football scrum tactics that the AEF used in the Meuse-Argonne; tactics reminiscent of the Somme which the Germans penalised similarly. Certainly the AEF was more successful in gaining ground on the more loosely held Meuse-Argonne front than the BEF had been on the Somme two years earlier; but AEF tactics were crude in comparison with those being used in August 1918 by the British, Canadian and Anzac troops in the BEF.

Pershing does not seem to have grasped that the very large unwieldy American divisions were unsuitable for the war of manoeuvre on the 1914 pattern on which his mind was set, let alone the new tactics exploiting improved artillery techniques, air support and tanks to break the deadlock of trench warfare and penetrate the *Siegfriedstellung* (called the 'Hindenburg Line' by the British.) In these semi-mobile operations, the opponents used the ground to fight *on*, rather than fighting *for* it yard by yard. Although the US 27th, 30th, 33rd and 80th Divisions had taken part in these operations under British command, there seems no contemporary evidence that the significance of the Battles of Hamel and Second Amiens (July and August 1918), and still less of the all-British operation by the Third Army at Cambrai in November 1917, had been noted in GHQ AEF. This may have been because the French, with whom the bulk of the AEF was attached for training, regarded them as green troops, suitable only for garrisoning trenches, to free the more tactically minded French to act as assault divisions.

Exploitation by his allies, even if it best served the Allied cause, was Pershing's fear. Indeed, his suspicions were perfectly justified. At the beginning, the British had proposed that Americans should be drafted into the British Army, arguing that there would be no language barrier. When the location of the American forces was being considered, Haig suggested that they should be positioned between his own right and the French left. No doubt he calculated that they would save him from taking over line from the French at the end of 1917. In the event, logistics decided where the Americans would have to be positioned if they were to be an independent force. The northern and western part of the Western Front was served by congested ports and railways, and it was clear that, to avoid these, American communications should flow from the southern Brittany and Gironde ports, south of Paris to the Lorraine front. From there, Pershing could see that there was a strategic objective in the German rail system from Metz through Mézières which served German troops further west. Hence it followed that the Americans' neighbours, the French, would be their main tutors – and also potential exploiters.

However, the British still held a trump card. Only they could provide the shipping to carry the Americans across the Atlantic and keep them supplied. Also, it had been understood from the beginning that as much of the material required for the AEF as possible should be acquired in Europe. Eventually, over half its requirements were provided from England and France. These two factors set up a degree of AEF dependence which weakened Pershing's hand. The Bolshevik revolution in October, the defeat of the Italians at Caporetto in the same month, and the German offensives over the Somme in March 1918, on the Lys in Flanders in April and on the Aisne in May, together made American manpower potentially the decisive factor on the Western Front. How, and in what order it should be brought over, equipped, trained and employed, became the centre of an interesting three-sided tussle in the first six months of 1918. In this Lloyd George played his familiar role of irresistible force and Pershing took over Haig's as immovable object.

After nine months of war, only 183,896 Americans had landed in France. The German General Staff had predicted that in a year not more than 500,000 equipped Americans would have arrived. They were right, for on 1st May the figure was still only 434,081. But two months later, a million men had left the United States for Europe and about 300,000 a month were arriving at western French ports. On 23 June, the flow of Americans and the French weakness led Clemenceau, Tardieu and Foch to visit Chaumont to urge Pershing to adopt a 100 division plan. At much the same time, the American War Department was planning on eighty as a minimum, although the G-3 section at GHQ had completed a study that showed sixty-six to be the maximum that could be trained, equipped and maintained in combat by 31 May 1919. Nevertheless, Pershing agreed to a 100 division programme by July 1919 in a cable on that day, the 23 June. This flurry of activity and the surge of troops arriving in France was a result of the tussle mentioned above. The surge put an added strain on the shaky logistics system, which the War Department had assigned Goethals to improve. It also led to two other predictable crises, of which the immediate causes were an unexpectedly high wastage of man-power in July and August and heavy casualties in September and October: hospital facilities were inadequate and there were insufficient replacements. Both had suffered in the rush to get combat troops, particularly infantry, to France. On 4 September, GHQ had to ask for no divisions to be shipped in October as 110,000 replacements were overdue. On that date combat divisions were 60,000 men short, mainly of infantry. On 12 October, thirty-six Base hospitals and thirty-one Evacuation hospitals, due by 30 September, had still not arrived, nor had fourteen urgently needed Base hospitals due in October. Forty-six Base hospitals had arrived since June without equipment, which was not provided for many weeks; 'situation so serious that it merits immediate attention', a GHQ cable urged at this time.

The time that President Wilson had allowed to drift by in 1916 and early 1917 without preparing to mobilise his forces could never be regained. In 1918, the Allies simply reacted to the changing tides at the Front between January and July by placing demands on the Americans to which they could respond only by upsetting the balance of their forces or overriding the perfectly legitimate insistence of Pershing that his instructions were to retain the independence of his force and to establish an American Army with an American mission as soon as possible. However, he had also been instructed to cooperate, as far as possible, with the French and British which meant, in practice, with the Supreme War Council, with the prime ministers, and with the two Cs-in-C until, in March, Foch took over the supreme command.

Pershing had planned to resist the employment of his divisions, particularly elements of divisions, within French or British formations. If he could keep divisions together he would eventually be able to claim them on the Lorraine front once they had been trained and introduced to front-line duties with the French and, perhaps, the British. The weakness in his position was that since he depended on the French for artillery equipment and training entirely and on both allies for training higher staffs, his divisions could not take the field as complete formations until they were ready. Infantry training took less time and some of it could be completed in the United States. Logically, then, infantry and machine gunners were available to be employed in detached roles at the Front before the divisions to which they belonged. By January 1918, when the slow arrival of Americans had become notorious, the British and French were in the middle of a manpower crisis that seemed likely to lead to a disaster when the Germans finished transferring about forty divisions from Russia to the Western Front. Whereas the French and British were well-supplied with artillery, they were short of infantry and machine gunners. The certainty that the Germans would probably attack them in great strength in March led them to demand that American infantry and machine gunners be shipped ahead of the other divisional components in order that they could serve with British and French divisions. This logical demand, which was in the Allied interest, was a threat to Pershing's independence as commander of the AEF.

On 9 and 10 January, Robertson, the British Chief of the Imperial General Staff, and the British Shipping Controller met Pershing in Paris and offered to provide the shipping to bring over 150,000 infantry in battalions, provided they were incorporated into British divisions. They argued that the British had plenty of divisional artillery so American infantry should serve in British divisions until their own artillery was trained. General Fox Conner later described GHQ's reaction. 'The shipping was in existence and the AEF problem was to get it without amalgamation.'

The next stage was a conference at Versailles on 29 January between Bliss and Pershing, Haig, Robertson and Henry Wilson (British permanent representative to the Supreme War Council), Prime Minister Lloyd George and Lord Milner, the British Secretary of State for War. From it came the so-called 'six division plan'. The British would provide the shipping to bring over six divisions which would train in the British zone. The sequel saw the British attempt to give priority to the infantry and machine gunners of this contingent, while arrangements for the training of complete divisions went ahead with Haig. Details of the latter were cabled to Washington on 10 March. The events of 21 March and the following days brought the Supreme War Council to override Pershing's resistance to bringing in infantry and machine gunners ahead of their divisions. Secretary Baker was then in France and he cabled the President that Pershing and Bliss had agreed to the arrangement with reservations:

> That the arrangement last only during the crisis, and 'keeping in mind always the determination of this Government to have its various military forces collected, as speedily as their training and the military situation will permit, into an independent American Army.'

In the next months, the British tried to extend the priority indefinitely while the Americans tried to end it as soon as possible. Pershing was accused of putting the Allied front at risk simply to form an American army of questionable value. On 3 April he proposed limiting the priority to four out of the six divisions, making it more palatable by including in the shipment 45,000 replacements, 18,000 of whom were immediately required. At the same time, Lloyd George opened up negotiations directly through Lord Reading, the British Ambassador in Washington asking Reading to confirm his information that there were only 400,000 infantrymen in the whole of the United States. If it were, his understanding that the agreement had been for 120,000 infantry for *each* month from April to July was not going to be fulfilled. Reading's reply was that, although March denied it, he thought that Lloyd George was correct. However, March had assured him that 480,000 men would be consigned during the four months, and that 150,000 men would be called up monthly from 26 April.

Pershing had not been informed of what had passed on this channel of communication, which was swifter than his own with Washington, and so was embarrassed when Lloyd George despatched General Whigham, Deputy Chief of General Staff to talk to him. Whigham told him that their understanding was that 120,000 infantry and machine gunners a month would be brigaded with Allied units and that they would not be withdrawn before October or November. When Pershing denied this and dug in his heels, Reading was sent to see President Wilson. On 10 April, wisely, Wilson declined to give an opinion until Baker had returned from France. When he had done so, the result was the 'Reading Agreement' of 19 April, which gave the priority to infantry and machine gunners for the four months. A cable giving this information was shown to Pershing on 20 April in London. His own War Department did not inform him until the 26th.

Having set the scene, Lloyd George handed negotiations over to Milner and Henry Wilson (who had by then relieved Robertson as CIGS) who were inclined to be more understanding. Furthermore, the German Lys offensive had been halted and the British had broken up some divisions to provide replacements. Their losses in artillery in the March retreat had been considerable and they were now more interested in balanced American divisions being sent to France. Also, the submarine threat of the previous year had been defeated and the British were releasing shipping in such quantities that it was possible to send far more than 120,000 men a month. There might, therefore, be enough to satisfy both parties. The London Agreement that ensued reflected the increasing readiness of the British to compromise, giving greater priority to divisional and brigade troops and headquarters, and limiting the divisions to six to be shipped in the month of May. Before the agreement was extended further, the original contingent, as agreed, would be completed, and the necessary Service of Supply troops despatched. In the event, 233,038 men arrived in May.

Nevertheless the Allied political heads were not satisfied. At Abbeville, Clemenceau and Lloyd George made a dead-set at Pershing, taking the view that matters had been taken out of his hands by the previous arrangements with Reading and Baker. But Pershing 'pounded the table' on behalf of the London Agreement and gained his point, at least to the extent that the priority for infantry, machine-gunners, headquarters, engineers and signal troops for six divisions was extended for one month only, to June, for which the British agreed to provide the ships. Cables to Washington from Lloyd George and Clemenceau sought the presence of Colonel House to overrule Pershing at a meeting at Versailles in June. House told the President that he thought he ought not to be used in this fashion, and he did not attend the meeting. At Versailles, fresh from his stirring address to the Chamber of Deputies, when the German Aisne offensive looked to be threatening Paris – '*Je me bats devant Paris; Je me bats en Paris; je me bats derrière Paris*' – Clemenceau, with Lloyd George in support, fought for the continuation of the priority scheme which would, probably, have deferred the formation of the AEF as a concentrated American army indefinitely. Pershing stood fast and gave only a little ground – the London . Agreement with six divisions less artillery and supply trains in June and four in July.

In June, the British attitude changed. On 28 June, General Walter Kirke, then Deputy Director of Military Operations at the War Office, wrote in a memorandum: 'The Americans have seen recently that their untrained troops have more fighting value than veteran French divisions', and he went on to recommend that as further efforts to retain American infantry would embitter relations, they should help rather than hinder the formation of an American army. The French, forced to concede that point, *first* tried to postpone the organisation of a distinct American army and *second* tried to employ its corps on different fronts once they came into existence.[13] A price the Americans had to pay for the piecemeal shipment of their divisions was that it delayed the integration of the infantry with their supporting troops and gave service troops a low priority. These two factors go some way to explain their failures in the Meuse-Argonne. When Baker was next in France in September, it was discovered that there was a gap of a million men between the War Department's eighty division plan and that of General Headquarters. There may have been two causes of this. First, the War Department plan omitted Supply from the total when it considered the Goethals plan; second, each corps initially consisted of four active divisions and two holding divisions but, on 30 August, five of the six divisions had been designated for combat, which increased the requirement for replacements. In early October GHQ had to break up divisions. In fact, the estimate of the replacements required had been miscalculated from the beginning. General Fox Conner informed the War College that each division had required 8,000 replacements before it got into the line. Put another way, 55,000 men passed through the ranks of some divisions before they reached France.

The comment of Peyton March about Pershing's unwillingness to accept directions from Foch is unfair, perhaps. Pershing had to show that good, red American blood flowed in his veins or he would have had no American army to command. When it came to which operations that army should undertake, Pershing did accept its committal to the Meuse-Argonne instead of exploiting the St Mihiel battle towards Metz as he wished. His reluctance to concede its divisions to French and British over-all command during the crisis months of March to May 1918 infuriated men who were hard-pressed to halt the Germans, but hold them they did, without substantial American assistance. However, American assistance was significant in two respects. AEF divisions that fought were blooded and successful, creating an invaluable expectation of success in American ranks everywhere; and the sheer numbers of Americans that were seen to have arrived in the summer refreshed the sagging French morale. In effect, American enthusiasm convinced the French that *Les Yankees* could achieve, albeit at high cost, what they, themselves, had not attempted since 1914.

What impression did its experience in France leave on the US Army's memory? Enthusiasm is a starting point. The Meuse-Argonne was a shock to American confidence, but the Armistice and victory ensured that it would have no lasting effect. Regular soldiers who studied all aspects of it after the war were convinced that had the fighting continued they would have corrected the weaknesses in the AEF. Fox Conner's list of lessons of the war included the observation: 'You need very few Napoleon Bonapartes in war but you need a lot of superb G-4s and above all you need good company and battalion commanders'. That allusion to the weak performance of the AEF in both departments, suggested his comment that any army with complete divisions ready in peacetime, in every detail, to fight, had an advantage which mere numbers could not overcome. 'The tail-end of a war is very unlike the beginning and we may not always be lucky enough to be tail-enders', was a reminder to War College students of the incompleteness of the AEF experience. The drift of his reflections, offered in 1933, was that the United States should not again raise an army from scratch at the outbreak of war and expect to be successful. It was a warning which professional soldiers have often sounded and which has, as often, fallen on deaf ears in Britain and America.

The last was a vital truth. Fortunately, it was one that George Catlett Marshall, who had been an operations staff officer at GHQ, at First US Army and in the 1st Division, had fully grasped. When he became Chief of Army Staff in 1939, he prepared the divisions that would inevitably be needed and as far as possible saw that they were equipped with American weapons. If he could ensure it, another AEF would not be dependent on its allies nor would its operations be subordinated to their chosen strategy. The two principal requirements mentioned by Fox Conner were less easy to supply. So it was that the American supply system in the Second World War in NW Europe proved seriously deficient. Nor was it possible to satisfy the huge demand for good junior infantry leaders – but that was common to both the British and American armies.

The 'enthusiasm' of the 1918 AEF was transferred to the American Forces in Europe a generation later, together with the disregard for casualties that would then, had it been continued into 1919, have led to a backlash in popular opinion. In some senses, neither the public nor the regular officer corps had quite grasped the realities of war at the battalion level in 1918. In Britain, it was quite different. The memory of the war was of failure and stalemate, and of the casualties that any attacker would suffer in the next war. The successes of 1918, and the means by which they had been obtained – no less than the development of land/air warfare – were overlaid by the gloom of the earlier years. Besides, the British casualty rates of 1918 had been as great as those of the years of failure. Americans had not experienced the bloody deadlock of 1915–17. They retained the offensive spirit with which the British had started their war in 1914. They had 'enjoyed' the successes of 1918 but since they had not had to extrapolate the statistics of their casualties into 1919 the price of their successes had not sunk in. They had paid only perfunctory attention to the details of British achievements in the Hundred Days of 1918, in which the decisive blows that finished the war had been struck.

What survived in the mental attitude to tactics and strategy in the American army's officer corps was akin to the French belief in 1914 in the offensive spirit. That was good but, unadjusted to reality, it had much to do with the severe casualties that their divisions suffered on the German frontier in the autumn and winter of 1944/45 a generation later.

We have now reached the half-way point in our study. We have seen how the

British entered the First World War without any properly constituted machinery for the higher direction of the nation's war effort or even for the formulation of national strategy. Yet their commitment to a continental war at once involved them, albeit as the junior partner, in a coalition which would dominate the nation's life for four long years of bitter conflict.

From a position in which French, as C-in-C of the BEF, was effectively controlled by the politicians at home, and particularly by the formidable figure of Kitchener, the Secretary of State for War, moved to the very different story of Douglas Haig's command of a greatly expanded BEF, revealing how his shrewd conduct of his relations with the French High Command and his deft handling of his arch enemy Lloyd George – first as Secretary of State and then as Prime Minister – put him in a virtually impregnable position. No British general had ever commanded such a huge Commonwealth-based force before and he soon became a towering figure and a national hero in the eyes of the British people. Despite the mounting criticism and tide of political opposition to his unshakeable policy of waging a war of relentless attrition against the German Army on the Western Front, and to the heavy price in blood that such a policy demanded, his dominating personality and his constituency of close supporters (which included the King), had made it politically impossible to remove him.

Back in Whitehall, the CIGS, Sir William Robertson, played a sterling role for two years as the guardian of Haig's back when the political battle was getting rough. A principal lesson from that period is the great danger inherent in a situation when there is no mutual trust between the military and political leaders of a country at war. It is impossible not to recognise the crucial and often decisive part played by personality, not only the personalities of the men at the very top of the nations' affairs but also of the senior commanders in the field. In our study of Third Ypres, for example, we saw how one of the root causes of the disaster which it became was Haig's stubborn refusal to listen to the sage advice of two of his army commanders, both of whom were far better tacticians than he. As for the working of the Coalition, it was the personalities of Joffre, Foch and Haig, in spite of their differences, which kept the ship afloat and ultimately made it possible to achieve a unified command structure under a French supremo. In contrast, it was the cunning, underhand personality of Sir Henry Wilson, working on the susceptibilities of Lloyd George, that very nearly put that ship on the rocks.

Whatever may be thought of Lloyd George's political manoeuvring, it has to be conceded that it was thanks to him that the bones of a structured system of control of the national war effort was built up during that first great war, a structure that would supply some of the elements from which an infinitely more sophisticated and efficient system would emerge in the Second World War, as we shall see in the coming chapters. We shall see too how the precedent of unified command within a coalition would be developed.

In Chapter 3 we considered the revolution in warfare that was brought about by new technology, creating a major stepping stone towards the much more complex and scientific pattern of war on land, in the air and at sea of the years 1939–45 – a war of movement for which many had longed in the First World War but which, for a host of reasons, which we have considered, was impossible until the resistance of one side or the other had broken.

The story of America's complete unpreparedness for war in 1917 and of Pershing's struggles with Washington to enable him to create a field army that was fit to fight on the Western Front, forms the background against which many of the attitudes, policies and decisions of the United States in 1941–45 should be seen. America's late entry into the First World War and her contribution to final victory at an infinitely lower cost than that paid by either of her principal allies, generated a certain conviction of American superiority and, perhaps, of contempt for those who had fought for so long and with only spasmodic success, growing physically and economically exhausted in the process. In the chapters which follow, we examine the strengths and weaknesses of a great new coalition in a war that was utterly unlike its predecessor but in which, once again, the personality factor was to overshadow all else. Of particular interest is the way in which the question of dependence had swung through a full 180 degrees. In 1917–18, the Americans had perforce had to depend very largely upon the French and British for many of their immediate needs. Now it would be America herself that became the universal provider and would thereby acquire enormous powers of persuasion over her Alliance partners with all the consequences that this would have not only upon the strategy of the Alliance and the relationship between its most senior figures but also upon the day-to-day conduct of operations.

CHAPTER 9

LEADERS AND COMMITTEES: WASHINGTON AND LONDON IN 1943

We, (the Americans) lost our shirts and . . . are now committed to a subterranean umbilicus operation in mid summer . . . We came, we listened and were conquered . . . From a worms-eye viewpoint it was apparent that we were confronted by generations and generations of experience in committee work and in rationalising points of view. They (the British) had us on the defensive practically all the time.

MAJOR-GENERAL A WEDEMEYER USA, SENIOR AMERICAN PLANNING OFFICER ON THE
CASABLANCA CONFERENCE, SYMBOL.[1]

SYMBOL, one in the series of Anglo-American conferences that began with ARCADIA in December 1941, was convened in January, 1943 to decide the strategy of the Allies after the defeat of the Axis forces in North Africa had been completed. The chief question to be settled was whether to keep up the pressure in the Mediterranean, with the aim of knocking Italy out of the Axis and the war, the British view; or to concentrate on the invasion of North-West Europe, the American view. The Americans had already deferred to the British by postponing the cross-channel invasion in favour of intervention in Africa, TORCH, and clearly a subsequent landing in Sicily would preclude a 'D-day' in Europe until 1944.

General Wedemeyer's chagrin at the outcome of SYMBOL and how the straight-forward, plain-dealing Americans were outwitted by the devious, self-seeking British illuminates a certain American (military) point of view, but it is mistaken. The British did not have 'generations and generations of experience in committee work.' In fact, their apparatus for coordinating

150

the formulation of grand strategy in a cabinet system of government operating through separate departments was new, its beginnings no earlier than 1916 as we have seen. The British bureaucrats and military staffs, alternately chivvied and inspired by Churchill, had only just learnt how to use it. We are not here concerned with the validity of the great strategic decisions taken at SYMBOL, or elsewhere. The question we propose to discuss is, in the perspective of high command, how the governmental machinery of the United States and Britain was organised to manage war, and the approach to it by the President and the Prime Minister (also Minister of Defence) respectively; closely connected and interacting when every great issue was discussed.

SYMBOL taught the Americans a lesson they were quick to learn. In future, beginning with TRIDENT (the second Washington conference. May 1943), they put forward their views in a more coherent and convincing way, but there remained a difficulty at the very summit of the hierarchy of command. President Roosevelt did not admit his two great and powerful chiefs of staff into his confidence. The fundamental principle of United States grand strategy had been decided: that the liberation of Europe and the defeat of Germany should have priority over the war against Japan. ('Germany First', or 'Plan Dog' (D).) The first was the province of General George C Marshall, the second of Admiral EJ King, and the two were at loggerheads.* Only the President could make them pull together evenly in double-harness. In the US army's eyes King, (who as a sailor was, understandably a 'Pacific-firster') was a wrecker. As Colonel Eisenhower, then head of the Army Operations Planning Division (OPD) in Washington confided to his diary: 'One thing that might help in this war is to get someone to shoot King. He's the antithesis of cooperation – a deliberately rude person – which means that he is a mental bully.[2]

When Marshall testified before Congress in May 1943, he hinted at this difficulty, agreeing that his immediate task was to build up supporting staffs to assist Chiefs of Staff in their principal task of formulating strategy. He explained that the British Chiefs of Staff were linked to the British War Cabinet, presided over by the Prime Minister, by a large and efficient secretariat. As a result, the views of the BCOS were in tune with government policy. In the United States such a channel of communication between the JCS and the President had so far not been established. A little later Marshall proposed to James Byrnes, then Director of Economic

---

* The US Chiefs of Staff were known as the 'Joint Chiefs of Staff (JCS) the British as (BCOS) and when sitting together, as the 'Combined Chiefs of Staff (CCS).

Stabilisation and a kind of Assistant President that this should be done. Extending the same theme, an officer in the OPD observed that British planners could count on all the departments of state and agencies to act according to an agreed policy[3], but that 'the great play of partisan politics in our government militates strongly against integration between our services and other departments except the State Department,' adding that even with the State Department the way plans were coordinated left much to be desired.[4]

It was generally believed that Churchill was too apt to interfere in operational matters that were not, strictly speaking, his concern, while Roosevelt erred in the other direction. Such criticisms are too facile. When dealing with grand strategy Roosevelt was arguing from strength, since the United States was the arsenal of the Alliance, and controlling the sinews of war he could control its strategy using a 'hands off' style of management. He could leave purely military matters to Marshall, although that may not have been his expressed intention. Churchill was a client, and therefore he, and the BCOS, had to argue with force and logic that the courses of action they put forward, requiring American resources to be put into effect, were in the common interest. British anxieties hinged around manpower, shipping and oil. Of these three shipping was the key.

In a nutshell, the British had available 30 million tons of shipping to import all the resources she required to fight a war including the invaluable manpower from India and the Commonwealth. In peace the British economy depended about equally on trade with Europe and with the rest of the world. Therefore, the loss of the European market was a colossal disruption. The preoccupation of the British with the Empire obscured from foreign eyes the importance of Europe to her and also that apart from her imperial interests, some economic, some not, Britain had other long-standing commitments world-wide outside the Empire. In strategic terms, she had struggled since the eighteenth century to reconcile her non-European with her European relations and found them to be continually in conflict. Since 1940, her European trade dead in the water, Britain's very life depended on trade with the rest of the world and on the ships in which it was carried. In a larger sense, the war forcibly brought home to Britain, as it had in 1914–18, that she was a European power and that she could no longer support her imperial role as well. The Americans were slow to draw the essential conclusions from these facts. Though the United States was a great maritime power, economically she was self-contained. Therefore the Americans could devote most of their mercantile fleet to the support of military operations, mainly in the Pacific. The British required most of theirs to maintain their war economy.

These realities have to be considered in light of the respective personalities of the Prime Minister and the President, their perceptions of the war situation as it actually was, and the post war situation as they hoped it might be. Churchill never ceased to attempt the impossible; to preserve Britain's position as a powerful voice in the future of post-war Europe, and at the same time to secure her imperial interests, especially in India, South-East Asia and the Far East. (He was, of course, emotionally incapable of contemplating, let alone accepting that the image of the Empire that possessed him was obsolete, and that the real Commonwealth and Empire was in the early stages of dissolution.) Churchill's vision extended beyond a mere war-time alliance to when the United States would become the leading power in a free world with Britain as a partner, and brought all his eloquence and imagination to bear on the propagation of this grand (if chauvinistic) idea. It was a prospect enticing to any American for whom the British did not live permanently under the shadow of George III and the American revolution. Others, whose world-view was narrow and traditionally isolationist, saw Churchill's interventions in Allied strategy as ploys to further British interests, ignoring their real motives.

Churchill's position arose from and was ruled by political weakness. He was master of a coalition government only so long as it was confident that he would in the end lead the country to victory. He was the suppliant and client of the United States. He had had to strike ruinous deals with her in 1940 and 1941 after British credit and trade had collapsed under the demands of a war impossible for Britain to meet. Roosevelt, in contrast, while he had to feel the pulse and be sensitive to the mood of Congress, was under no obligation to justify the strategy recommended by his military advisers to any third party. Military victory, defined as the unconditional surrender of the Germans and Japanese, was all that mattered. Like President Wilson, he had no territorial ambitions for his country, but if, when the fires had died down and the smoke had cleared, the Stars and Stripes could be seen flying triumphantly in Europe and the far Pacific, no American would fail to rejoice. Nevertheless, when it came to the brass tacks on consultation and decision, the President was, in the eyes of his Service chiefs, far more erratic and just as enigmatic as the British found Churchill.

By the end of 1942, the Americans were ready to assert their predominance, having started with the moral disadvantage of being, compared with the British, green in the actual practice of warfare. (Dunkirk and Singapore had been eclipsed by Pearl Harbour and Manila, and the first clashes of American troops with the Germans had not redounded to the credit of American arms.) That was now behind them, but what they lacked was, as the sagacious Marshall had perceived and the jealous Wedemeyer had noted with resentment, machinery for coordinating the management of a global war. The Americans arrived at Casablanca as if for a pow-wow, each war-chief ready to expound his views; the British with briefs prepared in advance and one of HM ships in attendance as a floating command post and communication centre, ready to supply Churchill and the BCOS with any fresh evidence or information that was required in the course of the conference. No one can seriously argue today that at Casablanca the Allies took a wrong turning, or that an invasion of northern France was practicable in 1942. What the Americans felt, and felt bitterly at the time, was that they had been out-smarted over TORCH and at Casablanca, by superior British advocacy.

As we have seen, in the earlier war the British had developed a promising if rudimentary organisation for the higher control of the war and the war effort, while the Americans, learning on the job, were still learning at the Armistice. In fact, the British expertise that made so sharp an impact at Casablanca was a post-1918 development stemming from the Committee of Imperial Defence, first established in 1904. The CID, originally a cabinet committee chaired by the Prime Minister, served as an advisory, not an executive body. It was relegated to suspended animation during 1914–18 although Hankey's secretariat was modelled on it. In 1923 the Chiefs of Staff Committee was established as a sub-committee of the CID, which gave rise to dependent all-military committees for Joint Planning in 1927 and Joint Intelligence in 1936.[5] This was logical and far-sighted, these being 'joint' concerns, while personnel, equipment, supply and logistics were single service.[6] In time the CID spawned sub-committees to deal with all aspects of national defence. Ministers chaired those concerned with their departmental responsibilities. To deal with the Abyssinian crisis of 1935, when it appeared as if Italy and Britain were on a collision course, the CID with the Prime Minister in the chair became a war committee with executive powers. By 1939, a complex of committees covered finance, industrial matters, the administration of the country in time of war, and made plans for re-armament and mobilisation. Flexibility was the system's great assct.

Another strength of the CID as an institution was that it was educative. Dealing with national defence in the widest sense, its military members learnt to look at the political dimension of defence questions, the politicians at military realities, and both at the economic and industrial infrastructure. The criticism so frequently levelled by Americans at 'making war by committee' was not valid, since it ignored the obvious:

modern warfare was too complex an affair for any one man, however brilliant, to manage and at least he required a flow of accurate information and estimates. In any case an organisation is only good as the men who are available to work it. Admittedly, the work was very demanding. Those involved had to be blessed with nous, patience, mental stamina, a wide knowledge of affairs outside their own field and view strategy in a national context, and indeed in a coalition war, the interests of the Alliance as a whole.

The capstone of the system was positioned only in 1940. In the inter-war years, when defence was seldom the pre-occupation of a prime minister, a cabinet office was needed to implement the recommendations of the CID and coordinate the three services on his behalf. The question was examined by the Salisbury* Committee which had recommended setting up the Chief of Staff (COS) committee, conspicuously lacking in 1914–18. Its further and far-seeing recommendation for a Minister of Defence, to be the deputy chairman of the CID, and to be a 'super-chief of a War Staff in Commission' consisting of the First Lord of the Admiralty and the Secretaries of State for War (Army) and Air together with the COS was not accepted, or only in part, and gradually. The heads of the ministries of state (the three Services, the Home Office, the Board of Trade and so on) continued to be individually responsible for executive action. In 1936 Sir Thomas Inskip was appointed Minister for the *Coordination* of Defence, but without the power to take executive action. It was not until the eve of war in August 1939 that a Ministry of Supply (i.e., war supplies) was created, and not until Churchill assumed the office of Prime Minister and Defence Minister, in April 1940, that the Salisbury recommendation was adopted. It was Churchill who finally breathed life and energy into the system. When he returned to the Admiralty he, looking as usual beyond his strict departmental responsibilities, set up a committee under his chairmanship to consider war strategy, (referred to in the Admiralty as 'The Crazy Gang'). Churchill, so often seen from the military and popular angle as imaginative and impulsive and an orator in the old style, was in fact a firm believer in order and system, and concise, precise written work. Like Lloyd George, he set up his own secretariat, but Lieutenant General Sir Hastings Ismay, as its head, also sat with the COS committee as his liaison officer. He ran the war as Prime Minister and Minister of Defence through a small War Cabinet, relying for intimate advice on the COS (notably the CIGS) and a few cronies; Beaverbrook,* Brendan Bracken,[†] and Professor Lindemann.[‡]

* JEH Gascoyne, 4th Marquis of Salisbury (1861–1947), Lord President of the Council and Lord Privy Seal 1922–23 and 1924–29, Conservative politician.

The CID, or rather its title, disappeared. However, in effect it lived on in the well-thought-out structure of secretariat committees linked to the war cabinet. The Chiefs of Staff allocated responsibility for consultation and executive action in military matters.§ To say this is not to imply that everything became perfect at a stroke. It took time for the system to work up to full efficiency, to avoid such fiascos as the British interventions in Norway and Greece, reconcile differences between rival chiefs of staff, and for Churchill to find men to stand up to him, yet with whom he could work, like Alan Brooke (CIGS and Chairman of the COS) and Charles Portal (Chief of Air Staff). Powerful though Churchill's position was, the role of the COS as his professional military advisers and, when necessary, as a restraining hand on some of his wilder ideas and ambitions, was crucial to the outcome of the war. Bully and rave though he might, there is no record of his ever deliberately flouting their advice. As in politics, so in the direction of Service matters, character played an enormous part. Both nationally and internationally the sheer professionalism of Alan Brooke and the quiet wisdom of Charles Portal made a vital contribution – as, of course, did the magisterial figure of George Marshall for the Americans. But how different things were in Washington, we shall soon see.

The literature of the Second World War, vast in itself, includes volumes of criticism directed at Britain's failure to prepare either mentally or in material terms for modern warfare. However, in terms of War Planning, the British were not as ill-prepared and, in consequence, armed themselves remarkably quickly. The national war effort was fully developed by 1942 but British achievements up to 1940 are not to be dismissed lightly, bearing in mind that the decision to prepare a new British Expeditionary Force to send to France was only taken after the Munich crisis in September 1938. What is sometimes overlooked is that the mobilisation of British industry for war was able

* WM Aitken 1st Baron Beaverbrook (1879–1964). b. Maple, Ontario. Businessman, newspaper magnate, Conservative politician, Minister of Information under Lloyd George, Minister of Supply under Churchill 1941–42.

† Brendan Bracken (1901–1958). 1st Viscount, journalist (*Financial Times* and *Economist*), Minister of Information 1941–45.

‡ FA Lindemann (1886–1957). 1st Viscount Cherwell, of German ancestry and education. Distinguished scientist with wide interests and Churchill's adviser; responsible for encouraging many scientific innovations in the war.

§ There was, it should be noted, no Chief of Staff of the Armed Forces; that and the unification of the Service departments only took place, after intensive debate, in the post-war era. The 'super chief of staff' was Churchill himself.

to overtake the German, though starting far behind it. British military expenditure as a proportion of the GNP, less than half that of Germany in 1938, had risen to 80 per cent in 1939 and was a third more in 1940.[7] This rapid growth did not, obviously, mean that the quality of the equipment produced was ideal, though it can be said that where there had been previous research and development, some of it, notably aircraft and artillery, was excellent. The fundamental difference between the German and British positions in 1939 was that the *Reichswehr* was well-prepared for a short war while the British were beginning to convert their economy for a long haul. That Hitler failed to prepare for a long haul too, until his invasion of Russia turned into a war of attrition, was a decisive material factor in his final defeat but as important was the superiority of Britain's war management over Hitler's individual intuition and audacity which was proved from 1942 onwards.

A comparison between the British and American systems of war-management should take into account the constitutional relationship between the executive arm of the government and the legislature. In the British, the Prime Minister and the ministers of the departments of state are members of the legislature, open to questioning in Parliament and able to explain and defend their actions. Legislation has to be carried through by a slow process of discussion from the first tabling of a 'white paper' to enactment, but as long as the Prime Minister and his Cabinet enjoy the support of a majority of the House of Commons they are free to take whatever executive action they consider necessary. In war time, Churchill, although scrupulous about making himself available in the House and in keeping his ministerial colleagues informed, was free in his double capacity as Premier and Minister of Defence to take such initiatives as the situation demanded, and the heads of ministries and service chiefs to manage their affairs as they saw fit.

Balance through conflict rather than cooperation is one of the underlying principles of the American Constitution. It militated against an unchallenged concentration of power in the executive, as might have been the result if a single, supreme director of the war effort, assisted by a secretariat supplying facts on its every aspect as in the British model, were allowed to arise. Hence the President, as chief executive, was restricted by the jealous supervision Congress was able to exert over military affairs using its right to vote funds in detail, divided under the various budgetary heads ('Votes' in British usage). This enabled Congress to interfere in matters such as internal service policy, organisation and appointments, which in other countries are left to the head of the department concerned and his professional Service advisers. Congress had the power to call senior officers before it for questioning, as we have seen George Marshall was called. The other side of this constitutional struggle was that the chiefs of the Armed Services saw themselves as servants of the Republic under the President as their commander-in-chief but also as semi-independent war-lords, fighting for their share of the pie before Congress. Cooperation with each other did not come naturally to them. As we shall see, the committee system in which cooperation might have been practised, was vestigial. An end product of the Americans' political conditioning was that they over-simplified the differences between their own and the British way of running the war into 'making war by committee' as opposed to their own more virile 'war by command decision'. More to the point was the different perception of the British and Americans of the aims and nature of the combined war effort. The British, and this was before Churchill's advent as 'war lord', hoping that the war against Germany would be a re-run of 1914, sent a small expeditionary force to France, hastily organised and far inferior in relative terms to the 'Old Contemptibles' in training and equipment. This hope died with the collapse of France in 1940. British and German strategy then diverged. The Luftwaffe was neither strong enough nor suitably equipped to subdue Britain by air-power alone. Hitler, always preferring the quick kill, feared to put his fortune to the test by invading Britain, for a number of reasons. Instead he embarked on BARBAROSSA, his massive invasion of the Soviet Union, hoping for another lightning success.

Churchill was therefore committed to a holding strategy, and even that had to be carried on with resources inadequate for its modest objectives; building up the army at home and the strategic bomber force and, most difficult of all, a re-run of the anti-submarine war. The war in the Mediterranean was essential, but ancillary. Its purpose was to engage the enemy, and to be seen to be engaging him. Hope of strategic success there was none, short of some violent change in the nature of the war. Churchill's tremendous boast: 'Give us the tools, and we will finish the job' seems empty, but in political terms nicely calculated. He had at all costs to avoid alarming the powerful isolationist element that existed in the United States. (Not only isolationist, but anti-British, or anti-Imperialist. An America that had stood aloof when France fell was hardly likely to rally to the cause of England.) It was a strategy that paid. By 1942, after BARBAROSSA, and after Pearl Harbour had rudely propelled the United States into war, the British war-machine, schooled by adversity, was working well. Churchill had never, even at the nadir of British fortunes, lost sight of the strategic imperative, that sooner or later Britain would have to assume the offensive. The question was when and where.

The American perception agreed with the British whole-heartedly as regards the paramountcy of the offensive principle, but being more impetuous and more direct, mistook the British preference for 'appreciating the situation' and weighing the merits of different courses as pusillanimous. The British were all for cooperation and acting in concert. The Americans detected in this the underhand motive of harnessing American muscle to serve British strategic aims, and worse, *subjecting* it to British aims. We must remember that their experience in 1917–18 had made a lasting impression on the American military mind. It is hardly necessary to remind the reader that the American Expeditionary Force had been faced with all the difficulties that the British had overcome with great travail in 1914–16 – of how to make a staff work, of devising tactics and building an administration – and on top of that it had been the client of France for up to date weapons and equipment and training, and of the British for shipping and training and horses. Pershing had had to fight hard to protect the integrity of the AEF, and to resist specious demands that its units should be used as reinforcements for the French or British.[8] Pershing had also had to fight a hard battle within his own camp over the question of where the final authority for military decisions lay: with him as commander-in-chief, or with the Chief of Staff in Washington.

Those experiences survived most strongly in the Chief of the United States Army, George Catlett Marshall. To take the last point first, recalling the destructive struggle between his great predecessor, C Peyton March and Pershing, he was determined to be the master. In that he was supremely successful. He retained the confidence of the President (not an easy feat), he prevailed over Admiral King and the 'Pacific First' lobby, judging correctly that Hitler had to be defeated and the Russians sustained, and that the Japanese war could wait. He won Pershing's battle before it could be re-started, asserting the integrity of US forces in Europe and their clear-cut, single mission, the defeat of Germany. As we are recounting a clash of interest between Britain and the United States we emphasise that General Marshall was not only an outstanding soldier. He was also a man of great integrity and fair-mindedness. He did not suffer from the insularity and chauvinism that marred say, able commanders like Bradley, Patton or Stilwell. On the contrary, he understood the British position and, recognising Field-Marshal Sir John Dill as a man with the same qualities as himself, formed a relationship with him that was, until Dill's tour in Washington ended in his death through illness, of the utmost benefit to the Alliance.[9]*

* F-M Sir John Dill was CIGS until his commonsense and caution irritated
Churchill so much that he relieved him of the post, appointing Alan Brooke in his
place, and sending him off to Washington as head of the British Staff Mission and
secretary to the Combined Chiefs of Staff. So greatly was he honoured in the US
that he is buried in Arlington and his grave marked by an equestrian statue.

Marshall was a patriot whose ambition was to see the United States Army prove its worth in Europe, and under an all-American command. Balked, like his British counterpart, Alan Brooke, from exercising high command in the field because he was indispensable to the head of his government, he used his great authority and the respect, even fear, in which he was held by American generals, including his protégé Eisenhower, to ensure that no delegation or dilution of American authority took place, unless it was essential and unavoidable, and temporary. He had also sound political reasons for this. As he had bested the Pacific lobby, it was important for the American public to see the US army playing the leading role in Europe in pursuit of the specifically American goal.*

Such were the soldierly pre-occupations and patriotic ambitions of George Marshall. They have to be seen in the wider perspective of American foreign and domestic policy, the responsibility of the President. By temperament and ability, Marshall was uniquely fitted for the delicate balancing task that faced him from 1939, when he was appointed Chief of the Army Staff, until December 1941, when Pearl Harbour brought the Americans into the war. Roosevelt had no doubt that though, by virtue of her power and resources and geographical isolation, the United States was not endangered as Britain and Soviet Russia were endangered, their downfall and the consequent German hegemony over Europe was not in America's interest, as President Wilson had seen in 1917. All the same, Roosevelt had to proceed with the utmost circumspection, taking care not to alarm the isolationists amongst the general public and more importantly, in Congress. He had also to avoid provoking the Japanese, and the Germans in particular by overt cooperation with the British, such as the security of the Atlantic sea-routes.

Whereas Marshall was the advocate of cooperation, a full exchange of information and a defence secretariat on the British model, his Commander-in-Chief, the President, adroit politician as he was, was disposed to keep his grand plan in his own head, his cards close to his chest, and confide in no-one. Until lines of battle on both sides were declared, he kept the activities of the various departments of state insulated from each other. The scope of military liaison with the BCOS was not coordinated with political missions. (These were sometimes supplementary to the formal diplomatic link.) The Armed Forces with a necessary interest in war

---

* E.g., when in Tunisia, the US formations in the British army were united under US command for the final offensive, and in Italy, when Clarke, without reproof, disobeyed Alexander's instructions and broke away to liberate Rome with a US Corps.

production, were distanced from the supply of food, machine-tools and war equipment to Britain. Roosevelt's progress on an all-out war effort was by the methods of 'grandmother's footsteps',* disguised by the anodyne catch-phrases: 'Hemisphere Defence', 'The US as the Arsenal of Democracy' to 'All action short of war'.

To explain how this constrained the work of the Chief of the Army Staff and the War Department, it is necessary to return briefly to the Department's predicament in 1917–18. It will be remembered that Pershing had claimed that he served directly under the President as AEF Commander-in-Chief. Although the channel of communication was through the Secretary of the Army Department, he regarded himself as the superior of the Chief of Staff of the Army. After the war, Congress followed his line when it limited the size and responsibility of the General Staff in Washington, but left the staff of the Field Force commander alone. A policy already outdated in 1918, it would be entirely impracticable in a multi-front war, in which there would be several overseas commanders-in-chief. Nevertheless, the idea lived on in the mobilisation plans, which assumed that the Chief of Staff would take to the field as Commander-in-Chief and be replaced in the War Department by his deputy.[†] He would take the War Plans Division (WPD) with him as his staff, while the peace-time commander of the field force became his chief of staff. In 1914, this procedure had left the British War Office denuded of its principal staff officers and incompetent for nearly eighteen months. Fortunately, that outmoded plan was discarded by Marshall when war finally came in 1941. After two years of preparatory work by the General Staff and other departments and with an immense programme for mobilising an army of over a hundred divisions to implement, Marshall had to remain in the War Department to manage it. By remaining in Washington he made it clear that the position of the Army Chief of Staff was paramount. He made his office in Washington into a command post and, instead of taking his War Plans Division (WPD) into the field, he renamed it the Operations Planning Division (OPD) and allotted it the Pacific and Atlantic theatres, responsibility for which had previously been divided between the WPD and the War

---

* The children's game, in which the players move with short steps when the eyes of the observer are not on them, freezing when they are. A player fairly detected in motion is 'out'. Also called 'Statues'.

† This procedure derived from the original Prussian model, the reason being that the author of the war plan was the best man to carry it out. Von Moltke (the 'Elder') moved from the Defence Ministry to take command at Königgratz, his nephew did the same in 1914, as did Sir John French, and General Gort in 1939.

Department General Staffs. Marshall made himself a commander-in-chief in Washington and the indisputable head of the United States Army.

Marshall's reorganisation strengthened his position in the Joint Chiefs of Staff (JCS) *vis-a-vis* King and the Navy and his power to influence events in Europe where the Army would be the main agent of American policy. The JCS was only established in February 1942 as a result of the first meetings with the British the previous December in Washington (ARCADIA). Its origin was the Joint Board (JB) which had existed since 1903 to discuss problems common to the Army and Navy and to recommend action.[10] The JB consisted of four officers from each service who were first appointed by name and later designated by office, which institutionalised the Board. In 1914, in pursuit of his policy of unpreparedness, President Wilson issued verbal instructions for its meetings to be suspended. After the war the JB was reformed and in 1919 a Joint Planning Committee was added to it as a sub-committee, in which the WPD was represented. In July 1939, President Roosevelt placed the Board, together with others dealing with economic and supply matters, under his own direction and supervision as Commander-in-Chief. Just before Pearl Harbour, a Joint Intelligence Committee was formed and the system began to take the shape of a rudimentary inter-service advisory body. However, as the Board avoided matters which could only be settled by a superior authority, it was not linked to the Administration as was the BCOS. Its powers within the military community were no wider than those of its individual members. It was not until February 1942 that, following the British example, the JCS replaced the JB and inherited its committees.[11]

The JCS still lacked an organic link with the President such as the BCOS had with the Prime Minister. Admiral D Leahy, the President's chief of staff, had a function similar to that of Ismay in London, but his position was not the same. As chairman of the JCS he was on the military side of the fence, never able to bridge the gap when Roosevelt chose to keep his own counsel about his conversations with individuals outside the Cabinet, such as Harry Hopkins, or those within it such as Secretary of the Treasury, Henry Morgenthau.[12] The President chose not to pin himself down by placing himself at the centre of a committee system. As Marshall had observed to Byrnes, the President had no executive secretariat to keep records of presidential decisions that he ought to have passed to the JCS as a matter of routine. He frequently kept the JCS in the dark and his relations with it were neither regular nor frank. On a number of occasions, Marshall learned of communications between Churchill and Roosevelt from Sir John Dill. Dill sympathised with Marshall's position and briefed him.[13] The time devoted by Marshall and his colleagues in the JCS plotting how to steer the President away from undesirable initiatives could have been better spent.[14]

The disadvantages in conducting important business along such lines seems so obvious that the reason why sensible men adopted it requires an explanation for those other than Americans, who are unfamiliar with constitutional history. It was not until long after the American Revolution, or the War of Independence when the Americans finally abandoned the notion that the defence of the United States could best be entrusted to a militia of citizens in arms and created a standing army, together with a corps of educated and trained officers. They feared that a standing, professional army might become an instrument of tyranny, as the British Army had appeared in American eyes. The Army therefore, and more importantly the General Staff, required to be constantly scrutinised and checked by Congress, a system which led naturally to general officers acting with one eye on it and the other on the military chain of command. The tyrant had been George III, and the temptations of absolute power in their own executive had to be prevented. To obtain a measure of liberty of action, a President like Roosevelt, faced continually by a war situation demanding foresight and immediate action, was forced to adopt political manoeuvres of Byzantine deviousness. Compared with him, a British Prime Minister, though answerable to the Cabinet and the members of the House of Commons, was relatively free and untrammelled. The British system has been not inaccurately described as an 'elective dictatorship'.

American interdepartmental and interpersonal relationships were in part a power-game between rivals which was, to the British, an invisible factor in their international relationship. The experience of the two sides in the many committee meetings and conferences contradicted the stereotype each had of the other. The British were expected to be formal stuffed shirts. In fact the security of the British Prime Minister's position made for informality. The first impression of the Americans was that they were flippant. The British expected the Americans to be rugged individualists with a candid shirt sleeves manner; they appeared formal and ponderous. Nevertheless, the administrative training of the British had taught them the value of formal channels and regular meetings. They prepared their cases carefully and argued patiently and logically on their merits. The frequency of their meetings taught them that strongly expressed but unsubstantiated opinions were wasted in committees, whose members were easily fatigued by sermons instead of facts, but a certain lightness of touch was also essential. The Americans were used to a dog-eat-dog struggle between the Services. Lobbying congressional committees and White House officials on their own behalf did not require closely reasoned military arguments and

163

did not advance the cause of national defence which should have been regarded dispassionately and as a whole. Now they had to join a game that was already being played according to British rules which they did not particularly like. They were used to politicking, but not to the kind that tried to run wars by committee. Americans believed, as a matter of principle, in solving a problem by appointing one man to handle it, as in business management: i.e., the paramountcy of *command*. The British regarded the conduct of war at the top as political; the art of the possible. Compromises and flexibility were required to deal with its uncertainties. They felt that the Americans liked to ignore war's uncertainties caused by the enemy as though a command decision somehow made them irrelevant. Patton, typically, once exclaimed that intelligence and possible enemy intentions never worried him: it was what *he* was about to do to the *enemy* that mattered. Stilwell despised conferences, which he called 'walla-wallas'. To Americans, a decision was action, and they liked action because it demonstrated character. Dwight D Eisenhower, who was to be appointed to supreme command, followed this line of thought; ironically, since he himself was essentially a committee man who left operational planning entirely to committees, and was anything but a man of action. Eisenhower may have expressed his theoretical objections to command by committee, but later, his style in North-West Europe, as we shall see, was characterised by his inability to reconcile the command of a great field force with his position as chairman of a committee. (Arthur Nevins, journalist and SHAEF staff officer in the COSSAC period and afterwards, observed that British Joint Planners were joint service officers whereas US planners were used to producing plans for their own arm and then having to persuade representatives of each service to accept them, which was next to impossible.)[15]

It is necessary to contrast these differences between the Allies in their attitude to war management, so incompatible at first, but equally necessary to emphasise that gradually, in joint committees and in joint headquarters, their ways of thinking fused; where their methods differed, each made allowances for the other. However, senior American officers continued to be frustrated by the British way of looking at problems, particularly when they avoided definition and demarcation until it became essential. Then they rationalised contradictions in a manner Americans considered perfidious. The British complicated and dispersed command responsibility by blurring it, another symptom of committee mentality, thereby gaining more influence than their individual contribution to the war effort warranted. Americans, the British observed, reacted by pressing principles upon them before the example to which they were to apply had arisen. The Americans, it seemed, were always looking for a formula to pin down the slippery British. The British believed that the precipitate Americans ignored the practical difficulties of large scale, complex operations. The Americans believed that the British magnified difficulties and 'took counsel of their fears', in the words of an old military adage.

The scene of this clash of culture, education, politics and experience was the Combined Chiefs of Staff (CCS). It first met in January 1942 as an outgrowth of meetings between the heads of state and the senior officers of the Allies which had begun earlier with the America-Britain Conversations (ABC) in February and March 1941. A permanent British Joint Staff Mission had been established in Washington in June 1941, under Lieutenant-General HCB Wemyss and Air Chief Marshal Arthur Harris, the future commander of Bomber Command, nominally to help handle the procurement of war material, and it became a liaison staff which acted as the representative of the BCOS in Washington under Sir John Dill. The CCS usually met in Washington thereafter, but Dill represented the British case when the BCOS members could not cross the Atlantic to attend. Ranged facing one another on either side of a table, the Chiefs generally avoided long speeches but allowed personalities full scope in discussions that at times became heated. Of the Chiefs, Brooke, Portal and Marshall were the most influential. Agreement was often a compromise stalked warily and expressed in stealthy language that painted over differences until the next meeting. The drafters' hope, and sometimes expectation, was that by then circumstances might have changed the terms of the argument.

It should not be assumed that the CCS was always divided into national camps. There were 'cross-benchers, particularly when air force and naval questions were discussed. Unanimity inside the JCS in preparing American position papers for CCS meetings could not be counted on without some give and take either. Marshall's position was powerful. He had prepared his own base by establishing himself as a commander and distancing himself from the day to day business of the War Department so that he could study the issues that came up in the JCS. To that end he followed Peyton March's example by appointing Lieutenant General Brehon Somervell to be virtually the commander of the Service of Supply, as March had appointed Goethals in the earlier war. He made the airman Lieutenant General Henry ('Hap') Arnold one of his deputy chiefs of staff; giving him several hats to wear; Commanding General Army Air Forces, Chief of the Air Corps, and the US air representative on the CCS, where he gave Marshall an extra vote. Finally Marshall made Lieutenant General Lesley McNair commander of the ground forces in the continental United States. It remained only for commanders in all theatres to be appointed (Douglas

MacArthur being already in place in the South-West Pacific), to give Marshall a command structure with clear lines of command at home and abroad. OPD increased in size and importance under General Eisenhower, who headed it in the spring of 1942 before he was assigned to London. It was during his tour in OPD that the relationship between Marshall and Eisenhower was forged. Eisenhower's knowledge of OPD's workings stood him in good stead when he eventually became an Allied supreme commander.

When these reforms received presidential blessing, Roosevelt asked the Secretary of War, Henry Stimson, to write into the executive order '. . . The Chief of Staff is the executive through whom the President of the United States, as Commander in Chief, exercises his functions in relation to strategy, tactics and operations . . . is the immediate adviser of the Secretary of War . . . exercises general supervision over the Army of the United States and the Military Establishment . . .'

'These statements', wrote Ray Cline 'placed the Chief of Staff on the pinnacle towards which the successive incumbents of that office had been moving steadily since 1921. Inevitably, the power of the General Staff through which the Chief of Staff fulfilled this vast responsibility also increased.' Marshall's authority was established within the Army and he had created the means by which to exercise it. Nevertheless, it is remarkable that this basic statement about the management of a war was made only in 1942 because Congress had not allowed a workable system for the employment of armed forces to be prepared in peace. That seems to belie Cline's reference to 'steady movement'. It may also strike the reader that three Services and the whole might of the American people were engaged in war and that Marshall was but one of its directors with a rather tenuous entry to the Oval Office of the President. For the Pacific war, a largely naval war, Ernest King was the more important executive. Only in Europe by virtue of the subordination of the Army Air Forces and the relatively minor role of the US Navy, would Marshall be *the* executive of the President. One of his tasks was to ensure that Europe had priority in American strategy. It was to be a hard one.

CHAPTER 10

GEORGE MARSHALL'S TWO-FRONT WAR

... The task [for the supreme commander] is to hold the situation firmly to the straight road which has been agreed to and which it is now on. He should tolerate no departures from the program ...

NOTE BY HENRY L. STIMSON, SECRETARY OF WAR, 10 NOVEMBER 1943.

Samuel Eliot Morison, the great historian of the US Navy, called the Second World War a war of two oceans for the Navy and of five theatres for the US Army. The resulting competition for resources between Europe and the rest of the world, the Pacific in particular, was at the centre of almost all strategic disputes. Logistics were on Marshall's mind when he argued against operations in the Mediterranean in favour of North-West Europe and, later, when he influenced Eisenhower's actions as Supreme Commander Allied Expeditionary Force (SCAEF). The Army's South-West Pacific front was led by Douglas MacArthur, a previous Army Chief of Staff and the most celebrated American serving. He was a persistent and influential advocate for his front but it was in North-West Europe, not in the Pacific, that the US Army and the competition for logistics, combined to shape Marshall's policy in Europe, which may be described as the concentration of all American resources allotted to the European theatre against the German Army in France. His purpose was to finish the European war as soon as possible in a manner that redounded to the credit of the Army. Marshall was the father of the wartime Army and, like Haig and the BEF a generation before, he had a proprietary interest in its performance.

When the Grand Alliance had been conceived but Pearl Harbour had not yet brought it into existence officially, Plan DOG envisaged that, if and when the United States joined the war, she would devote most of her resources to the defeat of Germany. After Pearl Harbour that remained the policy in principle. Japan would be held by a defensive strategy, but

167

Americans wanted immediate revenge for the 'Day of Infamy'. Furthermore, the Pacific war did not go as expected. The Japanese advance was not limited to the Philippines but gobbled up the South Pacific as far as New Guinea, very close to Australia, and penetrated into the Dutch East Indies, British Burma and the Indian Ocean. India was threatened and there was talk of a pincer movement by the Germans from the West and the Japanese from the East. The Americans wanted the British to take offensive action in Burma to open the Burma Road to China. China, which had been at war with Japan since 1937, was to be prepared as a base for action against the Japanese islands. Persia had been cleared of German sympathisers by the British in 1941 and now had to be secured and prepared as a channel for supplies to Russia. Northern Europe and the Mediterranean became fronts whose demands had to be considered in what was not just a 'two-ocean war' but a world war. The queue for resources in 1943 and 1944 was long.

In the Pacific, how to *stop* the Japanese was at first the urgent problem. After the US Navy, with its effective air component, held the Japanese at the Battle of the Coral Sea, 3–8 May 1942, and defeated them at Midway on the glorious 4th of June, American strategy ceased to be defensive: its aim was to drive back the Japanese wherever they had made a lodgement. The cry went up, 'we won't wait for Europe'. In the summer of 1942, the small American force in Britain had so far seen no action. 'Japan First' was an option that Marshall considered seriously in the CCS, knowing that it was favoured by many Americans who were equivocal about Europe now that the United Kingdom was no longer threatened. He could not resist the flow of air, shipping and army resources to the Pacific following the build-up of naval forces there, nor could he check the President's tendency to please both lobbies, when no Americans were engaged against the Germans except for sorties by the United States Army Air Force (USAAF) against French targets. It was much easier for the American people to hate the Japanese than the Germans. Furthermore, the Pacific war was easier for the American military to understand. The US navy was imbued with the doctrines of Admiral Mahan.* The Pacific was a Mahanist war of great fleets: defeat the Japanese fleet and their sea communications and trade would wither: the home islands would then be indefensible. No politics were involved. In contrast, the Atlantic war against the U-boats was a

---

* Alfred Thayer Mahan (1840–1914) was author of many books about the influence and practice of seapower. After examining British maritime strategy in the 18th Century and noting the lack of American naval power in the war of 1812 with Britain he devoted himself to advocating a strong navy. Great battles enabled the victor's trade to flow freely and closed the seas to his enemy.

trade war: it was a defensive war with unremarkable successes, 'inglorious' in Mahanist terms. On the European and African mainland, politics complicated every operation and European politics were anathema to many in Congress and in the Army, though the Army could not forget that France had been the scene of the AEF's victory over the German Army in 1918; a victory unappreciated by French and British alike. Marshall, who had played an important role in that year, was determined that 'his' US Army should cover itself with glory and compel the respect of its allies. The sooner it got to grips with the enemy, the better.

An invasion of France was impossible in 1942 because most of the troops would have been British and they declared it to be a forlorn hope, one they did not intend to risk, unless Soviet Russia was on the verge of defeat or, an unlikely event, the Germans faced a massive revolt in the occupied territories. At that date the JCS was curiously naive about the complexity of an opposed assault landing and of the scale of the build-up in Britain required for one across the Channel. The Americans did not need vast amounts of shipping to import essentials. Most of their shipping was military and employed in the Pacific. As explained in the previous chapter, they failed to grasp that the only shipping available to carry American troops was British, and limited to what was not required to sustain Britain's economy and war industry. Thanks to the refusal of Admiral King to adopt the convoy system in the six months after Pearl Harbour, 2.34 million tons of shipping had been sunk off the eastern seaboard of the United States, more than in the whole of 1941 before America entered the war. The total loss from all causes in 1942 was 6.2 million tons. During the build-up of the American base in Britain, code name BOLERO, the shipping tonnage required for the equipment, as opposed to their manpower, proved an unpleasant surprise and one which resulted in reductions in the lavish establishments of mechanised US divisions. Debates in the CCS about invasion in 1942 and 1943 were uninformed about logistics and consequently were pursued in an Alice in Wonderland atmosphere. The disaster at Dieppe, where the 2nd Canadian Division attempted a raid in force in August 1942, had a deterrent effect on the tactical Micawbers in the American camp but taught them nothing about logistics . In 1943, the British members of the CCS, by dragging their feet over invasion, forced the Americans to consider such essentials as shipping in detail. In late 1943, American ship-building began to outstrip losses by a wide margin, but most of it was still directed to the Pacific. Only then did the JCS realise that there was a *double* imbalance in the figures they were considering: as yet there were insufficient divisions and supporting units ready to fill the shipping capacity available. In 1943, Churchill took Roosevelt to task for treating Britain like Australia, Greenland and Noumea, as simply another forward base, a trans-shipment point which should require nothing but military supplies, and ignoring Britain as a producer of war materials for which substantial imports were essential over and above military supplies.

Instead of pressing for SLEDGEHAMMER, the putative invasion of the Continent in 1942, which had always been a lost cause, despite the diplomatic wording of CCS minutes about it, Roosevelt supported Churchill's choice of French North Africa, GYMNAST, later renamed TORCH, as the first commitment of the Americans to active operations. He wanted them to be fighting by the time of the mid-term elections in November, so as to fend off the isolationists and Pacific-firsters, and also the pressing Soviet demand for a Second Front which Roosevelt had practically promised the Soviet Union's Foreign Minister, Vyacheslav Molotov. It was a political decision but militarily the right one too. The JCS did not agree. They would not accept that other than doing nothing, which would encourage the demand to transfer sole attention to the Pacific, TORCH was the only alternative to a disastrous or merely futile invasion of France. Nor did they admit that Dieppe had demonstrated that a direct assault on a port, Cherbourg for instance, would be repulsed and that there was insufficient assault shipping for landings on a wide front over the beaches.

Patience was not a virtue in the JCS at this stage. Its attitude to TORCH, even after it had been mounted, was equivocal. TORCH was seen as a hazardous operation largely because of its political aspect; it was designed to bring the colonial French into the war. If the French resisted it would become operationally hazardous. Because the Americans had to play the most visible part, the British being *persona non grata* with the French, thanks to their various assaults on the French fleet in African ports in 1940, Dwight Eisenhower was appointed supreme Allied commander and concentrated his attention on the political aspects of his task. The military function of TORCH, to cut off the retreat of the Africa Korps facing Montgomery in Libya from Tunisia, received too little attention in his planning. The Germans hurriedly reinforced their forces in Africa and successfully defended Tunisia until May 1943.

Throughout that year, Marshall maintained pressure on the British to scale down Mediterranean operations and to invade across the Channel. He could not press his argument to a conclusion as operations unfolded as planned in the Mediterranean and there were too few American troops in Europe to invade France with any hope of success. That would still have been true even if operations in the Mediterranean had reverted to the purely defensive and the handful of American divisions employed there sent back to England in the spring of 1943. Marshall's political motives

170

seem to have ruled his military logic concerning operations in the European theatre of Operations (ETO). However, by taking the TORCH decision out of Marshall's hands, Roosevelt enabled his Chief of Staff to show King that he had at least tried to mount a direct assault on Germany. It is questionable, though, whether Marshall ever understood what was a reasonable and what an unreasonable risk when fighting the Germans on the mainland. The arguments he advanced during the long struggle in the CCS over ANVIL (the invasion of the South of France by American and British troops which we shall examine in the next chapter) suggest that his grasp of the practical corollary of strategy, 'operations', was superficial, as in General Sir Alan Brooke's unkind verdict. Nevertheless, he kept his simple political objectives in view and eventually reached them in the fullness of time by sheer persistence. With hindsight, it seems that events created their own momentum and led to D-day on 6 June 1944, and not before, without benefit of Marshall or Brooke or the politicians. They argued, and even made 'decisions', but they were not decisive. Until then the Mediterranean campaign was simply a continuation of British strategy – indeed, the only possible option in 1940, 1941 and 1942, and still the only feasible one until 'D-day' in June 1944. After that the story is different. It was due to Marshall's persistence that the final decision for ANVIL was made in late June 1944. It was, arguably, a political decision in operational garb.

Marshall's admirers have granted him strategic and tactical ability. We are among his admirers but point out that those qualities were never tested in the field except, perhaps, as a general staff officer for a short time on the Western Front. In the Second War, his advice and comments on operations seem to bear out Brooke's opinion. Marshall's suggestion to Eisenhower that he should cross into Sicily from Tunisia 'on the heels of withdrawing Axis forces' to 'cash in on the resulting confusion to gain a great success' smacks of the armchair strategist. He was too sanguine about the efficacy of air power and his suggestion that it could contain the Germans in Italy and the Mediterranean more economically than ground forces and compensate for a shortage of troops to invade northwest Europe was specious. In 1944, during the planning of OVERLORD (the code name for the Normandy landings) his proposed use of airborne divisions in an offensive role deep in the German defensive system was visionary and would have proved disastrous, but it served Marshall's current concern to save shipping. Orde Wingate and his Chindit operations using air-landing and infiltration on the ground in Burma fired his imagination, as it had Churchill's. He determined to give Wingate air support even if the Chindits met scepticism in their own camp. At the time, he was trying to persuade the British to mount major offensive operations in Burma in the interests of

American policy over China. In fact, though Wingate's operation deserves the adjective 'heroic', it consumed scarce resources with negligible benefits. Marshall seized on Wingate as an example and perhaps an exception to cautious British military commanders.[2] That is an oversimplification, constantly repeated in the literature of the Second World War. Superficially it is a contrast between American daring and British caution, even timidity. The real argument was over the question of what, at any given stage in the war, was operationally feasible and what was not. Marshall by virtue of his office was above the tactical and operational aspects of the war. He may, on occasion, have thrown out ideas, but he could do no more than guide the field commanders in a broad, general way. His role was to be a statesman-like soldier.

Marshall was pre-eminent among his peers and treated with awe by his subordinates, as the following comments reveal. 'First, of course, his supreme integrity . . . he was a developer, he encouraged, gave leadership, knew when to dispense authority and to delegate it . . . a plastic mind . . . grasped things completely foreign to his line of experience . . . He had no work papers on his desk, his mind was apparently completely free and open to attack a new subject, uncluttered, unhurried . . . keen interest in our viewpoint . . . Altogether my superior in character and intellect and in the lucidity of his mind and his tremendous control over himself . . . I heard William Jennings Bryan at almost his best, but (he) could not hold a candle to General Marshall when he wanted to make people do things . . . (Speaker of the House, Sam Rayburn). 'He has the presence of a great man. He doesn't dissemble . . . Congress always respected him. They would give him things they would give no one else.' All this, and a cold blue pair of eyes that looked right through bluffers, self-seekers and the pretentious. A man with the strength to be kind and to admit when he was wrong.[3]

Brooke and Marshall were both highly respected and both aspired to field command in the great adventure which eventually began on the beaches of Normandy on 6 June 1944. Throughout the second half of 1943, Marshall was widely tipped for supreme command: Brooke was only told that he would not have it by Churchill at the QUADRANT meeting in Quebec in August 1943. Churchill had proposed to Roosevelt that Marshall be offered the appointment of Supreme Commander Allied Expeditionary Force (SCAEF). The projected balance of forces between the two armies in 1944 had tilted decisively in the American favour and Churchill saved Roosevelt from having to make the proposal himself.[4] Marshall declined in December. He and Brooke, both holders of the highest military position, would have preferred active command in the field, but:

Oddly enough, when the prize he coveted seemed definitely within reach, Marshall refused to put forth his hand to grasp it. It was not Hamlet-like indecision that held him back, but strong pride. In the days when he was being considered for the Chief of Staff position, he had deliberately insisted on avoiding all publicity as the most politic way of handling the situation. His silence now was not due to any such calculated reticence. If this appointment was to be his, he wanted it without any effort on his part . . . Once the press disclosed the possibility of his appointment, Marshall became even more aloof.

Secretary of War Henry L. Stimson* thought that he had persuaded Roosevelt to allow Marshall to leave Washington but his lack of response when Roosevelt approached him on the subject was to be decisive in the final choice of the Supreme Commander.[5]

Marshall s biographer Forrest Pogue suggests that he, rather than refusing outright, reacted in such a way that made it easy for Roosevelt to decide to keep him in Washington. It would have been completely in character for Marshall to do what he believed best for his country and, perhaps for the Allied cause, however intense his desire to hold high command, in spite of his understandable and intense desire to command the US armies in the field. By 1944 there was another inter-Allied factor that influenced the choice of a SCAEF. After the assault phase, the strength of the US armies would build up until they outnumbered the combined British and Canadians by about four to one; hence the choice of Dwight D Eisenhower a man who was not a strong leader and who had no pretensions to be a field commander, instead of Marshall. This entirely changed the command aspects of the most important military operation of the war. Marshall certainly gave that angle of the matter more thought than anything else in his life. In his own game-plan for Europe he had planned that he would be the Supreme Commander of the *whole* European theatre. In a memorandum to the JCS on 5 November which was discussed at their 123rd meeting on the 15th, the possibility of securing a single air command and a joint command for the Italian and French theatres was discussed and a compromise position proposed which envisaged separating the ground commands, as Churchill would never agree to an American commanding virtually everything.[6] Now it was his protégé Eisenhower who would have to attain the goals that Marshall had set himself, and with severely restricted powers, since it had been agreed that SCAEF's sphere of

---

* Stimson had been Secretary of War as long ago as in the Taft presidency, when General Leonard Wood was Chief of Staff. He knew the Army's internal politics intimately. (Pogue, *Marshall*, 266).

command would be linked to northwest Europe and exclude the Mediterranean theatre. If Marshall remained in Washington, a supremely correct and high-minded decision, the question that arose was whether Eisenhower, self schooled as a supra-national commander, favouring no component of his force above another, could be relied on to work for Marshall's private and national goals. Marshall would have to control his protégé carefully but firmly.

As we have said, the concentration of all American resources for OVER-LORD and the subsequent great battles in France was central to Marshall's strategic concept. Concentration of air-power was part of it, and relatively the easiest to realise. The air war was indivisible, unlike the war on the ground which had to be divided into theatres. Marshall controlled the USAAF, a large part of Allied air power, through Arnold. Relations between the RAF and the US Army Air Forces were good, much better than those between the armies, which gave Marshall concern, and even between the air forces and the armies which improved in 1944 but was not yet satisfactory in the American case in the spring of 1944. Solidarity between the USAAF and the RAF might serve Marshall's purpose to concentrate both on OVERLORD. A short diversion into the question of air-power is necessary to clarify this point.

Disagreement over the control of the Royal Naval Air Service, of which the Royal Navy had been deprived until the Fleet Air Arm was returned to naval control in 1937, and the neglect of tactical air support for the Army still affected British inter-service relations. The RAF retained their pre-war belief that victory could be won by an offensive bomber force. Air Chief Marshal Sir Arthur Harris of Bomber Command still believed that invasion was not necessary. As long as Bomber Command was his only effective weapon against the Germans, Churchill sided with the RAF: after the summer of 1942, when the USAAF 8th Air Force began to operate from England, he guarded the RAF as an independent, British-controlled weapon. To a large extent, the USAAF shared the British belief that strategic bombing could be decisive but to attain it they pursued the goal of unified command for all Allied strategic air forces. This, the British, and particularly Churchill, resisted. Both armies demanded the support of strategic aircraft from time to time but neither air force wanted to divert heavy bombers from their role of bombing German industry and the German population. As to tactical air forces, by the middle of 1942 there were sufficient aircraft for the relatively small Eighth Army in the Western Desert to develop effective inter-service techniques for close support. British doctrine, if not British practice, was adopted when the Allies fought together in Tunisia but the US Army complained, because air superiority and interdiction took priority over the close air support of the army. Though the USAAF was an *Army* Air Force, its commanders preferred British doctrine and made common cause with the RAF; the bond between airmen transcending national prejudice. (An attitude manifest even at the level of the CCS.) Marshall sympathised with the USAAF ambition to be independent of the Army, like the RAF, and to have its say in grand strategy. One reason for appointing Arnold as his deputy Chief of Staff was to further that policy. The USAAF had achieved virtual independence when it took part in the joint Allied bomber offensive against Germany, POINT BLANK, designed at SYMBOL to weaken German resistance to the invasion of France. But Marshall did not accept the thesis that the war could be won by a strategic bomber offensive alone. His immediate short-term aim was to strengthen the authority of SCAEF, who would require all air forces, British as well as American, to support his ground forces.

At the end of 1943, Marshall gathered the two American strategic air force commands, 8th in England and 15th in the Mediterranean under the operational control of Lieutenant General Carl Spaatz, recently Eisenhower's American air commander in the Mediterranean. He attempted, but found it unacceptable to the British, to have Bomber Command included in a single command for all strategic air forces in Europe. He intended to use them as he and Arnold pressed Generals Alexander and Mark Clark, the American Fifth Army commander, to use the 15th Air Force heavy bombers to blast open the front at Cassino in February and March 1944. That had not proved a success, but the idea remained an attractive alternative to prolonged and costly battles on the ground. Had Marshall accepted the post of SCAEF, his authority would have extended over the entire European theatre, his subordinates being a British commander-in-chief in Italy and an American, Eisenhower, in North-West Europe, with Spaatz as overall air force commander. Marshall would not have met the same resistance to giving the armies direct air support as did Eisenhower.[7]

How did Marshall intend to exercise supreme command? Lieutenant General Frederick Morgan, COSSAC (Chief of Staff to the Supreme Allied Commander), was appointed in 1943 after SYMBOL to be the putative chief of staff to SCAEF. His plan was for SCAEF to be a strategic commander, not an operational one, and that in the initial stages of the battle in Normandy Montgomery, British 21st Army Group commander, would control all troops on the ground. Marshall, briefing Lieutenant General Jacob Devers, then Commanding General, European Theatre of

Operations, US Army (ETOUSA) on his own views on command, said that SCAEF would take command from the beginning, leaving Montgomery to command 21st Army Group and Bradley to command 1st US Army Group. When Morgan talked to Marshall in Washington in late October 1943, after it had been determined in principle at the QUAD-RANT conference that OVERLORD would take place in the spring of 1944, the detailed arrangements for command were unresolved. Marshall, Morgan gathered, thought that 'he should in some way control the assault-ing army although I am quite certain that his conception falls far short of what we understand by the term "command".' Surprisingly, Marshall was under the impression that SCAEF would have complete 'communications to forward units to allow him to participate directly in the battle when it took place.'[8] Simultaneously, an OPD plan prepared for Marshall had him still located in Washington until late in the planning for OVERLORD, and retaining his place on the CCS during operations. Needless to say, Morgan, who had been struggling for months to plan without a commander to direct him, asserted that Marshall could not manage complex inter-service and inter-theatre military and political matters for which SCAEF would be responsible before the operation unless he were in London. After the oper-ation was launched Marshall could not personally manage the battle as well, which seemed to be his intention. Morgan had two ideas about how SCAEF would command OVERLORD. If he intended to control opera-tions he would have to operate from a small headquarters like Foch, and his function would be to give general direction to commanders of army groups as Foch had done, and not enter into details. Most of his time would be occupied in the higher direction of the European war through a large supreme headquarters. The alternative was to have a land force com-mander to run the battle while Marshall himself devoted his time to higher matters and to orchestrating the strategy of the two European fronts. The question was not resolved by Morgan before Eisenhower was appointed who, as we shall see, deliberately left it unanswered, except that a single land forces commander, Montgomery, was to control the assault phase of the operation, as Morgan intended. Eisenhower wisely distanced himself from operational matters until the invading armies were securely lodged in the bridgehead.

Unity of command was a principle frequently on American lips. Marshall disapproved of the committee system adopted at the supreme level in the Mediterranean by which three co-equal service commanders served under Eisenhower. They were often located in different places, behaved independently and were not given firm orders. The problem, though, was not in the system itself but in Eisenhower, who did not function as a commander. The complexity of coalition campaigns that started with an assault landing were supplied from the sea and required air force support was not part of Marshall's experience. The men from the Mediterranean who had absorbed all the practical lessons of the landings in Africa, Sicily, Salerno and Anzio were the best qualified to undertake and execute NEPTUNE/OVERLORD. All the same, there is merit in Marshall's firm opinion that a supreme commander should not have to negotiate for essential resources, or humbly request the commander of another service for support. Had Marshall accepted the post of SCAEF, he would have given orders and expected them to be obeyed without demur, enjoying as he would have done, the blessing of the two heads of state and the support of the CCS. Both Marshall and Eisenhower were men of strong character, but it is fair to assume that Marshall would not have tolerated the pressures that bore on Eisenhower so sorely from above and below. Ironically, an irresistible one was from Marshall himself, who made the best of both worlds by remaining in Washington, and ensuring that Eisenhower acted as if he were the great Chief of the Army Staff's deputy, and his loyal agent.

CHAPTER 11

THE MAN WITH
THE CUDGEL

The owner of the buffalo is the man with the cudgel –

INDIAN PROVERB.*

The CCS agreed in principle at QUADRANT to land a force of several divisions in the south of France in conjunction with the main invasion in the north (OVERLORD), planned, subject to certain conditions, to take place in the spring of 1944; code name ANVIL. The JCS saw it as a means of siphoning US and French divisions from the campaign in Italy, which they regarded as a wasteful diversion, in order to concentrate all American and American sponsored forces in France. The Italian front, which was about to be opened with landings in Calabria and at Salerno in early September, was to be controlled by the BCOS who stoutly maintained their view that pressure on the Italian mainland could contribute more to OVERLORD than a diversion in the south of France. In their opinion, an agreement in principle on ANVIL so far ahead of events could not be binding in terms of timing, location and strength. The decisive factor was how best to assist OVERLORD. In practice, ANVIL became the nexus for wider disagreements between the Allies, concerning the distribution of resources, the respective importance of OVERLORD and the Mediterranean, the shape of Europe at the end of the war and, of course, the priority of Europe over the Pacific. When ANVIL was finally carried out on 15th August 1944, Churchill gave it the derisive code name DRAGOON, to replace ANVIL, a punning protest against the arbitrary way in which the Americans had forced the issue. 'They had used the cudgel of their logistical power – their ownership of men, material and assault shipping – to impose their own strategy.'

* *Jiski lathi, uski bhain.* i.e., Disputes are decided by *force majeure.*

178

Britain's so-called 'Mediterranean' strategy is a bone from which historians have gnawed all the flesh but they return to it because they must. The long-standing dispute between the Allies may have been, in strictly strategic terms, 'much ado about nothing', but it is a fact and is part of the history of the war in Europe. At first, historians argued that the British prevented OVERLORD taking place in 1943, and would have done so indefinitely by embroiling large American forces in the Mediterranean. Building on unguarded phrases of Churchill referring to Italy as 'the soft underbelly of Europe', for example, and his declared and natural fear of 'blood on the beaches' of Normandy, and even of Brooke who spoke at TRIDENT of having to delay OVERLORD to '1945 or 1946', a picture was painted of the British wanting to defeat Greater Germany by attacking her southern perimeter from the Mediterranean, while the Americans wanted to take the direct route to the heart of Germany by way of Normandy. There were 'two opposed strategies'. That seemed to reflect the impression of Marshall and King, if all that was said and written at the time is taken at face value.[1] Later historians pointed out that, in the light of events, the Americans came to recognise that Italy had a part to play in the success of OVERLORD and the British committed themselves to OVERLORD when they thought that it could succeed. What had been differences were fused into one strategy by events in the Mediterranean and shipping shortages. The Allies were not engaged in a morality play in which the American strategists were betrayed by British 'peripheralism' and struggled to win the war by mass and concentration, as had been said. Nor was it true that Churchill was betrayed by short-sighted American strategists who eventually lost the peace. Nevertheless, by the time ANVIL was mounted, its original strategic purpose had been replaced and it was designed and served to transfer American troops fighting under the British in the Mediterranean to American command in France.[2]

Recently this fusionist interpretation has been modified in turn. Even if their strategies were reconciled, differences in the strategic philosophies of the two allies were not. The British mobilized and deployed their forces in the belief that opportunities would arise for the decisive engagement. The Americans decided where the decisive engagement should take place and tailored their deployment and mobilization to fit. The British claimed that American means did not fit their ends: the Americans that the British, haunted by the Somme and Passchendaele, overestimated the difficulties of a direct assault.[3]

Our purpose is simply to examine ANVIL, which is at the centre of the matter, in detail, in order to learn more of Marshall and Eisenhower, and the part played by the CCS. Our contribution to historiography is, perhaps, incidental. We conclude that the sometimes acrimonious exchanges in the CCS, of which so much has been made, had little effect on major events until after D-day when Marshall, King and Eisenhower intervened to transfer American controlled resources from Italy to Southern France.

The QUADRANT decision that ANVIL should, in principle, be adopted was referred to Eisenhower for him to suggest how it should be applied while he was still in the Mediterranean, in October 1943. The story then unfolded in three phases. Eisenhower advised against a firm decision to land a force in the south of France because a better use might be found for it and the shipping required nearer the time. The Russians were informed of ANVIL by Sir Anthony Eden during a meeting of the Allied foreign ministers in Moscow 19–30 October, in a session discussing OVERLORD. At EUREKA, the conference with the Russians in Teheran at the end of November, Roosevelt introduced ANVIL into conversations with Stalin over the timing of the Second Front in Northern France, intending to invoke his assistance to apply pressure on the British. Stalin, gratuitously involved, showed no interest in the details of ANVIL. Provided OVERLORD was effective he did not care whether ANVIL was to be only a feint, a diversion, a prelude to OVERLORD or a sequel to it; indeed, whether it should take place in France or Italy.[4] EUREKA was not held to settle any of these points. Stalin was much more concerned by Roosevelt's failure so far to designate a commander for OVERLORD. 'Could he be serious about the invasion'? he asked. (The notion that Stalin was 'promised' ANVIL in southern France dies hard but is not, as far as we can determine, borne out by the documents nor is it probable. Wishful thinking was its parent.) This forced the President to make up his mind about Marshall's future. Immediately after EUREKA, Roosevelt declared that he would retain Marshall in Washington, and he and Churchill agreed to appoint Eisenhower Supreme Commander, Allied Expeditionary Force (SCAEF). At the beginning of 1944 it was intended that OVERLORD should take place in May. It would have priority over all other operations in Europe. ANVIL's location, timing, purpose and strength were to be chosen so as to make maximum contribution to it. As far as the British were concerned, that was the principle agreed at QUADRANT. The unanswered question was how to apply it.

The second phase in the story lasted until April 1944. OVERLORD needed more shipping than it had been allotted because the assault wave had been increased from three to five divisions and the frontage widened. Extra shipping could be brought from the Mediterranean, taken from United States production and reserves be transferred from other theatres. After acrimonious exchanges and revised estimates British shipping was transferred from the Mediterranean. (There were 300 Landing Ships Tank (LSTs) worldwide; the only ocean-going ships capable of landing vehicles over beaches. 139 of them were in the Mediterranean, of which 67 were RN. 26 of these were sent to the United Kingdom and 62 more from other theatres for OVERLORD.) Consequently, as an offensive (DIADEM) was planned to start in Italy in May, to culminate precisely by D-day for OVERLORD in June, neither the troops nor the shipping could be removed from the Mediterranean theatre in time for ANVIL to coincide with OVERLORD, so its timing was postponed for review in June. Hence, if it took place at all, it could not be until well after the landings in Normandy.

Finally, when the review did take place in late June, operations in Normandy were developing rather slowly, while DIADEM had broken the stalemate on the GUSTAV Line and seemed to be on the brink of a great victory. At that moment the Americans demanded that OVERLORD be reinforced by ANVIL. When it was mounted on 15 August, although it was irrelevant to Normandy, where victory was already assured, it still reinforced Eisenhower's command at the expense of Italy, as Marshall had always intended.

To take up the story in more detail from the beginning of January 1944: by this time the standpoints of the two parties to the long debate were fairly established. Although ANVIL was conceived as an essential part of the invasion strategy, at first intended to precede OVERLORD, the Italian campaign as a whole also furthered it by defeating or containing German forces that might otherwise have been moved to Normandy. (About fifty German divisions were retained in Italy and the Balkans in 1944 after the surrender of Italy, amounting to roughly 20 per cent of German effectives in the field.) Indeed, operations in Italy were planned with OVERLORD in mind. In his reply to the CCS from the Mediterranean in October 1943, Eisenhower pointed out that ANVIL would serve OVERLORD just as well if it were a landing behind the German lines in Northern Italy. In treating ANVIL as an Italian operation in support of the main effort in Northern Europe, he took the British view that the European Theatre was divided into a predominantly British front in Italy, and what would be a predominantly American one in France.

After it had been decided that he would stay in Washington, Marshall continued to share with the British the principle that all operations in Europe should be coordinated, have a common aim and not compete with one another. That required military decisions about the disposal of forces to each front to be made without regard to nationality. Nationality was the rub and the gloves almost came off over that aspect of ANVIL. The British were aware that had Marshall been SCAEF he would have milked Italy of its American and French divisions and consigned them to the South of France. But the Italian front was not under Eisenhower's control as it might have been under Marshall's, and the strength of the Allied forces in it continued to be jealously guarded by Churchill. He was determined to preserve it as a predominantly British political fief to balance the predominant position of the Americans in North-West Europe. Although he used military arguments to maintain allied strength in Italy it was evident, when military victory in Europe became inevitable, that his purpose was political and focused on the post-war settlement of Europe. With that subject the American military appeared unconcerned although they wanted to participate in any glory that might accrue to the victors in Italy and to maintain enough strength to keep an eye on British meddling in the post-war politics of southern Europe.

Here we find that ANVIL lay on the hazy frontiers between military operations and strategy, and between strategy and politics. A lacuna, caused by the agreement at SYMBOL that the ultimate purpose of Allied operations was the unconditional surrender of Germany, underlay the bitterness that ANVIL provoked in military circles because 'unconditional surrender' was treated as a military statement by the Americans. Actually, it was a political statement: treated as a military one only it foreclosed political considerations when formulating strategy, limiting its aim simply to the military defeat of Germany.

Clausewitz defined strategy as the use of battles to serve the purposes of war. The way battles served the purpose of the war was as the decisive events in 'Operations' (in the sense defined in our second chapter, and part of the Russian and German military vocabulary.) ANVIL was a 'battle' but the word 'Operation' was not used in the wider sense by the Americans and British at that time.* In practice, political motives invariably intrude when 'Operations' are planned.

The Allies remained at cross-purposes over ANVIL. Neither side declared its real motives openly, each advancing, instead, sometimes spurious military reasons for the course it preferred. Each indulged in its accustomed modes of argument; the Americans from principle, the British pragmatically from the situation as it existed. The Americans looked at their objective and used any facts that served to make it seem attainable: the British, their feet more firmly on the ground, used the same facts to lead to a different conclusion.

---

* It is only in post-Second World War military studies that *Operation* has come to be used in this sense.

The British were disinclined to theorise about concentration of force and so on, but they had no difficulty in seeing the practical, political effects of landing a Franco-American armed force in the South of France, and they were against it. Its military value escaped them. Although fighting in Italy in the winter of 1943–44 had proved anything but a success story, the dry summer to follow held better prospects. Any decision on the most militarily advantageous course should be postponed until then.

The Americans, themselves masters of political tactics in their domestic controversies, discoursed widely on general theory; on the need for concentration of force at the decisive point (which no one denied was France), and the maintenance of that aim in face of diversions, such as operations in the Mediterranean. The theory was incontrovertible and straight out of the Field Service Regulations; it was also time-serving and might prove irrelevant in practice. CCS correspondence on the subject of strategy was not so much a dialogue of the deaf, as one between two sets of politicians who agreed only when they were compelled to by pressure of events.

Marshall's application of the principle of the unity of European operations was simple. He would concentrate the maximum force in France, whether in the north or south did not matter. To what end? His mission, as he saw it, was to put American politicians in the driver's seat by defeating the German armed forces. To that end, as he could not dictate the operational use of British forces, he was determined that the Americans should be concentrated in France under American command and play the decisive role in defeating the enemy. The British could see the consequences of this approach on the so-called Second Front. The Americans' superior military power would give them a dominant say in directing operations. The political purpose of strategy would be over-borne by military expedience. Marshall's remarkable statement in the final month of the war in connection with the seizure of the political objectives Berlin and Prague, that lives should not be expended for political ends, was to illustrate what the British learned during the ANVIL disputation. It was to the benefit of the American Army to adopt the unsophisticated doctrine of keeping military strategy and operations quite separate from their political purpose. The future of Europe was not in the forefront of the mind of its Commander-in-Chief, Franklin Roosevelt, so it could devote itself to seeking the military honour and glory that was denied it in 1918.

ANVIL was the preliminary skirmish over the strategy to be adopted in the Second Front campaign. To counter the simple American position, formidably buttressed by *force majeur,* the British played for time hoping that events in Italy would make ANVIL impracticable or unattractive. They had one initial advantage. ANVIL was bound to be a Mediterranean operation:

183

it was not going to be mounted from the United Kingdom or the United States, as TORCH had been, but from a well-established British theatre. Hence its timing was geared to the progress of operations in Italy and depended on resources available in the Mediterranean. When Marshall perceived that the British could make ANVIL completely dependent on operations in Italy he suggested that they be halted south of Rome so as to free divisions for a landing on the Riviera coast. The few divisions retained in Italy would stand on the defensive. In reply, Algiers and London both pointed out that General Alexander's armies in Italy had been directed to maintain pressure on the Germans until the OVERLORD forces were firmly ashore. They must be active until then, at the least. Although the ANVIL assault force was only two or at most three divisions, the follow-up might bring the total to ten. After the New Year of 1944, when seven Allied divisions had returned to the UK to prepare for OVERLORD as agreed at TRIDENT, there would be insufficient forces in the Mediterranean to maintain two active fronts continuously until OVERLORD. If ANVIL was adopted, Italy would stagnate.

But the crux of the matter lay in two ineluctable factors which Marshall conveniently ignored: first, that in October 1943, Ultra intelligence had made it clear that the Germans intended to fight every inch of the way back to Rome and beyond; second, that there would always be a six week gap between operations in Italy and a landing in the South of France, while the divisions and substantial air detachments from Italy prepared for the landing. The conclusion from the first fact was that Italy was an active mincing machine for German divisions. The second determined that the mincing process, at best, would certainly be interrupted and at worst terminated by ANVIL, weeks before its D-day. This was much the same case as Eisenhower had made in answer to the QUADRANT proposal in October 1943. Until OVERLORD was firmly ashore, he had argued, offensive action in Italy was its best support; therefore ANVIL should not precede OVERLORD but might take the form of a landing behind the German front in Italy in conjunction with it.

In practice, the poor alternative to this proposal for helping OVER-LORD by a vigorous offensive in Italy, which would include landings from the sea, was to go over to the defensive as early as 75 days before OVER-LORD to allow the three divisions in the ANVIL assault and perhaps seven in the follow-up to be released in time. If ANVIL was to coincide with OVERLORD in early May, the rest of Alexander's forces would have to adopt a purely defensive stance on about 15 February.[5] At that time, only if all the American and French divisions in Italy were assigned to ANVIL could ten divisions be drawn from the Mediterranean. Allied forces would then be dangerously weak on both fronts, divided in the face of the enemy. Furthermore, a major landing in France, by relieving the Germans of their fear of short range, tactical landings behind their Italian front, would facilitate German concentration against either Allied front. In fact, from September 1943 until ANVIL was finally launched in August, 1944, the Germans kept about half their forces in reserve to guard against such a threat, which they appreciated was the one manoeuvre likely to force them to accelerate their retreat.

At the beginning of 1944 then, ANVIL both in Algiers and London was regarded as a strategic mistake, unless the resources to permit both ANVIL and the offensive in Italy to go forward were provided from the United States. (In Cairo, Eisenhower spoke on 26 November on behalf of the 'established theatre since much time was invariably lost when the scene of action was changed . . . [and pointed out] the arduous task of building a fresh base.') The British could have contributed to that only by retaining in the Mediterranean those divisions they had already assigned as their contribution to OVERLORD, a condition unacceptable to both sides. As it was, OVERLORD would tax British manpower to its limit. Only the Americans possessed the necessary additional resources. King, the man who controlled American assault shipping and knew how much there really was, would deny it to any European operation that he himself judged would not contribute directly to the defeat of Germany. The South of France passed this test; Italy did not. So, for the British, the hard fact was that the Americans enjoyed the decisive advantage: all the troops earmarked for ANVIL were American, or French equipped by the Americans. At first glance, that gave them control but they were in two minds about exerting it if it meant replacing the divisions they consigned to ANVIL from Italy by fresh ones from the United States. If the Americans failed to do so, the British might point out that merely shifting troops from one part of the Mediterranean to another was not in the spirit of 'Plan Dog' – the Germany First strategy – as it did not increase their commitment to Europe.

Nevertheless, the British bargaining position though weak was not entirely hopeless, as the appeal to the principle of 'Plan Dog' might indicate. British and Commonwealth strength in the Mediterranean was substantially larger than the American. (So much so that the US Fifth Army could not exist as an army without a British or Commonwealth corps, or the powerful French contingent of four divisions.) A British commander, Maitland Wilson by agreement, succeeded Eisenhower in December 1943. The British fleet of landing craft and ships in the theatre. equalled the American. Above all other factors, the British hoped that a successful offensive in Italy and a German withdrawal to the plain of Lombardy might persuade the JCS to see the merits of an Italian strategy and the European theatre as a strategic whole.

All this was in Winston Churchill's mind when he initiated the ploy of embroiling the Allies in operations in Italy so successful that disengaging forces for a separate ANVIL would be unthinkable. In December 1943, he breathed new life into an abandoned scheme for landing a reinforced corps at Anzio-Nettuno behind the right of the strongly defended Gustav Line. He intended to stir up the front and get it moving regardless of the difficulties of campaigning in the Italian winter. At his prompting the US 6th Corps (one US, one British division) landed at Anzio-Nettuno on 22 January (Operation SHINGLE), but was penned in its bridgehead and forced on to the defensive. The shipping for its support, which should have been released for OVERLORD and ANVIL remained tied up until the spring of 1944; an unplanned and unexpected consequence. The US Fifth Army offensive, intended to pass an armoured force over the Garigliano river simultaneously with the launch of SHINGLE, join hands with the 6th Corps and liberate Rome, was a total failure. The fighting continued through the winter without a decision until in April there had to be a pause for complete reorganisation and a fresh plan. Nevertheless, it had become plain to Americans and British alike that, having gone so far, the best contribution that the Allied armies could then make to the success of OVERLORD was a spring offensive in Italy to contain as many German troops as possible until D-day at least. Operation DIADEM began in May. By the beginning of June, Alexander was on the verge of a great victory; one which Churchill and the BCOS hoped would convince the Americans that ANVIL was irrelevant.

Ultimately, they failed. In December 1943, Churchill had sold SHINGLE to the President on a false prospectus in that what was to have been a temporary demand for shipping previously assigned to OVERLORD persisted into the late spring of 1944. By the time SHINGLE was launched, the newly appointed commanders, Eisenhower and Montgomery, had reviewed the OVERLORD plan in Europe and insisted on a larger assault force and more shipping. A tug of war between the two theatres over shipping began. The BCOS asked the Americans to make up the deficiency from the United States: the Americans, bitten over SHINGLE, insisted that it should come from the Mediterranean. In the months that followed, the BCOS tried to squeeze the Pacific and the JCS to squeeze Italy. An immediate result was the postponement of OVERLORD for a month from 1 May until 1 June. (The original date for OVERLORD was arrived at by splitting the US proposal at TRIDENT, 1 April, with the British one of 1 June. It was not an operational decision. At EUREKA it was 15 May. The postponement to the first week in June was operational.)

To mark his change of view over ANVIL when he became SCAEF, Eisenhower wrote officially to Washington on 23 January 1944: 'I regard ANVIL as an important contribution to OVERLORD. OVERLORD and ANVIL must be viewed as one whole.' Of course, that was the view of the JCS as Eisenhower well knew. On that day Eisenhower had to deputise for the JCS with the BCOS in London, which placed him in an anomalous position.[6] Marshall could reasonably expect Eisenhower to be his loyal agent in most questions and he could expect ANVIL to appeal to Eisenhower, since it increased the troops available to him. Marshall warned Eisenhower against agreeing with even operationally sound British arguments that undermined the policy of moving troops from Italy to France. Marshall was quick to squash 'localitis', realising that Eisenhower was by nature a trimmer, and impressionable. For his part, Eisenhower found his increasingly confidential, if one-sided, relationship with Marshall awkward. Marshall communicated to him only what was necessary but encouraged him to confide everything in return. When Eisenhower met the BCOS and his subordinate commanders face to face over operational matters it was sometimes difficult for him to reconcile their respective concerns with Marshall's and retain the confidence of all parties. Tension arose in London when it was clear that OVERLORD, the most important and difficult operation of the war, was not the *sine qua non* in Washington that it was in Supreme Headquarters Allied Expeditionary Force (SHAEF) and 21st Army Group, the two planning headquarters. Marshall had other fish to fry after the end of the campaign in Africa, when he told Eisenhower not to expect to have all his needs satisfied in future, as they had been in the past. The controversy over ANVIL was a second reminder that he lived in a world of divided loyalties and sharp competition for resources; there were to be others after D-day.

Eisenhower, as a trained staff officer, was accustomed to reconciling conflicts of opinion and interest, but now he was an international commander whose duty it was to do his best for the men who would fight and might die on the beaches. The CCS increased the pressure on him by its practice of handing to him unresolved questions of policy in a military guise so as to bring them within his jurisdiction. They, nevertheless, remained political questions and Eisenhower, treating them as such, sought to compromise rather than provide military answers. His subordinates, disappointed that he seldom took a firm stand, correctly attributed his indecision to lack of forcefulness, concluding that he was not his own master. He always played the part of the judicious staff officer, sitting on the fence between the BCOS view, often militarily sound, and Marshall's political advice, which he felt bound to follow.

The JCS never swerved from their version of ANVIL, a landing in Southern France to coincide with OVERLORD. Writing to Marshall on 6 February, after he had met the BCOS, Eisenhower tactfully presented, as his own opinion, the view of BCOS and the Allied command in the Mediterranean: that as there were insufficient landing craft, ANVIL should be reduced to a threat of one division until enemy weakness justified its employment. He said that he did not think it was possible to disengage the forces earmarked for ANVIL for the moment. 'Some compensation will arise from the fact that as long as the enemy fights in Italy as earnestly and bitterly as he is now doing, the action there will in some degree compensate for the absence of an ANVIL . . . but decisions involving OVERLORD and ANVIL must be quickly crystallised and given to us so that we may proceed definitely with our work.'

Marshall rejected the demand of the BCOS for more shipping for OVERLORD and for ANVIL to be cancelled rather than postponed. He replied, with calculated obtuseness: 'The British and American Chiefs of Staff seem to have completely reversed themselves and we have become Mediterraneanites and they heavily pro-OVERLORD.' He hoped that the British were not influencing Eisenhower and once more warned him against 'localitis'. Marshall was anything but obtuse. He knew that Eisenhower was angling for more shipping, but he had no intention of asking King for it until he was compelled to do so. (Alan Brooke had pointed out at EUREKA on 30 November that the lift for OVERLORD was too small. Indeed, it was smaller than for Salerno.) He advanced some dubious arguments for ANVIL which the BCOS would have swiftly demolished had Eisenhower been unwise enough to present them. Cancelling ANVIL, Marshall wrote, would lose eight or nine divisions that could not be employed either in Italy or north-western France because of inadequate port facilities. And, he added, as a makeweight, that the Resistance forces in southern France were stronger than in the north. This was the first time that port facilities had been mentioned as an argument in favour of ANVIL.

In this way a phase of haggling over shipping for OVERLORD and ANVIL began. As Marshall's real aim was to concentrate all American troops as far as possible under American command he was indifferent whether ANVIL coincided with OVERLORD or took place later, hence his point about ports. Marshall wanted Eisenhower, as the Allied commander, to press the case for ANVIL on operational grounds, rather than do so himself, since he was American and therefore not disinterested. So when

Churchill, ever persistent in arguing a case, requested that the whole JCS assemble in London to settle the ANVIL issue once and for all, Marshall's reaction was to send a team from OPD to London to play for time and, he hoped, demonstrate that SHAEF and 21st Army Group were wrong by proving that there was really enough shipping for both OVERLORD and ANVIL. He did not suggest terminating Alexander's operations in Italy. Eisenhower's predicament has to be viewed sympathetically. Representing both SCAEF and JCS, he was faced with the alternatives of accepting the OPD verdict, thereby running into trouble with the BCOS and endangering OVERLORD, or of arguing with Marshall and forcing him to fight King for more landing craft. Should he refuse to launch OVERLORD unless given the landing craft demanded by 21st Army Group? If they could only come from the Mediterranean, should he recommend the cancellation of ANVIL, or its postponement until after his forces were securely ashore in Normandy? Additional craft from the United States would solve the problem, but Eisenhower had not the power, either as SCAEF or the JCS representative, to insist. Nor, by asking for them, did he wish to convey to Marshall the message that he had been nobbled by the British. He knew perfectly well that the JCS would not agree to provide them unless assured that ANVIL would take place, sooner or later. Eisenhower was, willy-nilly, the agent of Marshall; not an independent, international commander.

The battle over assault shipping was fought at two levels. Neither Marshall nor Eisenhower were *au fait* with the tactics of assault landings or the complexities of loading tables.[7] Such technical details, as they believed them to be, could be safely left to the staffs concerned at HQ SHAEF and 21st Army Group. So far operational experience was based on amphibious operations in the tideless waters of the Mediterranean, but British estimates took into account the lessons of the many trials and exercises carried out by Combined Operations HQ in the rough waters round the British Isles, with their high rise and fall of tides, strong currents and summer gales. The visiting team from Washington, out to prove what Marshall hoped that there was enough shipping to mount OVERLORD and ANVIL simultaneously, used data drawn from operations in the Pacific and the Mediterranean to justify overloading craft and reducing follow-up capability. Marshall's euphemistic term for this was 'willingness to take risks'. Those who were actually responsible for the operation thought it folly. During a long wrangle in which OPD accused SHAEF of being 'chicken', relations inevitably became acrimonious, while the clock inexorably ticked away towards the hour when a final decision had to be made. Eventually the SHAEF staff surrendered to Washington pressure by offering a compromise.

On 17 February, frustrated by the mixture of politics and inexperience evident in the OPD team's calculations and SHAEF's offer to compromise, HQ 21st Army Group wrote a point by point exposure of the principles on which Rear-Admiral Charles Cooke, USN, a determined 'Pacific-firster' and a faithful lieutenant of Admiral King, had been working. Its 'Memorandum on Implications of the SHAEF Proposal to Reduce the Allocation of Landing Ships and Landing Craft' said that, in the opinion of 21st Army Group and the Royal Navy, to accept the compromise solution would require unwarranted risks to be taken as ships became casualties or hung about while men and vehicles waited for one another. The SHAEF-OPD compromise was a logistical not a tactical plan; the product of planners, not of commanders. Montgomery thought that they would not have been in their present situation had Eisenhower been a commander instead of a planner himself. A clash with Montgomery over both a principle and its application in this case was inevitable. Montgomery wrote:

> C-in-C 21 Army Group has never been asked to state his views as to the optimum allocation of landing ships and landing craft for the operation. The problem of mounting OVERLORD has been a matter of making the best use of an estimated allocation of craft. The normal method of dealing with such a problem would be to decide on how the object can be achieved practically, and from this basis to obtain the necessary resources for it.

The 21st Army Group memorandum stated flatly that the C-in-C's wishes could not be met with the existing allocation. In a separate letter Montgomery wrote: 'I recommend, definitely, that the proposal be turned down and that the craft and shipping essential for a successful OVERLORD be made available.'

A few days later a further compromise was adopted of which Admiral Ramsay, the naval C-in-C, remarked that 'it added to the complexity of an already complex naval situation.[8] It was now proposed to transfer LSTs and some other RN craft from the Mediterranean as an interim measure and re-examine the question of ANVIL and the provision of more ships for OVERLORD on 20 March. Eisenhower commented that 'he considered an agreement had been reached on the basis of preserving ANVIL', but that it might be necessary to withdraw additional British ships from the Mediterranean and replace them there by American ships. This was done late in March. Meanwhile much had happened in Italy. The winter offensive had petered out by the end of March when Alexander began to redeploy his forces for a spring offensive intended to defeat the German armies south of Rome by the beginning of June and drive them back to the Pisa-Rimini line. He submitted his plan (DIADEM) at the end of the month and urgently needed to know whether ANVIL was cancelled, or merely postponed.

The March denouement came about because Eisenhower had at last realised that both Montgomery and his own chief of staff, Walter Bedell Smith, were at the end of their respective tethers over the shipping question. His subordinates bore harder on him than Washington. General Wilson was also demanding to know whether DIADEM could go forward. Marshall took the hint and called off his OPD sleuths in exchange for future considerations and the shifting of British naval craft from the Mediterranean for OVERLORD. His was a considerable tactical success, as we shall see.

Eisenhower's handling of the March crisis revealed his method of command. When it came to operational matters, such as the planning of assault landings, he was modest and wise enough to realise that though he had been a midwife three times, he still did not understand conception and had never brought up a child. He was a godfather. He never did grasp the details of plans sufficiently to understand their purport unless they were pointed out to him; and then he soon forgot. For instance, in his correspondence with Marshall about the plans for D-day he observed that British airborne forces would seize the Caen area. Marshall had suggested it but there was no plan for such a coup, which was just as well. The details of loading ships for trans-shipment into landing craft for the final run into the beach, of tactical loading, the relative merits and accuracy of different forms of supporting fire, the particular as opposed to the general hazards that lay ahead on the Normandy beaches were subjects Eisenhower felt it was unnecessary for him to master. But he recognised when pressure from subordinates for a decision could no longer be denied and reacted to that, not to the military logic of the situation. The climax came when Bedell Smith and General Handy of OPD in Washington held a series of dramatic, and probably dramatised, transatlantic phone calls to settle the matter. In London, Bedell Smith yelled:

> It is enough to drive you mad with this uncertainty and these changes. When you have to sit down and figure the balances of the divisions, the loading tables and everything of that sort, and you don't know what kind of craft you are going to load them in or whether you are going to have as many as you think you're going to have, it is enough to drive a man insane . . .

He added that the SHAEF planning estimate was:

> the very lowest, skimpiest, measliest figure that you can possibly cal-
> culate to get by on the assumption there would be a strong landing in
> the Med. Any time anybody will guarantee us there will be a strong
> landing in the Med, we will stick by that measly figure, but time is get-
> ting short.

Eisenhower took the same line with Marshall simultaneously. Their compromise shipping demand had assumed a strong ANVIL, he said. Now
that it was clear that the best assistance that the Mediterranean theatre
could offer OVERLORD was an offensive in Italy, ANVIL was going to
have to be scrapped.

Of course, Bedell Smith's and Eisenhower's argument that ANVIL, if
activated, justified taking risks over OVERLORD was totally spurious.
Bedell Smith was patronising the Washington staff in using it but actually
handing responsibility to ANVIL's instigators. Nevertheless, the argument
and haggling continued briefly, with the Americans obstinately advancing
statistics and curious strategic arguments to prove that Wilson could still
launch ANVIL *and* continue his planned spring offensive in Italy. Then
they wanted an agreement to mount ANVIL by mid-July. Out of sheer
fatigue, the British agreed to have that re-examined in June, knowing it to
be improbable that the July date could be met. Only then was the shifting
of sufficient shipping to OVERLORD agreed. It is interesting that Bedell
Smith, who was hard-headed over such matters, discerned that by accepting landing craft from the Mediterranean instead of demanding an
infusion into Europe from elsewhere over and above that agreed earlier, the
Allied Expeditionary Force 'might reap the fruits of the additional landing
craft at the expense of facing arguments in the future.' He consistently
stood up for Europe against the Pacific and took an Allied line in the matter. The outcome of all this was that ANVIL was not likely to take place
until August, about two months after D-day. That changed its relationship
to OVERLORD entirely.

The debate over shipping was exacerbated by a fundamental difference
of approach to 'planning' by the British and US staffs. Both understood the
need for long term contingency plans, necessarily limited to a scenario,
time and space, logistic considerations and an estimate of the forces likely
to be required; the whole to be modified in light of the actual situation as
it transpired.

In real, immediate operations the US Army system was directive. The
staff developed a plan in considerable detail. If submitted to a superior

commander he was free to accept or reject it, but a subordinate commander was expected to accept it dutifully and without criticism or demur. The
British system relied on the principle that the commander on whom the
burden of success or failure rested had the authority to make the plan, or
else to be perfectly satisfied with the plan submitted to him as it stood. (A
principle that applied all down the chain of command.) To the Americans
this involved debate, was tantamount to insubordination, and abhorrent.
Montgomery, who became the *bête noire* of the Americans, astonished
and dismayed them by the vehemence of his objections to the initial plan
for the invasion of Sicily (HUSKY) and his radical alterations to the plan
made by COSSAC for OVERLORD, involving increases in the frontage and
weight of the initial assaults. Montgomery was a fundamentalist. Nothing
would induce him to compromise between what he considered militarily
sound and the politically desirable. The cost-cutting exercise by staff officers from Washington meant nothing to him: *they* were not landing on a
fortified coast-line held by the formidable German soldiery.

When the team of OPD shipping investigators descended on London,
they acted like invading Internal Revenue Service Inspectors, or a
Congressional Inquiry, not staff officers. Worse, their ignorance of the
subject of assault landings aroused scorn and resentment. They awakened
the dormant contempt of experienced soldiers for the stereotype 'gilded
staff' who had not heard a shot fired. Montgomery, insubordinate by
nature, suffered from a built-in disrespect for all headquarters superior to
his. Eisenhower was more pliant, since he had spent his service as a staff
officer. Montgomery had fought on the Western Front as an infantry officer and on the staff. More importantly, in the current war he had planned
and inflicted a major defeat upon the German Army in the field, as an
army commander. Eisenhower had no front line experience upon which to
draw. The two men were quite incompatible in character. Montgomery was
solitary, abrasive, anti-social, tactless and impatient with anyone who
could not see that his military appreciations were logically irrefutable. His
successful insubordination reinforced these traits. Eisenhower was emi-
nently reasonable, polite, clubbable and a compromiser by temperament
with a politician's sense of the possible. In Sicily and Italy, Alexander had
acted as a cushion between the two, but in SHAEF there was no provision
for a land forces commander, and a stormy confrontation between the
two men was inevitable.

The CCS had decided to reconsider ANVIL in June. On the 4th June,
General Mark Clark's Fifth Army entered Rome and Alexander had
achieved a great victory which he hoped to exploit. Clark had been reinforced by two divisions from the United States for DIADEM, not only for

military reasons but because the American component of the Fifth Army was outnumbered, including as it did a French corps of four divisions and a mixed British-American corps under American command in Anzio. The removal of four French and three American divisions for ANVIL would reduce the Fifth Army to a shadow and end any hope that the Allied Armies in Italy (15th Army Group) might have of completing the defeat of the Germans before they occupied the Pisa-Rimini line, let alone pursuing their remnants into the plain of Lombardy. When the CCS met in London in late June – two weeks after D-day for OVERLORD, the British wanted the Fifth Army to be left intact and ANVIL to be laid finally to rest, on the grounds that a victory in Italy would be of more assistance to Eisenhower than an ANVIL which could not be mounted until August. In any case, its possible benefit to operations in Normandy by then would be doubtful. The military facts before the CCS were those that Eisenhower had put forward in October 1943, when he had argued in favour of defeating the enemy in Italy rather than pausing to set up another theatre in southern France. The JCS, ignoring that argument, persisted in ANVIL regardless of its adverse effects.

King's extraordinary stipulation at a previous meeting of the CCS, that his price for sending American craft to the Mediterranean to replace British ones transferred to the United Kingdom for OVERLORD was that they should only be used for ANVIL, had been angrily rejected by the BCOS, and the JCS had withdrawn it. Now they changed their line of attack. The new argument in favour of ANVIL was that the Mediterranea port facilities, and Marseilles in particular, were required for the entry of forty to fifty fresh American divisions which could not be handled by Atlantic or Channel ports. The pressing of this argument happened to coincide with a storm off the beaches of Normandy on 19 June which placed the whole supply system of 21st Army Group in jeopardy. It lent force to Marshall's argument but ignored the fact that the earliest that Marseilles could be operational was mid-September, by when it could reasonably be hoped that the harbours of North-West and Western France would be available. However, as Marshall was disposing of American divisions under American command, he could choose their point of entry, and he chose Marseilles. He had lost all patience with the British but that did not justify his distorting the facts; that after the divisions committed to OVERLORD had been despatched, only *fourteen* operationally ready divisions remained in the United States. A total of forty-four was unlikely to be ready before the end of 1944. In the meantime, some 100,000 administrative troops were retained unemployed in the Mediterranean bases, waiting to provide back-up for ANVIL.[9] It was fair to say that Marseilles would be a valuable acquisition, but later, and not at the price of crippling Alexander's offensive capacity at that particular moment. Furthermore, the existing plan was for troops to land at the end of the Normandy battles at Brest, in Brittany, nearer to where they would be employed.

However, it was to prove futile for the BCOs to continue their objection to ANVIL on the basis of these or any other arguments. Marshall closed the debate for good by two clinching arguments. ANVIL was part of the general plan for the battle of France, and therefore the decision to launch it lay with Eisenhower, as SCAEF. Next, at the suggestion of the JCS, Roosevelt stated that ANVIL had been 'promised' to Stalin, and that to cancel it would require them to re-open the question with Moscow, which he had no intention of doing. This was a misrepresentation of what had happened at Teheran, but it effectively brought down the curtain on the long argument.

The landings, renamed DRAGOON, took place on 15 August. Military resources that might have decisively defeated the Germans in the Gothic Line in August–September were instead engaged in an irrelevant operation against a retreating enemy in the Rhone valley: irrelevant because the decisive front was then in France and Belgium.

The BCOS could not challenge Eisenhower's decision in favour of ANVIL without calling into question their confidence in him as the commander responsible. Eisenhower held the key, whatever his private view. Montgomery the commander actually engaged at that time, opposed ANVIL, but Eisenhower overruled him. He did so because he was swayed by the argument over additional ports of entry, and also at that moment he feared that there was a 1917-style stalemate developing in Normandy, which could only be broken by a fresh landing on the Riviera; trimming once more to oblige Marshall, thus confirming the fears of the BCOS that Eisenhower was not the international, independent, commander he pretended to be.

The BCOS felt that hitherto Eisenhower had not been allowed to dictate strategy, and that it would be a mistake to allow him to do so now, unless as a coalition commander he was able to take a more objective view. The final decision on ANVIL ran counter to the idea of how post-Normandy operations should develop, as conceived by the BCOS and COSSAC. They had counted on the apparently amiable partnership between Bradley and Montgomery with Eisenhower as referee, continuing. Now, Marshall's interference might compel Eisenhower to take a firmer grip and cut out the BCOS from future military operations, while he became a ventriloquist's dummy operated by Marshall. Churchill feared a dislocation between operations and political aims, a grievous mistake, especially when the end of the war was approaching. He fought ANVIL up to the last minute in August long after Brooke had decided that continuing the struggle was counter-productive. Churchill pleaded with Eisenhower to change his mind, tears of frustration rolling down his cheeks, but to no avail: he appealed, fruitlessly, to Roosevelt but the die had been cast in Washington.[10]

We have dwelt on the ANVIL issue at length not because it was a vital strategic question, for it was not. It was important, but all the factors and the possible courses deriving from them were simple and plain to see. Its interest lies in the tensions and constraints of coalition war. Among them can be discerned several strands. Setting aside the built-in dislike of American officers for their British opposite numbers as a class, and the insensitive attitude of the British, who saw themselves as knowledgeable, war-hardened veterans, the Americans had no intention of allowing American resources or American lives to be used to pull British chestnuts out of the fire or further British post-war aims.

Marshall himself had, from the American point of view, read the lessons of 1917–1918 correctly; that in a coalition, American armies should fight as a single entity under American command. That had not been easy when the US Army was dependent on France and Britain for vital major items of equipment and transportation. In 1944 the position was reversed. The United States was the motor that powered the Allied war effort, because it was its arsenal. Marshall was both a patriot and a realist. The United States owned the cudgel, and he was determined to assert its ownership of the buffalo.

CHAPTER 12

THUNDERHEADS: TWO SHAEF DILEMMAS

Men of ability and goodwill make even faulty organisations function.

MILITARY APHORISM

It will be remembered that in October 1943 Marshall had an exchange of views with COSSAC on how he proposed to command and control the Allied armies as SCAEF. General Morgan proposed two options and a suitable headquarters organisation for each. If Marshall intended to direct operations in the Foch style of 1918, he would need a small tactical head-quarters as an off-shoot from his main SHAEF. Alternatively he could dispense with a tactical headquarters and delegate tactical operations to a land force commander. No conclusion had been reached about these related matters when Roosevelt appointed Eisenhower. When Eisenhower arrived, Morgan expected him to settle his operational role before he organised his headquarters. Instead, Eisenhower simply incorporated COSSAC and some of his staff into a large headquarters modelled on the one that he had in North Africa with Major-General Walter Bedell Smith as Chief of Staff.* He said nothing about a tactical headquarters. Morgan and other senior staff officers conformed to his wishes, but wondered how he intended to delegate authority for operations.

The BCOS, who were responsible for coordinating the hand-over of COSSAC to SCAEF and the absorption of his staff into SHAEF, wanted to

---

* Bedell Smith had been on Marshall's staff in Washington as Secretary General Staff and then Secretary to the CCS. He was appointed Chief of Staff to Eisenhower in the Mediterranean. After the war he was Ambassador to the Soviet Union, commander First Army, Director of the CIA and Under-Secretary of State. His biographer is DKR Crosswell, *The Chief of Staff: The Military Career of General Walter Bedell Smith* (Greenwood Press, 1991).

know Eisenhower's intentions after he, himself, had landed in Normandy. No land force commander had been appointed, but Montgomery, as 21st Army Group commander, was to act as such initially. His command consisted of the British Second Army, the Canadian First Army that would form in due course, and the US First Army. When Patton's Third Army arrived, General Bradley, earlier commanding First Army, became Commander First US Army Group (FUSAG), later called 12th Army Group. For a short period, Bradley and Montgomery would be equals, with Montgomery as coordinator, 'equal and above' Bradley. Then, in a third stage, SHAEF's advanced headquarters would arrive and Eisenhower would take supreme command. The BCOS wanted to know how Eisenhower intended to manage thereafter. They assumed that he would let Bradley and Montgomery continue to conduct operations on a loose rein together. The large size and the rationale of SHAEF, the precedent of North Africa, where Eisenhower had been given Alexander as land force commander after he had found that he was unable to direct operations and manage the politics of his post as well, and his known inclinations made that his logical choice. Papers on command written in the COSSAC period and just before D-day bear out this conclusion. In *General Eisenhower's Comments on Command, 18 May 1944*' Eisenhower recorded the instruction: 'No mention should be made in the initial paper [concerning command for both allies as opposed to command of American troops only] to the fact that General Eisenhower will ever act as Senior Allied Ground Commander'.[1]

American opposition to this arrangement before Eisenhower arrived in London made him reticent about details and the BCOS did not press him for clarification. Marshall, had he been Supreme Commander, intended to control Bradley and Montgomery directly from the assault onwards. There would have been no interim stages of command and, therefore, no loosely structured sequel such as Eisenhower envisaged when SHAEF opened in Normandy. Before COSSAC spoke to Marshall, arrangements for the assault stage and the break-in battles had been thrashed out between COSSAC, the BCOS and General Devers* (then CG ETOUSA), in London. Devers advanced Marshall's idea but was worsted on the grounds that it was essential, in the first days and weeks ashore, to have one responsible commander for the whole front, the commander of the senior formation ashore, 21st Army Group. Devers' argument that Americans could not be subordinated to a British commander was also ruled inappropriate. After

---

* Devers was appointed as American deputy in the Mediterranean to Wilson in December 1943 and then to command 6th Army Group which was responsible for ANVIL. (ETOUSA: European Theatre of Operations, Fifth Army.)

all, Alexander was commanding the American Fifth Army and British Eighth Army in Italy and had had an American corps under command in Tunisia. Furthermore, Mark Clark had British and French corps and a New Zealand corps, consisting of an Indian and New Zealand division, in his Fifth Army. It was essential in the 1944 coalition, that Americans should be able to take British divisions under command, and vice versa, when necessary. When Eisenhower took over, these two points had been settled as the BCOS and COSSAC recommended. Consequently, in the SHAEF paper concerning Allied command, it was laid down that formations *smaller than a corps* would *not* come under foreign command, but it was envisaged that whole armies *would* and the US Ninth Army, which would be on the American left when the German frontier was reached, was mentioned specifically. The rub was that it seemed unlikely that a British corps would serve under American command whereas the reverse was likely because the geography of the front placed the *schwerpunkt* on the American left and the British right, at the junction of the army groups.

Eisenhower had made his views on Allied cooperation clear in the Mediterranean, and did so again in SHAEF. He had no truck with xenophobic super-patriots like Patton: 'Anybody who wants to divide the British from the Americans and try to say who gets the credit on Tuesday or the blame on Wednesday is helping Hitler,' he wrote.[2] But, echoes of the Western Front in 1918, Marshall was always averse to Americans fighting on British fronts under British command, and Patton and Bradley could be expected to voice the same objection. Eisenhower would also meet resistance if he allowed a dominant Montgomery, in his command partnership with Bradley, to dictate the course of operations. So, while Eisenhower did not commit himself to an active command role, of which SHAEF was structurally incapable, neither did he explain how he would manage the 'arms-length' relationship that he intended. Eisenhower never burnt his bridges.

The command issue was Eisenhower's sword of Damocles. SHAEF, itself, was being built into an Allied team on the principle that nationality was submerged for the greater good. American and British officers were placed alternately in senior positions, and woe-betide the man who showed national prejudice. Eisenhower had sacked an American for referring to a 'British' son of a bitch in Tunisia, and he hoped that the team spirit evident in his own headquarters and amongst the troops that he visited would also reign among their commanders. Bedell Smith was not so sanguine as his master about the arrangement between Bradley and Montgomery. While Eisenhower smiled and played for time, his ambiguity about the command system and the place of the General Staff in it aggravated his

Chief of Staff's ulcers. The shipping furore had also upset Bedell Smith, and for the same reason. Unlike Eisenhower, he put no trust in personalities. He tried to ensure his authority as Chief of Staff, and hence the authority of Eisenhower and SHAEF, by creating unambiguous command and staff relationships. The authority of SHAEF for operations had to be absolutely clear, and it was not. The way the management of logistics was being planned seemed even less satisfactory to him. Their smooth functioning, too, rested on the foundation of personalities and Eisenhower would not see how shaky that was.

In North Africa, Bedell Smith had conducted a guerrilla war against the senior Administrative Officer for the American forces, General Everett Hughes. Hughes successfully maintained the independence of the logistical services from the General Staff of which Bedell Smith was chief. Bedell Smith could not prevail upon Eisenhower to bring Hughes to heel, by which he meant subordinate him to the General Staff. Hughes continued to function as a commander, rather like Lieutenant General Brechon B Somervell, Marshall's head of the supply services in Washington, or Harbord on the Western Front, in 1918. His relationship to Eisenhower replicated Somervell's to Marshall. Furthermore, Hughes was a close friend of Eisenhower and acted as one of his 'eyes and ears'. Eisenhower, none too secure when it came to understanding what was going on, had used Hughes as spy and adviser. It was a custom which did not make for healthy relations and, naturally, it annoyed and upset Bedell Smith whose job it was to know everything and to be the Supreme Commander's adviser. As Chief of Staff, he was entitled to be the keeper of the door to his commander's office.[3]

Bedell Smith was thankful when Hughes was left behind in the Mediterranean and that in the share-out of senior posts between the British and Americans, Eisenhower's Chief Administrative Officer at SHAEF was from Alexander's staff, Major-General Humfrey Gale, a British officer. Brigadier-General Thomas J Betts, G2 at SHAEF, said of Gale: 'He would be my man to run US Steel. He's that kind of a type, a great manager practically a genius . . .'[4] Administration of the Lines of Communication, COMZ in American nomenclature, was divided along national lines. So it was necessary to have an American commander for the American COMZ. That was where Bedell Smith's trouble started. He had hoped to choose his own man and subordinate him, through Gale, to SHAEF but it was not to be. Somervell and Marshall ensured that Lt Gen JCH Lee, an officer already established in the UK in charge of ETOUSA supply services, was appointed. To add to Bedell Smith's unhappiness, Hughes arrived from the Mediterranean, having been given a loosely defined role as minister without portfolio by Eisenhower. Hughes found time and opportunity to make trouble. Lee had not, of course, been chosen by Eisenhower for his post, a point that was mentioned more than once by Bedell Smith during subsequent events. After the war he observed:

> Of course, Lee was a stuffed shirt. He didn't know much about supply organisation. I would have liked someone else and I got Eisenhower prepared several times to fire him. I got Lutes over and later Clay with the idea of putting them into Lee's place, but something would come up and Marshall and Somervell would intervene . . . he did a better job than I gave him credit for at the time . . . he was one of the crosses we had to bear.[5]

That was Smith's comment in 1947 on the logistical muddle in North-West Europe. It reflected Smith's inability and Eisenhower's refusal to sack a senior American over what they had, as a result of their impotence, to pretend was a whole 'bunch of petty things'.

They were not petty things for they amounted to logistical chaos in 1944. Marshall's and Somervell's influence was decisive in a replay of the logistical row between Pershing and March and between Harbord and the G4 branch of the General Staff in GHQ in 1918. This time Washington won the contest, for Eisenhower was no Pershing. It will be recalled that in Marshall's reconstruction in Washington in March 1942, he created a command system which included the Service of Supply, later called the Army Service Force (ASF), under Somervell, who was to be Marshall's Goethals.[6] ASF was both an integral part of the War Department and a field command in the sense that it dealt directly with Lee, Somervell being one of Marshall's commanders as well as a staff officer. ASF was 'hastily thrown together', though. The staff officers who wrote the new organisation followed Marshall's instructions to decentralise but 'they did not know much about the Army's supply system'. ASF was a 'more or less unplanned product' of Marshall's general idea to reduce the number of agencies with which he had to deal. 'It also reflected the tendency of combat arms officers to take logistics for granted, a tendency which had caused embarrassment during World War I, and would cause further problems in World War II.' Somervell was determined to become the sole logistics adviser to Marshall and cut out the G4 branch of the General Staff and the logistics planning committees of Marshall's Operations and Plans Division (OPD). His own Plans and Operations Division, under the aggressive direction of Major-General Le Roy Lutes, were experts, and Somervell said that OPD merely duplicated it. It did not 'pay sufficient attention to practical logistical problems, especially the lead time required to produce weapons and other materials,' and he appropriated a larger role in strategic planning. OPD naturally resented ASF's intrusion.[7]

Marshall encouraged Somervell to take complete control of Supply, as Peyton March had urged Goethals. He gave him freedom, intervening only when essential. Somervell, energetic and determined, responded by welcoming full responsibility. He made himself second only to Marshall in power and was always extending the boundaries of his logistic empire from industry in rear to Lee's COMZ in ETOUSA. He provided Marshall with a continuous flow of information useful in the JCS and CCS. But whereas Marshall had abolished the combat arms directors – operations bureaux – in favour of a linear system which brought their organisations under Army Ground Force or field force commanders, Somervell found the abolition of seven technical service bureaux, headed by the Quartermaster's Corps, beyond him. Except for the Transportation Corps, a recent creation, they all had a long tradition of administrative independence and a dual role as staff agencies and operating commands. Consequently he could not create the unitary supply service that Arnold had in the USAAF. Yet, 'all were archaic procedurally and needed to be rationalised'.[8]

Somervell set himself a very difficult task and made it more difficult by an abrasive manner which irritated Congress as much as it did the heads of the technical bureaux. As production was not unlimited and the total demand from all fronts was exceeding capacity, he planned to regulate supply and demand for ammunition, weapons, food and clothing, petrol, oil and lubricants (POL), and vehicles of all kinds. He also decided to control the supply systems in the theatres of war when and where he was able. Far and away the biggest army consumer was ETOUSA and he intended to control Lee and his system. With hindsight, Somervell was anticipating the idea of cost-effectiveness, which in practice conceived operations as part of an industrial process controlled and limited by logistics and measurable by statistics. It was the interference in operations by Somervell's empire that Bedell Smith feared and to which OPD had reacted with hostility. (Eisenhower spoke to Somervell in Washington on 13 January 1944. Somervell told him that he was going to have Lee promoted to three-Star rank. Somervell's real motive, Eisenhower believed, was that the pyramid promotion rule would elevate Somervell, himself, to four-Stars. Without consulting Eisenhower, Marshall approved Lee's promotion.[9])

Somervell had to grapple with a problem within his empire that seems inseparable from the management of logistics in war and industrial enterprises at all times. It is that the technical services, which have civil counterparts, run best on functional lines which cut across the hierarchical channels of military command. The latter, though, must be master, lest production becomes an end in itself for the logistic services. The task of 'management', of the 'staff' in the military context, is to ensure that the technical services are efficient and that they serve the field commanders. The General Staff, therefore, manages COMZ but it cannot 'command' each *component* of it. There were two workable systems for its control which were distinct, but not different. In one a staff served a COMZ *commander,* such as Harbord had been and Lee was to be in 1944, who was a subordinate of SCAEF and dealt with him directly through SHAEF. The other system was to treat Lee as a second chief of staff, although Bedell Smith would be the first among equals because he was the head of the *General* staff which is responsible for overall supervision. The final solution of the 1918 muddle in the AEF would have been to make Harbord a chief of staff to Pershing, co-equal with the Chief of General Staff at GHQ. That was not promulgated before the Armistice and the dispute ran on into the post-war years without resolution. One reason was that an artificial distinction was made between a commander and a chief of staff. In 21st Army Group Montgomery's senior administrative officer, Major General Sir Miles Graham, was a chief of staff but still managed the Lines of Communication through subordinate area commanders. His relations with Montgomery were similar to those of Major General Francis de Guingand, Chief of General Staff. In ETO Lee was to be a commander outside the control of SHAEF and Chief of General Staff Bedell Smith, as Hughes had been.

The bureaucratic battle in Washington, at SHAEF and by Lee at COMZ, was for mastery. The bureaux in Washington, Transportation, Quartermasters, Signals, Engineers and Ordnance, each maintained a command and communication link with ETOUSA for their various functions. Because the bureaux had maintained their independence in Washington, their subordinates in ETOUSA insisted on the same status. A muddle was in the making because Somervell intended to control Lee but neither he nor Lee had control of their bureaux. The General Staff at SHAEF could only control Lee if Eisenhower insisted on it. Perhaps none of this would have mattered if Lee had not been, as Bedell Smith described him, 'a stuffed shirt'.

At first glance, JCH Lee was unsuitable as commander of the COMZ because he had no experience of modern field conditions. Dubbed 'Jesus Christ Himself', because he was a lay preacher and inclined to read the Bible to his subordinates during journeys by air, he was also an autocrat. Mistakenly, he took the Western Front as his supply model but had not studied the uncorrected faults of the American system in 1918. He proved to have grave professional weaknesses. A poor improviser, he did not keep a balance between supplies on wheels and supplies on the ground. That was as important as it was difficult to effect, for it demanded a pool of transport and labour to be available at short notice to react to an imbalance caused by the sudden demands of large, fluid operations. Close liaison with operational staffs was essential to ensure intelligent anticipation. Lee was not prepared for rapid operations because the American armies had not, so far, experienced them and he had not read the lessons of the lengthy experience of the British in the Mediterranean. He seemed to have a peacetime quartermaster's mind: if an item was not on the authorised table of equipment it could not be issued. If a unit's demands exceeded its authorised scale, its operations should be modified, since obviously the scale could not be changed, which exasperated operational staffs and commanders alike. The expression 'The Tyranny of Logistics' exactly describes his régime, since he was like the salesman who assures the customer that he may have anything he wants provided it is on the list in his hand. Although all this actually lay in the future, Bedell Smith anticipated it with a gloom arising from his own experience of the results of faulty command and staff systems.

Lee's personality and lack of qualifications and the impotence of the General Staff to control him in the field was not the only aspect of logistics that worried Bedell Smith. Lee had been the manager of the UK end of BOLERO, the operational name for the build-up of American supplies and men in the UK. He controlled the UK end of the supply line before D-day, with Somervell at the American end. His was a static organisation in the UK with established ports, railways, roads, vehicles and a labour force. Somervell intended to transfer it to Normandy and run down the UK advanced base. He would then service Normandy directly from the United States by sea. Lee's ETOUSA organisation was, as he should have appreciated, unsuitable for France where the roads and railways had been shattered by air attacks in order to prevent German troop movements to the invasion beaches, and the port facilities expertly demolished by German engineers. Until these were restored, the armies ashore would have to be supplied over the beaches and by motor transport. By failing to recognise this, Somervell and Lee revealed how out of touch they were with the operational plan and ignorant of conditions in the field.

Bedell Smith's reaction to all this was to make the best of Lee but to rearrange command and control so as to bring him under Eisenhower's direct control. ETOUSA was, of course, a purely American organisation and Eisenhower became its commanding general. He commanded all Americans including Lee and his COMZ. In turn Lee was made deputy commander of ETOUSA as the senior officer in COMZ. Bedell Smith, as

Chief of Staff to Eisenhower, was also Chief of Staff to the commander of ETOUSA. One of his deputy chiefs of staff in SHAEF became Lee's chief of staff in COMZ. In this way Bedell Smith hoped that he and the American element in SHAEF would be able to control Lee, but in the last analysis all rested on Eisenhower's keeping Lee as his subordinate commander firmly in his place, and resisting Somervell if he interfered. If this solution sounds complicated it was, and the system had other curious twists. As Deputy Commander ETO, Lee was theoretically Bradley's superior in the American chain of command, but in the SHAEF (International) chain he and Bradley were equal because army groups and COMZ were rated equal commands.

Bradley as an army group commander had no responsibility for supplies. Lee dealt directly with Bradley's subordinate army commanders.* Worse, Smith could not persuade Eisenhower that SHAEF G3 (Operations) and G4 (logistics) staffs had to deal directly with Lee, as a commander of equal seniority to Bradley. Consequently Bedell Smith was doomed to have the running fight with Lee that he had with Hughes in AFHQ, and Moseley had with Harbord in 1918, despite this contrivance.

It is difficult to imagine a more fantastic structure of staff relationships. Eisenhower's command system both in operations and logistics depended on the goodwill of its members. The logistics side of it was faulty, the operational one was not necessarily so, but whether it was Bradley and Montgomery who were at loggerheads or Lee and the army commanders, it was Eisenhower who would have to exert himself to make decisions in both fields if things went wrong. Himself a man of goodwill, he believed that his subordinates were too. He never prepared himself for the stark decisions that might face him, if his confidence proved to be misplaced, by mastering the essentials of the operations and the logistics of the campaign. That would have entailed a continuous mental effort for which he was unprepared because, fundamentally, he was intellectually lazy. His nervous energy was dispersed by a radiant personality; not much was left for his intellect. Bedell Smith, the sceptic who worked seventeen hours a day to master his trade, for whom knowledge was power, hoped for the best but prepared for the worst.

Circumstances did bring crises in command and in logistics. Eisenhower did not foresee either and proved incapable of handling them. The command crisis was instigated by men with small parts to play in the battle of Normandy, but who enjoyed power and importance in London and Washington, where they were located before SHAEF moved to Normandy.

* In the US command chain, army group and corps headquarters were concerned only with operational matters.

Like Eisenhower, they paid too little attention to the nature of the wearing out battle in Normandy after the initial assault and consolidation, or to Montgomery's general idea for its conduct. Their views were narrowly centred on such things as the establishment of airfields and the maintenance of the tentative timetable sketched into Montgomery's pre-D-day plan. They were fixated on the danger of a Western Front-style stalemate developing.

Two RAF officers, Sir Arthur Tedder, Eisenhower's Deputy SCAEF, and Air Marshal Sir Arthur ('Maori' or 'Mary') L Coningham, the abrasive commander of the Allied Tactical Air Forces, both of whom had more power than responsibility in the inflated system of Allied command at the top, completely misread what was happening on the ground. Both should have known better but were prejudiced observers, since they had disliked Montgomery since their first clashes with him in the Western Desert. Eisenhower had not grasped that, by 1944, battles with the Germans were inseparable from attrition. He did not understand that the essential need was for the enemy to be destroyed and that gaining territory was unimportant, except as the means of grinding the enemy down. Consequently he was unable to stem the tide of ill-informed criticism that arose as, for six weeks, slow progress was made at the battle fronts. The very American chauvinism that he dreaded was being led by British critics, some of them within SHAEF. When the battle ended with a resounding success for Allied arms and within the time predicted, he had contributed, by his indecisive and equivocal stance, to the prevailing mood against Montgomery, so very much at variance with the feeling of the troops in the field. The mood, exacerbated by those responsible having been proved by events to have been quite wrong, was fed in symbiotic fashion by the way the progress and outcome of the battle was conceived by the American press and the War Department. Eisenhower, ever the politician, felt compelled to take a direct hand in the tactical command of the armies in the ensuing advance, lest Montgomery, as Bradley's recent superior, be seen by Americans to be still in charge when the Americans had more divisions in the field than the British. For the moment, Eisenhower's reluctance to assume operational command melted in the euphoria of victory, or a victory requiring only one good heave to end the war, an end that seemed imminent.

In three weeks that victory was followed by stiff battles on the German frontier which showed that neither the Allied command system nor the American logistics system had been able to respond to such a fast moving battle situation. The US armies first ran short of gasoline during the advance and later ammunition as German resistance stiffened throughout the autumn. Faulty organisation was not rescued by good leadership.

Eisenhower blocked Smith's attempts to replace Lee. The armies at the front suffered and so did relations between the Allies. The logistics muddle and shortages lasted until mismanagement in both command and logistics finally came to a single head when the enemy launched his counter-offensive in the Ardennes in December.

CHAPTER 13

THE CAMPAIGN IN EUROPE: PRIDE AND PREJUDICE

Thrice is he armed that hath his quarrel just . . .

KING HENRY VI, ACT III, SC. 2

The rosy glow of victory in Europe on May 8, 1945, had not faded when 'revelations' from journalists and the generals' versions of how it had been won started to appear. Historical accounts then began to flow and to erode first impressions. They clarified what had happened and started to expose the 'how' and the 'why' of the campaign. We are concerned mainly with the latter and will assume that readers are familiar with the general outline of 'what' happened: namely, that the campaign was fought in Normandy from June to August 1944, on the frontiers of Germany with France, Belgium and Holland through the autumn and winter, and after the cross-ing of the Rhine in force in March 1945, in a rapid advance through Germany to the Baltic, the Elbe and to Leipzig, 90 miles southwest of Berlin.

Analytical and synthetical history, such as ours, in uncovering the 'how' and the 'why', is necessarily critical. We could not undertake it until painstaking, narrative accounts of the events by official historians and thorough biographies of the main actors had been written. The former are national histories: histories of the coalition from one nation's vantage point. They avoid meeting controversies head on although they leave hints of them between the lines. The biographers, on the other hand enliven the narrative by bringing the controversies and the men who were involved in them into the open. With some extrapolation on our part, we have peopled our pages with men of pride and prejudice rather than unreal national heroes. Clashes between such men, all members of one English-speaking family, were to be expected. There is no need to speak of them in hushed voices nearly half a century after the event. They may be judged by professional, international standards. This chapter changes the lighting on some familiar historical scenes and warns the reader what to expect of the military leaders and their men in the campaign. Some preliminary remarks concern the relationship between the First and Second World Wars and the political nature of wars in general.

In war as in peace politics disposes of much of the time of military as well as political leaders. Soldiers who are competent politicians are often represented as being less admirable for their talent, and quite wrongly. We shall find that the politics of the First War cast a long shadow over the Second and that the memory of it influenced the soldiers continually, sometimes prejudicially. Both wars were *Materialschlachten*: tests of the industrial scientific and social strength of the combatants in peace and of their adaptability to war. The Americans learned the hard way about the politics of logistics in the First War and they exploited logistics in the Second as they perceived the French and British had in 1917 and 1918. The human raw material in the armies was shaped in peacetime societies and could not be completely altered by military training in war, reminding us that war and peace are part of a continuum. The First War was in most respects a more severe test of leadership. Consequently, we should judge its leaders with more compassion than is customary and those of the Second with more reserve. Both were coalition wars and the similarity between the problems that arose between allies should not surprise us, nor in fact that they provoked similar responses. In 1914–1918 the leaders of the Entente powers sought the independence and exploited the strength and military competence of their respective national contingents while simultaneously they were arguing for Allied strategy to be objective and unified and to eschew selfish national considerations. Attempts to reconcile these contradictory aims stirred up discord in both wars. In 1943–44 the Americans, as in 1917–1918, insisted that their armed forces should neither be subordinated to a foreign commander nor should they be used to further the post-war goals or interests of their partners, even if to do so benefited operations. (This xenophobic attitude was all very well but the realities of the campaign, as we shall see, made it inevitable that some form of compromise would have to be achieved and from time to time American formations would come under British command for a limited period). They had in mind British not Soviet imperial interests. The British, for their part, wished to end as quickly as possible another war that was bankrupting them and, again, had the survival of their imperial position in the forefront of their minds. The bases and communications of the Empire, a substantial although relatively waning military contribution and their greater experience of war gave them their influence on Allied strategy. The American influence came from the vast superiority of their resources and their determination to use them. How power was converted into influence in both coalition wars is the prevailing theme in our treatment of supreme command.

The First World War saw the emergence of the 'generalissimo', resisted by British soldiers at first and then by the Americans and only reluctantly accepted in the person of Ferdinand Foch in the teeth of a great emergency, the near rupture of the Allied front in 1918. Military victory came upon the heads of Allied governments suddenly and before they were much concerned about controlling Foch through the machinery of the Supreme Allied War Council. But the whole experience of government relations with field commanders made an impression deep enough to induce the British and Americans to create the system we have described for controlling Allied strategy generally, and supreme Allied commanders in the field in particular, early in 1942 before the campaign in North Africa started. They did not wait for the pressure of events as in 1917. The unchallenged authority of the Chiefs of Staff in the CCS over Cs-in-C in the field also flowed from the experiences of Generals C Peyton March and the British CIGS, General Sir William Robertson in the First War when neither Pershing nor Haig was under their control.

By 1943, the careers of the senior soldiers had spanned years of baffling change in the conduct of war. Some of these changes have been rehearsed in earlier parts of this book. Not the least important of them was the breaking down of barriers, ideological and rational, between the separate armed services and the civil and military domains. As a supreme commander in the Mediterranean and in North-West Europe from the end of 1942 until the defeat of Germany in May 1945, Eisenhower was in the middle of the rip between these civil-military tides. He was the link between operational commanders and the military men and politicians in Washington and London who really ran the war. His role was partly political, or diplomatic, since he was answerable to the British – that is to say Churchill – as well as Marshall in Washington, and he was responsible for civil-military affairs on the Continent as well as for military success or failure. He was concerned with Europe in war but had to prepare Europe for peace. He was an American but had to behave as an international figure. He was a soldier, but he had to wear the uniform of three services. We may imagine him as a principal character in the second act of a play in which the first act concerned the Western Front between 1914 and 1918, where some of his problems had first appeared, and the third act had yet to be played in the liquidation of the European colonial empires in Africa and South-East Asia, with Vietnam lying in the more distant future.

The idea of 'the four freedoms' was the moral war aim of the Allies.

The concept of 'United Nations' may have inspired the upper, idealistic, anti-imperialists in both English-speaking nations, but it did not impress the mass of American and British citizen soldiers, except insofar as the Americans equated being anti-imperialist with being anti-British. Similarly, the idea that Fascism was a great evil and a war against it just, based as it was on sophisticated moral and theological arguments rather than experience, cut little ice, in spite of the simplistic sustained propaganda of the Allied media. To the rank and file it was apparent that the unjust were as well armed, better even, as they and as efficient and eager in the fray.

Indeed, in this respect, the Germans had the advantage. The German people were patriotic, militaristic, authoritarian, with deep reverence for the state, and they were filled with a sense of injustice by the indictment of war guilt and the provisions of the Treaty of Versailles. The advent of Nazism exploited and amplified this deep discontent, acting through the Party on the adults, bourgeois and proletarian, and on those in or approaching the military age groups through the Hitler Youth Movement. When the time came, therefore, to build up the *Reichswehr,* the General Staff had malleable, even enthusiastic material to work on. German training was thorough and rigorous, with strong emphasis on minor tactics and aggression. German discipline was unique. A German officer would not hesitate to use his pistol to enforce obedience on the battlefield, but contrary to the popular image, there was an easy, comradely relationship between all ranks quite unlike anything in the Allied armies, except, perhaps, in the British Commonwealth Divisions. The Germans had the secret of combining strict discipline with initiative at every level, without which *Auftragstaktik* was unworkable. German soldiers were physically fitter and better educated than their opponents; some they respected, but their general opinion was that they were soft, morally and physically, unenterprising and reluctant to engage in close combat of machine-pistol and grenade. Until the last months of the war German morale held up under adversity in a way that astonished, indeed discomfited, the Allied High Command.

By contrast, the morale of the Allied armies never ceased to cause its commanders anxiety, although its decay had to be kept secret, and the full facts are hard to establish even today. All experienced soldiers know that there is a limit to the durability of the bravest individuals and the best trained and most highly motivated units. Morale can be expressed in effective combat-days, the result of investigation by army psychologists. Yet it has to be said that it was difficult to observe this process at work in the German Army, in which every man was a combat soldier, not only the infantry. The only objective, reliable statistical measure of morale is desertion, and in Egypt, North Africa, Italy and France the Allied statistics were dire. They included the wholesale absence from duty of men in the base and lines of communication units, who in the Allied armies were virtually non-combatants, as well as the weaker brethren who through neurosis, battle-fatigue or a healthy sense of self preservation strayed away from the zone of combat. The causes for this phenomenon were rooted in the social structure and therefore the training and organisation of the two Allied armies.[1]

The Americans did not give a great deal of thought to morale, in the sense of fighting spirit. Generals in all armies as a matter of faith and national pride believe that their soldiers are naturally endowed with courage. The younger American soldier was buoyed up by his national self-confidence, and the older by the memories of a war which for them had ended quickly in a glorious victory for American arms, or so it was perceived. Unlike the British, there was no folk-memory of the murderous attrition of 1916 and 1917: the AEF had emerged from the war in 1918 with its belief in unlimited objectives and aggression unshaken. The handicap the US Army was never able to shake off was the adoption of a logically justifiable but militarily inappropriate industrial model. The most economical use of the work-force was made by allotting recruits with special or potential skills to jobs where the fullest use could be made of them. As an inevitable consequence, the lion's share of the best and most intelligent went to the air force and the technical arms and services, leaving the combat arms, especially the infantry, starved of potential junior leaders. After basic training, men were trained in various simple special skills (mortar-man, machine-gunner, rifleman, signaller, and so on) to fill a vast number of slots, and units manned rather as if setting up a factory. It made replacement in battle deceptively easy, but compared with the inefficient British system it was a soulless process. There was no focus for *espirit de corps*. The reinforcement system gave Marshall continuous concern as it wasted manpower and upset morale. An officer who passed through 1st Division's replacement chain wrote: 'I'm struck by my own thought that fighting is like an athletic life; one is always hanging about in training for the next event. Somehow it's impossible to get on with anything else.'

The British suffered from the same problems of job allotment, and the same tendency to put too many of the lower categories into the infantry, a result of over-stressing armour after German successes in 1940 and 1941, but its effect was mitigated to a certain extent by over-officering (as compared with the Germans) and by traditional grouping by region and ethnicity into regiments, in which, as a general rule, a man stayed during his service and to which he returned from hospital or extra-regimental employment. One British problem was a legacy of the Western Front. As General George Marshall perceptively noted in another context, the shadow of the Somme and Passchendaele haunted British generalship. In the Second World War, no British commander could afford to buy victory at the cost of heavy casualties, for political reasons quite apart from the constraints imposed by lack of military man-power.

In the inter-war years, the British had been indoctrinated with anti-militarism, and it was too late to shake it off when the time came to re-arm. Between 1939 and 1942, when the new divisions were being trained in the United Kingdom, press and public maintained a jealous scrutiny of the Army's methods, and were quick to intervene at any sign of over-severe discipline or brutal training. British training and discipline were as a result less rigorous and more slack than the German, and discipline milder than in the US Army. The exception was élite corps such as commandos and parachute regiments where training and discipline were governed by what the Germans call *innererführung*, self-discipline based on pride, duty and comradeship. The morale of the regimental combat troops held up remarkably well during the long string of defeats in 1939–1942, but it was fragile. The mood was cynical rather than defeatist. British soldiers were quick to detect the false notes of propaganda portraying shameful reverses as heroic retreats. It was a tendency fortunately corrected in time by the close attention Montgomery paid to morale, and his carefully managed succession of victories in 1942 and 1943.

Having made these strictures, it has to be added that once the British and Americans had got into their stride, they soon became battle-wise. There was plenty of talent *at the top*, for the command of corps, divisions and regiments. The best American and British units were fully a match for the best of the German. Depth was lacking, though, and in the broad middle span the Germans had the advantage; not least because all German soldiers were trained for combat first and foremost. Clerks, storemen, *Luftwaffe* ground personnel and anti-aircraft gunners were all reinforcements for the fighting line.

The mutual perception of British and American senior commanders and their men has excited interest over the years. All soldiers run a critical eye over their rivals in their own army and their Allies. The criticisms they made of each other were no more severe than between the French and

British in the earlier war.* The Americans conceded that British soldiers could fight well, but their generals were unenterprising, even timid, unwilling to aim at distant strategic objectives, preferring a step-by-step operational method, and unwilling to attack without massive superiority in material and numbers, and then only after long and methodical planning. The British, over-cocky from their recovery from continual defeat, considered the American generals headquarter-bound, seldom visiting the front line troops or looking at the ground, and naive about the capability of their troops. Their methods were reminiscent of the Western Front. In their opinion the US infantry was reluctant to fight at night, had poor fire-discipline, and did not patrol or show curiosity about the enemy in front of them. None of this would have done any harm, with proper discretion. The fat was first spilled in the fire by a British senior officer in Tunisia. Ignorant of the perils of talking unbriefed to newspaper correspondents, when asked his opinion of the US army, instead of making an anodyne reply he offered his candid opinion. This was shortly after the rout of the green US II Corps by Rommel at the Kasserine Pass in February 1943.

The real reason for British insensitivity towards their ally was that British officers as a class had little or no understanding of Americans or of the history of the United States. They were largely ignorant of the fact that by virtue of the traditions of the Revolution and the bias in teaching history in their schools, Americans regarded the British as their hereditary enemy. If they had met any Americans they had in all probability been anglophiles, whose excellent manners would not have betrayed their prejudices, if any. The British were certainly unaware of the extreme American sensitivity to any hint of condescension. The melancholy fact was that the ordinary American was as insular as his British counterpart, his view of him being based on the Hollywood stereotype, and was quick, almost eager, to identify the British as an object for his dislike. James Gavin in his memoirs records that the staff of the US II Corps blamed the British (wrongly, in fact) for the dismissal of the inept General Lloyd C Fredenhall. He himself describes Lieutenant-General FAM Browning as 'a dapper, handsome man who in combat turned out to be a first class soldier in every respect', but disparages him on the basis of gossip thereafter. Russell Weigley, without identifying his source gives the American opinion of Browning as 'the sort of supercilious aristocrat (sic) for whom Americans are likely to feel an instinctive dislike: tall, moustached, well

---

* In the British Army the infantry looked down on the artillery, the Green Jackets and light infantry looked down on the infantry of the line, the Scots, Irish and Welsh on the English, the Guards looked down on all the rest of the infantry and airborne troops looked down on everybody.

poised. Too deliberate a smile, cool and polished manners of a British gentleman.' In fact, the American airborne leaders did strongly dislike him, especially Ridgway.[2]

The relationship was fraught with dislike and misconceptions. Anglo-French feelings were mitigated in 1914–1918 because the two armies were separated and had no common language but neither the British nor the Americans harboured affectionate thoughts for their ally by the Armistice. In 1942–1945 national prejudice was bound to affect a joint command with integrated staffs and units of both nations mixed up together. This was the real cause of what David Irving called 'The War Between the Generals'.

Fortunately, that deplorable conflict was unknown and unimagined by the men in units or even on most divisional and corps staffs in either army. At that level the Allies worked well together, accepting with good humour each other's idiosyncrasies. But at the top of the ladder, and mainly in the US Army, backbiting became endemic as the campaign proceeded. When the complaints of a senior commander against his ally remain a secret between himself and his diary, their recording may be cathartic. In the stress of battle, clashes of opinion between strong-minded commanders are unavoidable. It is only necessary to recall the heated exchanges between Pershing and Foch over the need to commit the Americans to operations before perfecting their training. Neither thought the worse of the other and their relationship survived, although not their friendship. In the autumn of 1944, the state of affairs was far worse. The rancour of a few senior American commanders for their British colleagues frustrated the objective discussion of strategic options altogether. It was a situation that Eisenhower utterly failed to correct, although Marshall had been concerned about it in Tunisia.

When Eisenhower moved from the Mediterranean to the supreme command in North-West Europe, he brought with him this old entrenched problem as well as new and intractable ones. The former, he may have believed, had been overcome, or, at least, that it was not as deep and corrosive as the antipathy between American and British commanders was to prove to be.

In North Africa, he had had a tight grip on his own headquarters but, preoccupied with the political problems of a coalition and of operating in French territory in which there was a quarrelsome government in exile, he had stood at some distance from clashes between his high mettled subordinates in the field. To an extent, Alexander, the Allied land force commander, shielded him there and later in Sicily and Italy but Alexander's post was not recreated in London. Eisenhower was never a man to seek out problems and he was not good at anticipating trouble. As SCAEF, he relied

215

on his power to mediate between parties or agencies, to conciliate, and to devise structures for command agreeable to all members of a coalition after conflict arose. He was supremely a master of organisational architecture whose various chiefs could be relied on to manage their respective enterprises, the nature of which Eisenhower did not fully understand or, indeed, did not consider it necessary for him to understand, while he looked after the high political questions. Everyone, including Churchill, but excepting the top leading British soldiers, was confident that he was a completely satisfactory choice for the supreme command. Only Montgomery discerned that a generalissimo who did not understand operations could not enforce his authority on subordinates who did.

Eisenhower's weakness was, in a word, his refusal to take command. Temperamentally, he was incapable of initiative. This was satisfactory if considered purely within the framework in which he himself elected to work. He would take advice, suggest compromise, arrive at an acceptable solution based on that advice. But he was appointed to be a supreme *commander*, i.e., one whose duty it was to see when trouble was brewing, and act at once, and to seize the fleeting opportunity before others nudged him to draw attention to it. It is essential for a commander-in-chief to delegate, but he must also keep himself in touch by informal contact and through the antennae that a good commander should have for sensing the mood of what is going on below, as well as through the usual channels of memoranda, reports and information copies of orders too long for him to read which are filtered by his staff. Another commander might have averted the muddle and consequent bad blood between Montgomery and AFHQ over the planning of the invasion of Sicily, and stepped in immediately to cure the friction between the American generals and Montgomery during its execution. A stronger man would have been more than a passive spectator during the closure of the Falaise Gap in Normandy, whatever his exact position was at that moment, and would have understood that his other business was unimportant compared with ensuring that the momentum of the Allied advance in August and September was maintained. Later, during the fighting on the German frontier, he would have called them to order when they not only questioned but sabotaged his own intentions. It should be emphasised that Eisenhower's quarrel with Montgomery was not, fundamentally, over operational principles, but Montgomery's curiously inverted insubordination in urging his chief to *take command*. Eisenhower's fundamental weakness was due to the fact that he had never commanded. During the formative period of his career he had been a loyal servant to two strong-minded masters: first MacArthur and then Marshall. Eisenhower understood perfectly that whatever his own title,

Marshall was *de facto* commander-in-chief of the US Army and Air Force.

RA Butler, the British politician, once observed that 'a prime minister had to be a good butcher, and know the joints'; that he had to be ruthless in dealing with his subordinates and to dispose of those who proved unequal to their task without mercy. Eisenhower shrank from such butchery; it may well have been a trait of the US Army officer corps as a whole. He was cautious, even devious in his sacking of General Lloyd D Fredendall, whose ineptness led to the embarrassing reverse at Kasserine; first sending an extra officer to his headquarters as an 'adviser', in reality to report on its deficiencies, and even asking the newly arrived Alexander for his opinion. (That enigmatic character replied tactfully that 'he was sure that the US Army had better generals'.) Eisenhower only relieved Patton as a result of the publicity the all-powerful corps of war-correspondents gave to his behaviour.* This may have been owing not only to the club-like solidarity of the US officers, but because their promotions and appointments were virtually in the gift of Congress. The publicity afforded by the press might make or break a US army general.† The same factor led to the distortion of American strategy by the obsession of US generals with territorial goals. To liberate Rome, be first over the Rhine or the conqueror of Metz were tangible news items more easily understood than such ideas as that the objective in Normandy was the annihilation of the German armies.

Apart from such constraints, Eisenhower was under pressure from above as well as from below. His great master, Marshall, was as fully determined as Pershing had been twenty-five years before, that sharing of effort was not to detract from victory in Europe being seen as a triumph of American arms, and that therefore the Americans should fight united under an American commander. It was Marshall who stiffened Eisenhower's resistance to suggestions that an Allied Land Force Commander should be appointed in northwest Europe: Marshall was determined that Eisenhower should command as he would have commanded had he been SCAEF. As long as that responsibility rested with his dutiful lieutenant, he could be confident that his wishes would be respected, as they might not be if a

---

* We would also cite the case of General Lewis G Brereton, who was directly and personally responsible for the USAAF in the Philippines at Clark Field being destroyed on the ground, who became commander of 1st Allied Airborne Army: a feeble, dismal little man, by all accounts. It is significant that in the many postmortems on 'Arnhem' his name is never mentioned.

† As it did Mark Clark, who was blamed for the casualties in the Texas National Guard Division at 'Bloody River' in Italy.

commander he could not control were interposed a link below in the chain of command.

We must bear in mind these various conflicting factors and undercurrents when Eisenhower met the great crises of the campaign: the initial stalemate, the unexpectedly sweeping nature of the victory in August, the virtual break-down of the US logistical system in France, the controversial strategy chosen for forcing the Siegfried defences and the passage of the Rhine and after the crossing, for concluding the war when the Allies were approaching the Soviet armies. When these episodes are described in subsequent chapters the reader should remember that the crucial traits that Eisenhower brought to his task had their good and bad sides. His amiability and tact were liked by the British, rather less by the Americans, and praised by most writers. This trait has to be balanced by his inability to force men who were not naturally disposed to be cooperative to work as a team. He knew of this weakness but thought that he had ensured against it. Denied a land forces commander like Alexander, he determined not to take direct operational command himself but to guide rather than command his two principal lieutenants, Montgomery and Bradley. That he deliberately concealed his intentions in that respect is significant when we examine his performance as a commander. His scheme collapsed because Montgomery's powerful reputation was tarnished in Normandy and Bradley would not cooperate with him thereafter. Required, thereafter, to control his subordinates Eisenhower could not do it.

Montgomery was not only the focus of American criticism, but also the target of detractors in the Royal Air Force and at SHAEF as well. He symbolised, for some senior American commanders, the worst British personality traits but in over-reacting to them they, in turn, exposed the shallowness of their own professionalism in failing to respond to his professional skill. Few successful commanders have been likable. When Americans experienced Montgomery's efficiency they recognised it. General Simpson, US Ninth Army Commander, who worked much of the time under Montgomery, appreciated being in 21st Army Group where he received clear orders, was given help when he needed it, and was visited frequently by Montgomery. Hodges too, found working under Montgomery in the Ardennes satisfactory. Indeed, in Normandy, earlier, Bradley himself had found that his relations with Montgomery had been amicable and that they made an effective pair. All three appreciated Montgomery's habit of going forward to visit and encourage them and not expecting his subordinates to reach back to him. That standard procedure was not practised by Bradley or Hodges in the Ardennes, both of whom lost touch with their subordinates. At that time, Eisenhower and Bradley allowed themselves to be virtually incarcerated at their headquarters for fear of German infiltrators. The collapse of his own command system in the Ardennes shook Bradley's confidence, never secure, and excited his ire against Montgomery further. Its disarray was increased by the bad example he had set his subordinates in circumventing Eisenhower's directives, and encouraging them to share his complaints against Montgomery, a surprising lapse in a man who has been praised for his quiet professionalism and loyalty. He behaved like a man with a grievance who talks himself into a storm when he is not face to face with his *bête noire*. How can we explain his behaviour further?

Part of the explanation lay in Patton, Bradley's subordinate. Like Montgomery, Patton needed to dominate and to be independent. Patton was senior to Bradley in army rank and in Sicily had been his army commander. He seemed to enjoy a psychological ascendancy over him. Yet their relationship was ambivalent. In Sicily, Bradley criticised Patton for his drive into the blue on Palermo and for allowing the situation to arise that gave him the excuse for it. Montgomery had demanded the use of one of Bradley's corps' roads when he shifted his drive from the east coast inland. Alexander told Patton to surrender it. Patton did not argue the toss, and Bradley, instead of negotiating the details of the hand-over with his British neighbour, Oliver Leese, halted his 45th Division and allowed a large German force to escape under its nose. For this incident, in which Bradley had cut off his nose to spite his face, he blamed Montgomery and Patton almost equally. For his part, Patton blamed Alexander and Montgomery and the affair became a *cause célèbre* for Americans.[3] It confirmed an American conviction, for which there was, unfortunately, ample circumstantial evidence, that the British had relegated them to a supporting role in Sicily because they distrusted their fighting value. The childish behaviour of both Americans was provoked by Alexander who had failed to explain the situation to Patton and, indeed, to control the operations of his two armies. It was he who permitted Patton to embark on his irrelevant drive on Palermo. The lesson of the incident, that commanders must control their temperamental subordinates or operations will go off the rails, was evidently lost on Eisenhower, for in Europe he behaved much like Alexander. Thereafter, Bradley and Patton assumed, what Montgomery always practised, that under weak leadership senior commanders should interpret their orders to suit themselves. In North West Europe it led to a tacit conspiracy to ignore Eisenhower if desirable. Soon after the incident in Sicily Patton was disgraced for slapping psychiatric patients in military hospitals. Bradley, his senior corps commander, was promoted over his head to command in OVERLORD. Later, restored to favour, Patton became Third Army commander under Bradley. As a subordinate, he was both wilful and irresponsible. Bradley, on the other hand, needed a superior to guide him, as Montgomery guided him in Normandy. He had been elevated too quickly from commanding a corps in Sicily to an army in Normandy and then an Army Group. Eisenhower was useless as a guide in operations: the blind leading the blind. Montgomery, on the other hand, was typical of some competent but abrasive men in being remarkably patient and understanding with subordinates and superiors when he had complete authority over the first and had gained ascendancy over and hence independence of the second. As Eighth Army Commander he dominated General Harold Alexander. They got on very well together because Alexander allowed Montgomery freedom of action. Montgomery demonstrated the same accord with Hodges, his subordinate in the Ardennes, as he had earlier with Bradley in Normandy. The key to understanding Montgomery's attitude to his American colleagues was his emotional necessity to be the dominant partner in any relationship. He had to convince them that the course he proposed was correct. In the meanwhile, he professed himself unable to understand how anyone could have doubts about the matter. His tragedy was that he was usually right but failed to understand the emotional roots of American dissent. What had been mild irritation became a virulent complaint, until Montgomery was the embodiment of everything that the Americans found objectionable in the British character.[4]

To suggest that had Montgomery behaved differently, had he been more pliant or more tactful, he might have persuaded Eisenhower not only to adopt his plans but to follow them through, and Bradley to cooperate with him, is to ignore this underlying Anglophobia; a satisfactory outcome would have required the three men to behave out of character and context. Eisenhower, though normally ever ready to see all sides of every question, was bound to take the American's side when he was pushed by Marshall from behind against a resistant Bradley in front. Marshall came to see Bradley as symbolising the US Army on trial and Eisenhower naturally supported that view. The reputation of the US Army was Eisenhower's legitimate concern, but in defending it he abdicated responsibility for guiding Allied strategy objectively in favour of allowing his American commanders free rein, even if they were subverting his own plans. He rationalised that the politically expedient was also best operationally. In consequence his fig leaf strategy amounted to no more than attacking everywhere to the limit of, and beyond, the capacity of his troops, like early French practice on the Western Front. It precluded the concentration and economical use of Eisenhower's available forces and prevented his armies from cooperating with one another.

The operational details of Eisenhower's conduct of the campaign must await the next chapter. Here we are concerned with the relations between the commanders which dominated operations. It is necessary, though, to point out that Bradley was caught in an operational as well as a psychological trap of his own making. He would have had to be a moron not to see that the broad northern thrust, roughly, Aachen-Cologne and Louvain-Wesel-Ruhr and across the German plain to the Elbe and on to Berlin and Hamburg which Montgomery advocated so strongly, was decisive. Operational logic demanded that his First and Ninth and Montgomery's Second Armies, which lay astride those thrust lines, be heavily reinforced and form a common front. That is how Eisenhower's own staff understood it; indeed it was their own plan. But as Bradley would neither surrender Hodges and Simpson to the loathed Monty, nor fight alongside him, he downgraded the northern thrust line and magnified the importance and feasibility of the southern one, south of the Ardennes. Although in the autumn Eisenhower told Bradley that he should either command his northern armies and fight beside Montgomery, handing his southern ones over to 6th Army Group under Devers, whose armies had entered the theatre via ANVIL, or allow Montgomery to take charge north of the Ardennes, he could not prevail on Bradley and would not insist on compliance. In this case Eisenhower displayed his principal weakness, that he could not command obedience to his orders.

Cooperation with Montgomery was difficult for Bradley after Normandy and impossible after he had failed to fulfil Eisenhower's hope of reaching the Rhine in the autumn and both had been humiliated by the collapse of Bradley's First Army in the Ardennes in December. Patton had succeeded in emerging from the Ardennes with credit, which made Bradley even more sensitive to the witticisms of his subordinate who described Eisenhower as 'the best general the British have' and continually criticised Montgomery, who had been given control of Bradley's First and Ninth Armies on the northern side of the Ardennes. Thereafter, Bradley was afraid of losing control of his northern armies.

It has been suggested that had Patton been the army group commander instead of Bradley, that great actor would have adopted a completely different attitude to Montgomery, whose professionalism he respected. Montgomery, another *prima donna*, might have teamed up with him to keep Eisenhower away from the fighting, something he could not achieve with Bradley who was encouraged by Patton to stand on his dignity as the commander of twice as many divisions. Montgomery could never get on equal terms with a man who he knew was not master of his trade. Patton, on the other hand, was an authentic American hero who represented a model of the outspoken and daring American leader who takes risks and pulls them off. In fact, his reputation had been earned by advancing rapidly against negligible opposition after First Army had broken out in Normandy – as he had in Sicily. On the Moselle, in the autumn, his accomplishments were bought at an exorbitant price. But Patton, like Montgomery, performed best when independent of men whom he did not respect.

The inadequacy of American leadership at the top might have been exposed by its mistakes by the end of 1944 had Bradley and Patton not obfuscated by turning the command issue into a popularity contest between themselves and Montgomery, which they were bound to win, and had Eisenhower not fabricated the broad and narrow front dispute, saddling Montgomery with the latter. Thus it has been interpreted ever since. Bradley and Patton nationalised the campaign where Eisenhower had tried hard to internationalise it. Unfortunately, as Marshall subscribed to their point of view, Bradley and Patton were on safe ground. Where they were less secure was on their record of performance. As we have pointed out, American generals attached great importance to territorial goals as proof, in terms understandable by journalists, of their superior skill and the achievements of their armies. By that measure they had certainly failed.[5] To American chagrin, the great superiority they enjoyed had been of little avail after Normandy. The Germans were fighting as hard as ever, and victory in Europe had been postponed, it seemed until late 1945.

Here we must return to an earlier subject that concerned the American commanders during the relentless and disappointing autumn and winter fighting of 1944: the operational limitations imposed by the quality and the quantity of their infantry, combined with a shortage of supplies, particularly ammunition. By the end of the year, both shortages were serious and increasingly the subject of confidential memoranda and signals. We emphasise the problems of the Americans because, whereas the insufficiency of British reinforcements had been an open secret since the autumn of 1943, the American manpower problem was a political as well as an administrative issue, and a surprise. It was, as we have remarked elsewhere, at the crux of Marshall's problems in the JCS in that it concerned the competition for resources between Europe and the Pacific. Furthermore, it was the American, not the British supply system that broke down in France. The political implications, if the shortages were publicised, were to question Eisenhower's leadership just when competition between the European and Pacific theatres was sharpening and the British were suggesting that Montgomery should play a more prominent part in operations. Exposure at the time of the Ardennes, would have weakened further the American position as the strategic leader of the two Western allies. Concealment was the order of the day (as we shall see in Chapter 15).

British observers of the US Army in action in North Africa, Italy and North-West Europe sometimes had the impression that they were watching a Hollywood production of 'A Triumph of the Will'. They could never be certain what had been achieved and was real and what was a stage set, a Potemkin village for the benefit of 'American Public Opinion'. The press made George Patton into a character from a Hemingway novel, and he played the romantic lead to the hilt. War had to be good drama which required red-blooded American heroes. Even if American performance was not perfect it must appear to be so. This could lead to deception and disillusionment if taken seriously. The dilemma arising out of the chaotic state of US Army logistics in the Autumn of 1944 was that remedial action could not fail to become known to the press and public, to say nothing of US senators with an axe to grind, and senior heads would roll for allowing this state of affairs to develop. It would prick the American balloon. If nothing were done, operational failures would result. From Eisenhower downward, commanders were acutely and inordinately aware of their public image. Montgomery certainly was. But American strategy was shaped by appearances, which meant by press coverage. Of course, Public Relations emphasised the positive and ignored poor performances. Men had to be sent into battle believing that their unit was well-trained, well-equipped and led, and would prove itself superior to the enemy. They needed a good press: there had to be subjective standards. The British were warmed by American enthusiasm and confidence in the final years of the war and appreciated the strength and comfort that it gave all the Allies. But Britons did not overlook American inexperience and incompetence either. They were, themselves, connoisseurs in detecting it in their own army which had suffered the same growing pains. So they expected, and found what they expected, that American units were very different from the public image of them. Remembering their own fumbling beginnings, though, and conscious of the never-ending struggle to correct repeated mistakes made by the inexperienced or the timid in their own ranks, the British could forgive those mistakes in their ally. What those at the higher levels who knew the truth could not forgive during the actual fighting was the systematic concealment of mistakes, exaggeration of achievements, and what seemed to be a campaign by some senior Americans to denigrate their British ally. At the end of the war, the extent of that campaign surprised and shocked even Eisenhower who had fought against it. When Bradley endorsed Ralph

Ingersoll's small-minded blackening of Montgomery in his post-war book *Top Secret* it spoiled both the image and the reality of Allied amity that Eisenhower had fought consistently to create. What he did not grasp was that the American custom of conducting operations in the full glare of publicity made senior officers competitive rather than cooperative, and concealment of the real state affairs very difficult.

The motivation of Marshall, Patton and Bradley, Hodges and Simpson, and of Eisenhower himself in their actions towards the British differed, although they were Americans and professional army officers with similar educations. The first three, and to some extent Hodges, were infected by the Montgomery virus which amounted, at times, to Anglophobia. Eisenhower's main task became to keep this destructive force in check. Bradley and Patton were, of course, personally anxious to claim success and establish their reputations through the media, a more effective agency than official reports when military appointments had to be endorsed by the Congress. Scrupulously, Eisenhower ensured that they, and the less aggressive Hodges and Simpson, received their reward for good service. Marshall, who was not at all personally ambitious, wanted the *United States Army* to have the main credit for defeating the Germans, something that it had not yet earned when the war ended in 1918. Eisenhower had to balance Marshall's prompts in his left ear with what he was hearing from the British in his right. It is not surprising that Eisenhower has been regarded as a chairman, a mediator, or, more aptly, as the conductor of an orchestra, rather than a commander. But even the last simile is inadequate to describe the complexity of his task or the drama within his command. Musicians play instruments in harmony and solo and follow a score. As professionals they undergo many years of training before they can perform in front of critical audiences. An observer of the military in 1944 could be deceived by the purposeful activity of a camp in the US or the UK into believing that all the 'trained' men who march out of it into battle had also become professionals. It was not so. Their first few performances would probably be indifferent if not disasters; for battles do not follow a score and rehearsals for them are never realistic. It takes many years of peace training, or many live performances, to make a soldier as it does a musician. Professional commanders have to admit the limitations in their human material until it is fully seasoned, and adjust their plans accordingly until then. They must also have the humility to admit to the limits of their own competence, to face facts and learn from them, and to be candid with their subordinates, their superiors and, above all, with themselves. A romantic view of war conducted by generals as celebrity actors is incompatible with this behaviour. Eisenhower's relatively inexperienced subordinates needed to hear the rap of his maestro's baton when they made mistakes or played unrehearsed solos. They seldom did.

We may regret discord among senior commanders, and Eisenhower certainly did, but they should not surprise us nor cause us to become indignant. Neither should we be angered by revelations of the imperfections of the soldiers in the ranks. We should admit them without national or class prejudice. So we reminded the reader at the beginning of these reflections that the softer rock of popular interpretation was being eroded by historians. This is being done in the interests of more realistic and less nationalistic history. With that as our aim, it is fitting that the central character in this part of our study, Dwight D Eisenhower, was a homespun Kansan American, a crusader for international accord,* but not one who was in the habit of calling a spade a spade.

---

* Eisenhower was a peacemaker and reacted warmly to cooperative colleagues. The story of Andrew Cunningham's intervention on behalf of an American sentry who shot a Royal Marine accompanying a British Army officer whose pass was unacceptable to him is instructive. The sentry had been sentenced to 10 years imprisonment. Sir Andrew's note, 'one of the most wonderful letters I've ever read', Eisenhower recorded, observed:

> 'One young life has been snuffed out; it would be a pity if another should be ruined.' Eisenhower reduced the sentence to 90 days. He saw the war as being managed by Gentlemen and Players and he preferred the Gentlemen. He tried to be one himself. 'With commonsense and goodwill, Allies *can* work together efficiently', he wrote. Cunningham and Alexander were his favourite British officers.

CHAPTER 14

EISENHOWER TAKES COMMAND: BROAD FRONT VERSUS SINGLE THRUST

By 1942 the war had brought forward the fighting generals and disposed of the failures: what was needed then was a political soldier who could coordinate a talented and often temperamental team of commanders.

EISENHOWER OBITUARY, *THE (LONDON) TIMES*, LEADING ARTICLE 29 MARCH 1969

The battle in Normandy was at its climax on the 19th of August when Eisenhower received a telegram from Marshall saying that the American correspondents in the United States and England were filing hostile criticisms of the command arrangement. The cause, as Eisenhower knew was a SHAEF censor's error in releasing a news item that the US 12th Army Group had been activated and that Bradley was now equal in authority to Montgomery. SHAEF's prompt explanation that Montgomery was continuing to direct Bradley as before until Eisenhower took over had only made things worse. The Washington *Times-Herald* urged the end of 'British dominance' and even the *New York Times*, friendly to Roosevelt, asked why Eisenhower had not superseded Montgomery already. The British press, of course, was angered by Montgomery's 'demotion'. Under pressure in Washington, Marshall complained that he had not been kept in close touch with the details of the battle or Eisenhower's command arrangements. Like the American press he was under the mistaken impression that Montgomery's Second British Army had been intended to break out towards the south-east but had failed, and that Bradley's Americans had rescued the operation by an improvised break-out on the St Lo front. The sense of Marshall's message was that it was time that the Americans, who had obviously won the battle, freed themselves from the grip of the plodding Montgomery. Eisenhower should take charge of operations,

226

ensure that Bradley received due credit for his achievement and allow him to play the major role henceforth.[1]

It will be recalled that Eisenhower had been evasive about how he intended to exercise command. Now, he explained to Marshall that command relations had worked well so far. He had been *au fait* with Montgomery's conduct of operations and approved of them, but there had been no room for himself and SHAEF in Normandy to date nor could the technical communications equipment be established for him to command the battle immediately. Nevertheless, he still intended to take over on 1 September[2], but the speed and extent of the German collapse – 400,000 casualties in Normandy – and the need for rapid exploitation had taken him by surprise. DRAGOON had brought a Franco-American force to the vicinity of Toulon and Marseilles on 15 August and it would soon advance northwards up the Rhône valley to join the Normandy armies coming from the West. Patton's Third Army was beginning its swing round Paris. A rapid advance across France to defeat the German Fifteenth Army in the Pas de Calais and to cut off other Germans in the south-west of France had already been planned by Montgomery and Bradley. Nevertheless, prompted by Marshall and the press, Eisenhower started that day, the 19th of August, to intervene in their arrangements to exploit the German débâcle.

Eisenhower had jumped on to a moving bus. Instead of confirming the plan that Montgomery had already made, or giving fresh but clear orders, he issued ambiguous directions that he subsequently changed. Thereby he shook the confidence of his subordinates in his judgment at the very outset and initiated an altercation which has subsequently been known as the Broad Front versus Single Thrust controversy. The label is usually attached to the initial advance from Normandy but in fact describes the whole campaign. It is a military axiom that a strategic plan should be flexible enough to be modified to take advantage of subsequent changes in the situation. Initially, a broad front may be appropriate, later it may not. The correctness of a strategy at any time can only be judged by the phase the operation has reached. It follows that an analysis of the controversy must identify the phases and determine whether the commanders followed this obvious principle. In short, while it is appropriate to pursue a beaten enemy on as broad a front as logistics allow, as soon as he offers resistance, concentration or a flanking move is required to dislodge him.

At the time that Eisenhower received Marshall's telegram of 19 August, Montgomery and the SHAEF staff agreed that the immediate objectives were the Channel ports and Antwerp, defended by the undefeated German Fifteenth Army. The next objectives were the Ruhr, which was beyond the

Rhine and was Germany's most important industrial region, and the Saar, which was west of the Rhine and Germany's second industrial region. Of these the Ruhr was the more important because Germany could not carry on the war without it. Montgomery had consulted Bradley on 17 August and they agreed that Second Army of 21 Army Group would be directed on Antwerp, the First Canadian Army on its left would secure the Channel ports, while on Montgomery's immediate right the First US Army would make for Brussels with its left, the Aachen Gap and Cologne with its centre and the Ardennes with its right. The US Third Army would guard the southern flank in the general area enclosed by Paris, Orleans, Troyes, Reims and Laon, and intercept Germans escaping from southwest France. The DRAGOON force, soon to be the 6th Franco-American Army Group, would eventually advance on Nancy and the Saar. The Third US Army would not move to join 6th Army Group since that would draw Patton away from Hodges whose First Army had the principal task.[3]

Bradley and Eisenhower met to discuss Marshall's concerns about command and the American role in operations on the 19th and Eisenhower called a conference on the 20th at which Montgomery was represented by Major-General de Guingand, his Chief of Staff. There, Eisenhower directed 12th Army Group to advance on the Saar and join up with the 6th. 21st Army Group alone would advance north-east on the Channel ports, Antwerp *and* the Ruhr. This was obviously a mismatch of force and objectives, so at the end of the conference de Guingand suggested that Eisenhower not issue a directive along these lines until he had talked to Montgomery. On 22nd August Montgomery invited Eisenhower to call at 21st Army Group tactical headquarters at Condé-sur-Noireau the next day. In the meantime despite de Guingand's request, Eisenhower reported his plan to the CCS, but it was not quite the same plan that he had announced on the 20th nor did he express his intention as clearly. Eisenhower informed the CCS that 21st Army Group would make for the Channel ports and Antwerp, and that if the German forces 'were no greater' than he thought, 12th Army Group would move north-east of Paris and then eastward, passing south of the Ardennes. 'Otherwise it may assist' 21st Army Group in the rapid reduction of the Pas de Calais. The speed of Bradley's advance would 'depend on the clearance of the Brittany ports and the improvement in our supply situation.' If logistics allowed, he would send a column to 'help the advance' of 6th Army Group. This was a compromise, and not a good one, since the degree of resistance that 21st Army Group would meet in the Pas de Calais and at Antwerp could not be accurately forecast, and the thrust to the Ruhr required the participation of First Army in any event, whereas Eisenhower had directed it on the Saar, as in the plan which de Guingand had questioned and asked to be referred to his chief.

On the 22nd, the SHAEF operations staff recommended an advance on the Ruhr to the north of the Ardennes by a total of twelve British and American divisions, four others would pass through the Ardennes and two to the south. In the meanwhile divisions of the Canadian First Army would deal with the Channel ports. Logistics could support only 18 divisions in the main advance and the thrust against the Ruhr was to have a force ratio of two to one over the remainder of the advance through the Ardennes and south of it.[4] This is to be compared with a rather wild, earlier suggestion of Montgomery's that forty divisions should advance side by side to the northeast, fearing naught, and Eisenhower's plan on the 20th, which had directed both of Bradley's armies south of the Ardennes. However, it was virtually what Montgomery and Bradley had agreed on the 17th and the former intended to propose to Eisenhower when they met on the 23rd.

While SHAEF supported Montgomery, Bradley changed his mind when Montgomery sought his agreement before meeting Eisenhower, and declined to direct his armies north of the Ardennes. Montgomery had more luck with Eisenhower the next day, although the latter complained that American public opinion would say that Bradley had only one army involved. Montgomery responded: 'Why should public opinion make us want to take unsound military decisions?' As a result of their meeting, Eisenhower issued a directive on the 29th that appeared to be in line with his staff's recommendation, with Montgomery's wishes and to give his American subordinates reasonable freedom to advance without being tied to the 'slow' British.[5] Bradley's main task was to 'thrust rapidly north with the principal offensive mission of assisting the 'Northern Group of Armies', [i.e., the 21st Army Group], in the destruction of the enemy forces . . . to the north-east . . .' On the other hand, the directive explained, 'The Commander-in-Chief Central Group of Armies [the 12th] will build up our incoming forces generally east of Paris, prepare to strike eastward towards the Saar valley, to reinforce the Allied advance north and west of the Ardennes, and to assist the advance of the Seventh Army [of the 6th Army Group] to and beyond Dijon'. Montgomery was given the task of coordinating the movements of the 12th and 21st Army Groups and the three divisions of the Airborne Army, based in the United Kingdom, which were put at his disposal.

The effect of this order was that Bradley's First Army, under Lieutenant General Courtney Hodges, with ten divisions in the XIX, VII and V Corps from left to right, advanced north-eastward. On its left flank, Second British Army had XII Corps on the left and XXX on the right; the latter, with the equivalent of less than four divisions, two and half of which were armoured, was ordered to capture Antwerp and Brussels. The Canadians were to take Le Havre and the other ports, and the Third Army to advance on Metz, on the Upper Meuse, with seven divisions. That was within the letter of Eisenhower's directive but not its spirit. Montgomery and SHAEF had intended that Third Army should be a reserve to support the northern thrust or be directed towards the Saar, as events unfolded, but Patton was firmly committed to the Saar. The plan therefore became a broad front advance, although the main weight and its objectives, the Channel ports, the V1 and V2 sites and the Ruhr, were on the left. This came about because Eisenhower conceived the plan as a compromise between SHAEF and Montgomery on one side and his Americans on the other. Compromise or not, it was a pursuit, and since pursuits ought to be on as wide a front as possible, it was orthodox. Its tactical aim was to overrun successive defensive positions on the Somme, the Scheldt, the Meuse and on the German frontier before the still disorganised German formations could collect themselves and occupy them. That done, the advance into Germany would begin. The point that the SHAEF staff had considered but Eisenhower in his search for compromise had not, was that a few properly supported divisions could maintain the initiative more effectively than twice their number with shaky logistics. The small British XXX Corps was soon to demonstrate this truth.

Thus began the first phase of operations after Normandy. It was a hectic, exciting and rapid advance without precedent. Something of the emotions of the time must be recaptured if we are to understand what followed. Patton's initial inclination was to scythe in behind the Seine and the Germans fleeing across it, forming a deep pocket between himself and the rest of the Allied armies, but it was too late for that. The enemy had lost much equipment and most of their vehicles, so they could be overrun in a straight pursuit. New instructions were given to Patton at Bradley's headquarters at Chartres on the 25th. In his diary Patton recorded what occurred at another meeting on the 30th:

> I asked to present my case for an immediate advance to the east and a rupture of the Siegfried Line before it can be manned. Bradley was sympathetic but Bull [Eisenhower's G3] – and I gather the rest of Ike's staff – do not concur and are letting Montgomery overpersuade Ike to go north. It is a terrible mistake, and when it comes out in after years, it will cause much argument. The British have put it over again. We get no gas because, to suit Monty, the First Army get most of it, and we are also feeding the Parisians.[6]

(Paris required 3,000 tons per day. That was roughly what was needed to keep an army of three corps moving forward but not fighting intensively as well.) Much of this was boloney, but it marked the beginning of Bradley's settled policy of winks and nods at Patton's defiance of SHAEF directives. In a letter the same day Patton wrote: 'I am headed for the Meuse, which I will get . . . I have to battle for every yard but it is not the enemy who is trying to stop me, it is "They". i.e. . . . Eisenhower and his British cronies.' However, the truth is that Patton was no more deprived of supplies than anyone else. His advance to Metz has been lauded but it was no faster than that of the US First and the British Second Armies, and the distance he covered was actually shorter than XXX Corps' advance to Diest, beyond Brussels, in the same time. Montgomery had told Lieutenant General Brian Horrocks, XXX Corps commander, on the 26th: 'The Germans are very good soldiers and will recover quickly if allowed to do so. All risks are justified – I intend to get a bridgehead over the Rhine before they have time to recover'. Horrocks, like Patton, 'had his whip out'.

All Eisenhower's subordinates complained about the plan. If one can believe Patton, 'Bradley was madder than I have ever seen him and wondered aloud "what the Supreme Commander amounted to"'. Montgomery was angry that Patton had been allowed to proceed. His concern was that the broad front advance was simply a political plan inspired by Marshall and the press and that there was neither the petrol nor the ammunition to maintain it. The Americans in general thought that they would be held up by the British. Entries in General Hodges' First Army 'diary', maintained by a staff officer, reflect that view.

19 August. The gap [the Falaise Pocket] is now quite definitely closed and the British are advancing at what is, for them, considerable speed towards the east.

31 August. Rather to our surprise the British, for once, kept up. The Second British with the 11 Armoured Division captured Amiens during the morning including General Elberfeldt.

2 September. Both the Supreme Commander and General Bradley apparently are extremely worried over the gasoline situation which is becoming more instead of less critical. General Hodges in consequence ordered both VII and XIX Corps to curl up short of Tournai and Mons . . . The whole plan is not to the General's satisfaction since he believes he can whip the gasoline problem and that while the Germans are on the run there should be no halt for even a minute.

Instead of First Army having to cut in behind the Germans in front of the 'slow' British, the latter were moving so fast that by the evening of 3 September they were in Brussels, and on the 4th in Antwerp. Various airborne operations had to be cancelled when leading troops had overrun their intended drop zones. Using fewer divisions in their spear-head, the British had advanced more rapidly and maintained their petrol supplies more efficiently. First Army diary for 4 September comments: 'British continue their astoundingly rapid drive into Belgium completing the occupation of Brussels.' In fact they were on the Albert Canal beyond Diest on the 5th.[7] British XXX Corps' armoured cars, tanks and guns, infantry dozing in the backs of 3 ton lorries, had moved through one whole night, by-passed and isolated pockets of enemy and given them no opportunity to halt, let alone consolidate. After a seventy-five mile advance in one day, they reached Brussels in the evening of 3rd September. There was a night of wild celebration. The Gestapo cellars in the *Grande Place* had been broken into by the liberated Bruxellois, and two inches of wine were slopping about on the floor. (Wearing gumboots and using a flash light to read the labels, one of the present writers was able to select a crate of Chambertin 1929, which he presented to his Belgian hosts for the night). Slightly tipsy, and very tired Welsh Guardsmen sat at attention in their jeeps and armoured reconnaissance vehicles. Next morning his battery was in action on the *Champs de Manoeuvre* with a crowd of children and women in summer dresses all around the guns. In pauses between fire orders, he had to convince his gunners that the war was not over and the spectators that they were in some danger. Only with the scepticism bred by a long war could he believe his own words.)

Although First Army had more trouble with gasoline, because its advance was on a broader front than the Second, its VII Corps reached the Meuse at Liège on the 7th. It advanced with the same élan as XXX Corps, but having trapped a pocket of more than 20,000 Germans near Mons, it had to pause to round them up. On the left of First Army, the US XIX Corps became a flank guard as XXX Corps, moving through Louvain and Diest away from it northwards to the Dutch frontier, opened a gap between the left of the First US and the right of the Second British army. This gap was to remain a bone of contention henceforth, and a reflection of Eisenhower's compromising directive on the 29th that allowed Patton to advance in the South, instead of being centrally placed to reinforce the northern thrust, and Bradley had to concern himself more with keeping his two armies together than on filling the gap and driving to Cologne and the Ruhr through Aachen.

For a week, from the 7th until the 14th of September, when it reached the

Escaut Canal, XXX Corps' Guards Armoured Division fought tough daily battles for villages and small towns. Although the advance continued, it was at a slower pace, and as friends began to disappear at the rate they had in Normandy, no one in the battalions spoke of the end of the war any more. As the gap widened, German resistance increased, but Eisenhower and Bradley were oblivious to or ignored the signs that the turning point had been reached in the campaign, and that they should act decisively to retain the initiative by bringing the First and Second Armies together in Belgium and on the Dutch frontier, and reinforcing them. That they did nothing was, in part, owing to the headquarters of both the American commanders being too far from the front. They were out of touch with the battle. Eisenhower's advanced headquarters was near Granville, on the west coast of the Cotentin peninsula in Normandy and Bradley's, which had been at Chartres, was now at Versailles. Eisenhower had been in England between the 29th and 31st August. On returning, he had strained his knee on 2 September when his light plane made a forced landing on a Normandy beach, and he was bedridden near Granville when he wrote a directive on the 4th, a crucial date. Montgomery's main headquarters was in Brussels but his tactical headquarters was near Diest; Hodges' was near Charleroi. Montgomery was in close touch with his corps and divisions fighting the battle, and with Hodges. Eisenhower had given him the task of 'coordination', but with Bradley in Versailles that was difficult, and after 1st September, when Eisenhower formally took command of operations, impractical and unwelcome as far as Bradley was concerned. Bradley visited his front, but he did not want to believe that he must concentrate on the northern part of the front, as Montgomery was saying, because it could only be done at the expense of his Third Army. Neither he nor Eisenhower had grasped that after the liberation of Brussels the happy days of carefree advance were over, and that concentration of force to maintain the initiative was imperative. This was to be the root cause of their disagreement with Montgomery over strategy in the next months. The gap in comprehension was even greater, not unnaturally, between Marshall in Washington, who gleaned his information largely from Eisenhower and the press, and Hodges commanding First Army at Charleroi. On 13 September, Marshall, under the impression that the final stages of the war in Europe had arrived, signalled his guidance to twenty-one of his senior commanders, including Eisenhower:

> While cessation of hostilities in the war against Germany may occur at any time, it is assumed that in fact it will extend over a period commencing any time between September 1 and November 1.[8]

On the 6th, Hodges' impression was still 'that given ten good days of weather . . . the war might well be over as far as organised resistance is concerned', a view echoed in XXX Corps, but by the 10th, Hodges' tone had changed as German resistance and short supplies started to cloud his optimism. That day his G4 revealed at a staff conference that the supply situation was desperate:

> There were no large reserves and they were scraping together enough for issue every twenty-four hours. Trains are running to Soissons but he cannot obtain any accurate information ahead of time as to what they are carrying or when they will arrive. [The first train was filled with PX goods, not the last instance of insanity in the COMZ]. Despite assurances that gasoline was arriving by C-47 at the large airfield at Juvincourt, none has as yet been flown in . . . This supply situation will undoubtedly delay, slightly at least, any concentrated attack on the Siegfried Line although Colonel Hart [a COMZ officer] promises five days intensive fire on hand by Friday night.

As German resistance stiffened, an ammunition shortage was added to the gasoline famine.

The nature of the operation changed from a pursuit to a fighting advance, and after the 17th both armies became engaged in a grinding battle, First Army fighting at an ever increasing disadvantage because of lack of supplies. Eisenhower and Bradley, remote from the scene of action and, perhaps, unwilling to admit that their strategy conceived to satisfy Marshall was not working, continued to talk of reaching the Rhine and taking the Ruhr and the Saar on a broad front as though nothing had changed since the 3rd of September. They had not accepted Montgomery's appreciation of the situation on the First and Second Army front when he had presented it on 4th September, the day after Brussels fell, and before German resistance had hardened, his aim being to reach the Rhine on the First and Second Army's front, keeping the initiative until the autumn rains began. On the 3rd, Montgomery talked to Lieutenant-General Browning, ground commander of the Airborne Army about a series of drops between the Escaut Canal and the Lower Rhine at Arnhem or the Rhine at Wesel. The scheme was designed to outflank the Siegfried Line's right flank and cross the Rhine where the Germans had no defences. Its success depended on supplies being available for it and for First Army's drive towards Cologne. He was still optimistic that the Rhine and then the Ruhr could be reached in the next phase if supplies were concentrated to that end. If the Rhine were reached on the front north of the Ardennes the

German front could be rolled up and resistance west of the Rhine would collapse. It would mean the end of the war and it was unnecessary to attack all along the line to achieve it. These ideas were in Montgomery's mind as he sent a crucial, but widely misunderstood, signal to Eisenhower at Granville next day.

I would like to put before you certain aspects of future operations and give you my views:
1. I consider we have now reached a stage where one really powerful and full-blooded thrust towards Berlin is likely to get there and thus end the German war.
2. We have not enough maintenance resources for two full-blooded thrusts.
3. The selected thrust must have all the maintenance resources it needs without any qualifications and any other operation must do the best it can with what is left over.
4. There are only two possible thrusts, one via the Ruhr and the other via Metz and the Saar.
5. In my opinion the thrust likely to give the best and quickest results is the northern one via the Ruhr.
6. Time is vital and the decision regarding the selected thrust must be made at once and paragraph 3 above will apply.
7. If we attempt a compromise solution and split our maintenance resources so that neither thrust is full-blooded we will prolong the war.
8. I consider the problem viewed as above as very simple and clear-cut.
9. The matter is of such vital importance that I feel sure you will agree that a decision on the above lines is required at once. If you are coming this way perhaps you would look in and discuss it. If so, delighted to see you lunch tomorrow. Do *not* feel I can leave this battle just at present.[9]

This telegram crossed with one from Eisenhower in Normandy to all commanders.[10] 'Enemy resistance shows signs of collapse', he observed, and went on to provide good evidence of it. First and Second Army would breach the Siegfried Line covering the Ruhr and then seize the Ruhr. The Third Army would attack the Siegfried Line covering the Saar and seize Frankfurt. It was important for that to start as soon as possible in order to forestall the enemy in that sector, but troops of Central Army Group (i.e., 12 Army Group operating with the Ruhr as its objective) had to be adequately supported. Clearly, on the assumption that the Germans were beaten, Eisenhower was continuing to place equal emphasis on the Saar and the Ruhr as objectives. On receiving Montgomery's signal of the 4th Eisenhower made that clear when he replied on the 5th.

1. While agreeing with your conception of a powerful and full blooded thrust towards Berlin, I do not repeat not agree that it should be initiated at this moment to the exclusion of all other manoevre.

2. The bulk of the German Army that was in the West has now been destroyed. We must immediately exploit our success by promptly breaching the Siegfried Line, crossing the Rhine on a wide front and seizing the Saar and the Ruhr. This I intend to do with all possible speed. This will give us a stranglehold on two of Germany's main industrial areas and largely destroy her capacity to wage war, whatever course events may take. It will assist in cutting off forces now retreating from South-West France. Moreover it will give us freedom of action to strike in any direction and we will force the enemy to disperse over a wide area, such forces as he may be able to assemble for the defence of the West.

3. While we are advancing we will be opening the ports of Havre and Antwerp, which are essential to sustain a powerful thrust *deep into Germany* [authors' emphasis]. No reallocation of our present resources would be adequate to sustain a thrust to Berlin.

4. Accordingly, my intention is initially to occupy the Saar and the Ruhr, and by the time we have done this, Havre and Antwerp should be available to maintain one or both of the thrusts you mention. In this connection I have always given and still give priority to the Ruhr, and the northern route of advance, as indicated in my directive of yesterday. Locomotives and rolling stock are today being allocated on the basis of this priority to maintain the momentum of the advance of your forces and those of Bradley north-west of the Ardennes. Please let me know your further maintenance requirements for the advance to and occupation of the Ruhr.[12]

An analysis of these three messages, in the context of 4 September and Montgomery's projections for the future, reveals the meat of the controversy over the so-called single thrust and broad front that now opened. The initial point to be made is that then and subsequently there was a contradiction in what Eisenhower seemed to be attempting; that is to cross the Rhine on a wide front, seize the Saar and the Ruhr and *give priority to the Ruhr*. Put simply, the Ruhr is beyond the Rhine so that to reach the Rhine on a broad front necessarily meant first taking the Saar which was west of the Rhine. Giving the Ruhr priority on one hand and, on the other, taking the Saar and reaching the Rhine on a broad front were mutually exclusive. Indeed, in saying that the Saar must be attacked without delay he was pointing the way to a broad advance to the Rhine, not to the seizure of the Ruhr which was beyond it.

In considering further these communications it must be remembered that they were written just before German resistance and Allied logistics brought the rapid phase of advance to an end. Montgomery referred to Berlin because the end of the war was on everyone's mind at the time and that meant 'Berlin'. However, Berlin had nothing to do with his argument or the immediate situation. The point, unanimously accepted, was that when the Ruhr fell, German resistance would crumble. That the priority objective was the Ruhr was also agreed by the SHAEF staff, and they wrote a paper to that effect on the 6th of September.[13] It followed that an attack on the Saar by Patton was inconsistent with this policy unless the Germans were still in disorder and sufficient resources were available for both wings of the Allied armies to advance. The question at issue was *how* the Ruhr could be taken. On the 29th, Eisenhower had been nudged into recognising what it entailed when, ostensibly, his directive held back his right to give First and Second Armies the resources for the task. By the 4th, Montgomery knew that Third Army was not being held back and that First Army was hamstrung for want of petrol. As we have seen, by the 10th it was acutely short of ammunition too. Commanders are expected to anticipate such problems and Montgomery was doing so on the 4th, when he wrote his message. But Eisenhower was still as optimistic on the 4th as he had been on the 29th August: he thought he could easily reach the Rhine on a broad front and even as Montgomery pressed for a more con-centrated advance, he gave Patton a directive to advance on the Saar 'at once'. Patton was, of course, already doing that, so he treated Eisenhower's directive as confirmatory.

Eisenhower's paragraph 3, which referred to Berlin, makes the point for the first time that Antwerp was required to supply the advance from the Ruhr deep into Germany: the final advance that would finish the war. As it was generally agreed that the capture of the Ruhr would end Germany's capacity to wage war, the final advance deep into Germany afterwards would be relatively fast and easy. Before it was undertaken, Antwerp would have been opened. At this time Eisenhower did not question that the Rhine could be reached without Antwerp but Montgomery was a step ahead of him in realising that unless existing supplies and divisions were concen-trated on the route to the Ruhr even the Rhine would not be reached on a broad front as Eisenhower seemed to intend. Montgomery's argument is really about logistics. He argues that there will be insufficient supplies to continue advancing on a broad front, against increasing resistance. The implication of this was to be apparent before the end of the month: Eisenhower's broad front approach to the Rhine made the immediate capture of Antwerp essential. The 1st Canadian Army's advance up what they came to know as 'the long left flank' had proved much more difficult than had been expected. Despite their withdrawals inland, the Germans clung tenaciously to the Channel ports and none had become available as points of entry for supplies. Thus the bulk of the fuel and munitions needed by the advancing armies was still coming in over the Normandy beaches or through Cherbourg.

Logistics came to the fore again when Montgomery proposed the operation that he had discussed with Browning on the 3rd, and remained the key issue in strategy thereafter, but before taking the story further it is necessary to clarify a relevant point. Montgomery was as much concerned with First Army supply as with Second, since the success of the northern drive to the Rhine depended on First Army being adequately supplied, and by 10 September it had run short. The British and Americans had separate systems but there were common-user items which were pooled and controlled by the Americans. The most important by far was petrol, oil and lubricants (POL) and transport, which distributed it. Normally the British were independent of American supplies, but a long advance such as that proposed required special arrangements. However, as POL was still coming from UK BOLERO stocks to which American and British divisions had an equal right, extra supplies sent to 21 Army Group did not come from the pockets of the Americans.

Montgomery took up this subject on 9 September.[14] He said that he had studied Eisenhower's directive of the 4th, carefully. (It had arrived in two bits, the second before the first, so chaotic were SHAEF's communications.) He said that he could not:

> see it stated that the northern route of advance is to have priority over the advance to the Saar. Actually, XIX Corps [on his immediate right] is unable to advance properly for lack of petrol. Could you send a responsible officer to see me so that I can explain things to him.

Eisenhower, himself, flew to see Montgomery next day.[15] He had sent a summary of the situation to the CCS on the 9th which mentioned that resistance had stiffened but that it was doubtful if the Germans could stop the Allies; though the supply situation would be stretched to the breaking point until the Channel ports were taken. He had decided that the Brittany ports were unnecessary and that he would take the gamble of attacking the Siegfried Line without a pause in order to take full advantage of German disorganisation. He was concentrating his main effort towards the Ruhr. 'After the crossing of the Rhine we will prepare logistically and otherwise for a deep thrust into Germany', he said. The remark confirms his complacence with his logistics until the Rhine had been crossed and, as he phrases his logistical intentions in terms of the 'Rhine' not 'after the seizure of the Ruhr' he seems to be under the impression that the Ruhr was *west* of the Rhine.[16] It was an example of Eisenhower's lack of precision which marred his dealings with Montgomery. (Indeed so consistent was Eisenhower in this respect that we are almost led to conclude that he confused the Ruhr with the Rhineland. That is not such a fantastic idea as it seems, for Americans were often uncertain about European geography.)

Eisenhower talked to Montgomery in his aircraft at Brussels airport on 10 September, being unable to walk. He was not persuaded to change his decision about Patton's drive, which he maintained was compatible with making the Ruhr his main objective. They talked about Montgomery's wish to drive north from the Escaut Canal via Eindhoven over the Meuse at Grave, the Waal at Nijmegen and the lower branch of the Rhine at Arnhem and to use the Airborne Army to seize the bridges. The final objective was Apeldoorn, a market-garden town north of the Lower Rhine at Arnhem. Hence, the airborne operation was to be MARKET and the XXX Corps drive up the axis Eindohoven-Nijmegen-Arnhem-Appeldoorn, relieving the airborne divisions as quickly as possible, would be GARDEN. Eisenhower agreed. Tedder, who was present at the meeting, reported to Portal:

> The advance to Berlin was not discussed as a serious issue, nor do I think it was so intended. The real issue is the degree of priority given to the American corps operating on Montgomery's right flank and the extent to which Montgomery controls its operations.[17]

Tedder was correct if he included the related subject of the logistics of the operations of the rest of First Army through the Aachen gap towards the Rhine at Cologne and from the Ardennes to Bonn. Next day, having received a copy of Eisenhower's directive of the 9th to the CCS and thought about their conversation at Brussels, Montgomery pointed out that by allowing Patton to continue to receive supplies urgently needed by First Army, Eisenhower made MARKET–GARDEN impracticable because it would be an isolated operation.[18]

Decision that the Northern thrust towards the Ruhr was *not* to have priority over other operations will have certain repercussions which you should know. The large-scale operation of the Second Army towards the Meuse and Rhine cannot now take place before the 23rd at the earliest and possibly the 26th September. This delay will give the enemy time to organise better defensive arrangements and we must expect heavier resistance and slower progress. As the winter draws on the weather may be expected to deteriorate . . . less results from our great weight of air power. It is basically a matter of rail and road and air transport and unless this is concentrated to give impetus to the selected thrust then no one is going to get very far since we are all such a long way from our supply bases. We will do all that is possible to get on with the business but the above facts will show you that if enemy resistance continues to stiffen as at present then NO great results can be expected until we have built up stocks of ammunition and other requirements.

Eisenhower responded by sending Bedell Smith to Montgomery on 12 September. On the face of it, Bedell Smith satisfied Montgomery. The terms of their agreement can be gleaned from Eisenhower's and Montgomery's confirmatory signals.[19] Bedell Smith told Montgomery that Hodges would get all the supplies he wanted. Eisenhower backed that up by assuring Montgomery that:

The US COMZ and General Bradley are responsible for this maintenance and I assure you that it will be adequate for the task assigned to the army on your right.

Montgomery had asked for 1,000 tons per day by airlift for Second Army, something that could not be promised as all air transport capacity would shortly be required for MARKET. Instead, he was offered 500 tons by road and 500 by air as long as transports were available. Eisenhower would ask Bradley to move his headquarters close to Hodges or allow Montgomery to communicate directly with Hodges. Eisenhower gave the impression that the Americans were sacrificing transport and supplies for Montgomery, 'to enable you to get across the Rhine and to capture the approaches to Antwerp'. This was when Eisenhower began to be concerned about Antwerp but one of the purposes of MARKET–GARDEN was ultimately to take Rotterdam, a larger and more accessible port.

Montgomery had ordered General Crerar to clear the Channel Ports and open the port of Antwerp at the end of August. The Channel Ports obviously had priority but he hoped that Crerar would tackle his tasks together. Crerar did not do so. From the 9th September Montgomery began to be impatient with Crerar's progress and on the 12th the logistical demands of Market-Garden caused him to signal Crerar that Antwerp was becoming of increasing importance and that he should tackle both his tasks together. Crerar was still unconvinced that that was possible with the two corps he had available, and it was not until the 6th October that First Canadian Army began its complicated operation on several fronts to clear the Scheldt. General Guy Simonds, by then commanding the operation in place of Crerar, carried it out in the face of obstruction from Tedder and, despite his rhetoric, little support from Eisenhower. Montgomery hoped to have an airborne descent on Walcheren, at the mouth of the Scheldt, but General Brereton, USAAF, the commander overall of the Airborne Army, refused the request. In this connection Eisenhower observed that 'when Belchem [BGS, 21st Army Group] discusses outline plans with Brereton's staff it may be found that these difficulties can be overcome. In any event I consider the use of Antwerp so important to future operations that we are prepared to go a long way in making the attack a success.' That was simply verbiage. (*vide* Dominick Graham, *Guy Granville Simonds: The Price of Command*, [Stoddart, 1993], 'Battles in the Polders'.)

Reassured by Bedell Smith's visit Montgomery agreed to start Market-Garden on the 17th, but in the event air supply was not forthcoming and ground supply started late, though reliable thereafter. Coordination of the operation was flawed. No 83 Group of 2nd Tactical Air Force, assigned to support the Second Army was forbidden to operate in the Arnhem area by Brereton, and HQ 21 Army Group were not consulted over choice of drop zones. The airlift was insufficient for so huge an operation. To compress and perhaps over-simplify a tangled piece of military history, MARKET–GARDEN was bedevilled by a faulty chain of command stemming from the original American refusal to appoint a ground forces commander subordinate to Eisenhower, and the deep-rooted Anglophobia of too many American senior officers. The business of coordinating the action of one set of air and ground forces based in England and another in Belgium would have been difficult enough with good will on both sides and a single commander overall with full authority. In the absence of such a commander the responsibility devolved on Eisenhower as SCAEF but he, remote from the scene, neither recognised the dangers of a divided command nor made any effort in the matter. The commander of the Airborne Army, Major-General Lewis H Brereton lacked grip and as already noted, Browning was unpopular with the Americans.

The initial advance of XXX Corps was rapid enough but 101st US

Airborne Division had failed to take the bridge at Son intact and when XXX Corps reached Nijmegen on the 19th, they found that 82nd US Airborne Division had not been able to capture the two bridges over the Waal at Nijmegen, cope with clearing the town *and* hold the high ground between the town and the German frontier. After the bridges had been seized, delay in bringing up British infantry for the advance across the Island between Nijmegen and Arnhem was the last straw. In the meanwhile, the 9th and 10th Panzer Divisions, which happened to be refitting at Zutphen, north-east of Arnhem, were able to destroy the British 1st Airborne Division at Arnhem, where only one battalion had reached the vital bridge over the Lower Rhine.

To declare MARKET-GARDEN a failure, as it too often is, is to ignore its achievements. Its aims were threefold: to obtain a bridgehead over the Rhine from which to attack the Ruhr in conjunction with an attack through Cologne by First Army; to enable the Siegfried Line further south to be outflanked by an advance between the Maas and the Rhine; and subsequently to take Rotterdam. Only the second aim was achieved, making it possible, thereafter, to drive south-east from Nijmegen towards the Rhine at Wesel in conjunction with an American drive from the south. Rotterdam was to have been taken by advancing westward from Arnhem. It was a great port more easily reached from the sea than Antwerp and its capture would have sealed the escape of the German Fifteenth Army from the Scheldt. As it was, the northward advance of XXX Corps put a cordon around the eastern escape route of the German Fifteenth Army, still fighting against the Canadians on the Channel coast. Much has been made of the narrow advance of XXX Corps and the frequency with which the road from Eindhoven to Nijmegen was cut. It needs to be pointed out that the string of American airborne units and British infantry and tanks that held it open most of the time were also one flank of the pocket in which Fifteenth Army was entrapped. Germans attacked the road as much to break out as the Allies fought to keep open the road to Nijmegen.

When the Arnhem operation was called off on 27 September, it was still hoped that with reinforcement and an aggressive drive by First Army through Aachen, Duren and Julich to Cologne and, further north, on the Second Army flank east of Sittard, the Rhine might be reached. That was not to be. Clearing the German pocket on the Scheldt approaches to Antwerp and in the area of wet and dismal farmland west of the main axis of XXX Corps' advance, occupied the British and Canadians until November. The process of clearing the Meuse-Rhine area was then delayed by the German counter-stroke in the Ardennes in December. It was not until February 1945, more than four months after the original target date that the operation to secure the west, or near bank of the Rhine began; the essential preliminary to the formidable task of the assault crossing of that river. Such were the fruits of a faulty strategy, misunderstandings and lack of grip at the top. In the meantime American operations to breach the Siegfried Line proceeded slowly in the face of stiffening German resistance, further handicapped by the muddle-'breakdown' is not too strong a word – in American logistic support.

The archives reveal that Bradley paid little attention to Montgomery's intentions and the operations of 21 Army Group. Had he maintained an effective liaison with Montgomery's headquarters he would not have recorded his surprise when Montgomery's first turned northwards in early September and the gap opened between his First and Third Armies on his left. Although it became visible and had been widening since 4 September, Bradley fought as if he had no ally on his left. After 4 September he had detached one division to reinforce Patton and a regiment to buttress the V Corps right flank. His attention was concentrated on the security of the inner flanks of his Army Group, Hodges' right and Patton's left. He took no positive action to rectify the imbalance between his supply situation and his operational intentions, continuing to urge Hodges and Patton to push on as fast as they could with what they had, oblivious to the fact that the Germans had recovered their poise and were fighting back stoutly.

Despite the repeated insistence on the importance of the Aachen-Cologne axis in Eisenhower's directives, Bradley continued to share his supplies equally between the First and Third Armies. Hodges, the hapless commander of the First, was tugged in two directions; Montgomery unsuccessfully striving to force him to order his XIX Corps to keep contact with him on Hodges' left, while Bradley dragged his centre of gravity southwards, ending by virtually controlling Hodges' right hand formation, V Corps, himself. As a result, the First Army front became over extended. Worst of all, Bradley did not make the Aachen Gap his main objective, his *schwerpunkt*. Eventually, after the two armies had valiantly ground their way forward with inadequate supplies of artillery ammunition and units increasingly depleted by casualties for which there were no replacements, exhaustion halted forward movement in December. It was then that the Germans struck in the Ardennes and made Eisenhower and Bradley pay for their errors.

We have here run ahead of events. These disagreeable consequences were unforeseen on 12 September, when Bedell Smith assured Montgomery that the First Army would be adequately supplied for the task in hand. He also informed Eisenhower that First Army was held up by enemy resistance and a bottleneck at the Liége bridges, not a lack of supplies.

> I believe that FM Montgomery over-emphasised to you the effect of this shortage. First Army states that they now have in hand sufficient ammunition for five days fighting and enough petrol to carry them to the Rhine.[20]

That was simply not true, being contradicted by the entries in HQ First Army War Diary. Third Army, wrote Bradley to Eisenhower, had been partly supplied by air, and had four days ammunition and sufficient petrol to reach the Rhine. On average over the last ten days the First Army had received 3,300 tons per day, and Third Army 2,500. (Their respective shares were proportionate to their strengths.) Patton was astride the Moselle and expected shortly to begin his advance to the Rhine on the axis Metz-Frankfurt. If held up there, he would shift his main attack north of the Moselle in conjunction with First Army's V Corps. Bradley assured Eisenhower that he would 'keep a close eye on supply and if necessary throw a larger percentage of supply to the First Army. However you cannot cut Patton much below 2,500 tons per day'. It looked as if 6 Army Group would be in a position to cross the Rhine between Karlsruhe and Mannheim, so the main axis of Third Army would be better aligned north of the Moselle in conjunction with V Corps. However, he did not want to 'shift [Patton] too much at present because it is necessary to cover the whole front in some way and secure positions into which to feed in the Ninth Army. In addition, the terrain on the axis Metz-Frankfurt is more favourable than the tortuous Moselle valley'. At this stage Bradley intended to feed General Simpson's Ninth Army (which would contain units moved from Brittany and new arrivals from the USA) into the centre of his front, not his left. MARKET forced him to put it into the enlarged gap on his left thus disrupting his plan to organise his battle around his centre, whatever directives he received from Eisenhower.

On 13 September, Eisenhower issued a directive 'to amplify', as he described it, what he had written on the 9th.[21] It was a clear document which, for once, did not require to be decoded into clear from 'Ike Speak', but it had a different message from that of the 9th, for the Ruhr was back in favour and Patton's actions were to be terminated quickly. There were only two courses open to them, Eisenhower wrote. First:

> a single knife-like and narrow thrust from our present position into the centre of Germany, hoping that the advance with whatever force

we would be able to maintain would bring about the capitulation of that country. The other course of action is to drive forward through the enemy's western frontiers to suitable positions on which we can regroup while preparing the maintenance facilities that will sustain the great bulk of our forces on the drive into Germany.

He went on to say that after recent conferences with Bradley and Montgomery he was confirmed in his conviction that:

the early winning of deep water ports and improved maintenance facilities in our rear are prerequisites to a *final all-out assault on Germany proper* [authors' emphasis]. The beaches are subject to storms which would become increasingly common and will paralyse our activities and make the maintenance of our forces even in defensive roles exceedingly difficult. Distribution of supplies once they have reached the Continent is still a major problem but is approaching solution through the improvement of the railway system . . . Inevitably the process of cleaning up the rear will involve some temporary slackening of our effort towards the front. Nevertheless, without improved communications, a speedy and prolonged advance by forces adequate in strength, depending on bulk oil, transport and ammunition is not a feasible operation.

The timing of efforts towards the attainment of '*immediate objectives along the German Western frontier is now of the utmost importance because we do not have sufficient resources to do even this much simultaneously,* [Authors' emphasis]. The intention was to close on the Rhine, seize bridgeheads and to take the Ruhr. The manoeuvre plan was to push hard over the Rhine in the north with Second and First Armies and the Airborne Army. Third Army, 'except for limited advance' to seize the bridgeheads over the Moselle and threaten the flank of the Germans facing First Army, and joining up with 6 Army Group, would be confined to holding and threatening action.

As quickly as this is accomplished, all possible resources of the Central Group of armies [i.e. 12 Army Group] must be thrown to the support of the drive of the First Army to seize bridgeheads near Cologne and Bonn, in preparation for assisting in the capture of the Ruhr.

Only then would the Third Army attack the Saar and push on to the Rhine. While all this was being done, either Rotterdam or Antwerp would be opened, the latter by the Canadian First Army. To finish an instruction that should have been perfectly clear to all commanders of good will and good sense, Eisenhower wrote:

> After attainment of the Moselle bridgeheads above directed, operations on our left will, until the Rhine bridgeheads are won, take priority in all forms of logistical support except for: a. adequate security measures and continuous reconnaissance by forces on our right; b. necessary resources for the securing and developing of ports.

Had this clear instruction been enforced it would have marked a turning point in Eisenhower's strategy. A term was set to Patton's activities. Logistics was recognised as precluding a broad approach to the Rhine. The Rhine was to be approached on the First and Second Army fronts. After it had been crossed on their front the Ruhr would be attacked. The missing thought was the shape of the battle that he envisaged, and clear definition of its phases. First, by reaching the Rhine in the north, the German front further south would be rolled up, which would ensure that the Germans would be defeated *west of the Rhine*. That, after all, was the object of the exercise. Secondly, reaching the Rhine, crossing it and taking the Ruhr were three separate operations, but Eisenhower still had not distinguished one from the other. In view of what followed, it seems probable that Eisenhower had not drafted this document himself and seen to it that its ideas were logically arranged. Eisenhower's imprecision allowed his subordinates their opportunity to sabotage his plans. Patton could only be halted by a specific order to dig in where he was. He read the directive as giving him the opportunity to draw German troops to his front by attacking continuously over and beyond the Moselle. Ironically, the situation resembled the strategic tug of war between the Italian and the North-West Europe theatres. Patton would, by fair means or foul, contrive to attack, drawing scarce resources away from First Army and he would be aided and abetted by Bradley.

Having issued a directive that seemed to indicate that he understood what had to be done, Eisenhower sent Marshall quite a different message next day.[22] They had always known, he said, that there would have to be a pause to allow logistics to catch up and he had decided that would be on the Rhine. (Whereas in fact he had said that would be after the Ruhr was occupied.) Hence his decision in favour of the broad front.

While this was going on Montgomery suddenly became obsessed with the idea that his AG could rush on into Berlin provided we gave him

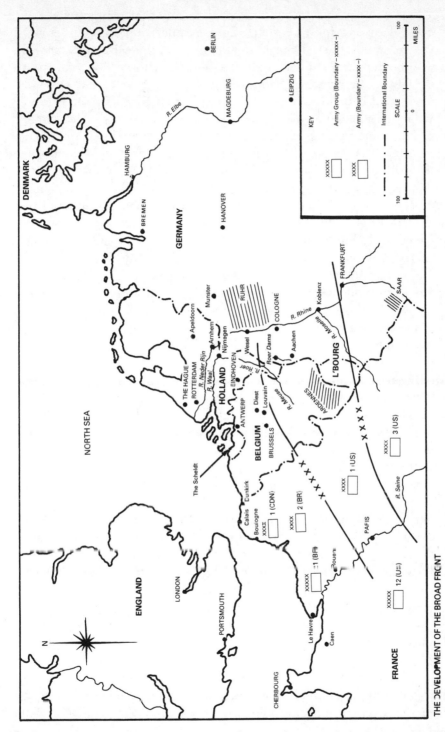

THE DEVELOPMENT OF THE BROAD FRONT

all the maintenance that was in the theatre – that is immobilise all other divisions and give their transport and supplies to his Army Group, with some to Hodges. Examination of this scheme exposes it as a fantastic idea. First of all, it would have to be done with the ports we now have, supplemented possibly by Calais and Ostend. The attack would be on such a narrow front that flanking threats would be particularly effective and no other troops in the whole region would be capable of going to its support. Actually, I doubt that the idea was proposed in any conviction that it could be carried through to completion: it was based merely on wishful thinking, and in an effort to induce me to give 21 Army Group and to Bradley's left every ounce of maintenance there is in the theatre. As opposed to this, the only profitable plan is to hustle all our forces up against the Rhine, including Devers forces, build up our maintenance facilities and our reserves as rapidly as possible and then put on one sustained and unremitting advance against the heart of the enemy country. Supporting this great attack will probably be subsidiary operations against the German ports on the left and against his southern industrial areas on the right. I have sacrificed a lot to give Montgomery the strength he needs to reach the Rhine in the north and to threaten the Ruhr. That is after all, our main effort for the moment. The great airborne attack which will go in support of this operation will be Sunday 17th, unless weather prevents. It should be successful in carrying Montgomery up to and across the Rhine; thereafter it is absolutely imperative that he quickly captures the approaches to Antwerp so that we may use the port.

He then gave a view of the shape of operations. They would have to fight –

one more major battle in the west . . . to break through the German defences on the border and to get started on the invasion. Thereafter the advance into Germany will not be as rapid as it was in France, because we won't have the FFI in the German rear, but I doubt there will be another full-dress battle involved. The big crash to start that move may prove to be a rather tough affair.

Eisenhower's letter seems to allude to Montgomery's signal on 4 September which had not demanded all resources to be given to Second Army but that Patton be stopped and the Ten Divisions of First Army be properly supported. Montgomery had been concerned about reaching the Ruhr at a time when everyone else, including Eisenhower and Marshall, was talking about Berlin and the end of the war. In that expectation Eisenhower had been trying to reach the Rhine on a broad front until his directive of the 13th, the day before he wrote to Marshall. Now, confusedly, Eisenhower is complaining that he has sacrificed a lot for MARKET – GARDEN, which was in keeping with that directive. From what Eisenhower was now telling him, Marshall must gather that MARKET – GARDEN was the knife-like thrust of which Eisenhower disapproved, for it was certainly contrary to the broadfront advance to the Rhine that he tells Marshall he is still pursuing. Much later, when his papers were being edited, he wrote of MARKET – GARDEN:

'I not only *approved* MARKET–GARDEN, I insisted upon it. What we needed was a *bridgehead* over the Rhine. If that could be accomplished I was quite willing to wait on all other operations. What this action proved was that the idea of 'one full blooded thrust' to Berlin was silly.[23]

Of course, MARKET – GARDEN was not aimed at Berlin when it started on the 17th. On the 4th, Montgomery, as we have pointed out, was concerned with reaching the Rhine and the Ruhr. He was not asking for all available resources for his XXX Corps which was far outnumbered by First Army which was to participate in the drive to the Rhine. Eisenhower, it seems, was toadying to Marshall and covering himself lest MARKET – GARDEN failed. The broad front, in satisfying Bradley and Patton would appeal to Marshall, who was suspicious of Montgomery's influence over Eisenhower.

Bradley ignored Eisenhower's directive of the 13th. A few days later, Montgomery drew Eisenhower's attention to a directive of Bradley's which appeared to be quite contrary to the conception of concentrating on the Aachen Gap. Eisenhower tried to reassure Montgomery by saying that 'only on the surface' was it at variance. Everything would turn out 'exactly as you visualised it.' This was simply deception. Bradley told Eisenhower that he was concentrating on his left, but actually Patton was by then fighting fifteen miles beyond the Moselle on the Nancy front. He himself was more concerned with V Corps' flank with Patton's XX Corps than with his left. Although Bradley promised to launch VII and V Corps attacks on the 17th, the day MARKET – GARDEN opened, the entry in Hodges' diary for that day reads:

Bradley comes for a more or less secret conference. General Plank and other COMZ officers in attendance. Supply still critical of POL,

249

ammunition and food and we are not now even holding our own. Whether we shall see any improvement is doubtful. It is not improbable that we shall have to slow up, even altogether halt our drive into Germany and this is in the very near future. The General met General Kean [his chief of staff] in the evening to somehow increase the supply of ammunition. Air activity washed out for the fifth day by dirty weather. Ground resistance is considerable. No advance on VII Corps front. Aachen nearly sealed off. XIX Corps still moving forward.

Eisenhower wrote to Marshall the very next day: 'Hodges is going well. His operations are coordinated with those of Montgomery. Hodges is driving straight on to Cologne and Bonn for the eventual purpose of attacking the Ruhr from the south as Montgomery swings into it from the north. Similarly, the plan calls for pushing Patton towards the left to support Hodges . . .' Shortly afterwards, General Simpson's Ninth Army, with the new XIII Corps and First Army's XIX Corps under command, was slipped into the line on Hodges' left but Troy Middleton's VIII Corps, which had been in Brittany, was put in on the right of V Corps and initially given to Patton. Marshall had told Eisenhower that he thought Patch's Seventh Army should be built up so that the American, as opposed to the French influence in 6 Army Group was predominant. To which Eisenhower now said: 'I put this project above the building up of Simpson's (Ninth) Army,[24] These details serve to show that only lip-service was paid to SCAEF's directive of the 13th and that Bradley was building up his centre, not concentrating on what was supposed to be his *schwerpunkt* in the Aachen gap. The deception being practised, to which Eisenhower must have been party, exacerbated Montgomery's relations with his American colleagues, for Montgomery knew what was going on.

Knowing that the others were ganging-up against him, and irritated by the Supreme Commander's abysmally sloppy habits on paper, put Montgomery in the mood for a show-down. The occasion was a paper dated 15 September from Eisenhower to his commanders about plans for *after* the Rhine.[26] It was an interesting letter in that it concerned cooperation with the Russians, and whether the Allies should make for Berlin, Leipzig or both. Eisenhower gave the impression that he favoured continuing the broad front on which, despite his last directive, he still intended to reach the Rhine. Since Montgomery had argued that in order to be poised ready for the advance deep into Germany they must first reach the Rhine, the argument slipped back into the previous rut about the northern thrust. They would not get there at all on a broad front, Montgomery said, yet again, whereas if they reached it in strength opposite the Ruhr they would roll up the front and be able to take the Ruhr. After that, the advance into Germany would be no problem. Eisenhower, by now thoroughly irritated by a problem that either he was incapable of understanding, or was unable to solve because of politics, wrote:

> As I read your letter, you imply that all the divisions that we have, except those of 21 Army Group and approximately nine of the 12 Army Group, can stop in place *where they are* and that we can strip all these additional divisions from their transport and everything else to support one knife-like drive towards Berlin. This may not be exactly what you mean but it is not possible.[25]

It was certainly not what Montgomery had said, although Eisenhower had told Marshall that it was. Berlin had been the subject of Eisenhower's letter, so Montgomery addressed it, arguing that by the time the Ruhr had fallen a two-army advance would be enough to be decisive. Most of his letter had been about reaching the Rhine and the Ruhr. The whole of 21 Army Group was not involved, and fewer divisions of Second Army than of the First Army. Clearly, that same dead horse was being flogged again. Bradley and Eisenhower were not playing straight with anyone. Eisenhower ended his letter by saying that he was sure that really all his commanders understood his directives and were in complete agreement.

All this equivocation was fast driving Montgomery to distraction. Unfortunately, when a meeting to discuss strategy was convened at Versailles on the 22nd, he sent his Chief of Staff de Guingand to put forward his views pleading absorption in the crucial stages of MARKET–GARDEN as an excuse for not attending himself. De Guingand was a conciliatory and well-liked man but it was unfortunate that Montgomery did not, in person, beard his opponents. Instead, he sent three notes that enabled them to see him as a trouble-maker and an empire-builder. Gale had been sent to him because the promised supplies for MARKET–GARDEN had not reached him and because his own Chief Administrative Officer, Major-General Miles Graham,* had told him that SHAEF administration was in a shambles.

> I have seen Gale. Since the change in command on 1 September I have not been in touch with the supply situation in 12 AG. From what

---

* Miles Graham, a graduate of Eton and Cambridge and a distinguished British publisher, had served in the First World War and rejoined the Life Guards as a reserve officer in September 1939.

Gale tells me it seems clear that 12 AG has been allowed to outstrip its maintenance and as a result we have lost flexibility throughout the battle as a whole. From my talk with Gale it seems to me that he is greatly to blame for not keeping in touch with the situation and ensuring things were in hand. My own administrative situation is not in blooming health but I can quite well continue the battle and am doing so. I suggest that it is now more than ever necessary that the inter-army boundary should be adjusted as recommended in my M 221 (211445) so that objectives can continue favourably in 21 AG. If the boundary is not so adjusted then the operations of 21 AG are bound to gradually peter out.[26]

Two other notes set the cat amongst the pigeons.

I consider that the organisation for command and control of the operation to capture the Ruhr is not satisfactory. It is a task for one man and he should have the operational control and direction of all the forces involved. He should be able to adjust boundaries as necessary to suit the changing tactical problem . . .

I recommend that the Supreme Commander hands the job over to me and gives me powers of operational control over First US Army.[27]

I cannot agree that our concepts are the same and I am sure that you would wish me to be quite frank and open in the matter. I have always said stop the right and go on with the left but the right has been allowed to go on so far that it has outstripped its maintenance and we have lost flexibility. In your letter you still want to go on further with your right and you state in your para 6 that all of Bradley's Army Group will move forward sufficiently etc. I would say that the right flank of 12 AG should be given a direct order to halt, and if this order is not obeyed we shall get into greater difficulties. The net result of the matter in my opinion is that if you want to get the Ruhr you will have to put every single thing into the left hook and stop everything else . . . Your very great friend Monty.[28]

The hectoring tone of these letters was not calculated to make friends. Worse, Montgomery was absolutely right.

On the 21 September, in a brilliant joint action, a sub-unit of the US 505 Parachute Regiment (US 82nd Airborne Division) in flimsy assault boats supported by an audacious frontal attack by the tanks of the armoured regiment of the Grenadier Guards captured the roadbridge over the Waal at

Nijmegen intact. The way to the Rhine was open, and had XXXth Corps been able to exploit this coup the US view of Montgomery might well have changed. Unfortunately the British 43rd Infantry Division, following up, was checked by enemy infiltration on the road, which was protected only by detachments of the US 101st Airborne Division in the ditches on either side. A few days later, 'Monty's' knife-like drive had 'failed', and with that failure he lost his remaining credibility with Bradley and Patton for whom 'face' was everything. That had not yet occurred on the 22nd when the Versailles meeting determined, to de Guingand's satisfaction, that the First Army drive should be given priority. Bradley was instructed to meet Montgomery to discuss First Army's part in the drive 'against the Ruhr'. Bradley, 'somewhat disgruntled' naturally enough since he had fought against it all along, went to see Montgomery next day. Eisenhower writing to Monty to say they had reached complete agreement, offered a mild rebuke.

> I regard it as a pity that all of us cannot keep in closer touch with each other because I find, without exception, when all of us get together and look the various features of our problems squarely, in the face, the answers usually become obvious.

That was well said, although Eisenhower was either deceiving himself or Montgomery. Montgomery, though, was just not prepared to argue it out calmly face to face with men who, he knew, disliked him and whom he now had good reason to distrust. Moreover, letters and telegrams, which continued to flow, were certainly not the way to run a battle. Assurances, whether verbal or written, continued to be breached.[29]

At the heart of the whole sorry disagreement was the fact that the supply and transport situation was in a state of desperate disorganisation, as Graham had revealed to Montgomery. On the 18th, Major-General Crawford, deputy chief of staff for logistics and head of G4, SHAEF, submitted a paper, written with the agreement of Bedell Smith, to explain the background and how the state of affairs on the COMZ could be put in order. It did not win Eisenhower's approval, and he blocked any attempt by his staff to bring its semi-autonomous commander, Lieutenant-General JCH Lee to heel.

On 6 October, George Marshall landed at Orly airport in the President's plane 'The Sacred Cow'. On his tour of the armies he learned how disgruntled they were about their supplies. Hodges told him that Collins of VII Corps and Corlett of XIX Corps had not the slightest doubt that, given sufficient petrol and ammunition, they could smash through to the

Rhine. On the 6th also Montgomery drew Eisenhower's attention to the matter:

> Dempsey went to see Hodges today and brought back a dismal picture. First US Army is, apparently, unable to develop its operations properly because it has not got the ammunition necessary. This does NOT repeat NOT promise well for our plans. Hodges' own view is that if he had the ammunition and the troops he could go right through to the Rhine easily. I considered I had better report this matter to you.[30]

CHAPTER 15

LOGISTICS: NEGLECT AND MISCHIEF

A little neglect may breed mischief: for want of a nail . . .

POOR RICHARD'S ALMANAC, 1757. BENJAMIN FRANKLIN

It will be recalled that the rapid advance from the Normandy battlefields to the German frontier had created a gasoline shortage. There was stiff fighting when the Germans recovered and First Army ran short of ammunition, a situation which Dempsey reported at the beginning of October. Montgomery passed on the information on the 6th to Eisenhower, who replied: 'Thank you very much for your M 260. Will put steam behind it at once,[1] Simultaneously, Montgomery made it clear that he could not clear the Scheldt, drive the enemy out of the area between the Maas and the Rhine south of Nijmegen, look after the Nijmegen bridgehead and clear the area west of the Maas on the First Army flank as well. Eisenhower agreed with him and told Bradley that his First Army should assume the commitment to clear the area on its left flank. To Montgomery he observed that 'in spite of some promise of improving logistics' Bradley might have to 'reduce still further the maintenance of Third Army.' The drive to the Rhine north of Bonn might have to be postponed until First Army accumulated adequate strength.[2]

Despite this last observation, Eisenhower did nothing to hasten the supply of ammunition beyond having his staff write a note to Lee. Marshall, though, heard the truth directly from First Army and then, when he visited Montgomery, had to listen to him expound on the weakness of First Army and its causes. Montgomery told Marshall that Patton had been allowed to continue attacking, despite Eisenhower's directive on the 13th September and the conference on the 23rd, which told him to halt. He had consumed the supplies that First Army ought to have received. The strategy that had been agreed at SHAEF was to concentrate on the approaches to the Ruhr. Indeed, the CCS had recommended that policy, but Eisenhower had allowed each army to attempt to reach the Rhine on its own. There was no concentration of effort. Unwisely, Montgomery added that he ought to be assigned the task of commanding on the Ruhr approaches, as he had proposed to Eisenhower recently. Marshall received these comments coldly because they were critical of Eisenhower and reflected on the American Army in general, which Montgomery did not intend. Besides, Marshall preferred Eisenhower's broad front to one that concentrated effort in the north, on the boundary between the 12th and 21st Army Groups, because it gave the American armies the limelight. Nevertheless, Marshall could not ignore the logistics muddle or its effects on First Army that Montgomery had noticed and passed on to Brooke in London. On his return to Washington he told Somervell to straighten things out.

The truth of the matter was that Montgomery was absolutely right on his point about concentration on the Ruhr approaches; indeed, the CCS recommended that strategy. No doubt that was the reason why Eisenhower repeatedly wrote in his directives that he favoured the Ruhr approach and seemed oblivious that the Ruhr conflicted with the Saar objective. And if it became known that American logistics and American strategy had been instrumental in bringing the autumn campaign to a standstill and, what was more, prolonging the war, a political row would ensue just at the time of the presidential elections. That was the main reason why Marshall's reaction to Montgomery was entirely negative. In 1956, when hindsight might have taught him that there had been some justice in Montgomery's complaints, he made the well-publicised comment:

> I came pretty near to blowing off out of turn. It was very hard for me to restrain myself because I didn't think there was any logic in what he said but overwhelming egotism.

Back in Washington, when he had set in train the investigation into logistics in the European Theatre of Operations (ETO) that we are about to recount, he sent a signal to Brooke expressing his confidence that Eisenhower would be able to finish the war in 1944. Brooke wrote to Montgomery expressing his amazement:

> Discussed with planners the wonderful telegram from Marshall in which he seems to consider that if we really set our heart on it we ought to be able to finish the war before the end of the year.[3]

Despite that piece of Marshall window-dressing, Somervell had despatched Major-General Lucius Clay to sort out the Normandy Base Area and Major-General Henry Aurand to investigate the ammunition supply in France. As we know, Bedell Smith had been angling for LeRoy Lutes, Somervell's efficient head of planning, to replace Lee, but Marshall and Somervell had no intention of advertising the situation by sacking the man chiefly responsible.

Aurand arrived in France in late October and reported to Bedell Smith in Versailles. Thence he went to COMZ headquarters which was ensconced in a luxurious Paris hotel. Lee's staff had moved into Paris when the advance started at the end of August. Aurand was briefed by COMZ before he proceeded to the front to start his investigation. An ordnance expert, he understood the supply business intimately, but he was not attuned to the political relationship between the men with whom he had to deal.[4]

The surest way for Aurand to have his head cut off was to present the truth too bluntly to the wrong people at the wrong time. Although Lee was unpopular at SHAEF, Aurand was considered a spy by both SHAEF and COMZ and an adverse report from him would be considered a criticism of both.[5] Clearly, as Eisenhower was ultimately responsible for allowing 12th Army Group to run low in ammunition, he and Smith were apprehensive about what the army commanders would tell Aurand, what Aurand would pass on to Somervell, and what would reach Marshall's ear. As we shall see, the shortage could also become a political issue in the United States. Lee treated Aurand with suspicion but also with care until he had taken the measure of Aurand's standing in Washington and seen how Smith, at SHAEF, handled him.

Lee feared that Bedell Smith, who wanted to get rid of him and clean up his organisation, would finally persuade Eisenhower to sack him, or at least to change the command system so as to bring COMZ directly under SHAEF. An adverse report on COMZ would play into Bedell Smith's hands.

Aurand did not understand these nuances in the political balance of power and influence until it was almost too late. At the end of his mission and after he had written his report, Aurand unburdened his critical views about the whole command set-up to Everett Hughes* at a cosy dinner in Paris. It was unwise of him, for Hughes tipped off Smith. Next day, Bedell

---

* Hughes appears an enigmatic character. He remained a friend of Eisenhower until his death in 1957. He has been described by a staff colleague: 'A very impressive man, tall, big, saturnine, quiet.' General Littlejohn, Eisenhower's QMG, thought 'he was great. He was one of the inner circle boys. In Paris, Hughes had an office over at the HQ of COMZ and nobody knew quite what he

Smith called Aurand in and took him apart, for he was a specialist in psychological bullying. He may have agreed with Aurand's views about SHAEF controlling COMZ but he was not going to accept Aurand's opinion that Eisenhower should either attend properly to operations and logistics, or hand them over to a ground forces commander for that was the British view. If the British press got hold of the story of the muddle in logistics and learned that Montgomery had complained, the fat would be in the fire; the British press was still sensitive about 'Monty's demotion' after the Normandy battle. Only when Aurand stood like a small boy before the desk of an angry Smith did he grasp that the idea of his mission was to put things right 'within the family'. There was to be no sacking and not a word to the British.[6] The affair was being kept away from the desks of the British staff officers at SHAEF; even Gale, Eisenhower's Chief Administrative Officer, was not involved.

Aurand learned a second point about the politics of command when he joined Lee's organisation as commanding general of Normandy Base Section and discovered how Lee's system of sticks and carrots controlled his subordinates. Lee punished anyone who pointed out the shortcomings of an over-centralised headquarters in Paris or told tales out of school about COMZ's inefficiency. He ran a kind of mafia with which he imposed obedience. Lee tried, without effect, to butter-up Bedell Smith by presenting him with crates of oranges and other goodies for distribution at SHAEF. The physical conditions in which most of Lee's senior commanders lived were luxurious compared to those of the rank and file, and paradise compared to the conditions endured by infantrymen on the roads to Aachen and Metz. The meals these men ate were provided by the black market and they lived not wisely but too well. Everyone thought twice about prejudicing such living conditions by outspokenness. The rank and file were less lucky and the jobs of junior officers could be miserably dull and grinding. Some had been wounded and posted from hospitals as no longer fit for combat. Others had been found unsuitable for combat units or had received adverse combat reports. A large percentage of the younger junior officers and men would rather have been in the forward area instead of working twelve hours on and twelve off in depots, shifting supplies by brawn, which some lacked, from one mud-hole to another, or completing

---

did, but he did a *lot* . . .' American WAC officers at AFHQ in Algiers were less complimentary, complaining that he prowled about criticising their sex life. Hughes was an ordnance Gunner who joined the Service of Supply in 1942. He was commissioned in 1908. In January 1945 he became Special Assistant to General Lee.

endless paper-work. The less scrupulous joined in the black market, where money could be made, girls obtained, and tasteless army rations supplemented by tasty French food. It was not surprising that many sought such perquisites as were within their reach.*

Lee fell foul of Eisenhower for moving COMZ, without his permission, into Paris hotels with such alacrity that the beds were still warm from Nazi occupation. His pretext was that he was getting nearer to the front and placing himself at the most important communications centre in France. But the move used quantities of transport which ought to have been employed taking gasoline to the front, and took his eye off the ball at a crucial moment. Soon the bad behaviour of COMZ troops became a scandal and it was an openly expressed opinion in Paris and a number of other cities that the Germans had been preferable to the Americans because they were better disciplined. There were embarrassing references to the American Occupation Forces and it was asked when the 'occupation' would end. Liberation was spoken of by the French as something they wanted soon and not at the end of the war. Finally, the black market operations of the American COMZ began to get out of hand and formation commanders complained that large amounts of supplies were disappearing on their way to the front. The Bois de Boulogne was the centre of the black market and ugly shoot-outs occurred there between rival gangs. Eisenhower threatened to move Lee out of Paris and he ordered him to clean up his troops and thin them out. Lee tried to comply and things improved after military police took a hand and Bradley had sent eight battalions to guard the lines of communication, but the conditions were not peculiar to Paris, nor were the COMZ troops the only ones who misbehaved. In March 1945, Brigadier George Kitching, Chief of Staff I Canadian Corps, on his way to Holland, spent a night at a US Army transit camp near the Somme. It was crowded with armed military police. He was told that they amounted to two full battalions, whose mission was to round up several hundred deserters who were skulking in the neighbouring woods, supporting themselves by systematically looting supply convoys. In many small towns behind the front the Americans were regarded as an indisciplined mob and were feared and disliked. LeRoy Lutes, who was to be sent out from Washington in December in a follow-up mission, noted the unkempt appearance and poor conduct of American soldiers in the towns and villages near the front and reported growing alarm among villagers. Eisenhower had to circulate a strong letter reminding officers not only of their duties regarding discipline but also of their responsibility for

*The film *Kelly's Heroes* is art imitating real life.

looking after their men. They should not leave soldiers in the backs of trucks without covers in pouring rain, for instance, and bivouacs were really not adequate shelter in winter, particularly when barns were available and officers were snug in farmhouses. Such a letter would have been unnecessary had officers been alert to their responsibilities. After Aurand had delivered his report and taken command of the Normandy Base Section in December, he recorded that he despatched a train of PX (Post Exchange) goods for the front. A platoon of infantry, part at the rear and part at the front, was to ensure that at long halts and in shunting yards, agents of the black-market would not get on board and rifle the wagons. That train disappeared, troops and all, he said, and was never seen again. Aurand wrote that he had no doubt that the men had joined the growing number of deserters living on the black-market, where a packet of American cigarettes was worth Frs. 200. The size of the deserter population was not something to be advertised, either. It may have been an open secret but anyone who arrived from outside and commented on it loudly and in public would be in trouble.

All this, the seamy side of COMZ, was not Aurand's business and although it was his concern, his pride in the Army made him more circumspect in criticising it than the professional work of the logisticians which was his assignment. He confined his description of it to his diary. Apart from criticising the chain of command, his report dealt mainly with the details of the failures of Lee's COMZ to provide ammunition, which also entailed commenting on transportation, communications, inventories – in fact all the subjects that are keys to effective logistics management.

Aurand traced the trouble in COMZ back to the procedure in the Normandy bridgehead. Supply in the field operated on an echelon system which originated in the French army before 1914, when it was copied by the British and became standard in most armies. The idea was to keep the echelons filled and supplies moving up the ladder to the fighting troops. There were three echelons in the COMZ part of the supply system; the Base Sections near the ports and beaches which comprised the Base Area, the Intermediate Section and the Advance Section. In front of the Advance Section, First and Third Armies and their divisions took over responsibility for handling supply. Neither the Army Group nor the Corps level of command was part of the chain of supply. The Advance Section was the COMZ echelon closest to the fighting troops. It was the first COMZ echelon to arrive in Normandy where it served First Army and, later, Patton's Third Army when it arrived. In the meanwhile, cells of the future COMZ headquarters and the rest of the rear organisation were included in HQ

21st Army Group, the senior headquarters in Normandy. COMZ head-quarter's job was to plan for the future deployment of the base and intermediate echelon units. In the meanwhile, Advance Section lived from day to day, clearing beach areas, building up dumps by categories and pro-viding fast moving items for First Army on demand. A state of improvised chaos soon arose as supplies were dumped on muddy fields as they were hauled off the beaches. Frequently, they were 'lost' before they had been properly inventoried. First Army's staff did not concern itself with what was going on, provided ammunition, food and military stores arrived on demand. Too often, commanders took no interest in supply problems until shortages inconvenienced their operations. In December, in the middle of his later mission, Lutes wrote to Somervell from France to that effect:

> Hodges is a man intolerant of supply shortcomings who has not stud-ied supply and does not intend to . . . (his attitude is) a hangover from the conservatism of the old First Army staff. (Reference to the AEF in 1917.)

Aurand recorded that when the port of Cherbourg opened, it became a base district of the future Normandy Base Section, a considerable distance from the original beaches at Omaha and Utah which were still being oper-ated by Advance Section. No one was informed what supplies were to arrive at Cherbourg and what were to be delivered over the beaches. Most significantly, all supplies in the hands of Advance Section were claimed as the property of First Army, so when the advance started and Normandy Base Section took over the beach operations, it received no clear instruc-tions of what was theirs and what was First Army's. From August, when the advance began until December, First Army sent scrounging parties back to Normandy in search of ammunition and scarce signals and vehicle spares which had been dumped in isolated places. They found scrounging a quicker way to obtain what they wanted than normal channels which were slow at best and moribund at worst. Nor did COMZ ever find out what First Army held, even in ammunition. Indeed, no one in the armies or at COMZ could state with confidence what was the theatre holding of any item of supply. Naturally, Washington grew sceptical about its reported shortages.

Congestion in the Normandy bridgehead had not permitted the estab-lishment there of Intermediate Section units, the echelon between the Base Area and the Advanced Section. Consequently, when the break-out occurred, the middle link in the echelon system, the Intermediate Section, was not on the ground. From then until the end of 1944, the US army, as it were, had a 'production plant' in the Base Areas and 'retailers' in the Advanced Section, but the 'wholesalers' in between, the Intermediate Section, with their transportation, dumps, stores and numerous specialists trained to handle, maintain and repair the hundreds of items a field army requires, was not, for the most part, in place. Indeed, when Lutes reported on the supply situation in December, the Intermediate Section was still not properly established. The reason, he was told, was the COMZ had been led to believe that as the invasion of Germany beyond the Rhine was at hand, there was no pressing need for it.

The echelon system was designed on the assumption that the expeditionary force would make an orderly entry into a theatre of war through friendly ports. The three echelons would be established together to form a chain of supply. An assault landing supplied over the beaches was a different matter. It made sense to land the Advanced Section first, since it operated closest to the fighting units. However, confusion arose when the Base Areas were established next, and the unwanted Intermediate Section had to take over from Base Area with one hand and reach out to Advance Section with the other, while Advance Section was striving to cope with an increasing load in front. The forward projection of operations and the administrative plan had not been reconciled. When the First Army broke the enemy front at St. Lo, the Third Army was landing and the Advance Section was in the process of handing over to Base Area. The Third Army wasted no time in passing through the gap created by the First, its VIII Corps turning west in Brittany making for Brest. 12 Army Group was now facing in two directions; the First Army fighting hard in 'artillery intensive' operations, the Third motoring fast in 'gasoline intensive' operations. Advance Section therefore had to carry stocks on wheels for delivery as needed, whilst its responsibilities were doubled.

In the meantime, on top of a chaotic start, Normandy Base Section suffered a stream of replacement commanders: none stayed long enough to sort things out; none was properly briefed about the operational situation. The scale of the German defeat in Normandy and the consequent Allied decision to advance rapidly to the German frontier had not been foreseen. The logistics plan for a pause on the Seine, while American maintenance was shifted to southern Brittany and the Biscay Normandy ports, had to be scrapped. Normandy Base found itself ill-prepared to support Advance Section in mobile operations two hundred and fifty miles or more away. Moreover, Base Section planned on the assumption that in the near future a string of ports further east on the Channel coast, particularly Le Havre, Marseilles on the Mediterranean and Antwerp on the Scheldt, would replace Normandy. It assumed that the crisis in supply would be temporary. COMZ took its lead from Eisenhower who expected his armies to reach and cross the Rhine in the near future. Eisenhower was convinced, even in late September, that since the German armies seemed to have collapsed, sorting out the logistic muddle could wait until the Allies reached the Rhine. With that in mind, and correctly appreciating that the enemy would defend St Nazaire, Lorient and Nantes to the last ditch, he decided that the cost of capturing them was not worth while.

As we have seen, Eisenhower and Bradley did not foresee and were slow to recognise the strength of German resistance in the frontier zone, nor had they any idea how poorly Lee's organisation in Normandy, using Cherbourg, Le Havre and the beaches and small ports, would cope with the problem of supplying armies engaged in stiff fighting at the end of ever lengthening communications. To give Lee credit, Eisenhower gave him the impression even in October and November that the war was about to end, or at least that the advance would continue to the Rhine before a logistical reorganisation based on Antwerp as well as Le Havre, became necessary. Throughout that long period Lee kept much of his Intermediate Section in railway cars because SHAEF led him to believe that to support an advance beyond the Rhine it should be located on ground that, eventually, was disputed all through the autumn. Of course, Lee ran out of railcars, the circulation between beach/port and Advance Section slowed up and rail tonnages were reduced. But there was more to it than that.

The lack of coordination in American logistics was evident soon after Patton had swung off into the blue around Paris, leaving his VIII Corps under Lieutenant-General Troy Middleton to turn west into Brittany. VIII Corps ran short of ammunition outside Brest, which the Germans held as part of their plan to deny the Allies all port facilities by demolitions and fanatical defence. Bedell Smith had to intervene to keep the peace between Middleton and Lee, and to give a direct order to Lee to get the ammunition forward. Middleton, a veteran of the Italian campaign, expected better service. Ammunition is ordered on a day to day, sometimes hour to hour basis to refill unit supply vehicles in the forward area immediately after firing. Its consumption is not a routine like food, nor can it be held in workshop inventories and replaced weekly, or sent up by express, like individual vehicle spare parts. All the echelons have to be kept filled all the time in case of sudden demand. The system must also allow for dumping programmes before big operations which make sudden surges in demand requiring ample reserves to be available. Again, ammunition is demanded by calibre and types, each of which is consumed at a different rate, so that impressive figures of tonnages shifted is not an indication that the right calibre has been delivered. Finally, ammunition is bulky and heavy and in the

Second War its handling was labour intensive and time consuming. VIII Corps' ammunition crisis was a sign of trouble ahead on the German frontier where demands would be much heavier. Middleton's ire was already aroused because he considered his assignment to advance into Brittany redundant anyway: he would rather have been galloping towards Berlin. Events proved Middleton right, Brest was a naval port and was never used for unloading follow-up divisions from the United States as intended.

In the meantime, instead of applying himself completely to the demands for POL pouring in from the rest of Third Army and First Army, Lee moved his headquarters to Paris which contributed to his losing touch with his supplies, with SHAEF and with 12th and 21st Army Group at a crucial moment. Many testified to the complete break-down even in telephone communications at this time. It will be recalled that Advanced SHAEF, according to the original operational plan, calling for a pause on the Seine, was at Granville on the west coast of the Cotentin Peninsula where it was, for all intents and purposes, *hors de combat* – although Eisenhower had taken over his ambiguous role as SCAEF on 1 September. The next day he suffered his leg injury and was confined to bed. It will also be recalled that under the curious SHAEF-ETO organisation Eisenhower was Lee's immediate superior. As Eisenhower was not giving clear directives to his field commanders, now in full cry for the German frontier, it is not surprising that he gave none to Lee either.

If there is one weakness above another that indicates inexperience in a commander it is being in the wrong place at crucial moments and being *incommunicado*. A commander without radio and telephone is like a unit without weapons. The SHAEF staff was quite aware that its organisation could not cope with Eisenhower's role as commander. General Bull, the senior operations officer (G3), stated that SHAEF forward 'must be cut to small, mobile elements and have only those personnel required to handle matters that cannot be delayed 24 hours'. General RWF Crawford, at the same time was arguing for control of COMZ.[7] Throughout September, Eisenhower conducted operational affairs by telegrams, fleeting visits and inconvenient 'conferences', repeating the error that had cost French commanders the battle in 1940. Like them he was out of touch, not just physically with his commanders, but with the 'feel' of operations. Consequently, he easily misunderstood the meaning of their written and even their verbal communications. Thus, when Patton and First Army's VII Corps (under the excellent and experienced General Joe Collins, a fiery and splendidly combative southern Irish American), advanced about fifty miles a day, and the British took up the cry and reached Brussels from the Seine in three days on the 3rd of September, every American commander was looking over his shoulder and asking for POL and orders. When the orders arrived they were, as we have seen, inappropriate. The POL arrived but not in sufficient quantities.

Thus was born the first logistics crisis, mainly in petrol, which was a natural sequel to Normandy, for great battles are supposed to be followed by great advances. They often disappoint in that respect, but the shape of the one in Normandy should have given logisticians warning enough of what was to follow, since it was a battle of annihilation. Normandy, from the logistician's point of view, had been an ammunition battle, and less so a POL battle. Tanks grinding about in the hedgerows had consumed POL in great quantities, but not in excess of scales. Consequently, even if POL stocks were not run up in anticipation of a long and rapid advance to follow, they were not run down either because of the fighting in Normandy. The POL needed by early September was there, in the Normandy beachhead. Lee's immediate problem was how to send it forward: to switch commodities and to adjust from a short to a long supply run. He had to find additional transport; but that was a matter of organisation for the transport, like the POL it was to carry, was available.

A 'Red Ball Express' was the standard American description of an emergency lift, by air, sea or road. So Lee organised all available transport in the Base Area and acquired vehicles in stock and from grounded units and sent them by one-way roads up to the front to deliver POL, starting at the end of August. Lacking intermediate dumps, with the advance base virtually on wheels and rail transport still in shambles that was all he could do. Airlift was also employed but it was a ferociously uneconomical way of moving petrol. In some cases it cost one and a half gallons of high octane fuel to deliver one gallon of 80 octane forward to depots.[8] Had the advance been better controlled, and the lift for divisions and corps followed some operational priority, shortages such as those which left American XIX Corps units on the left of First Army stranded on a crucial front could have been avoided.

This Red Ball Express operation, with black American drivers, eyes glinting behind the wheels of their 2½ tonners – 'dooce an'a haffs – speeding up the French roads, chickens flying for their lives, wary pedestrians gaping, was exciting stuff for the participants. By and large American blacks were not prominent in the Army's operations but here they could justly feel that they were important players, carrying an infusion of life blood to the armies. Between 25 August and 5 September Red Ball Express trucks carried more than 74,000 tons of supplies to 12 Army Group. By the middle of September, though, trains were running through to the Soissons area and carried a little more than the trucks. Unfortunately, the grand total of 150,000 tons that they provided was insufficient for 12th Army Group, then fighting on both its armies' fronts, all divisions up.

There were two closely related reasons for this short-fall, other than that too many divisions were engaged on too broad a front and that the French rail system had been thoroughly disrupted by the air offensive which preceded OVERLORD. The great effort, termed by Aurand the period of 'frantic supply' virtually destroyed the truck companies. The $2^1/2$ tonner was not as tough as it looked. It required regular maintenance but did not receive it, and workshop facilities could not keep the trucks on the road. Truck units were not rotated, so the back-log of trucks requiring repair was soon unmanageable. For every one on the road four were awaiting repair, standing forlornly in the muddy fields like derelicts in a car dump. The shortage for the long haul had to be made good from the pool in the Base Section in Normandy. In consequence the base depots were overstocked. Aurand reported that between 7 August and 13 December of the 2,859,893 tons unloaded in Normandy only 1,607,706 had moved closer to the front; the role of Intermediate Section. When enemy resistance stiffened and fighting intensified there was no reserve of ammunition between the Advance Section and Normandy.

In December as a dubious reward for his role as a critic, Aurand was appointed to command the Base Section himself, still in a tangle despite the efforts of his predecessor, Major-General Lucius Clay. At about the same time LeRoy Lutes arrived from Washington to make another inspection of the logistic situation. His report confirmed Aurand's in all respects. Although Antwerp had been recently opened, the system was still flawed. That demand was still out of kilter with supply was quite evident from a few statistics. The intermediate section was incomplete and the centre of gravity of all supplies other than vehicles and POL was still in Normandy where 47 per cent of them were held. Fifty-three per cent of fast-moving items, those urgently needed and rapidly consumed, were back there while 47 per cent of slow-moving items had accumulated in the forward area.

In short, the errors in the system within the theatre had not been corrected during the autumn. A grave result was that the shortage of ammunition noted in October continued to affect operations and now included tank gun rounds and mortar bombs for the infantry. A root of the trouble was that the scales or forecasts of rates of expenditure per day had been set too low, and that had been exacerbated by the abysmally slow flow of ammunition forward to armies. HQ 12th Army Group was still complaining about this to Lutes on the eve of the German counter-offensive in the Ardennes. Indeed, one of the reasons that SHAEF was in a state of panic and near paralysis during the first four days of the German attack (a state of affairs denied by Bedell Smith after the war) was its fear that the ammunition dumps in the Advance Section might be overrun, as many very nearly were.[9] Had they gone the nearest re-supply was in Normandy.

Even as late as December, Lee's excuse for all this was that SHAEF had assured him that the German armies west of the Rhine were shattered, and that the Advance Section should be stocked ready to maintain the advance of 12th Army Group east of the Rhine. Lutes was prepared to accept this, up to a point. HQ SHAEF was still absurdly optimistic even in November, by which time Bradley's armies had been fighting an increasingly obdurate enemy for two months, complaining of shortage of ammunition. Eisenhower had certainly said to Lee that he should build up as far forward as he could, since the Germans were incapable of a serious counter-offensive. None of this offered a valid excuse for Lee's neglect. He was, after all, the commanding general of a great and vital organisation, who could have read the signs of the autumn fighting and been sensitive to the mood in 12th Army Group. Perhaps because the US echelon system by-passed Army Group and Corps, he ignored their views. His failure to establish the Intermediate or back-up echelon was egregious and has to be laid at his door. Lutes found that COMZ had few friends in the forward area. Brigadier-General Ewart Plank, commander of Advance Section, was critical of Lee's headquarters and the support that he was receiving from the rear. Bradley complained that 85 per cent of his troops were in battle most of the time and deserved better support. Lutes recorded that Bradley.

said bitterly that 'the British would not consider an attack on only 60 rounds of 105mm ammunition per diem. He said that normally they would have 150 and that he wants 150–200 rounds per gun per diem for his offensive operations. This would require an overall average of 60 rpg throughout the year.' Bradley blamed Lee's staff for the US rate of 32 rpg saying he was never consulted on these plans. Moreover he was very bitter on the shortage of mortar ammunition.[10]

Bradley had not used such language back in October when, by his own admission, as quoted by Lutes, he was engaged in intense fighting across his front with inadequate supplies. The reason he denied that shortages were impeding the First Army in October was that to admit it would mean halting Patton, as Montgomery repeatedly insisted he should. Operational good sense dictated that Bradley ought to have matched his efforts to his means. As an Army Group Commander, he should have raised hell about the supply organisation, but neither in October nor November did he force the issue. His complaints to Lutes in December were made only after his efforts to reach the Rhine in the autumn had failed. Marshall first heard the true state of affairs from Hodges and Montgomery, not Bradley. The subject demanded careful handling by Lutes, not only because the outsider Montgomery was in the know, but because the basic miscalculation of mean artillery ammunition expenditure had been in Washington.

With this last point in mind, Lutes assured Bradley in December that all his problems would be solved by the spring, and he mentioned May. (A ghostly echo of the planners in London who promised Haig all the resources he required – for the campaign of 1919.) Instead of exploding, saying that May 1945 would, he hoped, be too late, Bradley began despondently talking about finishing the war in 1946. It really was no wonder that Montgomery at the time of this conversation in December, just before the Ardennes, was desperately afraid that the Americans were, indeed, thinking about 1946. But Bradley is an unreliable witness. What he went on to tell First Army did not quite match what Lutes told him or his own resigned reaction to it. 'The news from the US,' he told the First Army staff on 10 December, 'is that the ammunition situation is going to improve every day. They have made a thorough canvas of all stocks in the US and have cut down some weeks in average shipping time. By May, the amounts on hand will come very close to what First Army has constantly asked for.'[11] Less than a month before, when he ought to have been chafing about ammunition shortage, he told First Army that 'the last big offensive necessary to bring Germany to her knees had started' that day, the 16th November. Yet Brigadier General Moses, his chief administrative staff officer, had just uncovered statistics that showed 'the simple but appalling conclusion that the War Department had allowed Operation OVERLORD to proceed without any certainty that there would be enough ammunition to overcome prolonged heavy resistance . . . existing rates of fire would exhaust ammunition reserves by December 15 and force severe rationing thereafter.' Eisenhower's operations officer, General Bull, had gone to Washington to try to persuade General Somervell that ETO's ammunition shortage was critical. That did not stop Bradley committing his First Army, his Third and Devers' southern Army Group to offensives simultaneously, in the belief that, as in Normandy, a long period of slugging would lead to another Operation COBRA and break-through. Instead, it was to exhaust his armies, laying them open to the German counter-offensive in the Ardennes on 16 December.[12] No one was squaring with anyone else, as a matter of fact. Lutes had come out expecting to find that the muddles of October had been sorted out. And at first he behaved as though that were the case. But, like Aurand before him, he soon discoverd that the organisation was still 'creaking', as he termed it, becaues of Lee's failure to sort out basic mistakes.

For instance, the indenting system was insensitive to urgent demands and had become chaotic because indents were being resubmitted several times when the first one was not honoured. The processing of 'indenting', i.e., demanding items on a written pro forma, was done centrally.; large staff shuffling thousands of pieces of paper, many out of date. Items issued were written off by the despatching unit but of course not recorded as received by the demanding one until they arrived. Frequently they disappeared en route into the black-market or into that black hole, the French railway system. A standard operating procedure for responding to urgent indents was not being used. A separate demand and resupply system for ammunition was either in abeyance or not working properly. Ammunition trains had been known to take seven days just to make their way around Paris. First Army, having lost many consignments, sent their own guards for these trains with radio to report their progress. They also circumvented the defective indent system by sending their own teams back to Normandy with transport to collect radio spares, ammunition and vehicle parts. They often met Third Army pirates on the same mission who were unscrupulous enough to divert supply trains and truck convoys to their own formation. On 22 December Lutes wrote:

> The supply organisation is clumsy and, although it has greatly improved it still creaks considerably at all levels . . . COMZ is a tight corporation, determined to defend itself and sensitive to suggestions, but there is nothing we can do about that. It is probably natural and I am being as careful and tolerant as I can.

When Lutes pointed out all these things, the transportation corps quoted the great tonnages they shifted. Lutes had to explain that ammunition and many other items could not be measured by weight alone. In fact they were often shifting the wrong items and not responding to demand, a point that was borne out both by units and by statistics about the comparative distribution of fast and slow-moving items. The statistics of ammunition unloaded in Normandy and forwarded to the frontier confirmed that Hodges was justified in complaining that his First Army had been inadequately supplied for the autumn battles. The shortfalls included every sort of supply and warlike store as well as the vital commodities, ammunition and POL: winter clothing, spare parts, rations, signal equipment replacements and 'PX' – Post Exchange goods for the troops, cigarettes, razor blades, candy and so on (British NAAFI) – highly attractive on the black market. The most efficient form of transport is rail, using what the British 'Q' staff called 'pack trains', loaded with a variety of commodities in constant demand, or single commodity trains carrying ammunition or petrol. Some 150,000 freight cars were available in the French railway system, of which 38,000 were allotted to COMZ and 12,000 to 21st Army Group. The railroad tracks serving COMZ ran through or around Paris, the nexus of the whole northern system whose routes radiated from the city. Shortly before the Ardennes counter-offensive no fewer than eighty trains were caught in a hideous tangle around Paris which Major-General Appleton, railway expert of SHAEF (in peace Vice-President of New York Central Railroad) declared would take three weeks to a month to unravel.

Part of the trouble was deliberate and criminal. It almost seems as if the daring and often amusing escapades of the French Resistance had, after the liberation of Paris been directed at the liberators. Few if any of the US Army rail staff or operators were fluent enough in French to understand the traditional chalked scribbles on box cars indicating load and destination. Some were diverted to be plundered individually, others for nefarious reasons or simply through inept handling ended up in remote sidings all over liberated France. Lutes was informed that the traffic jam was due to the extra effort required to establish the Intermediate Section and stock it from the Base, and the opening of Antwerp as a port of entry, coupled with a shortage of labour for loading and unloading. That should have been foreseen, and more French civil labour employed. The combination of these adverse factors interrupted the essential flow of loaded trains going forward and empties returning, leading inevitably to congestion in the Base and shortages in the fighting formations.

Aurand's papers and Lutes' reports also have much to say about the management of the ports. That tonnages were accumulating in them shows that the slow clearance of supplies was the prime cause of the shortages at the front, not lack of ports of entry. All the same, this was bad management at the very source. Much of the delay in unloading ships was caused by arguments between the various services about where the port dispersal depots were to be. The Transport Corps ran the show which did not suit the other services. Consequently, the mistakes made at Cherbourg and Le Havre in the organisation of the dispersal of cargo to depots were repeated at Antwerp. Unloaded cargo piled up on the dockside until no more could be accepted for lack of space. Loaded ships were held up in the channel for want of berthing space; in effect, precious shipping was scandalously used as floating storage. In Normandy, the beaches continued to be used, as before, not because they were more suitable, indeed orders were issued that beach unloading must cease, but because the cargoes could be re-routed more easily from them than from the ports. The landing craft used were in short supply world-wide which caused the navies to complain bitterly that their ships were being mis-used.

V1s and V2s launched from Northern Holland made handling ammunition hazardous when Antwerp was opened in late November. That and congestion resulted in Cherbourg having to accept a backlog of ammunition to the tune of about 25,000 tons per diem in December. The long lines of communication from Normandy to the front and the accompanying railway snarl-up around Paris remained as an apparently insoluble situation, despite the long-awaited opening of Antwerp.

No doubt General Graham had been his informant when Montgomery warned Eisenhower towards the end of November that Antwerp would not solve his logistics problems. Montgomery blamed the British chief administrator, Humfrey Gale at SHAEF for the American muddle, not realising, perhaps, that neither SHAEF nor Bradley had any control over the COMZ. As regards command and control, the British and American systems differed. Lee was a commander who took orders only from Eisenhower, and Eisenhower, as we know, had not seen the need to bring him under the control of Bedell Smith, through whom he would have had to issue orders to Lee. In the British system, it will be remembered, Graham was a *staff officer* directly responsible to Montgomery but also a commander who controlled the linear hierarchy of areas and echelons in the Lines of Communication. He and de Guingand worked as equals, although as the officer responsible for operations and intelligence (G3 and G2) de Guingand had full authority, speaking for Montgomery and passing information and instructions directly to Graham. Graham's position was similar to Harbord's in 1918, had Pershing's GHQ been split in two, with the Chief Administrative Officer at 'Rear' HQ, the equal of the Chief of General Staff 'Main HQ', instead of being a separate commander under the C-in-C.* Unfortunately, Lee had inherited the latter relationship, which was the unreconstructed and failed system of 1918. Montgomery was in the same position as Eisenhower, being the operational commander of 21st Army Group *and* commander of the (British) ETO. Bradley, on the other hand, was 'only' an operational commander. He and Montgomery were not equal in status.

Lee and his men were forgiven their sins. Montgomery would have been staggered had he listened in at Lutes' final interview with Bedell Smith, who told him: 'No one can say supply has failed. At the front it is OK.' Earlier, on the 19th November, Everett Hughes had talked to Bedell Smith

---

* In the Second World War the British split their formation HQs in a small 'tactical' command group, 'Main HQ' (operations) and 'Rear HQ' (administration.)

when Aurand's report was on Smith's desk. The commanders, he insisted should demand the support of Eisenhower and should consider 'how the results of possible shortages should be made known to the CCS – or must we continue to prepare an alibi?' The answer was 'yes' to alibis. True to form, when Lutes presented his final report on 30 December in a one and a half hour interview, Eisenhower commented that 'nothing that Lutes had told him was news to him. That he had never felt easy about the COMZ set-up but that in spite of this uneasiness he did not desire to make a change nor to charge a lieutenant-general unless he had specific charges to make about incompetency.' Astonishingly, Lutes replied that he agreed that no one could say that there had been a definite failure in supply of the combat forces. The machine did not run smoothly but it did run, he suggested. He left it at that. 'Alibis' were the order of the day and Washington needed them as much as Eisenhower.

According to Lutes, Bradley and Eisenhower were caught quite unawares by the Ardennes offensive. However, his final interview with Eisenhower took place when the crisis of the Ardennes battle was over and when Eisenhower's mind was turning once more towards wildly optimistic schemes to turn the German offensive and the American débâcle into a great Cannae; a counter-offensive from North and South, the success of which would cover up what had gone before. It would serve a political purpose in giving all commanders a satisfactory role. There would be no need for American scapegoats. That version served as an 'alibi' for Eisenhower and Bradley and has done yeoman service ever since.

It has had three parts. The first has it that Eisenhower and Bradley predicted the German counter-offensive; that Bradley, having told Eisenhower how far it would penetrate, was proved exactly correct; and that the counter-stroke from North and South caused irreplaceable German losses, was an American victory, and a personal triumph for Patton who was in command of the southern pincer. The second part deals with Antwerp, the objective of the German offensive, and the logistics muddle. The shortages, it is alleged, would not have occurred at all had Antwerp been opened earlier. Eisenhower ordered Montgomery to capture it in September but instead he had gone off to Arnhem in his quest for fame. It is he, therefore, who has to take the blame for the supply shortages and for the over-extension of the front. Thirdly Montgomery's insistence that the front be divided geographically, north and south of the Ardennes, instead of nationally, was motivated by his own desire for aggrandizement and was not based on any sound logistic or operational considerations. This last gained credence when Montgomery, given control of the First and Ninth Armies, the northern pincer, urged Eisenhower to let him retain control of them afterwards, and also after a notorious press interview when he tactlessly gave the impression that he had rescued the Americans from disaster. His mistake was to claim that he had been correct in trying to persuade Eisenhower to appoint a single commander for the front north of the Ardennes, and implying that Eisenhower's flaccid conduct of operations was the cause of the original débâcle. That was unacceptable to Americans who at that time were acutely sensitive to the political situation. Naturally, they blamed Montgomery when he obstinately persisted in placing military imperatives before political sensitivity. American politics and Montgomery's conduct between them made it impossible either to sack Lee, or to fasten responsibility for the mismanagement of operations after Normandy on Bradley or on Eisenhower's politically inspired conduct as SCAEF. Conflict between Montgomery and Eisenhower would continue until Eisenhower devised a *modus vivendi* between Bradley, Montgomery and himself in the New Year of 1945.

When Lutes wrapped up his mission at the end of December, it was the political situation back in Washington that pressed more heavily on Eisenhower than the troubles of ETOUSA and COMZ. Before he left, Lukes had admitted to Bradley that there had been mismanagement over ammunition production in the United States. Apparently, Congress had seized on reports of extravagant ammunition expenditure in North Africa in 1943 as grounds for their taking a hand and ordering production to be reduced. An ammunition shortage had beset General Sir Harold Alexander in April 1944 when planning operation DIADEM to liberate Rome and advance to the Gothic Line. His demands had been met, but he was warned that the supply of American ammunition was restricted because it was necessary to build up stocks for OVERLORD. According to Lutes, a letter from SHAEF in March had stated that the scales used in Italy would be applied in France although Alexander had declared them inadequate. Thus insufficient ammunition was sent to Europe and production in the United States had been cut below what had been planned. Lutes was angry that the Administration had not enforced the priority of ETO over the Pacific. Unexpectedly high consumption in the Pacific by the US Navy and Marine Corps upset plans as mortar bombs and 105 mm gun-howitzer rounds were in great demand in both theatres. Lutes saw no hope of improvement before the spring when new production would come on stream. In the meantime they would speed up the supply line between America and France, squeeze ammunition out of the ground force establishment and correct the mistakes being made in ETO.

12th Army Group and General Aurand argued, then and after the war when the method of supply in ETO was investigated, that Lee was acting as the agent of his master in Washington, General Somervell, who was exercising too much control from there. Army groups were denied control over the supply of their armies. Naturally, Lutes disagreed, for like Lee he was Somervell's representative. It appeared from the evidence of Brigadier-General Moses that in order to control common user items which included Sherman tank ammunition, Somervell had run down the BOLERO stocks in Britain and opened new American supply lines direct from New York to the French ports. POL stocks were fed from the United Kingdom straight into American-controlled stocks in France, the British being given credit for Lend-Lease stocks transferred. In Moses' opinion, once the western end of the American system was located in Washington with New York as the port of exit, it became too centralised to react to operations. The UK-based BOLERO supply system was well established and well provided with railways and roads and transport, all in good working order, but the French end was not. Shipping direct to France from the United States saved transport and handling in the United Kingdom, but the advantages were outweighed by the removal of the British echelon in the American chain of supply. (In 1918 the same issue arose but as the northern part of France was crammed with administrative units and the United Kingdom had not been an American base, the AEF COMZ ran from the Biscay ports which made direct supply from the US more sensible, although a high percentage of the material handled was of European origin.) The short sea-passage across the Channel could have been undertaken by a variety of smaller ships working flexibly into small harbours, but had that course been chosen Somervell would have lost a large measure of his control over Lee and ETO in general. As it was, large convoys of ships crossed the Atlantic at the convenience of the shipping authorities and the navies and swamped ports which were unable to handle heavy traffic. Time was wasted at both ends. Somervell's drive to centralise and control supply in Washington made a bad situation worse. It was he who was the real instigator of the policy that made Lee virtually independent of SHAEF and 12th Army Group.

On Somervell's behalf, it must be said that he could not control 'the market' – that is operations that were determined by the strategic decisions of President Roosevelt, Prime Minister Churchill and the CCS, who paid only lip-service to logistics. The root of Somervell's problem was that the competition between the Pacific and Europe was unregulated and naval logistics were quite outside his control. He did attempt to control army logistics in so far as he could prevent demand rising beyond supply by centralising control of the latter. Hence his tight control over ETO. Somervell represented the school of cost-effective management, soon to be in vogue under Robert McNamara in the Vietnam era. He would have liked strategy to be determined entirely by the material considerations which governed the timing and locating of campaigns and great battles. He was successful in drawing power away from the commanders in the field to the administrators in the rear, and he would have liked to have sidelined the politicians in the same way. The struggle between the managers of material, the politicians and the field commanders was to be repeated in Korea and Vietnam.

Manpower planning is an essential element of modern logistics. Another mistake that had been made in Washington was to misjudge the casualty rate. Bradley was dangerously short of infantry well before the Ardennes counter-offensive. Would US divisions have to fight 'decimated and in half-strength like German *Kampfgruppen*?' Major-General William Kean (Hodges' Chief of Staff) asked Bradley on 10 December. 'Yes, I am afraid that is so,' replied Bradley.[13] Bradley and Eisenhower were partly to blame for exhausting their reserves by attacking simultaneously with Third Army and First Army, with inadequate replacements as well as inadequate supplies. When Devers' 6th Army Group was engaged, he was allowed to behave like Patton, continuing to attack after being ordered to halt and act defensively. In the spring of 1944, War Secretary Stimson informed Marshall of his unease about the available strength of army reserve units and replacements. He feared that by the summer, the American divisions would be on a par with the Germans, and by November would lack the margin of superiority required to finish the war, which might be prolonged into 1945. His anxiety was well founded. In modern war, untrained and hastily equipped men are of little use. Good planning demands that well-trained units or units in process of being thoroughly trained should be in the pipe-line well in advance. Marshall's reaction was to press theatre commanders to improve their replacement systems by combing out the *bouches inutiles* and avoiding unnecessary waste of manpower. (For his part, Lee resisted or ignored any orders to reduce his empire.) Marshall refused to ask for a larger intake or a larger share of the replacements allotted to the Pacific, not wanting to stir up a competition for manpower with King. Marshall, in Stimson's opinion, put too much reliance on airpower as a substitute for manpower. Stimson proved right and Marshall wrong.[14]

The high commanders and staff of the US Army seem to have been curiously blind to the fact that 'generals make plans, but quartermasters make them possible'. Perhaps this was due to the deep-rooted belief common to generals of every nation that in the last analysis will-power decided the outcome of battles. Perhaps it was the result of the self-confidence and optimism, the belief that obstacles are made to be overcome that is so attractive a feature of the national character. Be that as it may, by failing to match their operations and goals with their logistical means, Eisenhower and Bradley virtually bankrupted the American army that had landed in Normandy before a second wave of divisions started to arrive for the spring offensive. Fortunately, the reinforcements to rebuild in the late winter were at hand. And American industry slipped into a higher gear so that even Lee's incompetence could not prevent its largesse reaching the hands of the soldiers in the spring of 1945.

CHAPTER 16

OPERATIONS, STRATEGY AND POLITICS

I had never before heard him speaking in a large meeting and found myself bewildered between the tone and the content of the speech. The tone was inspirational and vigorous: the content was the meagrest intellectual affair.

DEAN ACHESON ON EISENHOWER, ROME 1951

The allies had already lost the operational initiative when Marshall visited France in October 1944. They might still have regained it by striking for the Rhine between Cologne and Bonn after a pause of several weeks to regroup and accumulate supplies and replacements. As Montgomery had tried to explain to Eisenhower, in reaching the Rhine on the First Army front the Allies would have turned all the German positions west of the river. In the meanwhile the Canadian First Army would have been clearing the Scheldt. In February 1945, First Canadian Army's offensive between the Maas and the Rhine in conjunction with Ninth Army's delayed drive to the Rhine on its southern flank, Operations VERITABLE and GRENADE respectively, eventually achieved what might have been possible in October had Eisenhower then set his mind to it.

Such a deliberate plan was uncharacteristic of Eisenhower who, to that date, had not once taken an operational initiative. Eisenhower was perfectly aware that the CCS, inspired by its British members, had recommended that he concentrate his offensive on the First and Second Army fronts. He would have had to pause to regroup to that end. An even less attractive course was to stand fast and prepare for an early spring or late winter offensive. Not for the first time, Eisenhower turned away from such deliberate plans in favour of drift, allowing operations to take their own course. His own inclination, that also had political advantages. Marshall explained to him that as he could not expect American replacements or new divisions ahead of schedule, for the time being he would have to make do with what he had. The 1944 elections made it inadvisable to

277

defy Big Business and Labour by increasing the draft but even if new men had been called up, they would not have reached the front until the spring at the earliest. Squeezing the Pacific to provide extra divisions for the West sooner was not a political option in the middle of a political campaign either. These factors urged a protracted pause but Roosevelt did not want the public's belief that the war was virtually won to be disturbed by inaction on the Western Front in the autumn because it would make it obvious that the war would extend far into 1945 and raise fears that the Russians would gobble up most of Germany while the Allies were still west of the Rhine. Eisenhower rationalised the political situation. As time was going to be on the Germans' side, not his, in the autumn, and as they must not be allowed the opportunity to rebuild their reserves, he would continue to attack although his own armies were not going to be reinforced or properly supplied. With nothing to justify their confidence, Bradley and he convinced themselves that they could reach the Rhine in the near future, without pausing to concentrate their strength on the northern front.

This was the background to the logistics enquiry and to the bitter autumn campaign of Bradley's and Devers' divisions. The Canadians, too, suffered from politics. W L Mackenzie King's government in Ottawa continued to send only volunteers overseas causing the three Canadian divisions to fight in the miserable Scheldt short of men. The British scraped up another 100,000 men, allegedly from the bottom of the barrel and, like the Americans, transferred unwilling, and often unsuitable conscripts to the infantry from other services.

It may be asked whether the influence of politics on Eisenhower's strategy after Normandy lengthened the war? Obviously, we cannot assert that Collins' and Corletts' corps would have reached the Rhine, as their commanders asserted, had they been properly supplied, reinforced and handled by Bradley, but the latter's obstinate refusal to concentrate his resources ensured their failure. It is also certain that the logistical miscalculations in Washington and ETO COMZ incompetence had as much to do with it as Eisenhower's lack of grip on Bradley. The sad result was lost lives and lowered morale.

British confidence in Eisenhower and Bradley, already shaken by the events of the autumn, was irreparable after the Ardennes. The BCOS felt that operations had been consistently subordinated to American politics and press-led public opinion. It seemed to them that Montgomery's handling of the northern flank of the Ardennes penetration, the subsequent retention in 21st Army Group of Simpson's Ninth Army and the joint success of Operations VERITABLE and GRENADE had justified his operational views, if not his personal behaviour. The finger was rightly pointed at Bradley as the fly in the ointment. For a time, the transfer of Alexander from the Mediterranean to be Eisenhower's land forces commander was in the wind. Even Marshall became defensive about Eisenhower's capacity, but Brooke knew that Alexander would not grip the situation either. Moreover, the Ardennes had finally shaken Eisenhower's trust in Bradley and he listened more carefully to what Montgomery had to say. Marshall did not want the British to have their way over the strategic plan or the land-force commander but could not escape the fact that the decisive front was where Montgomery commanded. Furthermore, the protracted struggle of the American First and Third Armies to cut off the Germans in the Ardennes had exhausted them so that they were not ready to fight until March. In fact, those operations distracted them from taking the Roer dams so that the Germans were able to flood Ninth Army's GRENADE battlefield and delayed Simpson's part of Montgomery's offensive for two weeks. As the rest was ready in early February, a tacit political deal took place. Montgomery retained Simpson's army, grown to twelve divisions by February, as his right hook until the end of March. Satisfied with this *status quo*, he decided that he preferred Eisenhower to Alexander. That also suited Marshall and Eisenhower. Bradley, though, was shaken by his experience during the Ardennes. Eisenhower had suggested to him that he ought either to concentrate his attention on his left or agree to take over all the front south of the Ardennes and leave Montgomery to manage the rest. Bradley refused but the German break-through forced that course upon him. Incarcerated during the Germans' Ardennes offensive in his headquarters for fear of German assassination and kidnap squads in American uniforms reported to be roaming freely behind the front, his influence on the battle was negligible and he had little else to do but grumble about Eisenhower and Montgomery to Patton. (Even Eisenhower had allowed himself to be placed in protective custody.) This absurd situation left the field clear for Patton and Montgomery to 'save the day' but that the whole US Army had received a jolt to its esteem, disturbed Marshall.

Ever a politician, Eisenhower evened the score in the final weeks of the war. In March, the German armies were defeated west of the Rhine. In the last week of the month, First Army advanced out of its Remagen bridgehead, seized during its quite rapid advance to the Rhine earlier in the month. North of it, Ninth Army and the British Second Army crossed the Rhine using an airborne corps to seize a bridgehead. The two forces surrounded the Ruhr as had been intended in the Autumn. On their right, Patton advanced on Frankfurt and Kassel. By the end of the month all were poised to advance to the Elbe and to Berlin.

At that moment, on the 28th March, Eisenhower rejected the seizure of

Berlin and Prague on the grounds that they were political and not military objectives, and redirected his armies allegedly to destroy the German field armies instead. It appeared that he believed that the German armies were still dangerous and that what remained of them might not equally well be destroyed by an advance on the two capitals. The same day, he informed the Soviet High Command in Moscow of his intention to drive on Leipzig, not Berlin or Prague, with the purpose of meeting the Russians there and of cutting the German forces in two. He did not consult his superiors and side-stepped the immediate objections of Churchill in London and of Montgomery. The former objected to what was a sudden, unexplained change of plan and pointed out that as the German armies were disintegrating, he ought to occupy political high ground. The British were not contemplating conflict with the Soviets but, in Churchill's words, thought that it was 'highly important that we should shake hands with the Russians as far to the East as possible.[1] The boundaries of the occupation zones in Germany had been settled but it was not intended that each should be a separate kingdom. Germany was to be jointly governed with the Russians; the more cards you held when you sat down at the table with them the better.[2] Montgomery pointed out that the plan made no military sense either, for it halted Simpson's Ninth Army which was confident that it could advance rapidly on Berlin, was needlessly sensitive about Bradley's First Army flanks on its advance to Leipzig (which Simpson's new task was to protect), wasted time entering the Ruhr and pausing to regroup while Ninth Army was restored to Bradley's command, and was misguided about the significance of the German defence of their so-called 'Southern Redoubt', an allegedly final mountain position. This was the time for everyone to advance, caution thrown to the winds, although, as in the advance from Normandy the priority objectives were in the north, not the centre and south.

Thus Churchill and Montgomery summed up the political and military cases against Eisenhower's plan in April 1945. Of one thing we can be certain: the military factors on about 28 March, when Montgomery first learned of Eisenhower's intention to send Bradley on a concentrated advance to Leipzig, and stop Ninth Army going to Berlin, did not call for caution, or even concentration on a single front, but for speedy advances on every front. Of course, there would be fighting but none that was prolonged. Only 21st Army Group had important military and civil objectives, for Montgomery had to rescue the starving population of northern Holland and open the Dutch ports of Rotterdam and Amsterdam to feed them, dispose of the German troops there, capture the northern German ports of Emden, Bremen and Hamburg, each of which was defensible, and reach the Baltic at Kiel and beyond Lubeck to keep the Russians out of Denmark. All this while Simpson was on his way to Berlin. Eisenhower's plan exacerbated Montgomery's task. By halting Ninth Army and making it Bradley's 12th Army Group flank guard on the Elbe, Eisenhower left Montgomery with too much to do.[3]

In his *Crusade in Europe*, General Eisenhower did not explain his actions candidly or accurately. He departed from the truth in denying that he had changed his plan at the last minute from a thrust on Berlin to one on Leipzig. 'Frankly', he signalled Marshall on 30 March, when the British objections reached Washington, 'that I have changed plans has no possible basis in fact'.[4] In *Grand Strategy Vol. VI*, 134–7, John Ehrman commented on the case made by Eisenhower and Bradley for their plan.[5] 'This was a reasoned case. But, as on previous occasions, the Supreme Commander's first telegram unfortunately failed to cover all its aspects, and thus suggested that he had not, in fact, considered it as a whole.' Ehrman was suggesting, tactfully, that Eisenhower's directives were sometimes poorly argued, inconsistent and factually selective. Once more, Eisenhower offered dubious military explanations for his political actions. After the war, Eisenhower continued to assert that he had not changed his plan although SHAEF documents refuted his claim. '*Notes on Development of Operations North of the Ruhr*', dated as recently as 23 March, refers to 'objectives to anchor the advance towards Berlin'.[6] A paper of 24 September 1944, '*Advance into Germany after occupation of the Ruhr*', says 'the main object must be the early capture of Berlin, the most important objective in Germany', by the northern route from the Ruhr. Nevertheless, this paper went on to observe: 'If the Russians forestall us to Berlin', the advance in northern and central Germany should be limited to the major objectives of Hamburg, Hanover-Brunswick and Leipzig. It was this alternative that Eisenhower chose on 28 March although the odds on Ninth Army reaching Berlin had shortened since the 23rd and were infinitely more favourable than in September.

The new plan was a surprise to Montgomery who learned of it in Eisenhower's reply to a plan of his own that he submitted on the 27th. Eisenhower stated that his reasons for the change were military ones. The Russians were only about 40 miles from Berlin and, according to Bradley, it would cost his Army Group 100,000 casualties to snatch Berlin from them.[7] (It was a laughable figure unless Bradley intended to fight the Russians as well as the Germans. And the purpose was not to race the Russians so much as to put in an appearance in strength in the enemy's capital). Besides, Eisenhower observed, Berlin was 'only' a political objective and not worth any lives. And there was the Southern Redoubt to which, he was informed, die-hard SS troops were moving to resist until the last. A drive to Leipzig would cut the remaining German formations in half and intercept movement into the redoubt.[8]

Why did Eisenhower change his plan? Why did he deny changing it? And why did he offer false military reason for the change? The answers are political. In Washington, Roosevelt was dying and with Vice-President Truman unfamiliar with the way the war had been conducted, there was a hiatus in its direction during March and April 1945. Marshall, Eisenhower's mentor, was holding the fort in Washington. Politics had always coloured Eisenhower's actions as a commander and in the final months of the war he was more concerned with post-war problems, the disposal of Russian nationals, feeding refugees and the form of the occupation of Germany, than the final destruction of the German armed forces in his theatre. He felt strongly that the Anglo-American alliance and the SHAEF cooperative spirit had to be preserved after the war and amicable relations established with the Soviet Union as well. He was by no means soft towards the Soviets but his message to Stalin was, in part, intended to be a cooperative gesture as the armies met. A race for Berlin and Prague, particularly if it had led to a clash of arms, might have worsened relations.[9] David Eisenhower believes that his grandfather, perfectly aware that he would be called upon to play political roles after the war, was careful not to prejudice his relations with any of the leading figures in the wartime alliance, including the Russians. Dwight Eisenhower was a man of peace who saw trust and fair dealing as the hall-marks of his own style of management. Indeed, the personal friendship between Churchill and himself had been one of the anchors of the Alliance. Churchill, was a romantic who trusted his favourites, sometimes further than was wise. His belief in Eisenhower's goodwill mollified his frustration with his Washington superiors at various times, for instance over ANVIL. It might be asked, then, if Eisenhower did not defer to Churchill's wish for the armies to advance on Berlin, Prague and Vienna, objectives which, whether attainable or not, ought to have been attempted in Churchill's opinion, why he did not, at least confer with Churchill before announcing his plan and informing the Russians? Instead he had finessed the decision past the BCOS members of the CCS by informing the Russians, denying that he had changed his plan, and insisting that it was an operational, not a political, decision. He knew that if he presented it as one within his *military* sphere as SCAEF, Marshall would support his line. Furthermore, there was no one else in Washington to challenge it.

Eisenhower's quite natural contact with the Soviet armies made his decision irreversible. In effect he played the 'Stalin Card' as Marshall had got Roosevelt to play it over ANVIL. Eisenhower was entitled to liaise with the

Soviets over military matters. On this occasion he had approached Stalin, as Soviet Generalissimo, through John R Deane at the American Military Mission in Moscow on 28th March, the day he wrote his directive. He had not consulted Stalin but merely informed him of what he intended *post facto*, as any commander should when his armies approach those of his ally. The Cold War has influenced our interpretation of this gesture as though it was ill-advised because of subsequent events. Eisenhower and Marshall were later criticised for it. Indeed Marshall was a target of the McCarthy campaign during the Eisenhower presidency. 'Years later, Marshall would endorse Eisenhower's actions as understandable at the time, which implied regret,' wrote David Eisenhower.[10] Eisenhower remained sensitive to criticism on the subject. Later he informed Marshall that Zhukov had told him:

> He regretted that when he shifted the principal effort of his final drive from the Dresden direction to the area just south of Berlin, he failed to inform me instantly of his intentions. He explained in detail the military reasons for the last minute change but said that I had the right to charge him with lack of frankness and this he would not want me to believe.[11]

Zhukov seems to be saying that Eisenhower opened the door to him to drive to Berlin.

In Marshall's view, the Army's view, in effect, the new plan was politically sound. The armies of the two great powers which had won the war would meet in the middle of Germany to symbolise the new geopolitics. If the British complained they would be in a minority of one. It had been Marshall's consistent aim to have the United States armies under Bradley and Devers take the leading role in the European war and Eisenhower's plan served to restore the morale of 12th Army Group, and the morale of its commander, damaged in the winter battles. It did not please Ninth Army, of course, but had it rushed for Berlin under the command of Bernard Montgomery's 21st Army Group, as had been intended originally, it would have been another Montgomery 'triumph.' It would have been blatant to send Simpson there under Bradley's command, having just removed him from Montgomery. So no one went to Berlin. We should put Marshall's remark about his being loath to hazard American lives for 'purely political purposes', made concerning Prague, in this context.[12] To stir up trouble with the Russians, whose assistance the Americans might need against the Japanese, and to sacrifice further lives in a German war already won, was madness. The Americans needed all the full-strength divisions in service, perhaps more, for Japan. In short, Eisenhower and Marshall were in complete agreement in ignoring a possible post-war power struggle in Europe in favour of terminating the war in a fashion that made good publicity. Familiar film stills of that period show American, not British, soldiers embracing Russians somewhere on the Elbe. Eisenhower had a sure sense in these matters. Indeed, he had good historical and political sense. The two are closely related. Eisenhower's idea of a political Cannae was not the complete annihilation of his opponents but an all-embracing compromise which was unassailable from every direction.

According to David Eisenhower, the new plan was hatched out at Cannes, where Bradley and Eisenhower were both resting in the week after the 20th March. There Eisenhower mended his fences with Bradley. His role as political broker between his commanders had strained relations between the two men. Bradley was still sore that Eisenhower had accepted Montgomery's Rhineland plan and allowed Montgomery to retain Simpson's twelve divisions to attain it. Although, before D-day, it had been expected that Ninth Army would be assigned to 21st Army Group, Bradley took the view that the hateful Montgomery had won an undeserved victory with the American divisions. At Cannes, Eisenhower promised Bradley a good and easy finale to go with his promotion to four star general. Good relations with his fellow officers, the restoration of the collegial spirit, were important to him for his senior officers might carry a grudge against him as the 'best general the British had' to the grave. Eisenhower had already taken the wind out of Churchill's sails by gaining Montgomery's support for the command set-up. He knew that he would weather any storm over his deal with Bradley in the final weeks of the war, even if Montgomery should object to it.

The matter was closed characteristically and for the time being, by Churchill, ever susceptible to Eisenhower's reasonableness, with the Latin tag *Amantium irae amoris integratio est*.[13] Churchill does not seem to have considered Eisenhower's parochial motivations but to have been concerned with Britain's future relations with the Soviet Union and that Eisenhower's procedure marked another step in squeezing out British influence. However, the completion of his victorious campaign and the fact that Churchill judged Eisenhower as a soldier and not as a politician healed the wounds. Within the Army, Eisenhower had saved his reputation, an important consideration when the office of Army Chief of Staff fell vacant. Internationally he had gained a useful reputation as peacemaker. He would have to work with the Russians in the occupation of Germany and his action in the final weeks would make that no rougher than necessary.

Judged solely as a soldier, Eisenhower would eventually be found wanting by soldiers and historians, and by politicians, too, perhaps. It can be said in his defence that despite his infirmity of command in 1944 which, some said, was a cause of the Russians being so much nearer Berlin than the Allies when the March 28th directive was written, the agreed demarcation line with the Russians was reached without friction. For the public and junior ranks who were thankful that the war was over and hoped that Japan did not loom ahead for them, it seemed petty-minded, even pointless, to complain that the war might have ended sooner, been won with more éclat or to more advantage in the Cold War. Those points cannot be resolved in any case. What is certain is that although Eisenhower cannot be recorded as one of the Great Captains, he does provide an interesting study in the problems of supreme command in coalition war.

We have been offered two adverse views of his performance by Alan Brooke and Bernard Montgomery. Critical professionals, they depicted him as an unlettered commander, incapable of realising that he had to concentrate his military effort, create reserves and use them on a decisive front. The experience of the Western Front demonstrated the advantage the Germans held over the Allies in being able to concentrate their divisions. Indeed, it was envisaged in SHAEF plans before D-day that American armies would have to serve under British command because the geography of the front and the decisive thrust lines demanded it. Nigel Hamilton, Montgomery's biographer[14] goes so far as to say that Eisenhower's management style was to play off one subordinate against another and try to please everyone. He believed that Eisenhower could not lose if he kept the peace between them. In other words, operations were less important than politics. The Ardennes brought a moment of truth, perhaps, when it seemed that he was going to pay the price for this technique, but the moment passed. Hamilton points out the pettiness of his subordinates, Bradley in particular, and brings us to realise that Eisenhower had to acknowledge that they represented a sizeable electorate in the Army. He was, in any case, a clubbable man who enjoyed the company and regard of his fellows. Eisenhower's American biographer, Stephen Ambrose, in his *The Soldier and the Candidate*[15], has found it difficult to criticize his subject's operational decisions as may a military professional, or to differentiate between his political and military motives. By neglecting the former, he has been unable to judge military operations which can only be explained politically. David Eisenhower candidly recognises his grandfather's political motivation but is torn between excusing it and criticising it. Indeed he goes too far in suggesting that Eisenhower deliberately allowed Montgomery to undertake MARKET GARDEN with inadequate resources knowing that he must fail and be placed thereafter in a subordinate role. David Eisenhower's contribution is to make us regard Eisenhower as a political general and even to accept his role as necessary.

Although the American official histories of logistics gave them a lead, none of these writers has stitched logistics, operations and politics together in their story. Yet, the dispute between Montgomery and the American generals cannot be understood unless the main argument against Eisenhower's so-called broad front, that it was logistically unsound, is centrally placed. Nor have they made clear that Eisenhower had no strategy except that of non-intervention, which, as he had no positive plan backed by a strategic reserve, necessarily became his so-called 'broad front.' Whatever may be said about Montgomery's tactlessness, the dispute in which he was embroiled was between professional and military amateurs. Eisenhower, the man himself, was complex and can only be seen in the round if we look at him as a politician in a military environment. The essential Eisenhower was less calculating than he was prevaricating. He delayed decisions until he could maximise his profits. He was a trimmer, but not to the last inch. Perhaps 'moderation in all things – including moderation' might have been his motto. That he so often sought to deny it, even having Bedell Smith draw up a specious paper explaining the major decisions that he had taken, suggests that he was well aware of this character trait and of both the criticisms outlined above. One of his endearing traits was his naturalness and ability to live with himself. But he regarded trimming as a weakness because it was unmilitary; a political credit, perhaps, but a military debit. And he thought of himself as a soldier and not a politician. Yet his ability to arrive at compromises, his political commonsense, was a trait that the job of Supreme Commander reinforced and was expected of him.

The successful commander of troops is a simplifier. Simplification is a technique that helps him make decisions. Conservative and sceptical, realistic may be a preferred adjective, he does not expect the best of all worlds but takes the worst case and prepares for it. He has to decide, often quickly, to reject one course and single-mindedly pursue another. His aim must be single or he will be defeated in detail. The politician, on the other hand, does not decide an issue until he is forced to do so. To delay is usually the wiser course. He presents his decisions as combining the best of both worlds but they are usually compromises. An optimist, apparently, he embarks on contradictory courses, advances on all fronts, is all things to all men. Avoiding head-on conflict, he prefers the tactic of B H Liddell Hart's indirect approach and 'expanding torrent'. Certainly, he is in the habit of ignoring dreary logisticians when they tell him that he cannot have his cake and eat it. In all these matters Eisenhower behaved like a politician rather than a soldier. He made a virtue out of allowing his armies to attack all along the front, convincing himself that he was pursuing a military strategy. It strengthened this conceit that American Army generals, whatever their text books might advise, indulged in the Western Front practice of attacking on as wide a front as possible, for as long as possible, in search of tactical rewards, even when no strategic ones were attainable. They fought tenaciously for resources to maintain their offensives, and indulged in deception to prevent their removal to other fronts. Eisenhower treated them indulgently because they behaved as *macho* soldiers ought. His own habit of having his cake and eating it, aided and abetted his subordinates' inclination to do the same. Not having commanded in a battle, he never learned that his means would always be limited, and insufficient if he did not restrict his aims. He always hoped something would turn up. Whether we are talking of means as human, material or temporal, concentration and economy are always *de rigueur*. But Eisenhower never formed a reserve and never made a plan that required him to do so, let alone carried one out. That would have required him to shut down the operations of one of his subordinates, an unpopular step.

All of this points to Eisenhower's principal dilemma. His position was political but in conducting the campaign in a political fashion he mismanaged its military operations and encouraged his subordinates, as well, to behave like politicians instead of soldiers or players, in the current analogy.* They had to be players not politicians if they were to command properly. However, Bradley, Patton and Devers appeared to believe that if they behaved as players, like Simpson and Hodges, perhaps, they would be run over by other politician soldiers who were prepared to act without scruple when the cards were down and they could get away with it. Clark under Alexander, Bradley, Patton and Montgomery under Eisenhower were not gentlemen. Can a supreme commander in a coalition *command* while eschewing politics? The answer is a resounding 'No'. He needs a land forces commander as a player to manage the battle without fear or favour. And it was a land force commander that Eisenhower was denied because of politics. Ironically, that was the idea he brought back from the Mediterranean in January 1944 and hoped to apply as SCAEF. None of his biographers and none of the campaign historians has pointed out that he never intended to follow Marshall's intention in 1943 to direct operations himself.

Coalitions set the Supreme Commander a further problem in that his superiors expect him to serve his nation's interests as well as those of the

* In first-class cricket the categories were once 'gentlemen' and 'players', meaning amateurs and professionals.

military alliance. Marshall expected Eisenhower to serve the interests of the US Army in dealing with Montgomery, Bradley and Patton, even when they referred to Montgomery as a second-rater, a sentiment which Eisenhower, himself, disputed. Under the circumstances, that Eisenhower retained his reputation as a manager of men whom everyone liked, if not as an operational commander, was a remarkable achievement. It is true that after the war had been won, the details of battles were of less interest to the general public than the personality of the leader who had won not only victory, but also the hearts of Londoners and New Yorkers. Judgment between the ability of one commander and another usually becomes a personality contest. In that contest Eisenhower will continue to be a winner, as he must have known. It is when he is judged as a field commander by professional standards that he will be found wanting. He would not have satisfied a previous age and the players of today will continue to disapprove of him. As a model for the future he may be found equally wanting. Yet he served the special circumstances for which he was appointed in 1944.

CONCLUSIONS

POLITICIANS AND MANAGERS

In the Introduction we observed that both World Wars were *Materialschlachten* in which the combatants acquired and expended huge quantities of war material. In considering the logistical control of the material destined for Western Europe in both wars, we concluded that strategy in the coalitions was decided by the *force majeur* of logistics, in the wide sense of the production, control and distribution of men, money and material, rather than by reasoned argument in committees and at conferences. On the battlefield, logistical superiority determined results, sooner or later, and within the coalition, which operational plan was adopted.

This was the conclusion of American soldiers after the First World War, when their allies had the advantage; after the Second, in which the Americans settled most issues to their own satisfaction as soon as they, in their turn, held the logistical cudgel, it was the unavoidable conclusion of the British. In both wars, in its simplest form, the coalition partner with most field divisions in a theatre of war controlled alliance strategy in it; the French on the Western Front, the British in the Mediterranean in 1942–44, and the Americans in North-West Europe in 1944–45 and the Pacific from 1942–45. Of all materials, it was shipping, particularly the production and control of assault shipping in the Second World War, that weighed most in making strategy, for all the allied armies were transported to their various theatres by sea and supplied and reinforced by sea. Most campaigns included at least one assault landing from the sea. Once battle was joined, logistics in the field were normally apolitical. They were an applied science, part of the anatomy of each Allied army which had its own system for the delivery of weapons, equipment, supplies of food, fuel, clothing and so on, and of reinforcements. It was when the quality of its logistics adversely affected an army's ability to perform its operational task in the coalition that, perforce, logistics took on a political hue. We have described how the failure of ETO USA logistics poisoned the complex relationships between the Allies in the field in North-West Europe. There, logistics did not become an overt cause of dissension because the Americans kept secret the investigations into ETO logistics by Generals Aurand and Lutes. As their findings were unknown (at least officially) to their ally, they never became *historically* a relevant factor in operations. The single thrust versus broad front became an unresolvable, academic argument turning upon personalities because the operational argument had been denied its logistical core.

In attempting to untie this historical knot we found the traditional role of logistics as a mere handmaiden to operations to be an impediment. Typically, commanders treated logisticians as if they should be seen and not heard. They were given tasks and not expected to answer back. Commanders were reluctant to acknowledge the help they received from efficient logistics, and never admitted that they won because they had the most shells and guns and more men with better weapons than their enemy. However, they were usually quick to excuse themselves when the boot was on the other foot. Few logisticians gain a place in the pages of history unless things go as wrong as in Lee's COMZ in North-West Europe. Add to this that the public is repulsed by the idea that material wins battles and we find that logistics and operations are seldom, if ever, integrated in historical accounts or related causally to the outcome of battles, as are the training and armament of troops on no more secure a foundation. In both cases, though, the evidence is mainly circumstantial and depends on expert witnesses rather than on the smoking gun.

Our evidence that logistics was a prime cause of the failure of the 12th Army Group to penetrate the German front between September and November 1944 comes from those expert witnesses, the commanders at the front. No less than the stalwart corps commanders, Generals Collins and Corlett, blamed ETO logistics for their failure to reach Cologne. Their opinion was supported in 1945 by '*The Report of the General Board, U.S. Forces European Theater: Organization of the European Theater of Operations, Study 2.*' Bradley, their Army Group commander, responsible for committing their VII and XIX Corps to battle inadequately armed and reinforced, blamed logistics too, but he did so *post facto,* not during the battle, as did Collins and Corlett. It is true that his shortages gave Bradley an alibi for his own failure.

In giving logistics a central place we have attempted to correct the tendency of historians to deal with it either as an *hors d'oeuvre* to the operational *entrée,* or to present it as a separate meal. An example of the former is Churchill's 'Battle of the Atlantic' – his name for the drama of U-boat sinkings and convoy battles which have been divided into phases and campaigns like land battles. The positive treatment of the convoy war has satisfied dyed-in-the-wool Mahanists who spurn the *guerre de course*, and entertained most readers who like battles but are bored by uneventfulness. The truth is that 'Safe Arrival', without U-boat engagements, was the aim of Royal Naval and Royal Canadian Naval convoys. The Americans had a more offensive outlook, since they were not concerned with provisioning the United Kingdom. Sinking U-boats only became the prime aim of the battle when the victory over the U-boats had been won in late 1943. No contact, no sinkings, no battle was a logistical victory for the convoy. Such victories enabled the battles of 1943–45 to be fought and won on land and in the air in Europe. In that sense the 'Battle of the Atlantic' has not become an integral part of a coalition history in which shipping and the demands of strategy would be the theme.

The story of logistics in North-West Europe in 1944 deserves attention not only because it is the dimension that is missing from accounts of the dispute over the single thrust and broad front but also because it shows that some of the weaknesses in the American command and staff system in 1917–18 had not been corrected. Although Eisenhower was primarily a staff officer by experience and training, and was served by an excellent chief of staff, Walter Bedell Smith, he was unable to sort out his own command and staff problems and unwilling to make the effort to master detail or place it in its correct context when other more attractive duties beckoned. Rather than talk an administrative problem through with his staff and give them a clear directive he preferred to place it, unsorted, in the hands of some trusted individual as a 'command assignment', and then expunge it from his mind. According to General LeRoy Lutes, Eisenhower's reaction to administrative tasks was typical of American commanders. Pershing reacted to his logistical problems in a similar manner, although he was not as lazy as Eisenhower and had the urge to command, which Eisenhower lacked. Pershing believed that the commander should both propose and dispose; the staff whether in Washington or in the field was to serve him. Had Eisenhower understood the 1918 problem, the events in Chapter 15 might conceivably have taken a different course, but we doubt it. It is impossible to imagine a repetition of the 1918 clash between Washington and Pershing in 1944. The issue would have hinged, not on the supply of a single theatre, the Western Front, but on a global logistical short-fall caused by the competition between Europe and the Pacific and the miscalculation of the size of the task in the former. It was an explosive and intractable problem in which Eisenhower had no intention of meddling. He was well chosen, not only in his familiar role as the peace-keeper between American and British commanders, but as Marshall's defensive flank in his most difficult task of all, balancing the demands of the Pacific and Europe against finite American resources. (see Chapter 10). That the American resources were finite, that miscalculations over the number of trained divisions required to defeat the Germans in the Autumn of 1944 had been made, was not revealed in the CCS. Marshall could not have had a better obfuscator of these logistical facts in France than Eisenhower.

In neither war was logistical capability used by the politicians and managers in London, Paris and Washington to argue convincingly for or against a strategic course, except in the most obvious cases. Rather, in making policy, resources for it were released as from a bank when their owner had the deal he wanted. Shipping was used in this manner in both wars. Shipping, arms and ammunition production, and manpower danced to a tune already being played on the Western Front and the Mediterranean battlefields in the First World War, although it may be said that the users of the material that was so successfully produced ended by dancing to the devil's pipes in succumbing to the idea of the *Materialschlacht*. In the Second, Montgomery's complaint that the commander's plan for OVERLORD had to conform to a predetermined shipping allotment was justified. ETO was a victim of American logistical over-extension, itself the result of continual offensives in Europe and the Pacific undertaken on an assumption that resource abundance could support them.

Somervell reacted to the way commanders treated logistics as the unconsidered servant of operations. He was an early advocate of the cost-effective strategy forced on top administrators in the limited wars in Korea and Vietnam by several related factors. The first was the incredible economic extravagance of modern war which had taken an exponential leap forward between 1914 and 1918 and in 1939 to 1945 had become ruinous. There had to be 'budgetary' constraints on operations. The second was that the 'limited' wars since 1945 have been highly political and have demanded that logistical support be apportioned between fighting fronts and the peacetime economy. The third has been that military achievements, rightly or wrongly, have not been seen as stages on the high road to political achievement, as in the earlier part of the century. An attempt was made to get both political and military value for money, as was the custom in peacetime.

The aims of war are political and the destruction of the enemy's economy, his social fabric and his governmental structure, may be within the capacity of a state to achieve, but it is not to its advantage, particularly if it also leads to its own bankruptcy. Since 1945, there has been a change in the function of armed force and in the aims of war: there has been a reversion to a more conservative view held before the age of total war when political aims were dominant. The change has been accelerated by a number of factors. First, the twentieth century's wars broke Britain's economic back, removed world leadership from Europe and saddled parts of the world with Soviet-style Marxism. When the betterment of standards of living became a priority, a repetition of the material profligacy in the world wars seemed prohibitive and immoral. Second, the conflicts since 1945 have been ideological and, since Korea, have been concerned with wars within societies rather than between them. They require a carefully graduated response rather than the use of unrestrained force as employed in the two World Wars. An unexpected new factor was nuclear weapons which rendered huge concentrations of material vulnerable to total destruction. Finally, the enormously high cost of electronically sophisticated weapon systems returns us to the position in the Napoleonic wars in which the cost of large armies, long intense wars and high casualties to equipment and men was prohibitive.

All this was beginning to be clear in the inter-war years, prompting Germany to build an army capable of very short wars against their neighbours accompanied by intense political action to reap some benefit from military success. Armed action or the threat of it and political action worked together. This required the close political control of the armed forces including their operations. The conception that once war started, operations and even strategy were the responsibility of the military, was no longer acceptable. In this sense the First World War had been a watershed and, as we pointed out, in the Second the politicians and the managers controlled the commander and not the reverse, as in the First War. There were to be no more Joseph Joffres and Douglas Haigs. Instead, we had Eisenhower who was a new phenomenon, midway between the commanders and the managers.

The new breed of politicians and managers had experienced the First World War and the stormy and motley state, neither war nor peace, of the interlude before the Second War began. We have seen how the British committee system developed out of the experience. To ensure military strategy and operations served policy, machinery and communications had to be created to serve wilful and knowledgeable politicians and managers who kept their political aims always in mind. For the British, an aim was to retain their independence in the face of French land-power in 1914–18 and American power in 1943–5. They sought as equal a say in strategy as possible in both wars, and initially, in 1942–3, with a preponderance of the forces available and superior planning machinery, that was not difficult. The post-war settlement in Europe and the Empire was always in their mind when strategy was discussed. Necessarily, they had to be more political in their dealings over policy as the balance of logistical power passed to the Americans who were inclined to divorce the battlefield from the council chamber.

Some interesting parallels may be drawn between Haig's view of strategy in 1917 and Marshall's in 1944 and 1945. Haig was determined that the more capable British should take over Allied leadership from the ailing French and his ambition was that the British Army should prove itself as a professional force. It had, too long, suffered from the patronising attitude of the French. He perceived that the belligerent with the strongest army with unshaken morale would be able to dominate the peace negotiations. It was Haig who pressed for an armistice when the German armies collapsed, because to continue the offensive would have weakened the British Army and caused chaos in a Germany threatened by a Bolshevik takeover. Marshall, too, was ambitious that the American Army should decide the war in Europe and be the one that met the Russians and decide the shape of the peace. He did not want to be involved in European politics at the behest of Britain and so the less opportunity the British had to appear as a principal contributor to the final victory in Europe the better. Furthermore, to preserve the US Army for use against Japan he had to avoid an altercation with the Russian Army.

Most of Eisenhower's sins of commission and omission as a commander, appear in a different light if we think of him as Marshall's agent guarding the interest of the United States rather than a supreme commander with a will of his own. Nevertheless, he had his own political agenda which happened to mesh with Marshall's. Except briefly during the Ardennes, he never thought that he could lose his war militarily. If he supported his own military colleagues he would be able to live with them after the war. His relations with Montgomery did not matter so much once victory in Europe was certain. So the mask was off in the final two months of the war when he changed his plan for the drive across Germany and showed where the power really lay. A generation earlier, Haig had had his moment of doubt during Passchendaele, the only time that he took the initiative and responsibility for a major offensive, and he nearly paid for that campaign when the Germans attacked him in March and April 1918, as they later attacked Eisenhower in the Ardennes after his autumn offensive in 1944. Otherwise, Haig managed to hide behind French commanders, as Eisenhower contrived to avoid any operational initiative until 1945.

Haig is open to serious criticism as a director of operations, but though Third Ypres weakened the BEF almost to the point of defeat, he has been given credit for the tenacity which led to the final, victorious offensives of 1918. He was also a sound military administrator; he had built the Army's staff system and was highly respected, indeed feared in the Army. Eisenhower was admired and liked; he was not an initiator of policy and in no sense a leader. There was little intellectual substance behind his actions or statements. However, he fitted admirably the system that evolved for running the war, and was instrumental in preventing cracks widening in the relations between its politicians, managers and soldiers. Haig has been harshly judged in matters in which Eisenhower is awarded most points. But that is unfair. No such machinery existed behind Haig as the JCS and COS committees, let alone a CCS. He was, in fact, an advocate of a COS committee. His base in London could only be secured by friends in political places, not a happy situation. In France, his relations with the other commanders (Joffre being also a manager) were not unfriendly, and perhaps that, above all others, was the negative factor that impeded the construction of some kind of forerunner of the CCS in 1916 or 1917.

There was another negative factor that prevented a mature command system being created. France was a continental power fighting mainly a continental battle for continental aims. She regarded Britain and then America as her subordinate aids in reaching her goals. Neither Britain nor America shared her ambitions and so the political underpinnings of military strategy were likely to be, and were, divisive when discussed. More important, France was not a maritime power and was not as dependent on imports and trade as Britain. The central place that shipping, trade and credits held in British strategy from 1914, when she started off to encourage the Russians to fight her battles with British credits, was of much less interest to France* Indeed, the dimension of the wars that we have subsumed under the term logistics, an essential feature of the Second Coalition, was not of great moment in Paris in the First, although it was central for the British and Americans.

---

* But see C B A Behrens' classical study, *Merchant Shipping and the Demands of War.*

CHAPTER NOTES

The following abbreviations of source titles have been used in these Notes:

AWC	Army War College
BCOS	British Chiefs of Staff
COSW	Chiefs of Staff, Washington
DDE	The Papers of David Dwight Eisenhower
fn	Footnote
MHI	Military History Institute, Carlisle Barracks, Pennsylvania
OCMH	Office of the Chief of Military History, Washington
OH	Official History (British)
SAC	Supreme Allied Commander
WO	War Office, London

Chapters 1–3 The Military Mind, The Operational Art, The Long Thin Battlefield

There is a vast literature available for an author attempting the three introductory essays, each of which could well be expanded into a book.

Those of special relevance are:

For Chapter 1: Goerlitz, W *The German General Staff: Its History and Structure*, (Hollis and Carter, London 1953). Demeter, K *The German Officer Corps in Society and State 1650–1945*, (Weidenfeld & Nicolson, London 1953). Ritter, G *The Sword and the Sceptre: The Problem of German Militarism*, Vol 1, *The Prussian Tradition 1740–1890*, Vol 11, *The European Powers and the Wilhelmine Empire 1890–1914*, (The university of Miami 1969). On German tradition and military outlook Gooch, G P *Frederick the Great, the Ruler, the Writer, the Man*, (Longmans, Green, London 1947). Guderian's references to the General Staff in his *Panzer Leader*, (Michael Joseph, London 1970) and Seaton, A *The German Army 1933–1945*, (Weidenfeld & Nicolson, London 1982) are essential. Studies of the British Army staff in which the new was grafted on to the old are scarce and, it has to be said, lacking in understanding of the nature of staff work. Fortunately the student of the British way

296

in warfare can rely on Professor Brian Bond's admirable *The Victorian Army and Staff College 1854–1914*, (Eyre Methuen, London 1972). Both authors of this book attended the British Army Staff College and one served a tour as an instructor, so we have an insight into its ethos and system of self-instruction and evaluation. On the evolution of the United States Army Staff, Ball, Harry P *Of Responsible Command: A History of the US Army War College*, (The Alumni Association, Carlisle Barracks, Pennsylvania 1983) and Hews, James E *From Root to Macnamara Army Organisation and Administration*, (Centre of Military History, US Army Washington D.C., 1975). *The French Army*, Gorce, Paul-Marie de la, subtitled *A Military Political History*, (Wiedenfeld and Nicolson, London 1953).

Any writer attempting the subject of Chapter 2 has to begin, even if only as a mark of respect, with the fragmentary *On War* by Clausewitz (we used the version edited by M Howard and P Paret (Princeton University Press, New Jersey, 1976). M Howard's *Clausewitz*, (Oxford University Press, 1983) is more compact and to the point. We relied on Foch's *Des Principes des Guerres* English translation by Hilaire Belloc, (Chapman & Hall, London 1918), and Frederick Maurice, *British Strategy: A Study of the Application of the Principles of War*, (Constable, London 1929) for 'principles', but of course the operational doctrine of all the armies engaged was determined implicitly if not explicitly by the same maxims or guide-lines. General JFC Fuller, the most radical and challenging mind to appear in the inter-war era was, after all, the codifier of the 'Principles of War' embodied in the British Field Service Regulations. For Fuller, see Brian Holden Reid's excellent *JFC Fuller: Military Thinker*, (Macmillan, London, 1987).

It is when he turns to the field of technological innovation that the student of modern warfare finds a shortage of texts. The cause is that few if any academic historians (using the term in a literal and non-pejorative sense) have any understanding of science or technology, or the practical determinants of the operational art. Neither of the authors of this work had the benefit of higher education in science, but as former regular officers in the artillery arm we had a good grounding in its technology, and belonged to a combat arm whose feet were firmly on the scientific basis of its art while their eyes were on the tactical battle. It is easy enough to compile a list of gadgets and inventions. What we hope the reader will find in our third chapter is how a blind reliance on the technological innovations of the nineteenth century led to the deadlock of 1917, and rational analysis of applied science in the first two decades of the twentieth pointed to the way out of it.

The reader will notice one major omission: any reference to chemical warfare. That is deliberate. Chemical agents, subject as they were to adverse weather conditions, failed as a break-through weapon, and rapidly generated effective counter-measures. 'Persistent' agents, like mustard gas, tended to stagnate rather than accelerate operations. Only non-toxic smoke served a useful tactical purpose, and was disliked by tanks and artillery if used on a large scale. (Nerve gases and biological weapons of mass destruction, invented later, were mercifully never used in the Second World War, both sides shrinking from mutual genocide.) References are few, apart from the technical manuals. The only account of the mysteries of artillery intelligence is the 43 page pamphlet *Artillery Survey in the First World War*, with contributions by Sir Lawrence Bragg, Major-General AH Dowson and Lieut-Colonel HH Hemming, (privately published by the Field Survey Association, London, 1917). In 1968 Colonel R Macleod read a paper on artillery employment in the 3rd Battle of Ypres, published in the *Proceedings of the Royal Artillery Historical Association*, 1969. J Marshall Cornwall's *Haig as a Military Commander*, (Batsford, London, 1973) provided facts and figures in his concise account of the opening moves in France in 1914. For Helmuth von Moltke the Younger we relied on Correlli Barnett's *Swordbearers,* (Eyre and Spottiswoode, 1963). To these can be added S Bidwell's Gunners at War: *A Tactical Study of the Royal Artillery in the 20th Century*, (Arms and Armour Press, London 1970),and S Bidwell and D Graham's *Fire-Power: British Army Weapons and Theories of War 1904–1945*, (George Allen & Unwin, London 1982).

Chapter 4 A Coalition Bedevilled

1. These conclusions emerge from recent studies. In particular David French, *British Strategy and War Aims, 1914–16*, and Keith Neilson, *Strategy and Supply: the Anglo-Russian Alliance, 1914–17*, (London, 1986 and 1984, respectively): 'The Mobilization of Anglo-American Finance during World War I', by Kathleen Burk in *Mobilization for Total War*, NF Dreisziger, ed.: *War Aims and Strategic Policy in the Great War*, Barry Hunt and Adrian Preston, eds., (London, 1977): Michael Howard, *The Continental Commitment*, (London, 1972): Norman Gibbs, 'British Strategic Doctrine, 1918–39' in Michael Howard, ed., *The Theory and Practice of War*, (London, 1965). We are indebted to Keith Neilson for his comments on drafts of this chapter in 1987.

2. *History of the Great War: Military Operations, France and Belgium, 1914:* compiled by Brigadier-General Sir James E Edmonds, London, 1937. Appendix 8, p. 499, 'Instructions to Sir John French from Lord Kitchener, August 1914.

3. From France Sir William Robertson, General French's Chief of Staff, described the uncoordinated activities of the members of Asquith's cabinet in a few 'brutal and laconic sentences.' Robert Rhodes James, *Gallipoli*, (London, 1965), on Dardanelles planning, pp. 14–38.

    > The Secretary of State for War was aiming at decisive results on the Western Front; the First Lord of the Admiralty was advocating a military expedition to the Dardanelles; the Secretary of State for India was devoting his attention to a campaign in Mesopotamia; the Secretary of State for the Colonies was occupying himself with several small wars in Africa; and the Chancellor of the Exchequer was attempting to secure the removal of a large part of the British Army from France to some Eastern Mediterranean theatre.

4. Roy A Prete, 'Joffre and the Concept of Allied Command, 1914–16', originally a paper presented at the 16th Annual Meeting of the Society for French History, 1988. We owe a debt to Roy Prete for his comments on drafts of this chapter in 1987 and showing us his work subsequently published.

5. The events at the Calais Conference in February 1917, when Lloyd George attempted to subordinate Haig to Nivelle, which conflicted with his instructions from Kitchener in December 1915, similar to those given to Sir John French in August 1914, are mentioned in Chapter 5. In the opinion of John Terraine in his documentary history of this period of the war, *The Road to Passchendaele*, (London 1977), pp. 42–3, Lloyd George would have reduced Haig to a 'glorified Adjutant-General.'

Chapter 5 Lloyd George: Man in a Frock Coat

1. HH Asquith, became 1st Earl of Oxford and Asquith (1852–1928). Academically brilliant, QC and Liberal MP. Became great reforming premier in 1908, but in 1914 proved too wedded to peace-time routine, indolent and pleasure-loving as the leader of the country at war. Superseded by Lloyd George in 1916.

2. D Lloyd George, became 1st Earl (1863–1945). Solicitor, Welsh patriot, pacificist and radical reformer, he was Chancellor of the Exchequer under Asquith in 1908, then after the outbreak of war Minister of Munitions, Secretary of State for War and premier in

1916. Fell from power in 1922. Wrote his war memoirs in 1933–1936.

3. A Milner, 1st Viscount (1854–1925). Distinguished colonial civil servant and administrator, first in Egypt and then in South Africa, where he was High Commissioner in 1897–1905. War Cabinet 1916, Secretary of State for War 1918.

4. GN Curzon, Marquis of Kidleston (1859–1925). Aristocrat, traveller and expert on Asian affairs, Conservative MP, Viceroy of India 1898–1905. Re-entered politics as Lord Privy Seal when coalition was formed, War Cabinet 1916.

5. A Henderson (1863–1935). Labour MP and politician who played an important role in building up the Labour Party as a political force to be reckoned with. Coalition War Cabinet 1915–1917.

6. JC Smuts (1870–1950). General in South African ('Boer') Army, Field Marshal in British Army. Successfully commanded British operations in East Africa against Germans, invited to join War Cabinet in 1916, Premier of Union of S. Africa 1919.

7. MPA Hankey (1877–1963). Commissioned Royal Marines 1895, staff officer Naval Intelligence Dept. 1902, retd. as Colonel 1929. Secretary War Cabinets 1916–1918. Thereafter distinguished career as a public servant. Author *inter alia* of *Supreme Command 1914–1918* (1963).

8. JR Jellicoe, 1st Earl (1859–1935). Royal Navy, had a distinguished career on sea and on land, leading a military expedition to rescue international legations in Peking in 1900. He was as Third Sea Lord and Controller of Navy fully involved in the modernisation of the RN and appointed C-in-C of the Grand Fleet in 1914 and First Sea Lord in 1916, dismissed in 1917. His career aroused intense controversy, many feeling that he was unfairly blamed for the escape of the German Fleet from Jutland, and unfairly dismissed by Lloyd George.

9. Stephen Roskill. 'The U-Boat campaign of 1917 and Third Ypres', *RUSI Journal*, November 1959, 441–2, offers the naval alternatives.

10. Sir Edward Henry Carson represented Dublin University as a Conservative from 1892–1918 and then the Duncairn division of Belfast until 1921. He was Solicitor-General 1900–1906, led the campaign against the Parliament Act and Home Rule. He joined the Coalition in June 1915 as attorney general but resigned in October. He became First Lord of the Admiralty under Lloyd George but quit at the end of 1917 although he remained in the WPC.

11. AJP Taylor, *English History, 1914–45*, Oxford, 1965, 84–7.

12. The military disadvantages of the Flanders operation had been argued by General Maurice in 1915. Maurice was now Director of Military Operations at the War Office so that his views on the subject were easily available.

13. Stephen Roskill, *Hankey: Man of Secrets, Vol. 1*, (London, 1970), p. 379.

14. AJP Taylor, *op. cit.* p. 87.

15. W Robertson, baronet (1860–1933). QMG and Chief of Staff to Sir John French in BEF and CIGS 1915–18. Sacked by Lloyd George in January 1918 and succeeded by General Sir Henry Wilson.

16. A Bonar Law (1858–1923). Of Canadian origin, industrialist and Unionist MP, Colonial Secretary 1915–16, War Cabinet and leader of the House of Commons 1916–18.

17. For the campaign within the Admiralty to cleanse it Barry D Hunt's chapter 'Crisis at Sea: the Young Turks Revolt (1916–17)' in his *Sailor-Scholar: Admiral Sir Herbert Richmond 1871–1946*, (Waterloo, 1982). For Lloyd George's motives, Taylor, *op.cit.* p. 86.

18. The original source for what has been considered an intrigue by Haig is Lord Beaverbrook, *Men and Power*,(London 1956) in the chapter entitled 'The Ulster Pirate'. Arthur Marder in *Dreadnought to Scapa Flow*, p. 199, and Hunt, *op.cit.* follow his line. However, Haig was interested, as a staff officer, in inter-service staffs and, as always, was probably pursuing two goals at once – his campaign and Admiralty efficiency.

Chapter 6 Haig: Man on a White Horse: Passchendaele I

1. Wynne was a German linguist and student of the German Army and its tactics. His book *If Germany Attacks: the Battle in Depth in the West* (Faber, 1940) and several articles in *The Army Quarterly* between the wars analysed German tactics competently. He spent most of the war in a German prison camp which seems to have made him hypercritical of the higher commanders. Edmonds derided armchair critics who had not, at first hand, experienced or observed the strain of high command. By 1945, he was eccentric and impatient. The official correspondence concerning *Military Operations France and Belgium 1917, Volume II, 7th June-10th November, Messines (Passchendaele)* is mainly in PRO, Cabinet 45/140, 103/112 and 113. We have also used the Wynne papers and the Edmonds and Liddell Hart papers at the Liddell Hart Centre for Military Archives, King's College, London for conversations and correspondence between Basil Liddell Hart and Edmonds.

2. *France and Flanders, 1917*, Vol 2, (OHMS, 1948).

3. The most recent account of the writing of the official history is in THE Travers' *The Killing Ground*, (Allen & Unwin, 1987). In 1978 we reviewed the documents he used and referred to them in our *Fire-Power* in 1982. Good as is Travers' account, he has not compared the earlier plans of Rawlinson and Plumer for Ypres with Gough's, and GHQ's reactions to them. Had he done so, he would have discovered that Plumer disagreed with Haig over the same points as arose between Gough and Haig. Their differences were never reconciled. He would also have found that Haig placed his subordinates in much the same awkward position on the Somme and at Ypres. The differences point to the answer to Travers' own question (*op.cit.* 205) 'First, did Haig and his GHQ staff tell Gough, GOC Fifth Army, clearly what kind of offensive it was going to be – a step-by-step advance or a break-through?' with 'Yes' not the 'No' which Travers offers. GHQ had wanted a one-step break-through and Plumer and Rawlinson a phased operation. In his chronology of the review and acceptance of Gough's outline and final plan, Travers has mistaken the purpose of the meetings on the 14th and 28th June – to examine Gough's outline plan and to receive his final plan respectively. It was on the 28th that Gough tried to explain his problems, which were not subsequently resolved by Haig. Travers has not explained that the terrain made the GHQ plan, in which Plumer played a spectator's part, unworkable and caused Gough to quarrel with Plumer. Travers has neglected Haig's main motivation for fighting the battle – his ambition for the BEF in which he had a proprietor's pride. The disparity between Davidson's ideas, Haig's, and Haig's explanation to the War Cabinet/War Policy Committee in the week preceding the 28th June receives no attention. In truth, Travers set himself an impossible task. In a short chapter he attempted to sort out an official account without replacing it by a correct one, and to place it in the wider context of an informative series of essays on Haig's command methods on the Western Front.

4. On 30 and 31 March 1916, after he had been appointed to command Fourth Army in

the coming battle of the Somme, Rawlinson spoke to Kitchener about his plan. Kitchener told him that he preferred that the Somme should be a series of small offensives with the sole aim of inflicting casualties. An offensive *au fond* should be avoided. But Douglas Haig had set his heart on a large offensive, apparently, as had the French. Shelford Bidwell and Dominick Graham, *Fire-Power: British Army Weapons and Theories of War, 1904–45*, p. 80.

5. Rawlinson Diary, Churchill College, Cambridge. The Paris conferees came to the same conclusion on that day.

6. Quoted by David Lloyd George in War Memoirs, Vol II, and printed in John Terraine, *The Road to Passchendaele*, p.17, (Leo Cooper, 1977.) The Navy's idea at the time was for raids from the sea, such as that against Zeebrugge in 1918.

7. Lord Hankey, *The Supreme Command*, Vol II, (Allen & Unwin, 1961), p. 28. David Lloyd George, War Memoirs, Vol IV, (Nicholson & Watson, 1934) pp. 2133–35.

8. Although a trial convoy arrived in the UK from Gibraltar on 10th May and convoys were gradually formed hereafter, over 2 million tons of shipping was sunk in the quarter ending 30 June. Thereafter, the threat eased so that 1 million tons were sunk in the last quarter of 1917 and 2.7 million for the whole of 1918. CRM Cruttwell, A History of the Great War, 1914–18, (Oxford U.P. 1940.) pp. 384–7, 438–9 and 536–42.

9. *British Strategy*: a *Study of the Application of the Principles of War* (Constable, 1929), pp.4–5.

10. Wynne, *op.cit.*, and Bidwell and Graham, *op.cit.*, in particular the chapter entitled '*Ubique*'.

11. GS Notes on Operations 1915, (PRO WO 158/17).

Chapter 7 Passchendaele II
1. WO 158/18.
2. WO 158/19, 13 November, 3rd, 12th and 15th December 1916.
3. WO 158/20, 3rd and 6th January 1917.
4. WO 158/38, 30 January 1917.
5. WO 158/214, 22 January, 4 and 6 February, 1917. WO 158/38, fn 207, 208 and 214 in Second Army papers at the Royal Artillery Library, Woolwich, various dates in April 1917.
6. Rawlinson Diary, Churchill College, Cambridge. And Bidwell and Graham, *op. cit.*, 85–88.
7. OH, 1917 Vol II, p. 127 fn 2. Edmonds offers the rejected plan of Rawlinson and Plumer as the GHQ plan and says that Gough rejected it in favour of one that was more ambitious. Thereby, Edmonds set the scene for the idea that whereas Plumer and Haig agreed about how to fight the battle, Gough was the odd man out. As we have shown, Haig had rejected the Rawlinson-Plumer plan and had instigated Gough's plan.
8. The OH, pp. 88–90, has garbled this story. First it confuses the impromptu attack, which Plumer declined to mount between the 8th and the 14th, when Messines officially ended, with the set-piece attack on the Menin road sector planned by Plumer and Rawlinson and the attack that Gough finally made on 31 July. Secondly, it asserts that it was Haig's plan to mount a preliminary attack there, thus appropriating to Haig the Rawlinson-Plumer plan, which he had rejected. In fact, Gough is thereby saddled with changing GHQ's plan although it was at Haig's insistence that there were to be no preliminary attacks.

9. OH, pp. 105–6.

10. Cabinet 45/140, 2 February, 1944.

11. Cabinet 45/140, 31 May, 1945. Gough was shown the OH version by Wynne. On the 7th June he wrote to Edmonds to explain what had happened at the meeting on the 28th and suggested that Haig had been mistaken and that his diary was unreliable.

12. OH, p. 383.

13. WO 158/17, 13 June, 1917.

14. WO 158/300, 30 June, 1917.

15. OH, p. 131.

16. Cabinet 45/140, 7 May. Malcolm's reference to 'ambush' refers to seizing an objective which is then successfully defended against counter-attacks as the Canadians defended Hill 70.

17. OH, p. 101.

18. OH, pp. 105–6. That was not the plan and Staden, Clercken and Dixmude are not on the Ridge.

19. The casualty figures in the Wynne and Edmonds versions of the battle differed. In 1922 the statistics given were 324,000 British and 202,000 German casualties. The 1948 OH showed 244,897 British casualties and the German 'about 400,000'. Cyril Falls, the original narrator, offered 240,000 as the German figure. The figures reflect the use of statistics to buttress the cases for and against Douglas Haig.

Chapter 8 And a Thousand Stern Warriors

1. The main sources for this chapter are: Edward M Coffman, *The War to End all Wars: The American Experience in World War I*, 1986, and *The Hilt of the Sword: The Career of Peyton C March*, 1966, (both University of Wisconsin Press). *The United States Army in the World War, 1917–19*, (Department of the Army, 1948), Volume I, II and XII. James E Hewes, *From Root to MacNamara: Army Organisation and Administration, 1900–1963*, (Centre of Military History, Washington, 1975), Chapter I. Otto L Nelson, *National Security and the General Staff*, (Washington Infantry Journal Press, 1946), Chapter titled: 'The Test of World War I, 1916–1919'. Donald Smyth, *Pershing, General of the Armies*, (Indiana UP 1986). At the Military History Institute, Carlisle Barracks, Pennsylvania: The Diary of Major-General Johnson Hagood, one-time Chief of Staff HQ Lines of Communication, AEF; Major-General Fox Conner, War College Lecture, 21 March 1933, titled 'G-3 GHQ AEF and its main problems'; Army War College Historical Section Studies, particularly No. 29 by Major Charles H Collins, 'Line of Communication, Organisation and Operation 1917–18'. AWC Study, 1936/7 Course, G4 Report of Committee 8 titled, 'Organisation and Operation of a Communication Zone', 21 December 1936, chairman Major Matthew Ridgway.

2. James W Rainey, Ambivalent Warfare: The Tactical Doctrine of the AEF in World War I, Parameters 13 (September 1983), 34–46. But perhaps Pershing feared that the French would consign his divisions to a holding role if he complied.

3. Smythe, *op. cit.*, pp. 296–301

4. MHI WP No.5. Army War College lecture, 1940. by Hon. Lloyd C Griscom.

5. AWC file 68–58, Memorandum, 22 October, 1923.

6. Allan R Millett. 'Cantigny', in America's First Battles, 1776–1965, Charles E Meller and Williams A S eds., (U.P. of Indiana), pp. 3–4.

7. Nelson, op. cit., p. 256.

8. Nelson, 241, describes the gap in responsibility for production and supply at the War Department 1916–17. This interpretation has been followed by Hewes, perhaps to too great an extent, as has been pointed out by Terrence Gough at the Centre for Military History who wrote:

> 'While I agree with Hewes in general terms about the conflict between the General Staff and the bureaus, I believe that he over-simplifies. The bureau officers indeed performed civilian-like functions, and their close ties with Congressmen did little to advance the modernisation of the Army. But they were still soldiers, and some of them were hardly unaware of the requirements of large-scale war. For them, the problem was how to meet those requirements while maintaining their own standing within the Army. To give in to the General Staff was not a palatable alternative, for they believed that such a course would reduce them to a low estate in wartime – the soldier's finest hour. Nor were they so enamoured of civilian ways and what they perceived as the civilian ethos – as I argued in my paper on the founding of the Army Industrial College. (At the American Military Institute, April 1989). The argument that the bureaux were too committed to *peacetime army* ways, stands on firmer ground. Hewes strongly takes the side of the line officers (who manned the staff) and implicitly accepts their denigration of the bureau officers as little better than civilians in uniform. It might be more correct to say that the bureau officers saw themselves as a bridge between the civilian zone of the interior and the army, but were ill-positioned to make their vision a reality.' (*Letter*, November 28, 1989.)

9. Coffman, *War to End all Wars,* p. 167.
10. Nelson, p. 248.
11. The National Defence Act of 1916, to which Conner referred, provided only that the Army would be organised into divisions and brigades, and did not prescribe the exact composition of a division. The tables approved on 30 May, 1917, represented the War Department's interpretation and extrapolation of the law, prompted strongly by Pershing himself.
12. Nelson, p. 246.
13. Fox Conner lecture at the War College. His emphasis.

Chapter 9 Leaders and Committees: Washington and London in 1943

1. Maurice Matloff, *Strategic Planning for Coalition Warfare 1943–44.* (Office of Chief of Military History, Washington, 1959), p.107.
2. *Eisenhower Diary*. Items deposited by Dr Francis Lowenheim from Columbia University at the Eisenhower Library Abilene, Kansas.
3. Ray S Cline, *US Army in World War II. The War Department. Washington Command Post . The Operations Division* (OCMH 1951), p. 313.
4. Cline, *op.cit.,* p.104.
5. Norman Gibbs, *Grand Strategy Vol I Rearmament Policy*, HMSO, 1976, p. 768. The seminal work on the early days of the CID is Nicholas d'Ombrain, *War Machinery and High Policy, Defence Administration in Peace-time Britain 1902–1914,* (OUP, 1973).
6. Gibbs, *op.cit.,* pp. 773–4, 777, 491.
7. Gibbs, *op cit.,* p. 782. See also GAH Gordon, *British Sea-Power and Procurement Between the Wars: A Reappraisal of Rearmament,* (Naval Institute Press, Annapolis, 1988).
8. MHI Carlisle Barracks, Army War College Historical Section, 57, 'Anglo-American

and Anglo-French relations'.

9. Alex Danchev, *Very Special Relationship, F–M Sir John Dill and the Anglo-American Alliance 1941–44*, (Brassey's Defence Publishers, London 1986).

10. Cline, *op.cit.*, p. 45.

11. *Ibid.* p. 46. The JB continued to exist.

12. Forrest C Pogue, *The United States Army in World War II. The European Theater of Operations*, (OCMH, 1954), p. 36.

13. Danchev, *op. c it.*, p. 136.

14. A Standing Liaison Committee to link the War, Navy and State Departments had been Suggested to Cordell Hull, and 'heartily approved' by the President, but whatever influence it had declined rapidly after the outbreak of war and it ceased to meet after the middle of 1943. Cline, *op.cit.*, p. 41.

15. Abilene, Oral History, 1973, p. folio 380.

Chapter 10 George Marshall's Two-Front War

1. The subject of two important works, Richard Leighton and Robert Coakley, *Global Logistics and Strategy, 1940–43.* (Office of the Chief of Military History, Washington, 1956), and CBA Behrens, (*Merchant Shipping and the Demands of War*), (HMSO, 1955), is as unconsidered in current historical accounts as it was in the CCS debates during the war. The total estimated requirement for Britain at the outbreak of war was 47 million tons. That was reduced to 30.4 m in 1941 and to the bare minimum of 26 m in 1942. The losses in 1942 approached 25 per cent of that tonnage.

2. Forrest C Pogue, *George C. Marshall: Organizer of Victory, 1943–45,* (Viking Press, 1973), pp. 195 and 199, gives some early examples of Marshall's ideas, not, though, in a critical sense. The literature on Wingate is extensive. A critical account is Shelford Bidwell, *The Chindit War. Stilwell, Wingate and the Campaign in Burma: 1944.*(Macmillan, 1979).

3. Pogue, *Marshall*, pp. 128–137.

4. Pogue, *Marshall*, pp. 260–1.

5. Pogue, *Marshall*, pp. 227–8.

6. Pogue, *Marshall*, A Season of Rumours', pp. 272–3 particularly.

7. Matloff, *Op.Cit.*, pp. 271–4.

8. Forrest C Pogue, *The Supreme Command*, Washington, (OCMH, 1954). p. 43.

Chapter 11 The Man With the Cudgel

The main sources for the interpretation that we offer are the following document collections: The ANVIL files in the Bedell Smith papers at the Eisenhower Library, Abilene, Kansas which contain a complete chronology including the documents to support the narrative;

The Papers of Dwight D. Eisenhower, Alfred Chandler and Louis Galambos, eds, (Johns Hopkins UP) Vols I–V which include copious footnotes and extracts of Marshall's letters to Eisenhower. The Irving Papers are a microfilm collection that David Irving used for his book *War of the Generals*. They include papers of the JCS and BCOS In the National Archives, selections from Abilene and The Military History Institute. Carlisle, PA.

The principal printed sources used were:

David Fraser, *Alanbrooke*, (London, Collins, 1982).

Michael Howard, *The Mediterranean Strategy in the Second World War*, (London, Weidenfeld and Nicolson, 1968).

Maurice Matloff, *Strategic Planning for Coalition Warfare, 1943–44*. (Washington DC 1959).

Forrest C Pogue, *The Supreme Command*, (Washington DC 1954) and *George C Marshall Organiser of Victory 1943–1945*, (New York, The Viking Press, 1973).

Richard M Leighton. OVERLORD Revisited: An Interpretation of American Strategy in the European War, 1942–44, *The American Historical Review*, July 1963.

Notes in the Text

1. Hanson Baldwin, *Great Mistakes of the War*. Chester Wilmot, *The Struggle for Europe*, (London, 1952), provides a more balanced version that has stood the test of time quite well. Trumbull Higgins, *Soft Underbelly: the Anglo-American Controversy over the Italian Campaign, 1939–45*, (London 1968) is tendentious. Maurice Matloff, *Strategic Planning for Coalition Warfare Vol II*, (OCMH, Washington, 1953), and 'The Anvil Decision: Crossroads of Strategy' in Kent R Greenfield, ed., *Command Decisions*, (OCMH, Washington, 1960), subscribes to the two opposed strategies interpretation.

2. Richard M Leighton, 'Overlord Revisited: An interpretation of American Strategy in the European War, 1942–44, in *The American Historical Review*, July, 1963, discusses the assault shipping bottleneck. Also Leighton, 'Overlord versus the Mediterranean' in Kent R Greenfield, ed., *Command Decisions*, (OCMH, 1960).

3. Michael Howard, *The Mediterranean Strategy in the Second World War*, (London, 1968). Mark A Stoler, *The Politics of the Second Front: American Military Planning and Diplomacy in Coalition War 1941–43*. (London, 1977). David Frazer, *Alanbrooke*, (London, 1982).

4. BCOS to JSM Washington, 4 February 1944: 'As to Teheran and Stalin, he advocated a diversionary operation but was not interested in the particular place selected for it (and) would accept the change' (from the south of France to Italy). Irving Reel 2 File 2, COS (W) 1126. See also COS (W) 1156, 21 February, 1944. On this subject Marshall and Leahy disagreed about what was said. Marshall 'felt that what the Russians want is the large attack in strength.' Roosevelt's memory of the subject was hazy also.

5. See CCS minutes of *Eureka* meeting on 30 November. OVERLORD was then scheduled for 15 May. Concerning landing craft Marshall spoke of releasing them from the Mediterranean $2^{1}/_{2}$ months before that date. Andrew Cunningham said 'No, it's 100 days which means 15 February'. 68 LSTs was 3 months American production. This was about half the total Mediterranean strength.

6. King opposed this arrangement because it put Eisenhower 'in an anomalous position', by which he meant that he might be over-persuaded by the BCOS. JCS minutes 21 February. Irving Reel 2, File 2, JCS 658/3.

7. The JCS meeting with the President on the landing craft question is disillusioning. The President suggests sending a fleet of private craft over to join the fleet to supplement landing craft, a kind of Dunkirk in reverse. And King observed: 'with the terrific number of craft involved in the assault one would almost be able to walk dry-shod from one side of the Channel to the other.' COSW 1156, 21 February 1944. DDE No. 1562 22 February fn3.

8. The crucial point in the shipping argument was that LSTs were large ships that beached, allowing men and heavy equipment to go directly ashore. Lacking them it had to be first loaded in Motor Transport ships and then transferred to Landing craft

(LCT) to the beaches. The off shore assembly was vulnerable to enemy fire and air attack, and the OPD 'proposal' involved a delay of 24 hours. It was not the first wave or the overall lift that were affected, but the absolutely vital follow-up with the main force on D+1 and D+2. SAC conference 26 February, Irving Reel 3.

9. Pogue, *Marshall*, pp. 361, 363.
10. BCOS 603/3 COS (W) 135, 28 June 1944. Irving File 2.

Chapter 12 Thunderheads: Two SHAEF Dilemmas

1. The Nevins Papers, MHI Carlisle Barracks, Pennsylvania. Appreciations on Op OVERLORD and Composition of Land Forces,' autumn, 1943. General Eisenhower's Comments on Command, 18 May, 1944.'
2. Diary Items sent from Columbia University, Butcher Papers, Eisenhower Library, Abilene, Kansas.
3. Dr. Daniel Crosswell offered us material on Bedell Smith's relations with Everett Hughes from his, then, unpublished ms (1989) and lent his microfilm copies of Mr David Irving's collection of official documents including Hughes' diary notes.
4. Oral History 397, interview with Brigadier-General Thomas J Betts, G2 at SHAEF. Eisenhower Library, Abilene.
5. Interview of Bedell Smith with Forrest Pogue. MHI, Carlisle Barracks, Pogue interviews, 1947.
6. Hewes, *Op.Cit.*, 68.
7. Hewes, 69–77.
8. Hewes, 97.
9. Irving Microfilms. Extracts from the Butcher Diary.

Chapter 13 The Campaign in Europe: Pride and Prejudice

1. A recent study, *Battle Exhaustion: Psychiatrists and Soldiers in the Canadian Army, 1939–45*, by Terry Copp and Bill McAndrew deals with the problem in the Italian and Northwest Europe campaigns. (McGill-Queens University Press, Montreal, 1990).
2. Russell F Weigley, Eisenhower's *Lieutenants: the Campaigns of France and Germany, 1944–45*, (Indiana University Press, 1981), 425. Poor organisation was the cause of the trouble. The Americans believed that Ridgway, not Browning, should have been commanding the three divisions, two of which were American.
3. The Sicily incident which began the feud with Montgomery has been recounted very thoroughly by Carlo D'Este in *Bitter Victory, the Battle for Sicily*, (Collins, 1988). D'Este and the present authors have not reached agreement over the correct procedure of Bradley on that occasion. It was, in their opinion, to arrange with Oliver Leese, the neighbouring and concerned British 30th Corps commander, how and when to hand over the road.

Chapter 14 Eisenhower Takes Command: Broad Front Versus Single Thrust

1. *The Papers of Dwight D Eisenhower, The War Years: IV*, Alfred D Chandler ed., (Johns Hopkins, Baltimore), hereafter 'DDE', W-82265, # 1900 and fns.
2. DDE, # 1900, 19 August.
3. *The Memoirs of Field-Marshal the Viscount Montgomery of Alamein*, Collins, London 1958, pp. 266 *et seq*.
4. MHI, Nevins Papers. 'SHAEF Operations'. (file).

5. # 1909 24 August to Montgomery confirming their conversation on the 23rd and a directive # 1920 on 29th.
6. *The Patton Papers, 1940–45,* Martin Blumerson ed., 531, Diary, 30 August.
7. Hodges Diary, Irving Papers Reel 8.
8. DDE # 1933 fn 2.
9. DDE, M–160 4 September.
10. DDE # 1933, 4 September.
11. M–160 # 1935 fn 1.
12. DDe # 1933.
13. Nevins Papers. 'SHAEF Operations'. (file)
14. M–181.
15. DDE # 1945 fn 2.
16. DDE # 1939.
17. DDE # 1945 fn 2 and 4.
18. M 192.
19. M 197, 122000 and DDE # 1945, 13 September.
20. Eisenhower Papers, Principal File: Pre-Presidential; Box 13, Omar Bradley, 12 September.
21. DDE # 1939 and 1946.
22. # 1953, 14 September.
23. DDE # 1945 fn 5.
24. DDE # 1968, 18 September, Marshall's W 26119 of 7 September in fn 7.
25. # 1957.
26. M 222 211935.
27. Butcher Box 169, entry for 21 September.
28. refers to DDE # 1975 of 20 September. M 223 211955.
29. DDE 1979 22 September and 1989 23 September. Eisenhower's peacemaking note # 1993 24 September.
30. M 260, 6 October, Pre-Presidential Papers, Box 83.

Chapter 15 Logistics: Neglect and Mischief
1. DDE–M 7 October.
2. DDE # 2028 to Bradley, 8 October.
3. Nigel Hamilton, *Monty: The Field Marshal, 1944–1976,* 108, 133.
4. The main sources for the chapter are: 'The Report of the General Board US Forces European Theater: Organization of the European Theater of Operations Study 2, 1945.' This typescript report is part of an extensive enquiry into the way the campaign had been conducted within ETO. A board member was Bradley's senior logistician (G4), Raymond Moses, a critic of Lee and the way SHAEF and army groups had been denied control over logistics. A copy of the board report is at MHI, Carlisle, File 320.2/1. General Aurand was the commentator for the War College Report on Logistics in the AEF, 1917–18, presented in 1936 by Major Matthew Ridgway, the chairman (MHI Historical Papers). Aurand papers are at the Eisenhower Library, Abilene, Kansas. Graham is grateful to Dr Dan Crosswell, who was working on the papers of Walter Bedell Smith at the time, for pointing out the importance of General Aurand and also for allowing him to read his copy of the collection of David Irving which included the LeRoy Lutes papers, the diaries of General Hodge's (First Army) and Everett Hughes, and miscellaneous records of the JCS,

CCS and BCOS, used in Irving's, *War of the Generals*. Additional Aurand papers were seen at the MHI where Graham read further background reports on the logistics of the ETO by senior officers. The Irving papers offer examples of Eisenhower tackling administrative problems piecemeal, without consultation with Bedell Smith, by allocating individuals to tasks better undertaken by the proper staff branch. Interviews with senior members of SHAEF are to be found at Abilene, and earlier, and therefore more useful ones, many by Forrest Pogue, at MHI. The Nevins Papers at MHI contain COSSAC and SHAEF operations planning papers which have been used as background in this chapter and have already been quoted in the previous one.

5. Crosswell, *Op. Cit.* quotes from Everett Hughes Diary in June and July: 'The man is crazy. He won't issue orders that stick. He will pound on the desk and shout.' And Crosswell comments that Eisenhower wanted to avoid trouble with Somervell over logistics. Crosswell blames Bedell Smith for not dealing with Lee and says that Smith had as much control over logistics as he desired. General Aurand, in his account confirms Eisenhower's tendency to side-track staff channels and create muddles.

6. SHAEF – 21 AG 07113, 5 September. Bedell Smith papers, Box 24, Eisenhower Library, Abilene.

7. Bull Papers, 14 July. WBS–DDE Correspondence, 19 July. Eisenhower Library, Abilene.

8. Bedell Smith correspondence. DDE–War Department, 29 0409 September.

9. Lutes Report. Irving papers . Reel 7.

10. Lutes' reports to Somervell. Irving, Reel 7. The First Army version of what passed between Bradley and Lutes is in Hodges' Diary, Irving, Reel 8.

11. Irving, Reel 8.

12. Irving, Reel 8. First Army War Diary, 16 November 1944. Russell Weigley, *Eisenhower's Lieutenants,* gives a reasoned assessment in his chapter 'Inadequate Means'. pp. 826–37.

13. First Army War Diary. *Ibid.*

14. Pogue *Marshall* pp. 361–4 and 488–504. Lieutenant General Ben Lear, the Army Ground Forces commander was sent out in January to the ETO to sort out the manpower situation in the Theatre.

Chapter 16 Operations, Strategy and Politics

1. Eisenhower Library, Pre-Presidential Churchill correspondence and DDE, #2096 2 April.

2. Ehrman. *Grand Strategy Vol VI,* 150–1.

3. For the BCOS case see DDE #2379, 31 March, fn 1.

4. DDE # 2372, fn particularly.

5. DDE # 2373.

6. MHI, Carlisle Barracks, Nevins Papers.

7. *Eisenhower at War, 1943–45,* 729–45.

8. Montgomery's M562 of 27 March, 1945, Box 83 Pre-Presidential Eisenhower Papers, Abilene. Eisenhower's replay with the new plan DDE #2364 of 28 March and # 2378 of 31 March.

9. DDE, # 1957.

10. *Eisenhower,* 732.

11. n.d. 1945? Irving Papers, Reel 1 File 1.

12. AGWAR to SHAEF, W74256, 28 April, 1945.

13. DDE # 2400, 7 April 1945, fn 1.
14. This is Nigel Hamilton's general assessment in *Monty: the Field Marshal, 1944–1976*, Hamish Hamilton, London, 1986.
15. Simon and Schuster, New York, 1983. This is the authors' general assessment of Ambrose's book in this respect.

SELECT BIBLIOGRAPHY

Ball, Harry P, *Of Responsible Command: A History of the US Army War College*, (The Alumni Association, Carlisle Barracks, Pennsylvania, 1983)

Blumenson, M, *Mark Clark*, (Congdon and Weed, New York, 1984)

Bond, B, *The Victorian Army and the Staff College 1854–1914*, (Eyre Methuen, London, 1972)

Bruce, A, *The Purchase System in the British Army 1660–1871*, (Royal Historical Society, 1980)

Carver, F-M Sir M, *The War Lords: Military Commanders of the Twentieth Century*, (Wiedenfeld and Nicolson, London, 1976)

Clausewitz, C von, *On War*, ed. by M Howard and P Paret, (Princeton University Press, NJ 1976)

Creveld, M van, *Command in War*, (Harvard University Press, Cambridge, Mass. 1969)

Cunliffe, M, *Soldiers and Civilians: The Martial Spirit In America 1775–1865*, (Harvard University Press, 1985)

Demeter, K, *The German Officer-Corps in Society and State 1650–1945* (Wiedenfeld and Nicolson, London)

Dixon, Norman F, *On the Psychology of Military Incompetence*, 1965 (Cape, London, 1976)

Foch, F, *Des Principes de Guerre*, (1903, republished 1918, English translation Chapman and Hall)

Fraser, David, *Alanbrooke*, (Collins, London, 1982)

Gooch, G P, *Frederich the Great: the Ruler, the Writer, the Man*, (Longmans, Green, London, 1947)

Goerlitz, W, *The German General Staff: Its History and Structure*, (Hollis and Carter, London, 1953)

Gorce, Paul-Marie de la, *The French Army: a military-political history*, (Wiedenfeld and Nicolson, London, 1953)

Guderian, H, *Panzer Leader*, (Michael Joseph, London, 1970)

Hamilton, Nigel, *The Making of a General 1887–1942* and *The Field Marshal 1944–1976*, (Hamish Hamilton, London, 1981 and 1986)

Hews, James E, *From Root to Macnamara, Army Organisation and Administration 1900–1963*, (Center of Military History, US Army, Washington, DC, 1975)

Howard, M, *Clausewitz*, (OUP, 1983)

Kolakowski, L, *Bergson*, (OUP, 1985)

Machiavelli, N, *The Prince*, (Penguin, 1985)

Macksey, K, *Armoured Crusader: Major-General Sir Percy Hobart*, (Hutchinson, London, 1967)

Macleod, R, *Proceedings of the Royal Artillery Historical Society, 1969*, Record of Session of November 1968, Ypres 1917

Marshall Cornwall, J, *Haig as a Military Commander*, (Batsford, London)

Maurice, F, *British Strategy: A Study of the Application of the Principles of War*,(Constable, London, 1929)

Montgomery, F-M, Viscount of Alamein, *A History of War*, (Collins, London, 1968)

Parkinson, R, *Tormented Warrior: Ludendorff and the Supreme Command*, (Hodder and Stoughton, London, 1978)

Ritter, Gerhard, *The Sword and the Sceptre: The Problem of German Militarism, Vol. 1; The Prussian Tradition 1740–1890 Vol. II; The European Powers and the Wilhemine Empire 1890–1914*

Seaton, Albert, *The German Army 1933-1945*, (Wiedenfeld and Nicolson, London, 1982)

Smythe, Donald, *Pershing, General of the Armies*, (Indiana University Press, Bloomington, USA, 1986)

Trythall, AJ, *'Boney' Fuller: The Intellectual General 1878–1966*, (Cassell, London, 1977)

Utley, Robert M, and Washburn, Wilcomb E, *History of the Indian Wars* (The American Heritage Publishing Company Inc., 1977)

Weigley, Russell F, *Eisenhower's Lieutenants. The Campaigns of France and Germany 1944–1945*, (Sedgewick and Jackson, London, 1981)

Also Fire-Power and Tug of War by Graham and Bidwell, *passim*

INDEX